D1565316

Go Figure!

Go Figure!

New Directions in Advertising Rhetoric

Edward F. McQuarrie and Barbara J. Phillips, Editors

M.E.Sharpe
Armonk, New York
London, England

Library of Congress Cataloging-in-Publication Data

Go figure! New directions in advertising rhetoric / edited by Edward F. McQuarrie
and Barbara J. Phillips.
    p. cm.
Includes bibliographical references and index.
    ISBN 978-0-7656-1801-6 (cloth : alk. paper) — ISBN 978-0-7656-2133-7 (electronic)
    1. Rhetoric. 2. Visual communication. 3. Advertising—Language. I. McQuarrie, Edward F.
II. Phillips, Barbara J., 1966–

P301.5.A38G6 2007
808'.066659—dc22   2007022322

Printed in the United States of America

Contents

Go Figure!

1

Advertising Rhetoric

An Introduction

Edward F. McQuarrie and Barbara J. Phillips

Rhetoric is an ancient discipline that was fundamental to Western thought for over 2,000 years. Rather suddenly, it began to wither as the scientific revolution took root in the seventeenth and eighteenth centuries. By 1900, rhetoric had almost disappeared from the canon (Bender and Welberry 1990). Today in the twenty-first century, for reasons as yet poorly understood, rhetoric is flourishing once more. Practitioners have spread across a variety of humanities and social sciences disciplines, including consumer research (Deighton 1985), so that by the early 1990s, conceptual and empirical pieces applying rhetorical ideas to advertising had begun to appear with some regularity (e.g., McQuarrie and Mick 1992; Scott 1994).

At present we may say that rhetoric has established itself within consumer research and advertising scholarship as one among many valid perspectives on advertising phenomena. However, we believe that rhetorical perspectives can be taken much further and that their application to advertising can be fruitful both for illuminating advertising phenomena and for advancing rhetorical theory itself. Our intent in assembling the present volume was to showcase new thinking in the application of rhetorical perspectives to advertising phenomena. We recruited a range of established and emerging scholars to this enterprise. Chapter authors were encouraged to push their thinking to the edge and given a mandate to innovate. Rigor was maintained by having each chapter reviewed by a fellow author, and again by the editors. We asked for ideas that had never before seen the light of day, and encouraged risk taking beyond what more conventional scholarly outlets would allow. The goal was to push the frontiers of contemporary thinking about how advertising achieves its effects and to provide scholars with actionable ideas for future research.

To lay a foundation for what follows, this chapter provides an introduction to the rhetorical perspective, proceeds to contrast the rhetorical perspective against other, more established social science approaches, and then summarizes the contributions to be expected from applying rhetorical perspectives to the study of advertising. We then briefly introduce the individual chapters in the volume.

What Is Rhetoric?

Style Versus Content

Since classical antiquity, rhetoric has been more concerned with *how* to say things, than *what* to say. In its contemporary revival, rhetorical scholars have focused ever more closely on issues of style rather than content. The idea is that the impact of an utterance may depend in whole or part on the style selected for it. In the background is the presumption that in any given case, a palette of potentially applicable styles exists, and that one of these styles can be determined to be the most effective in a given instance. Systematic approaches to rhetorical scholarship seek to discover general rules and organizing principles for identifying the most effective stylistic choice in any specified context.

In an advertising context, *what* to say consists of a decision about what attribute or position to claim. Once chosen, such content can almost always be delivered via more than one style. One can state the claim point blank or give it an embellish-ment; command a response or invite it; express a claim pictorially or verbally; and so forth. All of these are *stylistic* choices. Each instance shares the same underlying content, but each constitutes a different communication attempt that may fare well or poorly in a specific context. It is important to recognize that although style can be distinguished from content, style also communicates. The separation of style from content, together with the valorization of style, are defining characteristics of the rhetorical perspective. In fact, it can be argued that advertising style was almost invisible until the rhetorical perspective began to be applied (see Scott [1994] for this argument).

In locating the contribution of rhetoric within the arena of style, we also put down a marker as to what (contemporary) rhetoric is not, at least as far as its ap-plication to advertising is concerned. As practiced in antiquity, rhetorical ideas governed the selection of content as well as the choice of style; rhetoric claimed to offer guidance with respect to both. Although not all contemporary practitioners of rhetoric would agree, we think that a rhetorical perspective has little to offer advertisers when it comes to the selection of what brand attribute to claim or what competitive position to own. Instead, perspectives developed in other disciplines govern these content choices.

For instance, the concept of personal relevance (i.e., "select the attribute that is most relevant to the target audience") is a psychological construct, as is the idea that one attribute is likely to be perceived as more instrumental to a consumer's valued goals than another. Similarly, the concept of segmentation and the idea that one brand position is more viable than another comes from economic theory concerning competitive advantage. Rhetoric does not question or challenge any of these ideas, nor does it substitute its own approach to content; it simply points out that decisions about content do not exhaust the decisions facing the advertiser.

What we are suggesting, then, is a kind of division of labor. The choice of what to say has migrated away from rhetoric and belongs now to disciplines such as psychology and economics, or more properly, their integration into marketing thought. The contribution of rhetoric is to point out first that there is another set of choices to be made, concerning stylistic elements; and second, to contribute to the understanding of how these stylistic elements in advertising operate.

To sum up, contemporary rhetoric probably has more to offer the advertising strategist than the product manager. The product manager, as a marketing decision maker, is tasked with decisions about attributes, benefits, positioning, and target consumer selection. To make these decisions she or he will continue to draw on the best psychological and economic thinking, as distilled in the literature on marketing strategy. However, the advertising strategist knows all too well that his or her job has barely begun after decisions about content are set, because any given content can always be expressed in a variety of different styles. The advertising manager will find little of assistance in psychological research when it comes to stylistic decisions; consequently, she or he is naturally open to the potential contribution of rhetorical perspectives.

Differentiation

The goal of rhetoric, as Aristotle put it, is to identify in any given case the available means of persuasion. The plural form of this statement is crucial to understanding what Aristotle was trying to say. That is, the rhetorician always assumes the existence of sets of discrete stylistic options—of palettes, if you will. The practice of rhetoric, when applied to a specific phenomenon such as advertising, consists of identifying and differentiating the various stylistic options available. The number of options cannot always be known in advance, but the rhetorician tends to assume that there are more rather than fewer. For example, in the print advertising case, we can differentiate ad layouts, identify various headline styles, distinguish multiple pictorial styles, assign body text styles to genres, and so on. In each case, we are setting out the palette of options from which the advertiser may (must) choose.

Making advertising style visible means identifying and differentiating discrete stylistic options, and all rhetoricians engage in this activity. Some rhetoricians, ourselves included, strive in addition to embed these differentiations within an integrative structure. The notion is that a system of differentiations will be more theoretically powerful than an unstructured list of alternatives. For instance, from antiquity onward rhetoricians were wont to compile lists of rhetorical figures (e.g., rhyme, anaphora, antithesis, syllepsis, and many, many more). These typically took the form of simple catalogs with examples of each entry. Once the scientific revolution took hold in Western thought, these catalogs lost their claim to represent real knowledge. A list does not stack up very well against an equation like $E = mc^2$. The practice of compiling unstructured lists, and leaving matters at that, led eventually to Samuel Butler's famous gibe: "For all a rhetorician's rules/Teach nothing but to name his tools."

An integrative structure goes beyond a simple list by providing an underlying conceptual network that links some elements of the list together and simultaneously distinguishes them from other elements. As an example, McQuarrie and Mick (1996) suggested that *verbal* rhetorical figures in advertising could be organized according to a three-level hierarchy. They first distinguished all figurative expressions from nonfigurative expressions, in terms of the property of artful deviation from expectation. Next, they distinguished schemes from tropes as discrete types of artful deviation, constituted by excess regularity of expression in the former case, and irregularity of expression in the latter. Last, within both the scheme and trope categories, they distinguished simple versus complex rhetorical operations, whereby these regularities or irregularities could be constructed.

Without dwelling on the details of the McQuarrie and Mick (1996) taxonomy, we can develop the positive implications that follow from constructing such an integrated structure of differentiations. Specifically, such a structure links the rhetorical system to other systems, most notably the system that underlies consumer response to advertising. McQuarrie and Mick do that by linking artful deviation to the psychological construct termed incongruity. They then draw on Berlyne's (1971) framework to derive testable hypotheses about the impact of artful deviation on consumer response. Results supporting these hypotheses have been recorded in a number of empirical studies (McQuarrie and Mick 1992, 1999, 2003a; McQuarrie and Phillips 2005; Mothersbaugh, Huhmann, and Franke 2002; Phillips 1997, 2000; Tom and Eves 1999).

This rhetorical procedure is general and not specific to the McQuarrie and Mick (1996) effort. Thus, Phillips and McQuarrie (2004) set out to differentiate the set of *visual* rhetorical figures. Their typology, like the McQuarrie and Mick (1996) effort, leads to a differentiation of the set of visual figures, but uses different concepts judged more appropriate to the visual modality. Phillips and McQuarrie propose a 3 x 3 matrix, created by crossing two dimensions: visual structure and meaning operation. Again, without going into the details of their typology, the thing to note is that visual structures are conceived to vary according to their complexity while meaning operations vary in their degree of polysemy. Phillips and McQuarrie then use the concepts of complexity and polysemy to tie their typology to alternative consumer responses so that they too are able to generate testable hypotheses about the differentiations that make up the typology.

To summarize, integrated sets of conceptually structured differentiations allow the rhetorician to claim the title of "scientist" as well. We think it is important to note how one can simultaneously be a rhetorician and a marketing scientist, in part because Samuel Butler's gibe remains timely; we have repeatedly encountered more or less respectful versions of it when presenting rhetorical differentiations to scholarly audiences. In any case, although *Rhetoric* and *Science* were once contestants in an earlier "culture war" (Bender and Welberry 1990), the point we wish to make is that there is nothing about the drive toward stylistic differentiation of advertising that is intrinsically unscientific. In fact, the practice of rhetoric and the pursuit of scientific understanding share a common interest in causation, as developed next.

Pragmatism

Almost from its beginnings, rhetoric has been criticized for the ruthless and uncompromising pragmatism of its practitioners. Rhetoric has always been concerned with what works, over and above what is true or right. Early Greek rhetoricians were extensively criticized on this count by their fellow philosophers. Rhetoricians learned early on that the unadorned truth might or might not be persuasive in a specific context and then spent most of their effort on discovering what would be most persuasive in that context. This stance was deemed offensive by truth-seeking philosophers. The resulting ill repute has stuck to rhetoric down through the ages.

Now consider contemporary advertising—do its practitioners not labor under exactly the same ill reputation as ancient rhetoricians did and for exactly the same reason? Advertising is also ruthlessly pragmatic. Ads need not be false, but ads deploy only as much unadorned truth as is consistent with their aims. What ads must do is achieve their desired impact on the consumers to whom they are directed. Rhetoric is above all pragmatic communication. Advertising is likewise pragmatic communication. Truth, comeliness, clarity, or any other desideratum is entirely secondary. The primary goal of advertising is always to cause a specified consumer response. Since this has likewise always been the goal of rhetoric, it seems likely that rhetorical perspectives can contribute substantially to the understanding of advertising.

We do not mean to imply here that rhetorical practice is inherently unethical, nor do we intend to justify false advertising as okay. We are simply asserting a fact: truth seeking is not part of the mandate of rhetoric or advertising. Knowledge of rhetoric and of advertising is instrumental knowledge: it is knowledge-how. A virtuous person will tell the truth, whether rhetorically enhanced or not; an unethical person will not, whether rhetorically skilled or not. An analogy may help to clarify the point: achieving rhetorical knowledge is like sharpening a knife blade. If the person using the knife is a chef in a kitchen, the sharper blade is almost certainly a good thing. If the user is a criminal in an alley, it is probably a bad thing. Rhetorical knowledge can make truth more effective, and it can likewise make falsehoods more believable. Rhetorical knowledge is simply unrelated to truth seeking.

"Pragmatic" has another, less pejorative meaning, as when it refers to the branch of linguistics concerned not with syntax or semantics, but with the action implications of speech—what the listener does with what he hears (Sperber and Wilson 1986). Advertising is a kind of pragmatic communication because it is primarily concerned with causing a specified action to occur (as opposed to, say, educating understanding, or entertaining the recipient). Rhetoric claims to know something about how speakers can elicit whichever response is desired from their audiences, and this is what makes rhetorical perspectives so interesting and relevant to the student of advertising phenomena. In fact, the action focus of rhetoric makes it arguably the most relevant of the many text-analytic disciplines, so far as providing a deep understanding of advertising is concerned.

By "text-analytic discipline," we mean the scholarly disciplines whose subject matter is texts of various kinds (including pictorial texts). All text-analytic disciplines are primarily concerned with understanding specific types of human cultural artifacts and tend to be more concerned with explaining aspects of the artifacts themselves than with giving an account of their producers or the culture or society in which they arose. Prominent examples would include poetics, art criticism, literary criticism, and semiotics, among others. Now contrasts among text-analytic disciplines are necessarily fuzzy, since their boundaries are not tightly drawn or widely agreed upon, and many concepts and tools are shared. Still, it seems worth pursuing the argument as to why rhetorical perspectives might have the most to offer students of advertising, if only to help delineate the distinctive characteristics of rhetoric relative to kindred text-analytic perspectives.

Consider poetics, for instance. Poetics arose as an attempt to understand poems. Now to what extent can knowledge of poetry help us to understand advertising? We may speak metaphorically of copywriters as "the poets of our age," but really, copywriters are not poets. Poetry is not their task. Similarly, it seems likely that individual advertisements may make use of poetic devices, and that concepts from poetics can alert us to their presence in advertising and helps us to identify and systematize such devices. However, in advertising, poetic devices are merely means to an end, and will be utilized or abandoned to exactly the extent they serve that end; and the ends of advertising are not the ends of poetry.

Similar arguments can be leveled against art criticism and literary criticism as perspectives for understanding advertising. Likewise semiotics—ads are constructed from signs, and advertisers, like all communicators, do assemble signs in an attempt to communicate selected meanings. But advertisers do not actually care whether they communicate a specific meaning or whether they communicate anything at all. An unthinking consumer response may be just as welcome as a thoughtful and reflective one, as long as it is the response the advertiser set out to achieve. Communication of meaning is secondary, audience response is primary. Certainly, effective communication of a particular idea is often a necessary prelude to obtaining some desired response; but if the response can be achieved more cheaply or effectively without communicating anything very much, then that is what the advertiser will do.

Only rhetoric shares the same aim as advertising: how to assemble words, signs, poems, and other text elements so as to maximize the probability of a specified audience response. This single-minded focus on causative speech is also the reason why a scholar of rhetoric may claim to be a scientist. The scientific revolution triumphed in Western society because it offered demonstrably causal knowledge (Hunt 2002).

Rhetoricians are eager consumers of scientific findings because rhetoricians, like advertisers and like scientists, require causal knowledge.

The question that arises at this juncture is why an advertiser would look to rhetoric for causal knowledge concerning advertising, as opposed to consulting a more conventional scientific discipline such as cognitive psychology. The key difference between rhetoric and more classically psychological approaches lies in rhetoric's emphasis on contextualization.

Contextualization

As we have seen, rhetoricians expect that style can be differentiated and they expect these stylistic differentiations to have causal power. In addition, rhetoricians expect the causal impact of style factors to be contingent upon context. It is not good rhetorical practice to claim, for example, that rhyme is (always and everywhere) effective; rather, the goal of rhetorical inquiry is to discover *when* rhyme is effective. This commitment to contingent formulations reflects the practical roots of rhetoric. All practitioners know that different situations require different stratagems if the desired outcome is to be achieved; "it depends" is a fact of practical life, however unsatisfactory it may be in a classroom setting. The assertion we wish to defend is that other scientific disciplines with a claim to the allegiance of advertisers are, by and large, more universalist in spirit, and hence, less helpful.

A universalist discipline is inclined to seek general truths. Contingencies will be acknowledged as necessary, but are to be avoided in the first instance. To a universalist, the best scientific thinking is the most general, and the best theoretical constructs are those that do not need to be modified to reflect different cultures, different societies, different types of stimuli, or different kinds of responses.

By contrast, rhetoricians are too ruthlessly pragmatic to be able to ignore contextual factors. Since the entire focus is on what works, and on what works best, contingencies are accepted as an intrinsic part of theoretical frameworks. A rhetorician keeps an open mind about whether persuasion outcomes in mass-media advertising contexts conform to persuasion outcomes in interpersonal contexts; whether pictures persuade in the same way as words; whether audiences striving with all their might to shut out and ignore advertisements can be persuaded by the same devices as audiences that eagerly seek out information; and so forth. This attention to context and openness to contingencies are among the most important advantages offered by rhetoric when the goal is to develop a scientific understanding of advertising. Attention to style, the impulse toward differentiation, and the drive toward causal knowledge are intrinsic features of rhetorical scholarship, but the particular conceptual schemes developed by rhetoricians may vary a great deal according to the particular kind of advertising being studied. Web banner ads may require quite different frameworks from magazine ads; radio ads might require different frameworks from billboard ads; and so forth. A rhetorician sees no problem with this diversity of explanatory schemes.

In sharp contrast, we can assure the reader, having floated these ideas in many scholarly venues over the years, that the reaction of devout universalists to the notions just described ranges from acute indifference to active repugnance. Universalism is one of those fundamental personal and philosophical predispositions that run deep. Many psychologists are committed to the idea that human behavior is human behavior, period, and that any sampling of human behavior will do about as well as any other sample when testing fundamental scientific theories about all human behavior. But to a rhetorician, context matters. The rhetorician returns always to the question of what works—what are the available means of persuasion, within this particular context?

Rhetorical Versus Psychological Perspectives on Advertising

With the distinctive features of rhetorical scholarship now brought clearly into view, we can delve more deeply into what distinguishes rhetoric from more conventional scientific approaches to understanding advertising phenomena. The fundamental difference between a rhetorical perspective and the social and cognitive psychological perspectives that have historically dominated scholarly work on advertising can be stated as follows:

1. Rhetoric assumes a few simple models of consumer response, and devotes effort at the margin to differentiating and structuring the *stimuli* capable of evoking one or another response.
2. Cognitive and social psychology assume a few broad distinctions among stimuli, and devote effort at the margin to elaborating more detailed and nuanced models of how consumers *process* stimuli.

Elsewhere the two perspectives have been contrasted as focusing on the ad system, on the one hand, versus the human system, on the other (McQuarrie and Mick 2003b). Here we might say that rhetoric studies the ads, while psychology studies the consumer.

In rhetoric, an effects model is assumed and fresh modeling efforts are directed at the stimuli, more specifically their stylistic elements. In social-cognitive psychology, a model of causes is assumed and fresh modeling efforts concentrate on different modes of consumer processing that might be triggered when these causes are encountered in different combinations. Thus, a psychologist will assume that ads can be distinguished as containing, say, strong arguments or weak arguments, and will then decompose the processing of these different types of arguments. By contrast, a rhetorician will assume that some hierarchy of effects governs ad response (e.g., attention–comprehension–acceptance–preference), and then proceed to develop a much more complex differentiation of "arguments" than the simple bipolar distinction that suffices for the psychologist.

A social scientist who also practices rhetoric remains committed to causal understanding, but makes the kind of simplifying assumptions about consumer processing described above. The promise of rhetoric is that new insights into the stylistic structure of advertisements may be gained, and that the differences so identified will make a difference to consumer response. It is again this commitment to causal understanding that permits one to call himself both a rhetorician and a scientist. The idea is that rhetoricians have spent centuries parsing different kinds of human discourse, with special attention to contexts where persuasion is the goal. Mass-media advertisements can then be understood as a relatively novel sort of discourse that provides fresh fodder and fruitful grazing for anyone with a rhetorical habit of mind.

In short, rhetoricians may be just as scientific in their effort as psychologists, but the focus of their efforts will differ. The reader can judge his or her openness to rhetorical versus psychological perspectives via this simple question: how adequate do you judge the aforementioned "strong versus weak argument" distinction to be, with respect to capturing theoretically important variation within the population of advertisements? If you find yourself asserting that strong versus weak arguments, along with a handful of similar distinctions (e.g., cognitively demanding or not, vivid or pallid), should be adequate to capture much of the theoretically important variation in the population of advertisements, then rhetorical ideas will likely hold little appeal. Your judgment that such distinctions are adequate is simply a statement that for you, all the really interesting questions concern what types of processing occur when a consumer of type X encounters a strong (weak) argument in situations of type Y. This simple distinction is perfectly adequate for studying the circumstances under which arguments do (or do not) get processed. You are not interested in arguments; your concern is with when and how consumers process arguments. You are a psychological scientist and not a rhetorician.

Career choices and one's choice of disciplinary affiliation are, of course, partly matters of individual temperament. However, within the context of scientific work focused on advertising, a substantive argument can be made that on an a priori basis, rhetoric is likely to be a more apt foundational discipline than psychology. This is because experimental psychology was initially forged in an attempt to understand how *physical* stimuli were processed. Theoretically relevant variation in physical stimuli is nicely captured by simple bipolar dimensions such as bright–faint, loud–soft, and the like. Even as social psychology evolved to address the much more complex nature of social stimuli, a great deal of psychological work continued to be driven by such simplified descriptors as "same race as me/not the same race." In short, psychologists have a century-old tradition of dealing with physical (and social) stimuli whose theoretically relevant variation (i.e., variation relevant to studying how consumers process) can be captured in simple dichotomies. Rarely, if ever, are these dichotomies linked together in overarching conceptual structures. That sort of elaboration of conceptual structure is reserved for processing.

To see why a set of simple, unintegrated, continuous dimensions like "strong–weak" might not be useful in understanding advertising, consider how a print advertisement out in the world differs from a classic laboratory stimulus. First, the ad is an artifact, a cultural product. A team of highly paid professionals, whose employment can be terminated at any point (especially if the advertising effort fails), works for a period of time to craft the verbal and pictorial character of an 8½ x 11 page. They work in direct competition against other teams who are simultaneously working to make other such pages. In the life of each such team, a given advertisement is the *n*th effort, where *n* may be a very large number. Each effort involves a myriad of stylistic decisions, as we have already discussed. The resulting population of advertisements clearly represents cultural artifacts ensuing from socially shaped collective effort. The idea that this population of cultural artifacts can be effectively characterized via a few simple dichotomies might strike a neutral arbiter as . . . absurd.

None of this bothers the psychologist, because s/he is not interested in studying artifacts (much less in making them more effective). The psychologist may simply wish to identify situations in which arguments do not get processed, and a simple way to do that is to construct strong and weak arguments, and then show that there is no difference in consumer response to the two kinds of arguments, under circumstances of type X—which is prima facie evidence that the arguments did not get processed there. But this is where the rhetorician hits the roof: "So what *will* the consumer process under circumstances of type X? What are the alternatives to argumentation, here, and which of these will be most effective, here?" The psychologist does not even hear the question; she or he is off building a conceptual model of the set of circumstances under which arguments are or are not processed.

Part of the promise of rhetoric is that it has always been concerned with the causally potent differentiation of complex human artifacts—a speech to a jury, an address to a legislative body, a propaganda tract. The procedure of rhetoric is to identify the manifold (but limited) number of possibilities or options available in a given artifactual context, and then to determine the probability of achieving a desired audience response, given a choice to employ option A or option B, in context C. To a rhetorician, every persuasive endeavor is like chess. There are a limited number of pieces (options), each with distinct capabilities; there is a larger but still limited repertoire of gambits, any of which might be a smart (or dumb) response, given the state of play. When investigating a new domain, a rhetorician contributes initially by identifying and differentiating the capabilities of, say, a knight versus a bishop, and also by establishing that pawns, rooks, knights, bishops, queens, and kings represent all the possibilities that exist.

As we saw above, the pragmatic character of rhetoric, which is intrinsic and definitive of the discipline, is one of the things that makes rhetoric so suitable as a foundation for the scientific study of advertising. Its history of inquiry into complex human artifacts, each of which is constructed by making a series of choices from a palette of options, is its other attractive feature. In short, the application of rhetorical ideas to advertising was and is inevitable, so much so, that it is an interesting historical puzzle why rhetorical perspectives came so late to marketing and consumer scholarship on advertising.

Potential Contributions of Rhetoric to the Study of Advertising

The first and most important contribution to be expected from applying a rhetorical perspective is that new aspects of the advertising phenomenon will come into view. For example, before the publication of Leigh (1994), and McQuarrie and Mick (1996), it was not widely recognized that contemporary print advertising makes use of exactly the same rhetorical figures initially described by Greek and Roman orators over 2,000 years ago. Similarly, before the publication of Phillips and McQuarrie (2004), it was not well recognized that the new computer graphics technologies of Photoshop and the like were being put to work by advertisers to create very specific types of nonrealistic photographic representations. Once a rhetorical perspective has been applied, scholars of all persuasions can set to work explaining *why* advertisers use figures of speech, or *why* they alter photographs in certain ways.

The second contribution of a rhetorical perspective is to raise the question of the relative importance of variations in style as opposed to variations in content. Simply to distinguish style from content, and to show how style can be differentiated, opens up new perspectives on how advertising works. But once style has been differentiated from content, the question of relative causal potency readily comes to the fore. The advertising decision is broadened to include *how* to say it as well as *what* to say. It is not at all clear that decisions about content will always be the most important decisions facing the advertiser. We can thank psychologists and their tradition of studying strong–weak arguments for this insight. When arguments are not processed, content is unlikely to be the most important factor in achieving persuasion.

A third contribution of rhetoric is to raise the question of why advertisements in the field take the form that they do. For instance, Pollay (1985), and Pracejus, Olsen, and O'Guinn (2006) demonstrate that in a trend lasting for over a century, print ads have used fewer and fewer words, and devoted more and more of their real estate to pictures. Why should this be so? This question cannot even be asked from within a universalist psychological stance. The change in actual advertising will not even be noticed within an experimental tradition that is committed to the use of typed texts that argue a point in words alone; for example, a recommendation, supported with arguments, that student graduation should be conditioned on a qualifying exam (a stimulus used multiple times in research associated with the Ohio State tradition; see McQuarrie [1998, 2004] for a discussion of the underlying issues). A universalist tradition using a very narrow (and mostly verbal) stimulus set will, if the change in advertising is noticed, simply dismiss it as an epiphenomenon—for what has the choice of pictorial versus verbal expression to do with the fundamental scientific laws of persuasive communication? Style is simply invisible to psychology.

This, finally, is perhaps the most important contribution of rhetoric: to challenge the validity of inherited conventional psychological perspectives on advertising. Consider again the oft-used manipulation wherein some experimental stimuli use strong arguments and others use weak arguments. As explained above, this treatment contrast makes perfect sense to the psychologist—it allows us to tease out circumstances where the consumer processes the arguments in the ad stimulus (producing a mean difference between strong and weak conditions), versus conditions where consumers do not process the arguments (no mean difference). But to a rhetorician, the whole enterprise is misbegotten. First of all, if an advertiser found him or herself facing a situation where consumers were unlikely to process arguments, she or he would employ some other stylistic element instead. Second, rarely does a contemporary print ad mount extended verbal arguments of any kind; in today's print ads, the expanded picture leaves no room for that amount of text. Third, of course there are situations where consumers fail to process arguments in ads—that is easy enough to arrange, and these may even be the norm today. The question the rhetorician sets himself is to discover what advertising device *would* be effective under these circumstances. In short, from the standpoint of the rhetorician, the psychologist is not actually studying advertising, regardless of the labels applied—he is parsing processing conditions under which a written text might produce one or another response. The relevance to advertising of the insights gained thereby is, strictly speaking, unknown, but arguably suspect—print advertisers could use large chunks of written argumentation if they wished, but it is a choice they now largely eschew.

We hope to have made clear that the issue is not that the psychological knowledge built up over the past decades is wrong or unsound; it is simply that psychology has abandoned the field, and chosen not to gain knowledge relevant to the task facing contemporary advertisers. Psychology and related cognitive science disciplines remain vigorous enterprises today, and can be expected to respond positively to the rhetorical challenge—if we succeed in catching their attention. Such further development of psychological perspectives would be to the benefit of all, and provoking this adaptive response is part of the mission of contemporary rhetorical scholarship applied to advertising. As noted, rhetoricians are omnivorous consumers of causal knowledge, and that portion of psychological research not bewitched by universalist precepts has much to offer students of rhetoric and students of advertising. The more we learn about consumer response—the province of psychology—the greater will be our ability to identify and evaluate the available means of evoking these now more thoroughly understood responses.

Potential Contribution of Advertising Phenomena to the Advancement of Rhetorical Theory

Finally, we would like to argue that the study of advertising phenomena has the potential to advance the larger enterprise of rhetorical scholarship. Mass-media brand advertising is the largest organized persuasive endeavor in the world today. Relative to other large-scale persuasive enterprises (politics, proselytization), it is the most focused on the use of artifacts as opposed to live speech and interactive events. This makes advertising a peculiarly fertile domain for the text-analytic strand within rhetorical scholarship. Many scholars of rhetoric are found in English and other humanities departments, and this will continue to be true so long as composition is taught there. And although there are many kinds of written text suitable for rhetorical analysis, it should not surprise us if literary scholars tend to pursue the development of rhetorical scholarship by applying rhetorical ideas to literary texts. However, persuasion is only one of many aims of literary texts and belle letters generally. By contrast, advertisements represent the epitome of persuasive text artifacts within contemporary culture. To the extent that rhetoric is a text-analytic discipline focused on persuasive outcomes, advertisements, and not belles lettres, ought to be considered the central or main domain for developing the rhetorical discipline going forward. Rhetoricians need to populate marketing departments as well as English departments. In short, studies of rhetoric in advertising aim to provoke the same sort of adaptive response from practitioners of semiotics, poetics, and aesthetics as from practitioners of psychology. Deeper insight into the phenomenon of advertising is the hoped-for goal in each case.

The other opportunity presented by advertising is that most print advertisements are no longer written texts. They are pictorial texts that include some words. Excepting radio, other advertising media are, if anything, even less focused on words. In principle, rhetoric, as a body of theoretical ideas, ought to be no less relevant to pictorial persuasion than to verbal persuasion. That is, it should be just as possible to identify "the available means of persuasion," or the palette of stylistic devices, in the case of two dimensional photographs as in the case of written text. Note also that nowhere else in contemporary culture are pictures so central to persuasion as in mass-media advertising. Now imagine, if you will, that rhetorical scholars en masse chose to eschew the opportunity presented by the widespread use of pictorial persuasion in advertising. Or suppose rhetoricians were to cling stubbornly to ancient classical ideas about the use of verbal stylistic devices, and insist on applying *only* these inherited ideas to the new pictorial artifacts. Would the revival of rhetoric as a scholarly discipline continue apace? We think not.

Rhetoric has to be able to generate new theoretical insights about advertising to retain its claim to bear knowledge. Advertising is the main show today. What public oratory was to the ancients, advertisements are to moderns (and postmoderns). The advertising enterprise is certainly ripe for rhetorical inquiry, but it promises much more to rhetoric than a fruitful domain for the application of existing ideas. Rather, exploration of the advertising domain is crucial if rhetorical scholarship is to be more than a recovery of lost insights of the ancients. Advertising offers rhetoricians the chance to build on what was inherited from ancient times, but also to develop new ideas.

Contributions to This Volume

Recall that the goal of this volume is to present new thinking. Hence, the remaining chapters in this volume should not be approached as a primer or review of current knowledge regarding the application of rhetorical thought to advertising practice. The rhetoric perspective is now firmly established within consumer research and interested readers can easily find published studies regarding advertising rhetoric in the leading journals. Such outlets generally require that articles contain a review of the relevant literature, and often insist on empirical evidence. In contrast, the chapters in this book offer what standard journal articles cannot—innovative ideas about where research in advertising rhetoric should go next, sometimes based on little more than expert opinion, blue-sky thinking, or clap-to-the-forehead insight. The authors of these chapters are well grounded in the literature, and have been the source of some of the empirical findings that shaped the field, but here, each presents a new approach to advertising rhetoric that pushes the field beyond what has already been conceptualized and done. Readers will find actionable hypotheses in each chapter that challenge or expand common wisdom about what advertising rhetoric is and how it can be used to enhance our understanding of the advertising phenomenon.

The volume is divided into four sections. The first section urges researchers to take a fresh look at past theories of rhetoric to inform new inquiry. In Chapter 2, Eric D. DeRosia asserts that although researchers pay lip service to the ancient Greek and Roman scholars who were the fathers of rhetorical thought, very few modern researchers treat their ancient admonitions as hypotheses to be tested in a current advertising context. For example, writers of antiquity valued the use of rhetorical figures because of their positive effects on listeners' attention, aesthetic judgments, inferences, and mental imagery, to name a few possible outcomes. DeRosia laments the fact that researchers have not gone further in marrying the art of ancient rhetoric with the science of modern inquiry, to test whether these ancient truths can inform the selection of advertising style in a modern world. To further this aim, he provides a list of ancient hypotheses yet to be tested.

In Chapter 3, Barbara B. Stern asserts that researchers have been guilty of narrowly focusing on ancient narrative or oratory rhetoric, the rhetoric of *telling,* as detailed by DeRosia in Chapter 2. Dramatic rhetoric, the rhetoric of *showing,* has been ignored. Stern applies dramatic rhetorical analysis to the study of soap operas to illustrate how this type of rhetoric can help us understand the message embedded in both the medium itself (e.g., genre, characters, and plot), and the modern product placement consumption scenario. Stern also suggests that rhetoric's ruthless pragmatism may sometimes be detrimental, especially to vulnerable audiences, and provides alternatives to its sole-minded focus on "what works."

Val Larsen, in Chapter 4, moves away from ancient rhetoric to dismantle the implicit assumptions embedded in the seminal publications in advertising rhetoric of the 1990s. He contends that in their initial zeal to demonstrate that advertising style had meaning, researchers narrowed in on the symbolic aspects of advertising images and dismissed the iconicity of these pictures. However, Larsen asserts that it is only by acknowledging an image's iconicity that the specification of a system to understand the effects of advertising images can be developed. That is, iconicity is the key to embedding rhetoric's differentiation typologies within an integrative structure rather than compiling a useless list of incompatible ad elements and effects.

The next three chapters of this volume examine the cognitive processing of advertising rhetoric. Each chapter attempts to marry cognitive theories developed in psychology for understanding consumer response with the rhetorical perspective that has proved useful in understanding advertising style. In Chapter 5, Bruce A. Huhmann models how the stylistic properties of ads affect psychological variables such as perceived openness and the cognitive resources required to process an ad. He uses a resource-matching perspective to explain how these structural properties ultimately influence consumer response. The outcomes examined by Huhmann match up well with those listed by DeRosia in Chapter 2, allowing cognitive psychology to explicate the processes underlying ancient rhetorical advice.

In Chapter 6, Paul E. Ketelaar, Marnix S. van Gisbergen, and Johannes W.J. Beentjes unfold the concept of openness, touched on by Huhmann in Chapter 5. These authors develop the properties that contribute to openness and empirically test consumer response to openness. Based on their findings, they argue that the concept of openness has been overrated in advertising, as they discover more negative outcomes of openness than one would expect from the theorizing of past researchers. These authors join Stern (Chapter 3) in calling for a new consideration of the negative effects of rhetorical techniques.

In the last chapter of this section (Chapter 7), Mark A. Callister and Lesa A. Stern examine the visual rhetoric that is growing in prominence in modern advertising practice, as explicated by Larsen in Chapter 4. They combine incongruity theory from psychology with rhetorical theory, to generate hybrid hypotheses regarding the types of schemas that are brought into play during consumer interpretation of advertising images.

The third section of this volume asks each contributing author to shine a spotlight on one specific element of advertising style to generate new research directions. In Chapter 8, Tina M. Lowrey examines the structural property of complexity, also touched on by Huhmann in Chapter 5. She develops a complexity continuum to reconcile opposing findings from past research and move the field past its current impasse.

Charles Forceville, in Chapter 9, calls for an understanding of the rhetorical figure of metaphor that goes beyond conventional examinations of pictures and words. He develops the idea of multimodal metaphor—metaphor that occurs in the interchange between pictures, words, movement, and sound—to use in furthering research with television commercials.

In Chapter 10, Kai-Yu Wang and Laura A. Peracchio explain the effects of basic visual stylistic elements, such as camera angle and orientation, on consumer response. Through their chapter, Wang and Peracchio illustrate a type of visual specification system called for by Larsen in Chapter 4, using the kind of cognitive responses developed by Huhmann in Chapter 5.

In Chapter 11, Alfons Maes and Joost Schilperoord develop a system for identifying and classifying visual rhetorical figures. They examine three existing typologies of visual rhetoric and highlight the foundational similarities and omissions of each. They then extend these previous typologies by proposing a series of analytical questions that help not only to identify visual rhetoric more distinctly but also to classify its interpretation based on its conceptual and structural categories.

The final section of this book provides specific advice regarding the processes of rhetorical inquiry that can help advance the discipline. In Chapter 12, Edward F. McQuarrie takes a workbench approach to the construction of typologies of rhetorical devices. The goal is to stimulate other scholars to develop their own rhetorical typologies and to help readers evaluate the success of proposed typologies and systems. He takes two rhetorical systems in which he has been involved and disassembles them with an eye to teasing out the distinctive characteristics of rhetorical typologies generally. He then essays a new set of distinctions to show, step by step, how the construction of a rhetorical typology might proceed.

Jonathan E. Schroeder, in Chapter 13, explains the importance of images to brand culture and introduces visual analysis as a way to make sense of rhetorical imagery in advertising. He provides three rich examples of the application of visual analysis to illustrate the method as well as to provide detailed hypotheses for future research.

The final chapter of this book (Chapter 14) returns to the themes of the introductory chapter. Linda M. Scott steps back to assess the fundamental nature of the rhetorical discipline, placing rhetoric and its contributions within related schools of thought. Scott argues that rhetoric is fundamentally concerned with power, and those who study rhetoric are well advised to understand the power structures that surround the "rhetoric of inquiry" that may advance or impede their efforts.

Conclusion

Advertising rhetoric has matured markedly in the few decades since it was introduced to the discipline. Having established itself as a valid approach to understanding how advertisements affect consumers, we think the time is right to deepen and extend its contribution. We hope the reader finds a wealth of insights, and takes up the invitation to pursue these ideas further. The territory is vast, and much remains unexplored.

References

Bender, J., and D.E. Welberry. 1990. *The Ends of Rhetoric: History, Theory, and Practice.* Stanford: Stanford University Press.

Berlyne, Daniel. 1971. *Aesthetics and Psychobiology.* New York: Appleton.

Deighton, John. 1985. "Rhetorical Strategies in Advertising." In *Advances in Consumer Research,* Vol. 12, ed. Morris Holbrook and Elizabeth Hirschman, 432–436. Ann Arbor, MI: Association for Consumer Research.

Hunt, Shelby. 2002. *Foundations of Marketing Theory: Toward a General Theory of Marketing.* Armonk, NY: M.E. Sharpe.

Leigh, James H. 1994. "The Use of Figures of Speech in Print Ad Headlines." *Journal of Advertising* 23 (June): 17–34.

McQuarrie, Edward F. 1998. "Have Laboratory Experiments Become Detached from Advertiser Goals? A Meta-Analysis." *Journal of Advertising Research* 38 (November/ December): 15–26.

———. 2004. "Integration of Construct and External Validity by Means of Proximal Similarity: Implications for Laboratory Experiments in Marketing." *Journal of Business Research* 57: 142–153.

———, and David Glen Mick. 1992. "On Resonance: A Critical Pluralistic Inquiry into Advertising Rhetoric." *Journal of Consumer Research* 19 (September): 180–197.

———, and ———. 1996. "Figures of Rhetoric in Advertising Language." *Journal of Consumer Research* 22 (March): 424–438.

———, and ———. 1999. "Visual Rhetoric in Advertising: Text-Interpretive, Experimental, and Reader-Response Analyses." *Journal of Consumer Research* 26 (June): 37–54.

———, and ———. 2003a. "Visual and Verbal Rhetorical Figures under Directed Processing versus Incidental Exposure to Advertising." *Journal of Consumer Research* 29 (March): 579–587.

———, and ———. 2003b. "The Contribution of Semiotic and Rhetorical Perspectives to the Explanation of Visual Persuasion in Advertising." In *Persuasive Imagery: A Consumer Response Perspective,* ed. Linda M. Scott and Rajeev Batra, 191–222. Mahwah, NJ: Erlbaum.

———, and Barbara J. Phillips. 2005. "Indirect Persuasion in Advertising: How Consumers Process Metaphors Presented in Pictures and Words." *Journal of Advertising* 34 (2): 7–21.

Mothersbaugh, David L.; Bruce A. Huhmann; and George R. Franke. 2002. "Combinatory and Separative Effects of Rhetorical Figures on Consumers' Efforts and Focus in Ad Processing." *Journal of Consumer Research* 28 (March): 589–602.

Phillips, Barbara J. 1997. "Thinking Into It: Consumer Interpretation of Complex Advertising Images." *Journal of Advertising* 26 (2): 77–87.

———. 2000. "The Impact of Verbal Anchoring on Consumer Response to Image Ads." *Journal of Advertising* 29 (1): 15–24.

———, and Edward F. McQuarrie. 2004. "Beyond Visual Metaphor: A New Typology of Visual Rhetoric in Advertising. *Marketing Theory* 4(1/2): 113–136.

Pollay, Richard W. 1985. "The Subsidizing Sizzle: A Descriptive History of Print Advertising, 1900–1980." *Journal of Marketing* 48 (Summer): 24–37.

Pracejus, John; G. Douglas Olsen; and Thomas C. O'Guinn. 2006. "How Nothing Became Something: White Space, Rhetoric, History, and Meaning." *Journal of Consumer Research* 33 (June): 82–90.

Scott, Linda M. 1994. "Images in Advertising: The Need for a Theory of Visual Rhetoric." *Journal of Consumer Research* 21 (September): 252–273.

Sperber, Dan, and Deidre Wilson. 1986. *Relevance: Communication and Cognition.* Cambridge, MA: Harvard University Press.

Tom, Gail, and Annmarie Eves. 1999. "The Use of Rhetorical Devices in Advertising." *Journal of Advertising Research* 39 (4): 39–43.

Part I

The Starting Box

Using the Past to Hypothesize the Future

2

Rediscovering Theory

Integrating Ancient Hypotheses and Modern Empirical Evidence of the Audience-Response Effects of Rhetorical Figures

Eric D. DeRosia

Chapter Summary

The rhetorical figures that are of increasing interest among persuasion researchers were first discussed by ancient Greek and Roman scholars. This chapter reviews the ancient Greek and Roman writings on rhetoric as viewed from a modern information-processing perspective to determine how the ancient scholars expected audiences to respond when rhetorical figures were added to persuasive messages. The modern-day literature is then reviewed to determine the extent to which empirical evidence supports the ancient hypotheses. The main finding is that many plausible hypotheses held by the ancients have not yet been empirically tested, giving new avenues of pursuit to modern persuasion researchers who are developing and testing hypotheses about audience responses to rhetorical figures.

□ □ □ □

A rhetorical figure is often defined as a method of expression that is an artful deviation from the literal (or expected) method of expression. Although rhetorical figures such as metaphor, metonym, and irony have been used in advertisements for many decades (Phillips and McQuarrie 2002), researchers have only recently begun to consider the rhetorical figures in advertisements from a theoretical perspective (e.g., McQuarrie and Mick 1996). One of the important questions still facing researchers is to determine what audience-response effects are brought about when rhetorical figures are included in advertisements. A variety of such effects have been proposed and tested in the literature (e.g., DeRosia and Batra 2002; McGuire 2000; McQuarrie and Mick 1999; Mothersbaugh, Huhmann, and Franke 2002;

Phillips 2000), but so far the question does not seem to have been fully answered. Research on audience-response effects continues, thus implying that the depths of the question have not yet been fully plumbed.

It was the ancient Greeks and Romans (ca. 400 BCE–100 CE) who first described rhetorical figures in a systematic and scholarly way. Based on an inductive process of observing many persuasion attempts in oratory and writing (particularly the former), ancient Greek and Roman scholars tried to identify a set of general principles of persuasion that described "the possible means of persuasion in reference to any subject whatever" (*Art of Rhetoric* I.ii.1), always with the goal to "secure as far as possible the agreement of . . . hearers" (*Rhetorica ad Herennium* I.ii.2) and to "produce conviction in the soul" (*Phaedrus* 271A). Many of the practitioners/educators/scholars who were most successful and famous in their time wrote texts describing their views on a variety of topics, including rhetoric. A number of the ancient texts have survived and are available in modern translations from the original Greek and Latin.

Admittedly, no single ancient author provided what today's researchers would call a well-defined theory of persuasion. Furthermore, none of the authors empirically tested the effectiveness of their recommendations. As a result, the ancient literature on rhetoric has been largely ignored by today's persuasion researchers (for a noteworthy exception, see McGuire 2000).

This chapter suggests, however, that the ancient rhetorical texts are more useful to modern persuasion researchers than previously thought. As part of their descriptions of rhetorical figures, the ancients proposed a number of hypotheses about audience responses to rhetorical figures. Some of these hypotheses are very similar to the types of hypotheses considered in the current persuasion literature. Indeed, as will be made clear, it can be said that many of the hypotheses in the current literature were originally proposed centuries ago by the ancient Greeks and Romans. Unfortunately, these hypotheses are scattered throughout many ancient works, and the hypotheses have not been collected and considered in a single review. One purpose of this chapter is to fill the gap in knowledge by reviewing the ancient literature to identify the audience responses that the ancients believed are brought about when rhetorical figures are added to persuasive messages.

Although some of the hypotheses reviewed here have already been empirically tested by modern researchers, other hypotheses are new in the sense that they have not yet been considered in the persuasion literature and have not yet been empirically tested. Because some of the hypotheses are new, drawing them together in a single review is beneficial as a guide to modern persuasion researchers who are developing and testing hypotheses about audience responses to the rhetorical figures currently used in advertising.

Scope of the Review

To facilitate this review, its scope is bounded in a number of ways. Most classical Greek and Roman authors did not comment on rhetoric; of course, such texts are

Table 2.1

Brief Description of the Ancient Texts Cited Herein

Title	Author	Language	Approximate date
Phaedrus	Plato	Greek	Early fourth century BC
Poetics	Aristotle	Greek	Mid-fourth century BC
The Art of Rhetoric	Aristotle	Greek	Mid-fourth century BC
Rhetoric to Alexander	Aristotle*	Greek	Third century BC
On Style	Demetrius*	Greek	Second century BC
Rhetorica ad Herennium	Uncertain*	Latin	Early first century BC
De Inventione	Cicero	Latin	Early first century BC
De Optimo Genere Oratorum	Cicero	Latin	Mid-first century BC
De Oratore	Cicero	Latin	Mid-first century BC
De Partitione Oratoria	Cicero	Latin	Mid-first century BC
Controversiae	Seneca the Elder	Latin	Late first century BC
On the Sublime	Longinus*	Greek	First century AD
Institutio Oratoria	Quintilian	Latin	Late first century AD

*Although this text is known to be of ancient origin, the identity of its author is disputed. The most commonly accepted author is listed here.

not reviewed here. No effort is made herein to inventory the many types of rhetorical figures identified by the ancients (e.g., metaphor, litotes, and anthimeria), nor is a review conducted of all the prescriptions for effective persuasion offered by the ancients (e.g., the proper order of arguments) because detailed reviews of these aspects of the ancient works already exist (e.g., Barthes 1988; Corbett and Connors 1999; Kennedy 1963, 1972). Because the purpose of this chapter is to rediscover the valuable insights of ancient Greek and Roman theorists, this review does not focus on comparisons and contrasts between ancient authors (e.g., dwelling on the similarities and differences between the views of Cicero and Aristotle). Instead, to provide value to modern persuasion researchers, this chapter reviews the ancient works as a whole and considers the variety of hypotheses regarding figures proposed therein. The hypotheses considered in the review are those the ancients specifically described as applying to figures, those that the ancients explained using figures as examples, and those drawn from a larger discussion involving figures.

It should be noted that each ancient text has a modern convention for citing quotations, and the modern conventions are used here. Table 2.1 provides more information about each ancient source.

Findings of the Review

The hypotheses of the ancient Greek and Roman scholars regarding the audience-response effects of rhetorical figures are organized here roughly in terms of the order of information processing (see Table 2.2 for a summary). First, the hypothesized effects on attention are addressed, followed by effects on comprehension, cognitive responses, and affective responses. Effects on the evaluations of the source are then described, followed by extra figurative effects that go beyond the single rhetorical figure.

Attention

One common theme in the writings of the ancients on rhetorical figures involved the attention of recipients. The notion of attention was understood by the ancients to be an important antecedent of persuasion. For example, the author of *Rhetorica ad Herennium* (I.iv.7) wrote that those who persuade wish to have their hearers attentive, and he made a series of recommendations for gaining recipients' attention.

Rhetorical figures, in the view of the ancients, had a particular influence on the attention of recipients. The ancients hypothesized that rhetorical figures increase attention to the message as a whole, increase attention to certain arguments in the message, and increase recipients' attention to future messages.

Figures Increase Attention to the Message as a Whole

The ancients frequently described rhetorical figures as capable of attracting and maintaining the attention of recipients to the message as a whole. For example, Longinus described figures as making the hearer "more attentive" (*On the Sublime* xxvi.3), and Quintilian wrote that the variety in expression that comes from using rhetorical figures will "rivet the attention of the mind" (*Institutio Oratoria* IX.ii.64).

As summarized in Table 2.2, the empirical results reported in the modern persuasion literature are strongly supportive of this ancient hypothesis. McQuarrie and Mick (2003) observed that under incidental processing—presumably a setting in which such an effect would be particularly difficult to observe—adding rhetorical figures to advertisements increased ad recall, thereby suggesting that the rhetorical figure increase attention to the ad. Mothersbaugh, Huhmann, and Franke (2002) observed that when compared with nonfigurative ads, figurative ads have higher percentages of recipients who report having read 50 percent or more of the ad's copy; they argue that this is a proxy for extent of ad processing, but at a more fundamental level, the observation implies increased attention to the ad. Homer and Kahle (1986) observed that adding figures to advertisements decreased specious recall of ad arguments, which they argue is indicative of increased attention to the ad. Furthermore, a number of researchers (Burnkrant and Howard 1984; Howard

Table 2.2

Summary of Findings

	Modern empirical evidence	
Hypotheses proposed by ancient scholars	Supportive	Unsupportive
Attention		
Figures increase attention to the message as a whole	Burnkrant and Howard (1984) Homer and Kahle (1986) Howard (1990) McQuarrie and Mick (2003) Mothersbaugh, Huhmann, and Franke (2002) Petty, Cacioppi, and Heesacker (1981)	Myers and Haug (1967)
Figures increase attention to future messages by influencing recipients' expectations	None	None
Figures focus attention toward certain arguments	None	None
Comprehension		
Figures require inferences to comprehend	Billow (1975) Biggs (1990) Hubbell and O'Boyle (1995) Inhoff, Lima, and Carroll (1984) McQuarrie and Mick (1999) McQuarrie and Mick (2003) McQuarrie and Phillips (2005) Mothersbaugh, Huhmann, and Franke (2002) Pawlowski, Badzinski, and Mitchell (1998) Phillips (1997) Toncar and Munch (2001)	Frisson and Pickering (1999)

(continued)

Table 2.2 (continued)

Hypotheses proposed by ancient scholars	Modern empirical evidence	
	Supportive	Unsupportive
Figures cause self-congratulation among those who comprehend	None	None
Figures cause self-generated veracity	None	None
Figures may cause comprehension failures	McQuarrie and Mick (1992) Morgan and Reichert (2005) Mothersbaugh, Huhmann, and Franke (2002) Phillips (1997) Reinsch (1971) Roehm and Sternthal (2001)	Forceville (1995) McQuarrie and Mick (1999) Mitchell and Olson (1981)
Figures with comprehension failures are useless and offensive	McQuarrie and Mick (1992) Phillips (2002)	None
Figures with comprehension failures cause admiration and acquiescence	None	None
Cognitive responses		
Figures reduce counterarguing	Brennan and Bahn (2006) Petty, Cacioppi, and Heesacker (1981)	Burnkrant and Howard (1984) Munch and Swasy (1988) Swasy and Munch (1985)
Figures cause mental imagery	Honeck, Riechmann, and Hoffman (1975) Gibbs and Bogdonovich (1999)	None
Affective responses		
Figures cause pleasure	Brennan and Bahn (2006) McQuarrie and Mick (1992) McQuarrie and Mick (1999) McQuarrie and Phillips (2003) Phillips (2000)	None

Proposition		
Figures cause other specific emotions (surprise, amusement, and anticipation)	None	None
Figures cause activation	None	None
Figures moderate the intensity of affective responses	None	None
Source evaluations		
Figures harm source credibility by suggesting thorough preparation	Ang and Lim (2006) Bowers and Osborn (1966)	None
Figures improve recipients' overall evaluations of the source	None	Burnkrant and Howard (1984) Swasy and Munch (1985)
Figures suggest the source highly esteems the recipients	None	None
Extrafigurative effects		
Multiple figures have diminishing effects	Ahluwalia and Burnkrant (2004) Howard (1990) Mothersbaugh, Huhmann, and Franke (2002) Munch and Swasy (1988)	None
Diminishing effects of multiple figures caused by satiety of pleasure	None	None
Diminishing effects of multiple figures prevented with affective responses	None	None
Diminishing effects of multiple figures prevented with proper ordering of figures	None	None
Figures require special refutation methods	None	None

1990; Mothersbaugh, Huhmann, and Franke 2002; Petty, Cacioppo, and Heesacker 1981) have observed that when a rhetorical figure is added to an advertisement, recipients are more sensitive to argument-quality manipulations. This finding suggests that rhetorical figures cause recipients to scrutinize ad arguments more carefully. That is, the finding suggests that rhetorical figures cause recipients to devote greater attentional resources to ad processing. One empirical finding is unsupportive of the ancient hypothesis: Myers and Haug (1967) observed that ads with figurative headlines had no better recall than ads with literal headlines, which Myers and Haug interpret as evidence that figurative headlines do not attract attention. However, it is clear that the balance of the empirical findings reported in the modern literature is supportive of the ancient hypothesis that rhetorical figures increase attention to a message.

Figures Increase Attention to Future Messages by Influencing Recipients' Expectations

Beyond simply hypothesizing that figures increase attention, Quintilian proposed a *reason* for this increased attention. As described more fully in a subsequent section of this chapter, Quintilian expected that effective rhetorical figures bring about pleasure among recipients. Related to attention, Quintilian (*Institutio Oratoria* XI.iii.60) hypothesized that recipients who experience such pleasure form an expectation that they will experience pleasure whenever they hear a message from that source. Due to this expectation, a recipient will devote careful attention to future messages from that source. It may be surprising to some modern readers that a scholar who lived almost 2,000 years ago proposed a hypothesis that involved recipients' interexposure expectations. Indeed, as summarized in Table 2.2, a review of the modern empirical literature finds no attempt to test this particular hypothesis for rhetorical figures. Quintilian's hypothesis seems plausible, and it is only the first untested ancient hypothesis among many reviewed here that adds to the modern literature on persuasion in general and rhetorical figures in particular.

Figures Focus Attention Toward Certain Arguments

In addition to drawing the attention of recipients to the message as a whole, the ancients suggested that the speaker can guide the attention of recipients toward the arguments most strongly supportive of the speaker's cause by using rhetorical figures to express those arguments. A number of ancients made this suggestion, including the unknown author of *Rhetorica ad Herennium* who wrote that when a figure is used to express strongly supportive arguments, "no opportunity is given the hearer to remove his attention from this strongest topic" (*Rhetorica ad Herennium* IV.xliv.58).

As summarized in Table 2.2, the modern literature on rhetorical figures does not contain empirical observations that directly test this ancient hypothesis. A somewhat related finding was reported by Sengupta and Gorn (2002), who observed that omitting expected information from a picture (the rhetorical figure of ellipsis; McQuarrie and Mick 1996) increased ad recall. In particular, an ellipsis that omitted information about the product category improved recall of the product category, whereas an ellipsis that omitted information about the brand improved recall of the brand. Although this finding is consistent with the ancient idea that increased persuasion could be brought about by using a rhetorical figure to guide recipients' attention to particularly strong arguments in the message, such a persuasive technique has not yet been empirically tested.

Comprehension

In addition to attention, the ancient Greek and Roman scholars recognized the importance of message comprehension. For the most part, they described comprehension as essential to persuasion, and they continually advised speakers to be clear so that their audiences would surely comprehend. As described below, however, the ancients thought of rhetorical figures as adding another level of complexity to comprehension.

Figures Require Inferences to Comprehend

The notion that some messages force recipients to make inferences during comprehension was not unknown to the ancients. For example, according to Aristotle, "An agreeable style may be achieved by the following method—by stating half of a consideration so that the audience may understand the other half themselves" (*Rhetoric to Alexander* xxii.35).

In particular, the ancients hypothesized that rhetorical figures require recipients to make inferential leaps during comprehension. Quintilian described a class of figures that have "a hidden meaning which is left to the hearer to discover," and he described figures of this type as so commonplace that many of his contemporaries "practically restrict the name of *figure* to this device" (*Institutio Oratoria* IX.ii.65). Quintilian also suggested that a figure "does not merely tend to make what is said understood, but causes more to be understood than what is said" (*Institutio Oratorio* VIII.ii.11). Apparently, the additional understanding described by Quintilian was the result of inference.

As summarized in Table 2.2, the modern evidence for this ancient hypothesis is overwhelmingly supportive. Studies among children (Billow 1975; Pawlowski, Badzinski and Mitchell 1998) have identified metaphors that are easily comprehended by older children but not easily comprehended by younger children, suggesting that metaphoric comprehension is related to maturing cognitive operations and, therefore, supportive of the idea that comprehending metaphors requires complex inferences. Further evidence comes from studies (Frisson and Pickering 1999; Gibbs 1990; Hubbell and O'Boyle 1995; Inhoff, Lima, and Carroll

1984; McQuarrie and Phillips 2005) that use response times in a variety of ways to find evidence of delays due to cognitive processing. The results of these studies suggest that figurative language requires more time for recipients to process than literal language (with the exception of Frisson and Pickering [1999], who used commonplace metonyms that were probably processed effortlessly, such as using "Vietnam" as a metonymic substitution of a place name for an event). Therefore, the overall finding of these response-time studies is consistent with the idea that inferential processing is required to comprehend rhetorical figures. Another relevant line of empirical evidence has been the observation that adding rhetorical figures to an advertisement increases recipients' elaboration as they attempt to comprehend the message. As explained by McQuarrie and Mick (1999), this increased elaboration is brought about when recipients attempt to resolve the incongruity of rhetorical figures (i.e., attempt to comprehend the figures). Thus, the frequent observation that adding figures to an advertisement increases elaboration (McQuarrie and Mick 1999, 2003; Mothersbaugh, Huhmann, and Franke 2002; Toncar and Munch 2001) can be interpreted as supporting the ancient hypothesis. More direct evident has also been reported. Phillips (1997, 79) observed participants in a focus group setting as they were exposed to ads containing visual metaphors, and she reported "a development or progression of inferences was observed, capturing the 'aha!' moment of understanding." In sum, the empirical studies reported in the modern literature are strongly supportive of the ancient hypothesis that comprehending rhetorical figures is not an automatic, effortless process but is instead a process that requires cognitive effort and inferential processes.

Figures Cause Self-Congratulation Among Those Who Comprehend

The ancients also suggested that because comprehension of figures can be difficult, recipients who successfully comprehend figures might experience a sort of satisfaction or self-congratulation. Quintilian was referring to the message ambiguity that can be created with rhetorical figures when he wrote, "There is even a class of hearer who find a special pleasure in such passages; for the fact that [hearers] can provide an answer to the riddle fills them with an ecstasy of self-congratulation, as if they had not merely heard the phrase, but invented it" (*Institutio Oratoria* VIII. ii.21). Similarly, Demetrius argued that if you allow the hearer to make inferences to complete your meaning, the hearer "reacts more favorably to you. For he is made aware of his own intellect through you, who have given him the opportunity to be intelligent" (*On Style* 222). More than simple pleasure, this hypothesis is that comprehension (presumably comprehension that was difficult to achieve) gives the recipient an opportunity for self-congratulation for having been sufficiently knowledgeable, creative, and insightful to comprehend the figure. As summarized in Table 2.2, no empirical studies have been reported in the modern literature that provides a specific test of this ancient hypothesis.

Figures Cause Self-Generated Veracity

Demetrius also suggested that because figures allow "some points for the listener to infer and work out for himself," the result is a kind of self-generated veracity: "For when he infers what you have omitted, he is not just listening to you but he becomes your witness and reacts more favorably to you" (*On Style* 222). In other words, recipients more willingly accept as true the meaning of a rhetorical figure simply because the recipient inferentially self-generated the meaning.

The only empirical observation in the modern literature that may offer a test of this ancient hypothesis is the empirical observation of Phillips (1997) that after viewing metaphoric ads, recipients "seem satisfied with their interpretations and feel they are correct" (80). However, correct in the context of Phillips's study referred to the recipient's judgment that their self-generated implicature truly reflected authorial intent. Phillips offers an example of a research participant who viewed an ad for eye drops and drew the implicature that the eye drops were cool and soothing. The participant disagreed with conflicting implicatures offered by others in the focus group and judged her own interpretation to be correct. Because "correct" in this sense may be completely unrelated to the recipient's evaluation of the veracity of the claim (e.g., the participant described by Phillips may not have actually believed the eye drops were indeed soothing), the finding by Phillips is unrelated to the ancient hypothesis that self-generated inferences brought about by rhetorical figures yield a self-generated veracity. As a result, the ancient hypothesis has not yet been tested.

Figures May Cause Comprehension Failures

The ancient Greek and Roman scholars frequently pointed out that recipients might fail to comprehend rhetorical figures. As the ancients described it, rhetorical figures can lead to ambiguity (*Art of Rhetoric* III.5), obscurity (*De Partitione Oratoria* v.19), a lack of clarity (*Institutio Oratoria* VIII.iii.15), and a lack of perspicuity (*Institutio Oratoria* VIII.ii.1), yielding speeches that contribute to additional darkness rather than throwing light on the facts at hand (*De Oratore* III.xiii.50).

The modern empirical literature is mostly supportive of the ancient hypothesis that comprehension failures are possible. The contrary—that recipients will not fail to comprehend figures—is justified by the claim in the modern literature that ad recipients will be so motivated to process rhetorical figures that they will work at comprehension until they arrive at an interpretation they find acceptably plausible (Deacon 1994). Indeed, some empirical results suggest this is the case. When McQuarrie and Mick (1999) compared figurative ads with literal ads, they observed no difference in the self-reported difficulty of comprehending the ads. When Mitchell and Olson (1981) offered participants an advertisement for facial tissue that included a colorful sunset, recipients interpreted the photo as a visual metaphor (Scott 1994) and comprehended it as a claim that the facial tissues were available in many colors. The observation that recipients derived an interpretation that is so uncommon in facial tissue advertisements is evidence that recipients worked at comprehension until they arrived at a plausible solution. Similarly, when Forceville (1995) asked study participants to offer interpretations of ads with metaphors, none of his participants failed to generate interpretations.

However, the more frequent observation reported in the literature is that recipients do sometimes fail to comprehend metaphors. In a pretest, Reinsch (1971) measured the self-reported extent to which recipients understood the meaning of metaphors, and he observed that many of the metaphors were poorly comprehended. McQuarrie and Mick (1992; study 2) created two figurative ads that were intended to be difficult to comprehend, and participants did indeed report that one of the ads was difficult to comprehend. Similarly, Mothersbaugh, Huhmann, and Franke (2002) used a self-report measure of comprehension difficulty (with items such as "I had to work to interpret this headline"), and they observed that ads with rhetorical figures were reported to be more difficult to comprehend than literal ads. Phillips (1997) observed that some of the participants in her focus groups failed to form any interpretations for some of the metaphoric advertisements. Morgan and Reichert (1999) observed comprehension failures, particularly among individuals who rely heavily on analytic (left-brain) processing. Roehm and Sternthal (2001) reported four studies with metaphoric advertisements that demonstrated participants who lacked either motivation or ability to devote cognitive effort while processing the ad were less likely to comprehend the metaphor. In sum, although the empirical findings are somewhat mixed, they mostly support the ancient hypothesis that recipients sometimes fail to comprehend rhetorical figures.

Figures with Comprehension Failures Are Useless and Offensive

Some of the ancients judged rhetorical figures to be ineffective if not easily comprehended by recipients. Aristotle wrote that if a figure is "difficult to take in at a glance . . . then it does not impress the hearer" (*Art of Rhetoric* III.x.6). Quintilian wrote of a "perverse misuse of figures" that leads to obscurity and difficulty of comprehension: "I regard as useless words which make such a demand upon the ingenuity of the hearer" (*Institutio Oratoria* VIII.ii.18).

Worse than making the figure "useless," Longinus (*On the Sublime* xvii.1) described comprehension failures as offending recipients: if a recipient fails to comprehend the meaning of a figure, "he is promptly put out," he feels "outwitted," and he construes it "as a personal affront." The consequence is that "he sometimes turns absolutely savage, and even if he controls his feelings, he becomes wholly hostile to the reasoning of the speech." Relatedly, Cicero (*De Oratore* III.52) described recipients who fail to comprehend figures as despising the speaker.

As summarized in Table 2.2, the modern empirical literature contains related findings. When McQuarrie and Mick (1992) tested a figurative ad that was specifically designed to be difficult to comprehend, participants reported lower attitude toward the ad (versus a literal ad that was easy to comprehend). Similarly, Phillips (2000) observed that with figurative ads, ease of comprehension was positively related to attitude toward the ad. Roehm and Sternthal (2001; studies 3 and 4) reported that the extent of comprehension of metaphors in ads was positively related to brand attitude. Although these findings do not address the specific ancient hypothesis that comprehension failures lead to recipients being offended and disliking the speaker, they are broadly consistent with the ancient idea that comprehension failures are undesirable for rhetorical figures.

Figures with Comprehension Failures Cause Admiration and Acquiescence

On the other hand, some of the ancients *prized* rhetorical figures for their ability to create ambiguity and a lack of clarity. Based on the literature available to him (but lost to us), Quintilian identified a teacher of rhetoric who "instructed his pupils to make all they said obscure," and to "darken" their persuasive messages. Relating this obscurity to rhetorical figures, Quintilian derided some of his own contemporaries for regarding "as a matter of complete indifference whether their meaning is intelligible to others, so long as they know what they mean themselves" (*Institutio Oratoria* VIII.ii.18). Although Quintilian regarded such ambiguity from figures as something to be avoided, his description implies that some of the ancients not only tolerated ambiguity from figures but also embraced it.

Two different justifications for seeking comprehension failures through the use of rhetorical figures can be found in the ancient literature. First, it was thought that ambiguity and impenetrable meanings suggest to hearers that the message is venerable. For example, Quintilian suggested that some of the rhetorical figures used in speeches were regarded by recipients "as ingenious, daring and eloquent, simply because of their ambiguity, and quite a number of persons have become infected by the belief that a passage which requires a commentator must for that very reason be a masterpiece of elegance" (*Institutio Oratoria* VIII.ii.21). Second, ambiguity was thought to bring about unquestioning acceptance among recipients. For example, Aristotle wrote that hearers who fail to comprehend rhetorical figures respond "with nods of acquiescence," much as they do when they listen to the vague advice of soothsayers (*Art of Rhetoric* III.v.3).

Other than the aforementioned empirical evidence that attitude toward figurative ads is positively correlated with the difficulty of the ad's comprehension (which would be broadly unsupportive of these ancient hypotheses), no modern empirical evidence offers a test of these two entirely plausible ancient hypotheses about positive consequences of comprehension failures.

Cognitive Responses

In addition to comprehension, the hypotheses of the ancients described the cognitive responses of recipients. The ancients did not refer to cognitive responses per se, at least not in the way they are currently described in the literature (e.g., Wright 1980). However, the ancients did refer to thought-based responses on the part of hearers, and these can be called cognitive responses when viewed from a modern perspective.

Figures Reduce Counterarguing

In terms of rhetorical figures, the most important hypothesis proposed by the ancients related to cognitive responses was that rhetorical figures reduce counterarguing. Quintilian wrote that figures "steal their way into the minds of the judges" (*Institutio Oratoria* IX.i.20), and he metaphorically described rhetorical figures in persuasive messages as subtle sword attacks against which recipients have difficulty defending: "For just as in sword-play it is easy to see, parry, and ward off direct blows and simple and straightforward thrusts, while side-strokes and feints are less easy to observe . . . the fighter who feints and varies his assault [such as is accomplished with rhetorical figures in persuasive messages] is able to attack flank or back as he will, to lure his opponent's weapons from their guard and to outwit him by a slight inclination of the body" (*Institutio Oratoria* IX.i.20). Quintilian further suggested that figures could be used to suggest meanings to hearers that they would thoroughly counterargue and reject if the claim were presented literally: "Some things, too, which we cannot prove, may advantageously be here and there insinuated by a figure; for a hidden dart sometimes sticks fast, and cannot be extracted for the very reasons that it is hidden; while if you state the same things plainly, they will be contradicted" (*Institutio Oratoria* IX.ii.75). As a result, a rhetorical figure was thought to have "the power of driving the hearers forward in any direction in which it has applied its weight" (*De Oratore* III.xiv.55).

The modern literature offers mixed support for the ancient hypothesis that rhetorical figures reduce counterarguing. One test of the hypothesis was provided by McQuarrie and Mick (1992), who tested it with self-report measures of counterarguing ("I argued/agreed with the ad," "I rejected/accepted the ad's point"). Two different studies demonstrated that when a rhetorical figure was added to an advertisement, viewers said they counterargued less (and also reported increased ad liking and more positive brand attitudes). However, one of the studies also included a rhetorical figure that was designed to be too complex for viewers to interpret. Counterarguing should have been inhibited for this figure also. However, in response to this figure, viewers reported high levels of counterarguing (as well as low attitude toward the ad and low brand attitude). It appears that the self-report measure of counterarguing was at least partially reflective of a more general evaluation by the participant, such as attitude toward the ad or attitude toward the brand, instead of the extent to which the participant counterargued. Therefore, the results from the self-report measure of counterarguing are inconclusive.

More direct evidence was obtained by Brennan and Bahn (2006), who used a traditional thought-listing task to determine whether including a rhetorical figure in an ad inhibited counterarguing. They found that among ad recipients with high in need for cognition (i.e., recipients who were sufficiently self-motivated to exert the necessary cognitive effort to comprehend the figurative ad), a figurative ad yielded fewer counterarguing thoughts than an equivalent literal ad. This observation supports the ancient hypothesis that figures inhibit counterarguing.

Other potentially relevant evidence comes from the many empirical findings that rhetorical figures are persuasive. After all, if a figurative ad is found to be more persuasive than a literal ad, the finding is consistent with the hypothesis that the rhetorical figure inhibited counterarguing. Such persuasive effects of rhetorical figures have indeed been frequently reported. Reinsch (1971) found that by adding a metaphor to a message, the message was more persuasive. Likewise, Tom and Eves (1999) observed that ads containing figures are more persuasive than ads that do not contain figures. Roehm and Sternthal (2001) reported four studies in which metaphoric ads are more persuasive than literal ads among participants with high motivation and ability. At the level of brand beliefs rather than brand attitudes, Mitchell and Olson (1981) compared an ad featuring a metaphoric claim with an ad featuring a literal claim, and they found that the metaphoric claim led to a greater change in the relevant brand belief. Unfortunately, these studies on the persuasive nature of figures do not test the ancient hypothesis that figures reduce counterarguing. The persuasive effects observed in these studies could just as easily support some of the other explanations proposed in the ancient and modern literature (e.g., figures attract attention or figures improve evaluations of the source). Even if these persuasive effects *are* related to cognitive responses, the persuasive effects observed in these studies can be obtained without any reduction in counterarguing. For a message with strong arguments—that is, arguments with which participants would be less likely to counterargue—more extensive processing should yield an increase in support-arguing and an attendant increase in persuasion. As a result, if the message contains strong arguments, an increase in persuasion is not necessarily an indicator of inhibited counterarguing. It appears that the ads used in these studies did, indeed, contain strong arguments. For example, as described by Roehm and Sternthal (2001, 267), the arguments expressed by the metaphors used in their studies will not be counterargued, but will instead bring about persuasion because the metaphor delivers information that is "more compelling" than the literal advertisement. Thus, evidence that figurative ads are more persuasive than literal ads does not provide an effective test of the ancient hypothesis that figures reduce counterarguing.

Fortunately, one of the methods used in the literature does provide an effective test of the ancient hypothesis: an argument-quality manipulation under high motivation. Ad recipients who have high motivation can be expected to cognitively respond to the ad, and if the arguments in the ad are weak, the recipient's cognitive responses can be expected to be counterarguments. Thus, if recipients with high motivation view an ad with weak arguments and are persuaded, it can be said that the recipients' counterarguing has been inhibited.

One study using this method found that adding rhetorical figures inhibited counterarguing. When Petty, Cacioppo, and Heesacker (1981) exposed highly motivated recipients to a message with weak arguments, they observed that adding rhetorical figures to the message caused an increase in attitude, a decrease in the number of counterarguing thoughts reported in a thought-listing task, and greater distraction as indicated by a self-report measure. These results clearly support the ancient hypothesis that rhetorical figures inhibit counterarguing.

However, other studies using this procedure have yielded different results. Burnkrant and Howard (1984) observed that among high-motivation participants viewing a message with weak arguments, adding a rhetorical figure increased the number of counterarguing thoughts and decreased attitude. Also among high-motivation participants using a message with weak arguments, Swasy and Munch (1985) found that adding rhetorical figures reduced attitude, increased the number of counterarguing thoughts, and increased the level of self-reported distraction. Using a different approach, Munch and Swasy (1988) examined the effect of increasing the number of rhetorical figures in an ad. When they tested advertisements with weak arguments among high-motivation participants, they observed that increasing the number of rhetorical figures in an advertisement did not yield an increase in attitude, and it decreased the level of self-report distraction experienced by recipients. With the exception of the self-report distraction observed by Swasy and Munch (1985), the findings of these three studies are unsupportive of (and in some cases directly opposed to) the hypothesis that rhetorical figures reduce counterarguing.

In sum, the ancient hypothesis that rhetorical figures inhibit counterarguing is an intriguing prospect for persuasion, but the empirical evidence available in the modern literature offers only mixed support for the hypothesis.

Figures Cause Mental Imagery

Mental imagery was a specific type of cognitive response hypothesized by the ancients to be brought about by rhetorical figures. Modern researchers define mental imagery as the representation of sensory experiences (such as visual representations) in working memory (MacInnis and Price 1987). The ancients referred to a similar imaginal phenomenon, suggesting that persuasive messages should attempt to "put the hearer in the presence of the action itself" (*On the Sublime* xxvi.2) and help hearers to "see what you describe" and "bring it vividly before the eyes of your audience" (*On the Sublime* xv.1).

Rhetorical figures in particular were seen as bringing about mental imagery, thus augmenting factual descriptions with illuminating and vivid mental pictures (*Institutio Oratoria* VIII.iii.72). Cicero wrote that such effects were thought to be accomplished because a figure "almost sets the fact before the eyes" (*De Partitione Oratoria* vi.20). Likewise, Cicero wrote that a figure yields an "almost visual presentation of events as if practically going on" (*De Oratore* III.liii.202) and a figure "makes us feel that we actually see it before our eyes" (*De Partitione Oratoria* vi.21).

Modern theorists (e.g., Paivio 1979) describe poetic metaphors as bringing about mental imagery, but little empirical evidence of this effect has been reported. The findings that have been reported do support the idea that metaphors (at least some metaphors) can bring about mental imagery. Honeck, Riechmann, and Hoffman (1975) observed in a pretest that some metaphoric proverbs generated more mental imagery among readers (e.g., "There is a great force hidden in a sweet command") than other proverbs (e.g., "Reputation is commonly measured by the acre"). Honeck et al. do not offer theoretical expectations that could determine a priori whether a metaphor is high or low in imagery, but their results clearly demonstrate that some figures yield high mental imagery. Gibbs and Bogdonovich (1999) exposed recipients to a poem with many metaphors and recorded participants' interpretations, along with any mental imagery they experienced during exposure. After analyzing the results, Gibbs and Bogdonovich concluded that comprehending the poem's metaphors involved the activation of mental imagery. Although neither of these reported studies were conducted in the context of persuasive messages, these studies do offer some support for the ancient hypothesis that rhetorical figures bring about mental imagery.

Affective Responses

Figures Cause Pleasure

Something the ancients considered wholly separate from the recipient's cognitive response was the recipient's emotional response. Pathos, the technique of appealing to those emotions, was a main tenet of ancient rhetoric. The ancients not only recognized the persuasive power of stirring up emotions among recipients (a topic that has received a great deal of attention in the modern persuasion literature) but also esteemed the ability to calm emotions among recipients as an essential tool in the persuader's toolkit (a topic that has received little attention in the modern persuasion literature).

Relevant to this chapter, the ancients described the inclusion of rhetorical figures in a persuasive message as one way of bringing about emotional responses. By far, the most commonly proposed emotional consequence of rhetorical figures was pleasure. For example, Quintilian described the majority of figures as having a goal of delighting the hearer (*Institutio Oratoria* IX.iii.102). Similarly, Aristotle (*Art of Rhetoric* III.i.6), Cicero (*De Partitione Oratoria* vi.22), Demetrius (*On Style* 164–168), and the unknown author of *Rhetorica ad Herennium* (IV.xxiii.32) all describe rhetorical figures as bringing about pleasure among recipients.

The modern literature contains evidence supporting this ancient hypothesis. A number of studies (Brennan and Bahn 2006; McQuarrie and Mick 1992, 1999, 2003; also Toncar and Munch 2001, but only among low-motivation participants) find that adding a rhetorical figure to an ad increases recipients' attitude toward the ad. Because all of these studies use "pleasant/unpleasant" or "enjoyable/not enjoyable" (or both) as measurement items for attitude toward the ad, it can be said that the studies offer support for the ancient hypothesis that rhetorical figures bring about pleasure among recipients. Even stronger evidence was provided by Phillips (2000), who observed that when testing ads with a visual metaphor and a headline that either partially or fully explained the meaning of the metaphor, ad liking was higher for the ads with a partially explaining headline. Phillips interprets this as evidence that providing recipients with a complete interpretation of the metaphor robs them of the opportunity to infer the meaning of the metaphor for themselves, thus depriving them of the opportunity to experience the pleasure of interpreting the rhetorical figure. Both this finding and the other findings in the literature on attitude toward the ad strongly support the ancient hypothesis that rhetorical figures bring about pleasure among recipients.

Figures Cause Other Specific Emotions
(Surprise, Amusement, and Anticipation)

In addition, the ancients described other specific emotions that can be brought about by rhetorical figures, including surprise (*On the Sublime* xxiv.2; *Controversiae* I.vii.15), enthusiasm (*Institutio Oratoria* VIII.iii.3; *Rhetoric* III.vii.11), amusement and laughter (*On the Sublime* xxxviii.5; *Rhetorica ad Herennium* I.vi.10; *De Oratore* II.lxv.261–264), and anticipation (*De Partitione Oratoria* xxi.73). The possibility of rhetorical figures bringing about these various emotions has not yet been tested in the modern empirical literature.

Figures Cause Activation

A broader aspect of the ancients' hypotheses about rhetorical figures can be described using the circumplex model of emotion (e.g., Larsen and Diener 1992), which proposes that any emotion can be described using two orthogonal dimensions: pleasure–displeasure (the hedonic quality of the emotion) and activation (the sense of energy or arousal imparted by the emotion). Activation is a continuum ranging from excitement (at the high end) downward through alertness, relaxation, and drowsiness (at the low end). According to the circumplex model, emotions such as elation and serenity are both pleasurable, but elation is high in activation, whereas serenity is low in activation. Conversely, emotions such as distress and depression are both displeasurable, but distress is high in activation, whereas depression is low in activation.

As described above, the most common hypothesis described by the ancients was related to the pleasure–displeasure dimension. However, the ancients also described an influence on the activation dimension of affect. Longinus wrote that figures "all serve to lend emotion and excitement" (*On the Sublime* xxix.2), and figures make listeners "full of active interest" (Ibid. xxvi.3). Longinus proposed that figures could fill listeners with a "divine frenzy" (Ibid. xxxix.2). Similarly,

Quintilian wrote that audiences of a speaker using figures can be "seized with a kind of frenzy" (*Institutio Oratoria* VIII.iii.3).

Relatedly, the ancients found that when they began their speeches, the attention of recipients was sometimes poor because the recipients were fatigued as a result of listening to previous speakers (*Rhetorica ad Herennium* I.vi.10). The ancients also found that even with fresh audiences, their own speeches could produce "weariness and satiety" (*Institutio Oratorio* IX.iv.142). Because of their activating effects, rhetorical figures were seen by the ancients as an antidote to this fatigue of reception (*Institutio Oratoria* IX.iii.27; *On the Sublime* xxvi.3).

The modern literature contains no tests of the ancient hypothesis that rhetorical figures increase activation among recipients.

Figures Moderate the Intensity of Affective Responses

The ancient scholars were well aware that some topics (e.g., descriptions of the suffering of crime victims) inherently bring about emotional responses among message recipients. In modern terminology, the ancients hypothesized that the effects of such topics on emotional responses were moderated by rhetorical figures. For example, a topic designed to make recipients feel pity would make them feel greater pity if the topic were expressed with a rhetorical figure. Longinus described just such an effect when he suggested that topics that would normally cause fear among people in an audience would make the audience feel "in the thick of danger" and would be more emotionally moving if the topic were expressed with a rhetorical figure (*On the Sublime* xxvi.1). Similarly, Cicero suggested that topics that bring about positive emotions can cause those emotions to be more strongly felt if the topics are expressed figuratively (*De Partitione Oratoria* xvii.58).

Furthermore, the ancients suggested that the moderation was due to more than simply the presence or absence of a rhetorical figure. They hypothesized that the figure's aptness or artfulness determined the direction of the interaction. If the figure were faulty, it would ruin the topic's emotional effect, whereas if it were artful, it would enhance the topic's emotional effect. Demetrius offers an example with a topic that should have made hearers angry, but because the topic was expressed with a poorly crafted figure, "the hearer loses all sense of anger" (*On Style* 247). Similarly, Longinus describes speeches intended to bring about pleasure that instead arrive at "frigid failure" because the figures used are childish and overly elaborate (*On the Sublime* iii.5; see also xxvii.2). On the other hand, well-crafted figures were thought to enhance emotional responses to the topic (*De Partitione Oratoria* xiv.53; *Institutio Oratorio* IX.i.21; *On the Sublime* xvi.2) Because of this moderating effect, Longinus describes the use of rhetorical figures as a dangerous tactic for speakers to attempt, and he describes figures as "the source and groundwork no less of failure than of success" (*On the Sublime* v.1).

No modern researchers have reported studies investigating a moderating effect of rhetorical figures on emotive message meanings. It could be argued that, as reviewed in a previous section, some findings (reported in the literature as attitude toward the ad) provide some support for this ancient hypothesis. However, this ancient hypothesis suggests an interaction between emotive message content and rhetorical figures, and such a relationship has not yet been considered in the modern literature.

Source Evaluations

Another of the basic tenets of ancient rhetoric was the persuasive power of ethos: the audience's belief that the speaker was credible, authoritative, and trustworthy. The ancients made explicit the fundamental assumption that recipients form evaluations of the source during the speech (*Controversiae* III.Preface.1), they recognized that hearers may have premessage evaluations of the source (*Rhetoric to Alexander* xxix.15), and they believed evaluations of the source had consequences for persuasion (*De Oratore* II.xliii.182). In the modern day, researchers have examined the ethos concept extensively in the source credibility literature.

Figures Harm Source Credibility by Suggesting Thorough Preparation

Relevant to this chapter, the ancients proposed that when speakers use rhetorical figures, recipients evaluate the speaker as less credible. The underlying mechanism they proposed for this effect is related to the ancient notion of artificiality. The ancients were very concerned with the appearance of artificiality and obvious preparation in their persuasive messages. The ancients believed that if the speech appeared to be natural and spontaneous, it would "make the judges more ready to accept our statements without suspicion" (*Institutio Oratoria* IX.ii.60). If, on the other hand, the message seemed artificial and to be the result of lavish preparation, such effort may indicate an attempt to skillfully perpetrate a deception. As a result, the ancients believed that if recipients perceived the persuasive message to be artificial, the recipients would become suspicious of the speaker. As Seneca the Elder described it, "Nothing is more prejudicial than obvious preparation: for it makes clear that something bad lurks beneath" (*Controversiae* VII.Preface.3).

Concerned about this effect, the ancients suggested that including rhetorical figures in a persuasive message was problematic because the creation of such figures "seems impossible without labor and pains" (*Rhetorica ad Herennium* IV.xxii.32). Similarly, Quintilian argued "abnormal figures lying outside the range of common speech . . . make it quite clear that they did not present themselves naturally to the speaker, but were hunted out by him, dragged from obscure corners and artificially piled together" (*Institutio Oratoria* IX.iii.5; see also *Institutio Oratoria* VIII.Preface.21).

The impact of rhetorical figures on source credibility has been measured in a few studies, and the results suggest that rhetorical figures can indeed harm source credibility. Bowers and Osborn (1966) added two different extended metaphors to two different persuasive messages, and they measured recipients' evaluation of source trustworthiness. They observed that one metaphor decreased source trustworthiness and the other metaphor had no significant effect. Ang and Lim (2006) added metaphors to advertisements, and participants in their study evaluated the brand (i.e., the sponsoring source of the communication) as less sincere. These findings are consistent with the ancient hypothesis that rhetorical figures reduce source credibility. However, these studies leave untested the ancient hypothesis that artificiality is the underlying reason for the effect.

Figures Improve Recipients' Overall Evaluations of the Source

In a broad sense, the ancient literature contains a paradox. Although the ancients hypothesized that figures harm the speaker's ethos, they also hypothesized that rhetorical figures would improve the audience's overall evaluation of the source. For example, Quintilian suggested that when figures are included in a speech, audiences approve of the speaker (*Institutio Oratorio* IX.i.20), admire the speaker (Ibid. VIII.iii.5), and give the speaker glory (Ibid. X.i.31).

Only two modern studies have tested this ancient hypothesis of a general effect on source evaluation, and the effect was not supported. Burnkrant and Howard (1984) observed that adding a rhetorical figure to a persuasive message made no difference on the overall evaluation of the source, and Swasy and Munch (1985) observed that adding a rhetorical figure reduced the overall evaluation of the source.

It should be noted that modern researchers have tested a number of other effects of rhetorical figures on source credibility that are only moderately related to the ancient hypotheses reviewed here. These have included investigations of the perceived pressure exerted by the source (Ahluwalia and Burnkrant 2004; Swasy and Munch 1985; Zillmann and Cantor 1974), the source's dynamism (Reinsch 1971), ingenuity (Bowers and Osborn 1966), politeness (Burnkrant and Howard 1984; Swasy and Munch 1985), authoritativeness (Reinsch 1971), expertise (Swasy and Munch 1985), competence (Bowers and Osborn 1966), and self-confidence (Burnkrant and Howard 1984). Although the findings are not reviewed here because these particular dimensions of source credibility are mostly unrelated to the ancient hypothesis (as indicated by the poor intercorrelations between these dimensions observed by Swasy and Munch [1985]), it can be said in passing that the findings in these series of studies are decidedly mixed, with some studies suggesting rhetorical figures have effects on the dimension of source credibility being tested, and other studies suggesting no such effect, with the end result that the entire question of the effects of rhetorical figures on source credibility is uncertain.

Figures Suggest the Source Highly Esteems the Recipients

An aspect of source evaluations uncommon in the modern source credibility literature is the recipients' judgment of how the source evaluates the recipients.

According to the ancient rhetoricians, if the hearers think the speaker esteems the hearers highly, there is a persuasive effect (*Art of Rhetoric* II.1.3). Because of this, the ancients suggested to speakers that they explicitly state that they are friendly toward the audience and hold them in high esteem (e.g., *Rhetoric to Alexander* xxix.30).

Relevant to the topic of this chapter, the ancients hypothesized that using rhetorical figures also accomplishes this goal by complimenting the audience (*Institutio Oratoria* IX.ii.78) and giving the appearance of friendliness toward the audience (*De Partitione Oratoria* vi.22). Why would using rhetorical figures imply that the speaker esteems the audience highly? One suggestion comes from Demetrius, who wrote that if a speaker explains everything in a literal and complete way, it implies that the speaker judges his audience to be fools who could not be trusted to comprehend something more complex (*On Style* 222). The converse should also be true: when a speaker adds a figure to a persuasive message, the audience should infer that the speaker judges the audience to be insightful and able to comprehend the figure's meaning.

As summarized in Table 2.2, the modern literature on rhetorical figures has not investigated recipients' judgments of the source's esteem of the recipients.

Extrafigurative Effects

Multiple Figures Have Diminishing Effects

In addition to the effects of adding a single rhetorical figure to a message, the ancients formed hypotheses that went beyond the single figure. The most prominent of these extrafigurative hypotheses was that when more than one rhetorical figure is used in a message, they have diminishing effects among recipients. For example, the author of *Rhetorica ad Herennium* wrote, "[Figures] quickly sate the hearing" (IV.xxiii.32). Similarly, Quintilian wrote that figures should not be "excessive in number nor all of the same type or combined or closely packed, since economy in their use, no less than variety, will prevent the hearer from being surfeited" (*Institutio Oratoria* IX.iii.27).

The ancients saw one consequence of using too many rhetorical figures as the loss of their positive effects. For example, "If a speaker use [figures] sparingly and only as occasion demands, they will serve as a seasoning to his style and increase its attractions. If, on the other hand, he strains after them overmuch, he will lose that very charm of variety which they confer" (*Institutio Oratoria* IX.iii.4).

Beyond rhetorical figures losing their positive effects, the ancients saw the excessive use of rhetorical figures as having negative effects. Quintilian wrote that using figures too frequently makes the audience "weary" (*Institutio Oratoria* VIII.vi.14), and the author of *Rhetorica ad Herennium* (IV.xxiii.32) and Quintilian (*Institutio Oratoria* IX.ii.72) wrote that including too many figures will make a message "offensive."

Some modern empirical studies offer tests of this ancient hypothesis by varying the number of rhetorical figures in persuasive messages. Howard (1990) found in two studies that adding a second rhetorical figure to a message made it no more persuasive than a single rhetorical figure. Munch and Swasy (1988) tested ads with strong arguments that included either four, eight, or twelve rhetorical figures. They found the ad with eight figures was no more persuasive than the ad with four figures, the ad with twelve figures was no more persuasive than the ad with eight figures, and the ad with twelve figures was *less* persuasive than the ad with four figures. Ahluwalia and Burnkrant (2004) found that when compared to a message with only one rhetorical figure, a message with multiple rhetorical figures was viewed as a lower quality message, with less appropriate tactics, higher pressure from the message source, and, most important, lower brand attitude. However, Ahluwalia and Burnkrant observed these effects only for a comparative ad; for a noncomparative ad, all of these effects were nonsignificant. Using a different approach, Mothersbaugh, Huhmann, and Franke (2002) found that multiple figures of the same type yielded no incremental benefit beyond a single figure of that type in terms of depth of ad processing (as measured by the proportion of recipients who reported having read 50 percent or more of the ad's copy). In combination, these findings support the idea that rhetorical figures have diminishing effects, although the mixed findings make it impossible to test the ancient ideas that multiplying figures not only ruins the positive effects of figures but also brings about negative effects.

Diminishing Effects of Multiple Figures Caused by Satiety of Pleasure

The ancients proposed that the root cause of the diminishing effects of rhetorical figures is that recipients reach satiety on the emotional response of pleasure. For example, Cicero wrote that rhetorical figures "must be so distributed that there may be brilliant jewels placed at various points as a sort of decoration. Consequently it is necessary . . . not merely to give [recipients] pleasure but also to do so without giving them too much of it. . . . The things which most strongly gratify our senses and excite them most vigorously at their first appearance, are the ones from which we are most speedily estranged by a feeling of disgust and satiety" (*De Oratore* III. xxv.98). None of the modern empirical studies offer a test of the ancient hypothesis that the diminishing effect of rhetorical figures is caused by satiety of pleasure.

Diminishing Effects of Multiple Figures Prevented with Affective Responses

The ancient literature contains another twist to the diminishing-effects hypothesis. Longinus argued that when the recipients strongly feel emotions (presumably pleasure and other emotions as well), the diminishing effects of figures would be prevented: "As I said in speaking of figures, the proper antidote for a multitude of daring metaphors is strong and timely emotion and genuine sublimity. These by their nature sweep everything along in the forward surge of their current . . . and do not give the hearer time to examine how many metaphors there are, because he shares the excitement of the speaker" (*On the Sublime* xxxii.4). The modern empirical literature offers no test of whether emotional responses forestall the diminishing effects of multiple rhetorical figures.

Diminishing Effects of Multiple Figures Prevented
with Proper Ordering of Figures

Another way the ancients suggested that the diminishing effects of rhetorical figures can be circumvented relates to the ordering of the figures in the message. When discussing an example of multiple metaphors, Demetrius suggests that authors should "place first those that are not specifically vivid, next or last the more vivid. In this way what comes first will sound vivid to us, and what follows more vivid still. Otherwise we will seem to have lost vigor" (*On Style* 50). It seems reasonable that this hypothesis would apply not only to the vividness of the figure but also more broadly to its artfulness. Although this ancient suggestion does seem plausible given the modern knowledge of contrast effects, no modern studies offer tests of whether such a technique can prevent the diminishing effects of multiple figures.

Figures Require Special Refutation Methods

Quintilian provided some commentary on how to negate the audience effects of rhetorical figures when they have been employed by adversaries in their persuasive messages. Quintilian suggested converting the opponent's figurative meaning into literal meaning: "Some hold that [figures] should always be exposed by the antagonist, just as hidden ulcers are laid open by the surgeon. It is true that this is often the right course, being the only means of refuting the charges that have been brought against us. . . . We may ask our opponents, if they have any confidence in the righteousness of their cause, to give frank and open expression to the charges which they have attempted to suggest by indirect hints" (*Institutio Oratoria* IX.ii.93). The modern persuasion literature has devoted little attention to methods of counteracting the persuasion attempts of opponents (for a noteworthy exception, see McGuire's [1964] inoculation theory). As a result, no modern empirical evidence is available to test these ancient hypotheses about methods of refuting rhetorical figures.

Summary

Rhetorical figures were thought by the ancients to have a wide variety of effects among recipients, including effects on attention, comprehension, cognitive responses, affective responses, source evaluations, and extra figurative effects. It seems likely that the ideas of the ancients related to rhetorical figures contain correct insights mingled with incorrect hypotheses. Consider, for example, how Cicero described good rhetorical style in a persuasive message as not only utilitarian but also aesthetically attractive: "But in oratory, as in most matters, nature has contrived with incredible skill that the things possessing most utility also have the greatest amount of dignity, and indeed frequently of beauty also. We observe that . . . the sky is a round vault, with the earth as its center, held stationary by its own force and stress; and the sun travels round it . . . while the moon receives the sun's light as it advances and retires. . . . This system is so powerful that a slight modification of it would make it impossible for it to hold together, and it is so beautiful that no lovelier vision is even imaginable. . . . The same is the case in regard to all the divisions of a speech—virtually unavoidable practical requirements produce charm of style as a result" (*De Oratore* III.xlv.178–181). Of course, Cicero was incorrect in his knowledge of astronomy: the sun does not revolve around the earth. However, it is difficult to argue with his insights that the solar system is maintained by powerful utilitarian forces and that its sight in the night sky is profoundly beautiful. Furthermore, Cicero's proposal that the night sky is beautiful *because* it is utilitarian, along with his implication that good style is beautiful because it is utilitarian, is an intriguing idea deserving of further reflection.

In a similar way, we may expect that the writings of the ancients on rhetorical figures contain some ideas that are incorrect, some ideas that are correct, and some ideas that are of uncertain veracity. Empirical investigations are necessary to identify the correct ideas. As reviewed here, a number of the hypotheses held by the ancients have been supported in modern empirical investigations. For these supported hypotheses, this chapter gives proper credit to the ancient scholars who conceived of the ideas centuries before modern theorists. Furthermore, as reviewed here, many ancient hypotheses have not yet been tested by modern researchers. These rediscovered ancient hypotheses give new avenues of pursuit to modern persuasion researchers who are developing and testing hypotheses about audience responses to rhetorical figures.

Acknowledgment

The author thanks Anne Traynor for her assistance, and also gratefully acknowledges funding support from a Marriott School of Management Research Grant and the JC Penney Research Program at Brigham Young University.

References

Ahluwalia, Rohini, and Robert E. Burnkrant. 2004. "Answering Questions About Questions: A Persuasion Knowledge Perspective for Understanding the Effects of Rhetorical Questions." *Journal of Consumer Research* 31 (June): 26–42.

Ang, Swee Hoon, and Elison Ai Ching Lim. 2006. "The Influence of Metaphors and Product Type on Brand Personality Perceptions and Attitudes." *Journal of Advertising* 35 (2): 39–53.

Barthes, Roland. 1970/1988. "The Old Rhetoric: An Aide-Memoire." In *The Semiotic Challenge*, trans. Richard Howard, 11–93. New York: Hill and Wang.

Billow, Richard M. 1975. "A Cognitive Developmental Study of Metaphor Comprehension." *Developmental Psychology* 11 (4): 415–423.

Bowers, John Waite, and Michael M. Osborn. 1966. "Attitudinal Effects of Selected Types of Concluding Metaphors in Persuasive Speeches." *Speech Monographs* 33 (2): 147–155.

Brennan, Ian, and Kenneth D. Bahn. 2006. "Literal versus Extended Symbolic Messages and Advertising Effectiveness: The Moderating Role of Need for Cognition." *Psychology & Marketing* 23 (4): 273–295.

Burnkrant, Robert E., and Daniel J. Howard. 1984. "Effects of the Use of Introductory Rhetorical Questions Versus Statement on Information Processing." *Journal of Personality and Social Psychology* 47 (6): 1218–1230.

Corbett, Edward, and Robert Connors. 1999. *Classical Rhetoric for the Modern Student.* New York: Oxford University Press.

Deacon, Peter A. 1994. "Investigating the Effects of Symbolism in Advertisements: A Framework Based on the Processing of Metaphor." In *Proceedings of the American Marketing Association Winter Educators' Conference,* 159–160. Chicago: American Marketing Association.

DeRosia, Eric D., and Rajeev Batra. 2002. "The Cognitive Processes Underlying the Interpretation of Visual Metaphors." In *Advances in Consumer Research,* vol. 29, ed. Susan M. Broniarczyk and Kent Nakamoto, 265. Valdosta, GA: Association for Consumer Research.

Forceville, Charles. 1995. "IBM Is a Tuning Fork: Degrees of Freedom in the Interpretation of Pictorial Metaphors." *Poetics* 23 (3): 189–218.

Frisson, Steven, and Martin J. Pickering. 1999. "The Processing of Metonymy: Evidence from Eye Movements." *Journal of Experimental Psychology* 25 (6): 1366–1383.

Gibbs, Raymond W. Jr. 1990. "Comprehending Figurative Referential Descriptions." *Journal of Experimental Psychology* 16 (1): 56–66.

———, and Jody Bogdonovich. 1999. "Mental Imagery in Interpreting Poetic Metaphor." *Metaphor and Symbol* 14 (1): 37–44.

Homer, Pamela M., and Lynn R. Kahle. 1986. "A Social Adaptation Explanation of the Effects of Surrealism in Advertising." *Journal of Advertising* 15 (2): 50–54.

Honeck, Richard P.; Paul Riechmann; and Robert R. Hoffman. 1975. "Semantic Memory for Metaphor: The Conceptual Base Hypothesis." *Memory & Cognition* 3 (4): 409–415.

Howard, Daniel J. 1990. "Rhetorical Question Effects on Message Processing and Persuasion: The Role of Information Availability and the Elicitation of Judgment." *Journal of Experimental Social Psychology* 26: 217–239.

Hubbell, James A., and Michael W. O'Boyle. 1995. "The Effects of Metaphorical and Literal Comprehension Processes on Lexical Decision Latency of Sentence Components." *Journal of Psycholinguistic Research* 24 (4): 269–287.

Inhoff, Albrecht Werner; Susan D. Lima; and Patrick J. Carroll. 1984. "Contextual Effects on Metaphor Comprehension in Reading." *Memory & Cognition* 12 (6): 558–567.

Kennedy, George. 1963. *The Art of Persuasion in Greece.* Princeton: Princeton University Press.

———. 1972. *The Art of Persuasion in the Roman World, 300 B.C.–A.D. 300.* Princeton: Princeton University Press.

Larsen, Randy J., and Edward Diener. 1992. "Promises and Problems with the Circumplex Model of Emotion." *Review of Personality and Social Psychology: Emotion,* vol. 13., ed. Margaret S. Clark, 25–59. Newbury Park, CA: Sage.

MacInnis, Deborah J., and Linda L. Price. 1987. "The Role of Imagery in Information Processing: Review and Extensions." *Journal of Consumer Research* 13 (March): 473–491.

McGuire, William J. 1964. "Inducing Resistance to Persuasion: Some Contemporary Approaches." *Advances in Experimental Social Psychology,* vol. 1., ed. Leonard Berkowitz, 191–229. New York: Academic Press.

————. 2000. "Standing on the Shoulders of Ancients: Consumer Research, Persuasion, and Figurative Language." *Journal of Consumer Research* 27 (June): 109–114.

McQuarrie, Edward F., and David Glen Mick. 1992. "On Resonance: A Critical Pluralistic Inquiry into Advertising Rhetoric." *Journal of Consumer Research* 19 (September) 180–197.

————, and ————. 1996. "Figures of Rhetoric in Advertising Language." *Journal of Consumer Research* 22 (March): 424–438.

————, and ————. 1999. "Visual Rhetoric in Advertising: Text-Interpretive, Experimental, and Reader-Response Analyses." *Journal of Consumer Research* 26 (June): 37–54.

————, and ————. 2003. "Visual and Verbal Rhetorical Figures under Directed Processing versus Incidental Exposure to Advertising." *Journal of Consumer Research* 29 (March): 579–587.

————, and Barbara J. Phillips. 2005. "Indirect Persuasion in Advertising: How Consumers Process Metaphors Presented in Pictures and Words." *Journal of Advertising* 34 (2): 7–20.

Mitchell, Andrew A., and Jerry C. Olson. 1981. "Are Product Attribute Beliefs the Only Mediator of Advertising Effects on Brand Attitude?" *Journal of Marketing Research* 18 (3): 318–332.

Morgan, Susan E., and Tom Reichert. 1999. "The Message Is in the Metaphor: Assessing the Comprehension of Metaphors in Advertisements." *Journal of Advertising* 28 (4): 1–12.

Mothersbaugh, David L.; Bruce A. Huhmann; and George R. Franke. 2002. "Combinatory and Separative Effects of Rhetorical Figures on Consumers' Effort and Focus in Ad Processing." *Journal of Consumer Research* 28 (March): 589–602.

Munch, James M., and John L. Swasy. 1988. "Rhetorical Question, Summarization Frequency, and Argument Strength Effects on Recall." *Journal of Consumer Research* 15 (June): 69–76.

Myers, James H., and Arne F. Haug. 1967. "Declarative vs. Interrogative Advertisement Headlines." *Journal of Advertising Research* 7 (3): 41–44.

Paivio, Allan. 1979. "Psychological Processes in the Comprehension of Metaphor." In *Metaphor and Thought,* ed. Andrew Ortony, 150–171. Cambridge, MA: Cambridge University Press.

Pawlowski, Donna R.; Diane M. Badzinski; and Nancy Mitchell. 1998. "Effects of Metaphors on Children's Comprehension and Perception of Print Advertisements." *Journal of Advertising* 27 (2): 83–88.

Petty, Richard E.; John T. Cacioppo; and Martin Heesacker. 1981. "Effects of Rhetorical Questions on Persuasion: A Cognitive Response Analysis." *Journal of Personality and Social Psychology* 40 (3): 432–440.

Phillips, Barbara J. 1997. "Thinking into It: Consumer Interpretation of Complex Advertising Images." *Journal of Advertising* 26 (2): 77–87.

————. 2000. "The Impact of Verbal Anchoring on Consumer Response to Image Ads." *Journal of Advertising* 29 (1): 15–24.

————, and Edward F. McQuarrie. 2002. "The Development, Change, and Transformation of Rhetorical Style in Magazine Advertisements 1954–1999." *Journal of Advertising* 31 (4): 1–13.

Reinsch, N. Lamar Jr. 1971. "An Investigation of the Effects of the Metaphor and Simile in Persuasive Discourse." *Speech Monographs* 38 (2): 142–145.

Roehm, Michelle L., and Brian Sternthal. 2001. "The Moderating Effect of Knowledge and Resources on the Persuasive Impact of Analogies." *Journal of Consumer Research* 28 (September): 257–273.

Scott, Linda M. 1994. "Images in Advertising: The Need for a Theory of Visual Rhetoric." *Journal of Consumer Research* 21 (September): 252–273.

Sengupta, Jaideep, and Gerald J. Gorn. 2002. "Absence Makes the Mind Grow Sharper: Effects of Element Omission on Subsequent Recall." *Journal of Consumer Research* 39 (May): 186–201.

Swasy, John L., and James M. Munch. 1985. "Examining the Target of Receiver Elaborations: Rhetorical Question Effects on Source Processing and Persuasion." *Journal of Consumer Research* 11 (March): 877–886.

Tom, Gail, and Anmarie Eves. 1999. "The Use of Rhetorical Devices in Advertising." *Journal of Advertising Research* 39 (4): 39–43.

Toncar, Mark, and James Munch. 2001. "Consumer Responses to Tropes in Print Advertising." *Journal of Advertising* 30 (1): 56–65.

Wright, Peter. 1980. "Message-Evoked Thoughts: Persuasion Research Using Thought Verbalizations." *Journal of Consumer Research* 7 (September): 557–580.

Zillmann, Dolf, and Joanne R. Cantor. 1974. "Rhetorical Elicitation of Concession in Persuasion." *Journal of Social Psychology* 94: 223–236.

3

Rhetrickery and Rhetruth in Soap Operas

Genre Conventions, Hidden Persuasions, and Vulnerable Audiences

Barbara B. Stern

Chapter Summary

This chapter examines the rhetorical strategies in soap operas and identifies the use of "rhetrickery" (Booth 2004) and "rhetruth" (my term) in genre conventions, hidden persuasions, and appeals to vulnerable audiences. It presents the Aristotelian perspective on the linkage between rhetoric and drama to justify the application of rhetorical inquiry—generally restricted to analysis of narrated genres such as orations—to dramas, here considered a vehicle for persuasive messages. The messages are performed in front of an audience (rather than spoken to an audience), and in soap operas consist of visual aspects of the setting, Aristotle's "spectacle," as well as plots (characters in action) that include consumption scenarios. Product placements and depictions of negative lifestyles are examined in terms of "rhetrickery," whereby naive or vulnerable audiences are exposed to hidden advertising plugs and alluring but unwholesome role models. In contrast, the inclusion of beneficial health and wellness messages—the strategy of "entertainment-education" (EE)—represents the strategy of what we call "rhetruth," here considered a theoretical base of EE and defined as a means of incorporating instruction for the public good in entertainment vehicles.

□ □ □ □

Wherever there is persuasion, there is rhetoric. . . . And wherever there is "meaning," there is "persuasion."

(Burke 1969, 171)

Rhetoric, defined by Aristotle as the art of discerning "in any given case the available means of persuasion" (Aristotle c. 350 BCE, 1355b) used to influence an audience's knowledge, attitudes, and behavior (Sood 2002), in itself is neutral. However, when persuasive appeals are covert and audiences are unwary, they can be manipulated or deceived by hidden consumption cues. Insofar as rhetorical inquiry is now viewed as the study of all human communication (Lunsford 1995) in fields as varied as economics (McCloskey 1985), science (Kuhn 1962), law (Gordon 1982), and advertising (McQuarrie and Mick 2002), we extend its application to research on soap operas, focusing on the hidden persuasions of product placements and depictions of unrealistic or harmful lifestyles. The rationale for our interest in soap programs is that their multicultural reach positions them as significant global influences on consumption, for soaps are produced and aired in most countries, including impoverished ones such as Rwanda, and attract a majority of viewers wherever they are shown. In the United States, daytime soaps also capture the majority of daytime audiences, and Spanish-language *telenovelas* are the most popular program type aimed at Hispanic viewers. In addition to overt advertising messages during the program breaks (Stern 1991a), persuasion also takes the form of embedded consumption cues enabled by the soap opera's structural elements, cultural conventions, and audience characteristics (Pfister 1977). What is unique about the rhetorical strategies in soaps and other electronic dramas is that persuasion can be conveyed nonverbally by what is shown in background elements such as settings, props, and costumes, as well as what is made manifest in a character's behavior. In this regard, rhetorical strategy relates more to the visibilia of drama, more prominently featured than the nonverbal behavior and design of orations or narratives. In order to analyze the hidden means of persuasion, we begin with an overview of the development of rhetorical inquiry and its relatively recent application to drama. We then examine the genre conventions of soaps that facilitate negatively valenced persuasive meanings built into the writing, production, and marketing of soaps and criticized as rhetoric messages aimed at unwary and vulnerable consumers. Finally, we present the education-entertainment strategy as a means for promoting "rhetruth" (my term) by embedding positive persuasive messages aimed at teaching disease avoidance and good health practices.

Classical and New Rhetoric: The Dramatic Context

Aristotle: Classic Rhetoric and Poetics

The theoretical justification for drawing from rhetorical criticism to analyze dramatic meanings is rooted in Aristotelian criticism, where the related arts of rhetoric and poetry are treated separately in the *Poetics* (Aristotle c. 320 BCE) and *The Art of Rhetoric* (Aristotle c. 350 BCE) for clarity of presentation. Even though Aristotle viewed rhetoric as a general art applicable to the persuasive aspects of any subject matter, later critics emphasized the formal distinctions between oratory and drama as different modes of communication, thus masking their underlying commonalities. The central distinction, phrased by Wells (1987) as "telling" (narrative speech) versus "showing" (dramatic performance), is that whereas the former is more abstract, requires less involvement on the part of the audience, and guides interpretation, the latter is more concrete, requires more independent thought-generation on the part of the audience, and provides greater immediacy. Showing is the essence of drama, a performative art that allows viewers to observe a mimesis of reality on stage; if the characters were to address the audience directly, the illusion of verisimilitude would be destroyed. The power of mimesis lies in its appeal to the basic human "instinct of imitation" that sustains both learning from imitation and taking pleasure in things imitated—in Aristotle's formulation, "to learn gives the liveliest pleasure" (Aristotle c. 320 BCE, 55). From this perspective, "the reason why men enjoy seeing a likeness is that in contemplating it they find themselves learning or inferring, and saying perhaps, 'Ah, that is he'" (Ibid. 55–56). In this regard, Aristotle's categorization of dramatic elements included "spectacle," described as "the production of spectacular effects," which despite being more a matter of "the art of the stage machinist" than of the poet, nonetheless has "an emotional attraction of its own" (Ibid. 64). When the "new rhetoric" school of literary criticism reconnected rhetoric and drama, they evaluated the emotional attraction of what is shown as more persuasive because of implicitness, stimulation of audience imagination, and reliance on the audience to interpret meaning on its own without narrative intervention (Wells 1987).

The "New Rhetoric" and Drama

The "new rhetoric" was based on the idea that literature was a mode of communication between author and reader and that the critic's task was to identify and analyze elements in a work put there to effect certain responses in readers. In its application to drama, characters were considered the agents of persuasion, and "identification" between rhetors (including characters) and audiences viewed as a means of persuasion actualized by nonverbal as well as verbal performative aspects (Burke 1969). Burke's ideas influenced the 1960s new rhetoricians, whose most prominent theorist is Wayne Booth. His works span four decades from the 1960s to the present, beginning with *The Rhetoric of Fiction* (1961), in which he explicitly linked rhetoric and drama, pointing out "rhetoric is by no means confined to what is spoken directly and exclusively to the audience or reader. In many completely dramatic works . . . there are scenes which are obviously rhetorical in intent" (Booth 1961, 101). That is, Booth emphasized the persuasiveness of entire scenes, viewing them as a gestalt means of influencing audiences by the totality of what is shown. Booth's latest work, *The Rhetoric of Rhetoric* (2004), emphasizes that "now is the time to start studying critically the floods of good rhetoric and rhetrickery that sweep over you daily" (172) and that may be committed by commission as well as omission. In order to guard against rhetrickery, Booth urges that we address the distinction between defensible and indefensible rhetoric wherever it appears.

The first modern critic to address dramatic rhetoric was Manfred Pfister (1977), but his work did not become well known in British and American literary criticism until it was translated into English in 1991. Pfister's theoretical grounding is classical, following the Aristotelian perspective in his comment that rhetoric "has as its primary purpose the art of persuading or convincing" (154). His model of basic strategies for achieving persuasive ends also adapts the Aristotelian tripartite system originally associated with oratorical techniques (Aristotle c. 350 BCE, I1.3.1356–1358b) relevant to the *speaker* (ethos), the subject (logos), and the listener (pathos). In dramas, speaker-centered techniques are primarily verbal, including the stylized speech commonly associated with the use of rhetorical tropes such as metaphor and metonymy (McQuarrie and Mick 2002) aimed at establishing his or her reliability and credibility. However, subject-centered techniques include not only verbal monologues/dialogues but also visual elements such as background action and hidden action aimed at establishing vividness and clarity. Viewer-centered strategy is "designed specifically to arouse strong emotions in the audience, with the intention of converting it to the speaker's position" (Pfister 1977, 156)—in dramas, the character's—and Pfister emphasizes that persuasive communication between characters and audiences depends on conveying familiar cultural conventions, recognizable lifestyles, and commonly identifiable settings. Nonverbal elements in the creation and production of dramas are important insofar as that genre alone is multimedial, distinct from other literary forms because it is "scenically enacted text" (7). Among the most useful performative techniques are "the showing of emotive objects" (156)—products in soaps—and using them to convey narrative information about the norms, values, and lifestyles typical of that world.

Soap Conventions and Rhetorical Strategies: Structure, Characters, and Settings

Structure: Longevity, Multiplicity, and Suspense

Product and lifestyle displays in soaps are sustained by marketer-driven genre conventions that determine a media vehicle's structure, characters, and settings, all of which are designed to facilitate a soap's ability to persuade and entertain audiences at the same time. The conventions serve as an "an easy-to-use creative toolbox" (Cawelti 1976) necessary so that the soap industry can produce cost-efficient and easily replicable formulaic programs resting on a culturally determined "system of orientations, expectations, and conventions that circulate between industry, text . . . subject," and audience (Neale 1980). The main structural characteristics are dailyness, longevity, open-endedness, and suspense, all of which engender the "intense and persistent loyalty" on the part of viewers that is responsible for making and keeping soaps "a vital part of commercial broadcasting in America" (Cantor and Pingree 1983, 18), and the most profitable program type on TV. As much as a half-century of airings signifies the popularity of soaps: *As the World Turns* dates from 1956, *Days of Our Lives* from 1965, and *All My Children, The Young and the Restless*, and *General Hospital* from the 1970s (Zenka 1995). Longevity is a consequence of structure, which is so unique—what Fiske calls an "infinitely extended" middle (Fiske 1987, 180)—that characters can live on for decades, succeeded by younger generations who replicate their behavior. The structure reflects the Gothic promise of an eternal status quo in which similar "characters and events reappear from one generation to the next" (Holland and Sherman 1986, 224), affording the opportunity for the extended viewer–character attachments that persist over time (Diener 1993). Soaps are the only serial dramas that can go on forever, for they have neither beginnings nor endings, replicated in each episode, which also has no beginning or ending, but simply stops when the hour is over. Within the programs themselves, attenuated time is replicated by the program tempo, which proceeds at the same slow pace of life (Levy 1962), a structural means of vivifying the illusion that the drama resembles real life in its pacing and immediacy. The use of time present also reinforces the drama's "realistic plausibility and its mimetic link with reality," as well as conveying the "semantic socio-cultural implications . . . between the setting and the contemporary world" (Pfister 1977, 282).

Multiple subplots, as many as six or eight per program, provide viewers with a steady supply of suspenseful events that keep the soap opera viewer "perpetually on tenderhooks, forever wanting to know what happens next" (Fowles 1982, 154). Suspense is said to "engineer" high loyalty, for in the absence of finality, each subplot stops at a cliff-hanging moment. For this reason, soaps have been called "cliché cliffhangers" (Ensign and Knapton 1985, 309) moving from crisis to crisis with unresolved conflicts left dangling at every turn. The point of the lack of closure is to keep viewers interested in tuning in the next day, and given that 260 daily airings (except for Saturday and Sunday), each of which has a minimum of four subplots, comprise an annual series, viewers can experience over a thousand suspenseful moments a year. As Irna Phillips, the creator of the first radio soap serial said, the law of soaps is "make 'em laugh, make 'em cry, make 'em wait" (MacFarquhar 2002, 64).

Characters

The multiplicity of subplots ensures the presence of many characters—occasionally more than forty—who lead exciting passionate lives that center on complicated sexual relationships and extended conversations about them. Both the male and the female characters are designed to appeal to women's desires for emotionally rich lives with men who are always available to talk about their feelings (Stern 1991b). The availability of male providers is a major factor in the genre's designation as women's escapist fiction, for soaps enable viewers to suspend ordinary life and enter a world where everyday life is pitched at a high level of thrilling personal interactions (Herzog 1941; Lavin 1995). In this way, for at least an hour a day, viewers can live along with characters who are "more picturesque, fantastic, adventurous, heroic" than real people (Abrams 1999, 260). Like their romance and Gothic predecessors, the main characters are often larger-than-life evil family members such as incestuous fathers, wicked stepmothers, or murderous uncles, all of whom threaten helpless women (Frye 1957). Mostly male villains marked by uncontrollable sexual desire (Day 1985; Holland and Sherman 1986) and clothed in seductive garb (Fleenor 1983) have long been a staple of soap society, along with the stereotypical image of the prefeminist "long-suffering Good Woman" (Buckman 1984, 46) as the norm. In this regard, the soap world is patriarchal and often punitive, with women not only restricted to "the private world of interpersonal relationships and excluded from more assertive roles in the public domain" (Barker 1997, 620), but also punished for deviations from expected behavior. Subordination of women is actualized in depictions of a social world in which the central value equates (Jhally 1990) the "possession of goods with possession of women" (Fiske 1987, 180), and women's identity is rooted in relationships with men who can provide them with "a materially satisfying style of life" (Schudson 1986, 82), no matter the price. The powerlessness of women emphasizes, to paraphrase Jane Austen, the universal soap truth that a single woman is in need of a mate, an innate convention carried over from centuries of the feelings and fear motifs in romance and Gothic novels (Geraghty 1991).

Settings and the Consumption Scenario

Audiences are said to be emotionally drawn into an imaginary life with characters who promise to enact social values centered on marriage, the family, and financial security (Holland and Sherman 1986), made manifest in realistic settings in which material goods serve as the visible emblem of the good life. No matter how fantastic the characters may be, realistic settings anchor them in recognizable milieus such as middle- or upper-middle-class American homes, offices, restaurants, and outdoor sites in suburban towns and small cities (Edmundson and Rounds 1976; Matelski 1990; Thorburn 1976). As the head writer of *Days of Our Lives* points out, "the towns on these soap operas" are "as real as any other town," created as "an alternative universe" designed to be as familiar to viewers as their own neighborhood (Weinraub 2004, E-8). The consumption panorama also reflects televised soaps' literary and electronic antecedents in romance and Gothic novels (Geraghty 1991), all aimed at women's interest in home furnishings, fashions, jewelry, food and drink, entertainment, holiday celebrations, and so forth. The settings and props consist of recognizable products and services that reflect the character's values (Coles and Shamp 1984) and social status (Fiske 1987). Products are perhaps the most defining element of the lifestyle community, serving both as emotive objects (Pfister 1977) in the genre's ubiquitous consumption scenarios and "psycho-cultural" cues to the construction of meanings about characters (Sherry 1995) who interact with products. Insofar as the dramas are "popular when their conventions bear a close relationship to the dominant ideology of the time"

(Fiske 1987, 112), the prominence of consumption is reflected in the importance of products (Cornwell and Keillor 1996). However, whereas these products may look as if they are just "there" as part of a naturalistic setting, in actuality they have been placed there by sponsors aiming at influencing audiences to develop positive attitudes toward what they see.

Product Placement and Unwary Consumers:
The Industry, the Genre, the Backlash

Formulaic Production and Industry Profits

Even though real-world consumer goods such as clothing, home furnishings, food, beverages (Cornwell and Keillor 1996), cars, jewelry, and electronics lend verisimilitude to representations of daily life, the driving force behind their presence is profits. The purpose of placements is to increase soap industry revenues by having sponsors pay for the inclusion of branded products that are shown, worn, touched, used, or seen in films and television shows (Balasubramanian 1994). The practice has become increasingly prominent in the past decade, with over a thousand U.S. firms (Marshall and Ayers 1998) sponsoring placements that have been predicted to outpace traditional television advertising messages. According to *PQ Media* (2005), the placement industry in 2005 accounted for revenues of $3.46 billion, with $1.88 billion spent on television placements alone (Russell and Stern 2006). Moreover, placements are poised to enter the Internet as well, where major sponsors such as Proctor & Gamble—the firm behind the creation of soaps in the 1930s (Lavin 1995)—plan to embed product promotions in soaps on the Web to make up for the loss of daytime television audiences (Elliott 2006). In this sense, it is accurate to call the genre a form of "industrial art" because it is a standardized entertainment product written rapidly by teams of writers who turn out episodes via an assembly line process.

Rhetrickery

In this context, placements can be viewed as rhetrickery (Booth 2004, 44) insofar as they represent the unethical intrusion of paid-for advertising designed to influence consumers who do not recognize that they are watching hidden plugs. Note that whereas sponsors such as Proctor & Gamble—the firm that gave radio soaps its name—were openly identified in the characters' dialogue (Lavin 1995), the same is not true for television soaps. Here, the sponsors are not identified, leaving audiences free to think that product presence is simply a realistic aspect of a character's attributes. The upsurge in placements has attracted condemnation by consumer advocacy groups, writers' unions, and the press as "stealth marketing" because no mention is made of sponsorship. Writers' unions (Writers Guild of America 2005) have issued bulletins pointing out that writers do not have free reign for creativity even within formulaic productions because they are forced to create scripts around sponsored placements, thus becoming unwilling copywriters who must "integrate sales pitches into story lines" (Ibid. 6). The union is currently lobbying the Federal Communications Commission for increased federal regulation to enforce disclosure regulations (Carvajal 2006), joining with advocacy groups such as Commercial Alert to emphasize the deceitful nature of "covert commercial pitches" (Waxman 2006). Despite marketers' insistence that products function as "part of the landscape of life" (Lubell 2006, 2), regulatory measures have been proposed to guard against deception by requiring full disclosure of product integration deals at the beginning of a program and on-screen notification whenever a placement appears. What disclosure does is to undermine the covert influence of "offering a product wrapped within an emotional story" (Keil 2006), and thus inform unwary audiences about why particular products appear on-screen.

Negative Persuasion: Inappropriate Role Models and Vulnerable Audiences

Even more subtle than placements aimed at surreptitiously persuading unwary consumers to develop positive attitudes to embedded products is the depiction of luxurious but unrealistic and often harmful lifestyles recently found to persuade vulnerable audiences that soap life is real, normal, and desirable (Stern, Russell, and Russell 2006). Television viewers, like radio audiences before them, show "fierce acceptance of the reality of soaps" (La Guardia 1983, 6), which has negative behavioral consequences for those who interpret them as arbiters of social reality (Cantor and Pingree 1983, 138). Cultivation theory supports the claim that persistent viewing of images on television influence "a viewer's perception of social reality" (Larson 1996, 98), especially the heavy viewers inclined to believe that the real world resembles the television one (Furnham and Bitar 1993; Gerbner et al. 1994). In this situation, viewers' beliefs about the way the world works are cultivated by means of "the sum total of interactions, behaviors, and values present in television content" (Cantor and Pingree 1983, 138). Insofar as television is the "central cultural arm of American society," it serves to socialize young people into standardized roles and behaviors" (Ibid. 139). In consequence, viewers may not perceive that the soap world does not represent social reality; that the lifestyles cloak danger, violence, and sadism under material sumptuousness; and that the dependence of women on men is taken for granted.

Studies in the past twenty years (Babrow 1987; Buerkel-Rothfuss and Meyes 1981) have traced the emotional damage to viewers resulting from long-term exposure to disadvantaged women (Signorielli 1989) caught up in a society characterized by an extreme reward–punishment system that perpetuates stereotypical gender roles. The "ritual of gender subordination" (Leiss, Kline, and Jhally 1986, 166) as a fact of life is viewed as an aspect of negative persuasion that is detrimental to viewers who accept soap life as real and characters as role models (Churchill and Moschis 1979; McCracken 1986). Survey findings (Cantor and Pingree 1983) indicate that heavy viewers were more likely to interpret soap families as models of correct behavior, notwithstanding the large number of dependent or abused women who sacrificed health and happiness for affluence (Churchill and Moschis 1979; O'Guinn and Shrum 1997).

Role Models

Let us imagine a soap character such as Barbara Ryan in *As the World Turns* as a realistic exemplar of life with a rich man:

> Barbara Ryan (*As The World Turns*) has not been lucky in love. She was dumped by her stepbrother for a jewelry thief who reminded him of his ex-wife, and later she dumped him for a pretender to the Swedish throne who turned out to be an Egyptian tomb-robber. She was jailed for the murder of her first husband until he showed up alive, she lost her second husband in a mysterious ballooning accident, and she married her third husband three times, but it didn't work out. As a consequence of her various marriages, she has been shot, drugged, kidnapped, committed to a mental hospital, afflicted by amnesia (twice), nearly gored by a bull, and nearly poisoned in a remote Scottish castle. (MacFarquahar 2000, 64)

Perception of the characters as role models is facilitated by the viewer tendency to perceive intimacy with fictional characters whom they have seen on a daily basis for a long time (Ehrenberg and Wakshlag 1987; Horton and Whol 1956; Sherman 1995). When viewers become parasocially attached to characters whom they interpret as role models (Bandura 1976; Bourne 1957), the characters are able to function as meaningful referent others—agents of socialization and sources of information who influence viewers' norms, desires, behaviors, and product choices (Churchill and Moschis 1979; Russell, Norman, and Heckler 2004). Audiences who have lower self-esteem and are less satisfied with their lives have been found the most likely to overestimate the number of soap women who are happy nonworking housewives (Cantor and Pingree 1983), infer that the characters behave in a socially approved manner (Bearden and Etzel 1982), and conclude that they themselves can behave the same way, all of which may be detrimental to a viewer's personal life satisfaction, realistic assessment of what the world is like, and the achievement of reasonable goals (Clark, Lennon, and Morris, 1992; Weitzman et al. 1972).

A decade's worth of studies have found that "the most regular soap opera viewer [is] a particularly vulnerable individual in that she is not working, less educated, has a smaller family income, and is an ethnic minority"(Gerbner et al. 1994; Greenberg and Woods 1999). From the demographic perspective, consumers who are lower in education and income as well as being members of a racial or ethnic minority group are considered more likely to experience a "disproportionate burden of preventable disease" and have more limited access to health care than would higher socioeconomic status and nonminority audiences (*Healthstyles Survey* 2000). Contemporary studies indicate that the audience profile has remained constant, with viewers still consisting of audiences who are mostly female (76.13 percent), ethnic minorities (31 percent African-American, 25 percent Hispanic), not college-educated (64.29 percent), not currently in the workforce (52.55 percent) (Mediamark Research Inc. 2001), and dominated by teen and elderly viewers. Disadvantaged teens are especially vulnerable, for their age and socioeconomic status makes them prey to constructing identity on the basis of what they see (Barker 1997). A study of adolescent girl soap viewers' responses to images of single mothers found a doubly distorted worldview in the teens' acceptance of the real world as a replica of the soap world. First, the teens took for granted that single mothers would be punished for sexual transgressions by experiencing an "inordinate amount of soap opera problems, such as incest, abortions, nervous breakdowns, and serious operations" (Larson 1996, 101). Second, despite the catalogue of ills, the viewers evaluated the mothers' lives as healthy and desirable because they enjoyed an affluent lifestyle supported by the babies' fathers or their own families, never had to work, participated in a vibrant social life minus bothersome infants, and brought up healthy children. The young viewers were neither informed about the social and medical support systems available for single mothers in a society that provides help, nor warned about what single motherhood is really like.

A *Healthstyles Survey* (2000) found another aspect of vulnerability in that regular soap viewers (those who watch at least twice a week) were found to show higher rates of risky behavior such as drinking, alcohol abuse, smoking, and unsafe sex practices, and disregard for good health practices such as low-fat diets, regular exercise, and medical checkups. In this regard, one of the most ubiquitous examples of the negative health messages in soaps is the presence of alcohol across programs and settings in a world in which drinking is an enjoyable activity associated with successful characters and a part of daily life (Diener 1993). The increasing frequency of alcohol cues in everyday locales such as living rooms, bars, and restaurants conveys the impression that its presence is taken for granted in the cultural milieu and regarded as "normal, appropriate, and innocuous" (Diener 1993, 252–258).

Rhetruth: Theories of Entertainment-Education and Areas for Future Research

Unlike rhetrickery, entertainment-education (EE), defined as a mixture of dramatic entertainment and educational content in a strategy aimed at inserting informational material and prosocial behaviors in soap opera plots, can also be considered an exemplar of "rhetruth". EE conveys ethical messages about consumer well being, delivering persuasive information about good health products (low-fat foods, nicotine patches), services (Alcholics Anonymous, free clinics), and disease prevention (AIDS, mental illness). In the social sciences, most researchers agree that messages aimed at changing behavior must be delivered in communication channels that audiences prefer in order to ensure awareness and attention, prerequisites of the information processing necessary for comprehension, recall, and ultimately behavioral effects. Theoretical grounding for the practice (Bandura 1976) has been found in observational learning theories (also called vicarious learning, modeling, imitative learning, and so forth), in which learning is attributed to the observation of others' behavior—particularly that of role models—whom observers then try to emulate. Vicarious learning is said to occur when the consequences of a role model's behavior are salient to observers who are able to be persuaded by a character about whom they care and to whom they are parasocially attached delivers a message (Kennedy et al. 2004). People are said to learn by paying attention to the role model's actions and consequences—rewards or punishments—which in marketing terms can relate to purchase decisions or lifestyle choices. The effectiveness of a role model is said to be increased when he or she is attractive, successful, credible, and able to overcome problems, and the audience is said to be most vulnerable when it is composed of those who have low esteem, low life satisfaction, and social isolation. Another theory, the "Health Belief Model" (Becker 1974), also posits audience vulnerability as a factor that, when associated with serious negative consequences of a disease or poor health practice, can lead to positive change in health behaviors. Other theories of EE have also been put forth, including self-efficacy, skill modeling (Kennedy et al. 2004), and parasocial attachment (Russell 2002; Russell and Stern 2006), to which we can also add involvement or identification with the characters, empathy and sympathy with them (Escalas and Stern 2003), the "Persuasion Knowledge Model" (Friestad and Wright 1995), and others. The sheer abundance of theories about EE effects suggests that different people make different claims for different reasons, thus arriving at different and noncomparable conclusions.

Balasubramanian, Karrh, and Patwardhan (2006) addressed the problem of fragmented theory regarding audience responses to product placements by developing an integrative framework that depicts audience outcomes in terms of four components: execution/stimulus factors, individual-specific factors, processing depth, and message outcomes. Even though the model was developed specifically for brand attitudes, we suggest that its reconciliation of various theories in a comprehensive model may provide new directions for reconciling different theories of EE, and ascertaining the way that EE messages achieve viewer effects. Among the variables that the proposed model framework includes are program type, nature of information presented, program involvement/connectedness, links between story characters and products, and links between the viewers and characters, all of which can be adapted to the study of EE. What is needed is a transposition of focus from embedded brand messages to prosocial ones, and from single placement instances to serial repetitive ones. Further, and perhaps at the heart of any theoretical advance in understanding EE, we emphasize the need to define constructs such as involvement, identification, imitation, attachment, role modeling, and projection for the sake of sorting out the terminological confusion that besets the field. Escalas and Stern (2003) have already defined "empathy," and Russell and Stern have defined "parasocial attachment" (2006), but the task of building a model applicable to EE requires much more definitional work to identify precisely what researchers are talking about.

Further, even when the terminology is defined and limited, the relationship between serialization of dramas in general and soap operas in particular, long considered particularly good vehicles for EE messages (Waugh and Norman 1965, needs to be more fully explored before a comprehensive framework can be constructed. The significance of time in temporally elongated serials has been discussed in reference to sitcoms (Stern and Russell 2006) and soap operas (Russell and Stern 2006), but the interaction among the major Aristotelian dramatic unities—time, space, and action—needs more consideration in reference to the influence of serialization on message responses. In this regard, even though both Bandura's (1976) social cognitive theory and the information processing literature suggest that EE embedded in plotlines developing over time facilitate viewer recall (Brinson and Brown 1997), the process is not yet well understood. The importance of the time viewer-character relationship is relevant to EE as a source of ongoing formats that engage audiences and facilitate receptiveness to the characters' educational messages. However, no unifying theory has been developed about the attributes of EE vehicles that sustain message placement, including visual/verbal means of conveying product and lifestyle information, structural techniques in dramas designed to play a part in persuasion, and the Aristotelian tripartite system (Aristotle c. 350 BCE, I1.3.1356–1358b) whereby persuasion is a consequence of integration of the *s*peaker (our character), the subject (our plot), and the listener (our viewer). In this regard, we suggest a turn to rhetorical inquiry as a theoretical base of EE, which we consider a modern variant of the Horatian injunction that the mission of dramatic poetry is to "instruct with delight" (Horace c. 20 BCE).

From this perspective, a major benefit of pleasure and persuasion working together is that it is able to present the "equipment of living" (Booth 2004, 76) that may persuade consumers to change their lives for the better (Beck, Pollard, and Greenberg 2000). In the *Healthstyles Survey* (2000), positive responses to informative and preventive messages were indicated by the finding that 38 percent of the regular viewers expressed a desire to see more health information on the programs, and 19 percent did seek out additional health information by contacting hotlines to request literature. Unfortunately, viewers who received the literature were less satisfied with print information because they found the written material difficult to understand, which suggests that the strategy of dispensing literature is not especially successful even in the case of viewers who actively seek to learn more. That is, the written word does not seem to be the best medium for actualizing educational goals. Rather, the electronic dramatic media have the advantage of being performative representations in which positive persuasive messages are delivered by characters who perform actions showing audiences the following: What to do (get regular medical checkups, exercise, make sure the smoke alarm is working); how to convert from poor to good health behaviors with positive outcomes (stop smoking and then stop coughing, stop being couch potatoes and then trim down; and how to overcome physical impairments to improve the quality of life). In this way, televised soap dramas are ideally positioned to function as EE by showing characters, actions, settings, and speech in an entertainment format that uses the art of rhetoric for the public good.

Insofar as soap production and consumption are global (Berger 2004) and the programs have achieved worldwide popularity, rhetorical inquiry is needed to investigate the means and effects of persuasion on unwary or vulnerable audiences in areas as diverse as India, Greece, Pakistan, Russia, China (Rofel 1994), and Latin America (Mayer 2003). Balasubramanian, Karrh, and Patwardhan point to the lack of comparative studies of brand placements in different program types, genres, and media vehicles (2006, 136), to which we would add different cultural and geographical milieus as well. We propose that the soap genre and its influence on characters and audiences in different cultures needs further investigation to ascertain the extent to which programs appeal to vulnerable women and portray vulnerable heroines. Different subcultures in the United States also require future research, for the ubiquitous appeal (Payne 1994) of soaps is further demonstrated by the popularity of foreign-language programs for immigrant audiences in the United States. Dish Network presents soaps on over fifty foreign-language cable channels in the United States, thus providing viewers with "an emotional outlet" (Berger 2004, B-1) at the same time as a touch of home. Not surprisingly, foreign-language soaps do not depict women in the same way that English-language ones do: for example, Pakistani and Indian soaps feature married couples who live in an extended household with the man's family. Indian soaps are watched by about one-third of the country's billion-plus population, and feature messages about the country's concerns such as the changing role of women, methods of birth control, materialism and the ideology of consumption, and other contemporary political issues (Gokulsing 2004). In contrast to U.S. soaps, which generally exclude references to the external world and are often watched alone, Indian soaps include current events, as do Chinese programs (Rofel 1994); are often watched in groups; and run for a limited number of seasons. However, little is known about the rhetorical strategies used in product and lifestyle depictions, the structural characteristics of programs with a defined ending date, and the means used to convey EE messages. Researchers also have not yet investigated whether or how transnational soaps play a role in the acculturation of immigrants to a new culture, and more research is needed to shed light on soaps as a vehicle important to the process (Peñaloza 1994). In consequence, we do not fully understand the impact of soap viewing in different cultures in relation to vulnerability, as well as the phenomenon of rhetrickery in a global context. Insofar as we currently have mostly impressionistic views of rhetrickery as more prevalent in the United States, but to move forward we must conduct additional comparative research to determine the accuracy of these opinions.

References

Abrams, Meyer H. 1999. *A Glossary of Literary Terms,* 7th ed. Boston: Heinle and Heinle.

Aristotle. c. 350 BCE [1991]. *The Art of Rhetoric,* trans. Hugh Lawson-Tancred. London: Penguin Books.

———. c. 320 BCE [1961]. *Poetics,* trans. S.H. Butcher, intro. Francis Fergusson. New York: Hill and Wang.

Babrow, Austin S. 1987. "Student Motives for Watching Soap Operas." *Journal of Broadcasting and Electronic Media* 31 (93): 309–321.

Balasubramanian, Siva K. 1994. "Beyond Advertising and Publicity: Hybrid Messages and Public Policy Issues." *Journal of Advertising* 23 (4): 29–46.

Balasubramanian, Siva K.; James A. Kharr; and Hemant Patwardhan. 2006. "Audience Response to Product Placements: An Integrative Framework and Future Research Agenda." *Journal of Advertising* 35 (3): 115–141.

Bandura, Albert. 1976. *Social Learning Theory.* Chicago: Aldine-Atherton.

Barker, Chris. 1997. "Television and the Reflexive Project of the Self: Soaps, Teenage Talk and Hybrid Identities." *British Journal of Sociology* 48: 611–627.

Bearden, William, and Michael Etzel. 1982. "Reference Group Influence on Product and Brand Purchase Decisions." *Journal of Consumer Research* 9 (September): 183–194.

Beck, Vicky; William E. Pollard; and Bradley S. Greenberg. 2000. "Tune in for Health: Working with Television Entertainment Shows and Partners to Deliver Health Information for At-Risk Audiences." Paper presented at the annual meeting of the American Public Health Association, Boston. www.cdc.gov/communication/healthsoap.htm.

Becker, M.H. 1974. "The Health Belief Model and Personal Health Behavior." *Health Education Monographs* 2: 324–473.

Berger, Joseph. 2004. *New York Times,* February 23, B1, B4.

Booth, Wayne. 1983 [1961]. *The Rhetoric of Fiction,* 2d. ed. Chicago: University of Chicago Press.

———. 2004. *The Rhetoric of Rhetoric: The Quest for Effective Communication.* Malden, MA: Blackwell.

Bourne, Francis S. 1957. "Group Influence in Marketing and Public Relations." In *Some Applications of Behavioral Research,* ed. Rensis Likert and Samuel P. Hayes, 208–224. Paris: UNESCO.

Brinson, Susan L., and Mary Hiler Brown. 1997. "The AIDS Risk Narrative in the 1994 CDC Campaign." *Journal of Health Communication* 2: 101–112.

Buckman, Peter. 1984. *All for Love: A Study in Soap Opera.* London: Secker and Warburg.

Buerkel-Rothfuss, Nancy, and Sandra Meyes. 1981. "Soap Opera Viewing: The Cultivation Effect." *Journal of Communication* 31 (6): 108–115.

Burke, Kenneth. 1969. *A Rhetoric of Motives.* Berkeley: University of California Press.

Cantor, Muriel, and Suzanne Pingree. 1983. *The Soap Opera.* Beverly Hills: Sage.

Carvajal, Doreen. 2006. "Placing the Product in the Dialogue, Too." *New York Times,* January 16.

Cawelti, John G. 1976. *Adventure, Mystery, and Romance.* Chicago: University of Chicago Press.

Churchill, Gilbert A., and George Moschis. 1979. "Television and Interpersonal Influences on Adolescent Consumer Learning." *Journal of Consumer Research* 6 (June): 23–35.

Clark, Roger; Rachel Lennon; and Leanna Morris. 1992. "Of Caldecotts and Kings: Gendered Images in Recent American Children's Books by Black and Non-Black Illustrators." *Gender and Society* 7: 227–245.

Coles, Claire D., and N. Johanna Shamp. 1984. "Some Sexual, Personality, and Demographic

Characteristics of Women Readers of Erotic Romances." *Archives of Sexual Behavior,* 13: 187–209.

Cornwell, T. Bettina, and Bruce Keillor. 1996. "Contemporary Literature and the Embedded Consumer Culture." In *Empirical Approaches to Literature and Aesthetics,* ed. Mary Sue McNealy and Roger J. Kreuz, 559–572. Norwood, NJ: Ablex.

Day, William Patrick. 1985. *In the Circles of Fear and Desire: A Study of Gothic Fantasy.* Chicago: University of Chicago Press.

Diener, Betty J. 1993. "The Frequency and Context of Alcohol and Tobacco Cues in Daytime Soap Opera Programs." *Journal of Public Policy and Marketing* 12: 252–258.

Edmundson, Madeleine, and David Rounds. 1976. *From Mary Noble to Mary Hartman: The Complete Soap Opera Book.* New York: Stein and Day.

Ehrenberg, Andrew S.C., and Jacob Wakshlag. 1987. "Repeat-viewing with People-Meters." *Journal of Advertising Research* 27 (1): 9–14.

Elliott, Stuart. 2006. "To Bolster Audience, Soaps Turn to the Web." *New York Times,* March 2.

Ensign, Lynne N., and Robyn Eileen Knapton. 1985. *The Complete Dictionary of Television and Film.* New York: Stein and Day.

Escalas, Jennifer Edson, and Barbara B. Stern. 2003. "Sympathy and Empathy: Emotional Responses to Advertising Dramas," *Journal of Consumer Research* 29 (March): 566–578.

Fiske, John. 1987. *Television Culture.* London: Methuen.

Fleenor, Juliann E. 1983. *The Female Gothic.* Montreal: Eden Press.

Fowles, Jib. 1982. *Television Viewers vs. Media Snobs: What TV Does for People.* New York: Stein and Day.

Friestad, Marian, and Peter Wright. 1995. "Persuasion Knowledge: Lay People's and Researchers' Beliefs about the Psychology of Advertising." *Journal of Consumer Research* 22 (June): 62–74.

Frye, Northrop. 1957. *Anatomy of Criticism: Four Essays.* Princeton: Princeton University Press.

Furnham, Adrian, and Nadine Bitar. 1993. "The Stereotyped Portrayal of Men and Women in British Television Advertisements." *Sex Roles* 29: 297–307.

Geraghty, Christine. 1991. *Women and Soap Opera: A Study of Prime Time Soaps.* Cambridge: Polity.

Gerbner, George; Larry Gross; Michael Morgan; and Nancy Signorielli. 1994. "Growing Up with Television: The Cultivation Perspective." In *Media Effects: Advances in Theory and Research,* ed. Jennings Bryant and Dolf Zillman. Hillsdale, NJ: Erlbaum.

Gokulsing, K. Moti. 2004. *Soft-Soaping India: The World of Indian Televised Soap Operas.* Sterling, VA: Stylus.

Gordon, Robert. 1982. *The Politics of Law.* New York: Pantheon Books.

Healthstyles Survey Executive Summary: Soap Opera Viewers and Health Information. 2000. www.cdc.gov/communications/surveys/surv2999.htm.

Herzog, Herta. 1941. "On Borrowed Experience: An Analysis of Listening to Daytime Sketches." *Studies in Philosophy and Social Science* 9: 65–95. New York: Institute of Social Research.

Holland, Norman N., and Laura Sherman. 1986. "Gothic Possibilities." In *Gender and Reading: Essays on Readers, Texts, and Contexts,* ed. Elizabeth A. Flynn and Patricia P. Schweickart, 215–233. Baltimore, MD: Johns Hopkins University Press.

Horace. c. 20 BCE [1978]. *Satires, Epistles, and Ars Poetica,* trans. H. Rushton Fairclough. Cambridge, MA: Harvard University Press.

Horton, Donald, and R. Richard Whol. 1956. "Mass Communication and Para-Social Interaction." *Psychiatry* 19: 215–229.

Jhally, Sut. 1990. *The Codes of Advertising: Fetishism and the Political Economy of Meaning in the Consumer Society.* New York: Routledge.

Keil, Jennifer Gould. 2006. "Shear Sellout." *New York Post,* March 19.

Kennedy, May G.; Ann O'Leary; Vicki Beck; Katrina Pollard; and Penny Simpson. 2004. "Increases in Calls to the CDC National STD and AIDS Hotline Following Aids-Related Episodes in a Soap Opera." *Journal of Communication* 54: 287–301.

Kuhn, Thomas 1962. *The Structure of Scientific Revolutions.* Chicago: University of Chicago Press.

La Guardia, Robert. 1983. *Soap World.* New York: Arbor House.

Larson, Mary Strom. 1996. "Sex Roles and Soap Operas: What Adolescents Learn about Single Motherhood." *Sex Roles* 35: 97–109.

Lavin, Marylin. 1995. "Creating Consumers in the 1930s: Irna Phillips and the Radio Soap Opera." *Journal of Consumer Research* 22 (June): 75–89.

Leiss, William; Stephen Kline; and Sut Jhally. 1986. *Social Communication Through Advertising: Persons, Products, and Images of Well-Being.* Toronto: Methuen.

Levy, Sidney. 1962. "Phases in Changing Interpersonal Relations." *Merrill-Palmer Quarterly of Behavior and Development* 8: 121–128.

Lubell, Sam. 2006. "Advertising's Twilight Zone: That Signpost Up Ahead May Be a Virtual Product. *New York Times,* January 2.

Lunsford, Andrea. 1995. *Reclaiming Rhetorica: Women in the Rhetorical Tradition.* Pittsburgh: University of Pittsburgh Press.

MacFarquhar, Larissa. 2002. "Oakdale Days: Why Do So Many Terrible Things Keep Happening in One Town?" *New Yorker,* April 15: 64–71.

Marshall, Norm, and Dean Ayers. 1998. "Product Placement Worth More Than Its Weight." *Brandweek* 39 (6): 16–17.

Matelski, Marilyn J. 1990. *Soap Operas Worldwide: Cultural and Serial Realities.* Jefferson, NC: McFarland.

McCloskey, Donald. 1985. *The Rhetoric of Economics.* Madison: University of Wisconsin Press.

McCracken, Grant. 1986. "Culture and Consumption: A Theoretical Account of the Structure and Movement of the Cultural Meaning of Consumer Goods." *Journal of Consumer Research* 13 (June): 71–84.

McQuarrie, Edward F., and David Glen Mick. 2002. "Figures of Rhetoric in Advertising Language." *Journal of Consumer Research* 22 (March): 424–438.

Mediamark Research Inc. 2001. *Television Audiences—Spring 2001.* New York.

Neale, Stephen. 1980. *Genre/Stephen Neale: British Film Institute—Film Availability Services.* New York: Zoetrope.

O'Guinn, Thomas C., and Shrum, L.J. 1997. "The Role of Television in the Construction of Consumer Reality." *Journal of Consumer Research* 28 (March): 278–294.

Payne, Monica A. 1994. "The 'Ideal' Black Family? A Caribbean View of the Cosby Show." *Journal of Black Studies* 25: 231–249.

Peñaloza, Lisa. 1994. "*Atravesadno Fronteras*/Border Crossings: A Critical Ethnographic Exploration of the Consumer Acculturation of Mexican Immigrants." *Journal of Consumer Research* 28 (June): 369–398.

Pfister, Manfred. 1977 [1991]. *The Theory and Analysis of Drama.* Cambridge, MA: Cambridge University Press.

PQ Media. 2005. "Product Placement Spending in Media 2005." www.pqmedia.com/product-placement-spending-in-media.html.

Rofel, Lisa. 1994. "Yearnings: Televisual Love and Melodramatic Politics in Contemporary China." *American Ethnologist* 21: 700–702.

Russell, Cristel A. 2002. "Investigating the Effectiveness of Product Placements in Television Shows: The Role of Modality and Plot Connection Congruence on Brand Memory and Attitude." *Journal of Consumer Research* 29: 306–318.

———, and Barbara B. Stern. 2006. "Consumers, Characters, and Products: A Balance Model of Sitcom Product Placement Effects." *Journal of Advertising* 35: 7–21.

———; Andrew T. Norman; and Susan E. Heckler. 2004. "The Consumption of Television Programming: Development and Validation of the Connectedness Scale." *Journal of Consumer Research* 31 (June): 150–161.

Schudson, Michael. 1986. *Advertising, The Uneasy Persuasion: Its Dubious Impact on American Society.* New York: Basic Books.

Sherman, Steve. M. 1995. "Determinants of Repeat Viewing to Prime-Time Public Television Programming." *Journal of Broadcasting & Electronic Media* 39: 472–482.

Sherry, John F. 1995. "Bottomless Cup, Plug-in Drug: A Telethnography of Coffee." *Visual Anthropology* 7: 351–370.

Signorielli, Nancy. 1989. "Television and Conceptions about Sex Roles: Maintaining Conventionality and the Status Quo." *Sex Roles* 21: 341–360.

Sood, Suruchi. 2002. "Audience Involvement and Entertainment-Education." *Communication Theory* 12: 153–172.

Stern, Barbara B. 1991a. "Literary Analysis of an Advertisement: The Commercial as Soap Opera." In *Advances in Consumer Research*, vol. 18, ed. Rebecca H. Holman and Michael Solomon, 164–171. Provo, UT: Association for Consumer Research.

———. 1991b. "Two Pornographies: A Feminist View of Sex in Advertising." In *Advances in Consumer Research*, vol. 18., ed. Rebecca H. Holman and Michael Solomon, 384–391. Provo, UT: Association for Consumer Research.

———, and Cristel A. Russell. 2006. "Aspirational Consumption in U.S. Soap Operas: The Influence of Parasocial Interaction on Consumers." In *Advances in Consumer Research*, vol. 23, ed. Linda Price and Cornelia Pechmann, Provo, UT: Association for Consumer Research.

———; ———; and Dale W. Russell. 2006. "Vulnerable Women on Screen and at Home." *Journal of Macromarketing Special Issue on Vulnerable Consumers* 25: 222–225.

Thorburn, Donald. 1976. "Television Melodrama." In *Television as a Cultural Force*, ed. Douglass Cater and Richard Alder, 595–609. New York: Praeger.

Waugh, Nancy C., and Donald A. Norman. 1965. "Primary Memory." *Psychological Review* 72: 89–104.

Waxman, Sharon. 2006. "Hollywood Unions Object to Product Placement on TV." *New York Times,* November 14.

Weinraub, Bernard. 2004. "Love Fest for Soap Opera Fans, in Two Languages." *New York Times,* March 22.

Weitzman, Lenore J.; Deborah Eifler; Elizabeth Hokada; and Catherine Ross. 1972. "Sex Role Socialization in Picture Books for Preschool Children." *American Journal of Sociology* 77: 1125–1150.

Wells, William. 1987. "Lectures and Dramas." In *Cognitive and Affective Responses to Advertising*, ed. Patricia Cafferata and Alice M. Tybout, 13–20. Lexington, MA: Lexington Books/D.C. Heath.

Writers Guild of America. 2005. *"Are You SELLING to Me?* Stealth Advertising in the Entertainment Industry." Los Angeles: Writers Guild of America West.

Zenka, Lorraine. 1995. *Days of Our Lives: The Complete Family Album.* New York: Harper Collins.

4

What the Symbol Can't, the Icon Can

The Indispensable Icon/Symbol Distinction

Val Larsen

Chapter Summary

*In recent years, Scott and McQuarrie and Mick have highlighted a critically impor-
tant deficit in research on visual persuasion: the failure to engage and understand
the richness and complexity of images. A science of visual persuasion cannot be
fully developed until our rudimentary understanding of the semiotic ad system,
within which stimuli are encoded, more nearly matches our relatively sophisticated
understanding of the psychological human system that processes ad stimuli. This
chapter suggests that the rejection or devaluing of Peirce's icon/symbol distinction
in past research partly explains why more progress has not been made in developing
an adequate understanding of the ad system. While acknowledging the symbolic
resonance of images, the chapter focuses on the deep structure/surface structure
relationship between referents and the icons that variously imitate them. It outlines
a research program that explores different levels of the ad system, including specific
transformations that link the deep and surface structures of images.*

In *Being and Time* (1962), Martin Heidegger famously alleged that philosophy made a
wrong turn at the time of the Greeks, that through most of its history philosophers had
missed the main point because they had not properly engaged the question of Being.
In a similarly devastating—though less grandly expansive—critique in her 1994 article "Images in Advertising: The Need for a Theory of Visual Rhetoric" (cf. Kenney
and Scott 2003), Linda Scott argued that research on visual persuasion has likewise
been fundamentally misdirected because consumer behaviorists have not engaged
the image. Virtually all consumer researchers who have explored visual persuasion,
Scott suggested, have done so with a simplistic understanding of what an image is.

This simplistic understanding has led to an unsophisticated use of "amateurish or dated" images. And it has cast into doubt the generalizability of research findings to the sophisticated contemporary practice of visual persuasion through advertising. To engage images as they are used in practice, consumer researchers must come to see them as complex artifacts richly endowed with multiple meanings.

Scott's radical critique in this insightful article could and should have been a turning point in the history of persuasion research, for if image is not everything as Sprite commercials once suggested, it may at least be the main thing in the persuasion of final consumers through advertising. McQuarrie and Mick (2003) point this out using a simple inequality. In magazines, the ratio *ad pictures* divided by *total magazine pictures* will almost always be greater than the ratio *ad words* divided by *total magazine words;* that is, images are a more important component in the ad portion of the magazine than they are in the magazine as a whole. And virtually any perusal of ads targeted at final consumers will confirm the point: space devoted to images generally dominates that devoted to words (cf. Childers and Houston 1984).

While it should have, Scott's manifesto has not yet precipitated an integrated and broadly supported program of research on the use and effects of images in persuasive communications. So it is unsurprising that, in a review of "the accumulated expertise on visual persuasion in American Society at the beginning of the 21st century," Malkewitz, Wright, and Friestad report, "our analysis suggests that practical expertise in applied everyday visual persuasion is not very well developed," that we remain in "a state of relative ignorance" (2003, 3, 7).

Scott's critique can be restated using McQuarrie and Mick's (2003) valuable distinction between the *human system* and the *ad system*. Consumer researchers have studied with great care and have developed a deep understanding of the human system, the mental apparatus that apprehends and processes an ad stimulus. However, they have devoted very little attention to the ad as an artifact that is embedded in a complex system of signifying variables. Thus, there is a debilitating asymmetry in our understanding of the two essential elements in visual persuasion—the ad and the mind that processes it. Given this asymmetry, the main impediment to major advances in our understanding of persuasion is the lack of an integrated theory of ad form.

McQuarrie and Mick's (1996, 1999, 2003) work on rhetorical figures in advertising is the main exception to the general rule of limited progress in developing practical expertise in visual persuasion. Their research makes a direct contribution in particular claims about the persuasive effects of rhetorical figures but a still larger indirect contribution by modeling the use of semiotics to develop a nomologically integrated taxonomy of ad executions. Their work demonstrates that semiotics, the science of signs, holds great promise as a theoretical framework within which ad form variables may be rigorously defined. Semiotics is the approach to images that is most likely to balance understanding of the human system with a commensurate understanding of the ad system and, thus, remedy the deficit in understanding that Malkewitz, Wright, and Friestad (2003) have highlighted.

But McQuarrie and Mick's work notwithstanding, the semiotic analysis of ad form has not progressed as much as one might have hoped when Scott first published her perceptive diagnosis of the essential problem of the forgotten image. One important reason for the lack of progress may be confusion sown by Scott (1994) and McQuarrie and Mick (2003) in their discussions of the fundamental semiotic distinction between symbols and icons. At the very moment in which she was so perceptively highlighting the need for a deeper understanding of the image, Scott was also challenging the validity of the icon/symbol (I/S) distinction that may be the essential key to any adequate description of the ad system. McQuarrie and Mick do not reject the distinction, but they suggest that it lacks scientific utility in the analysis of visual persuasion.

Through a critical review of Scott and McQuarrie and Mick's discussions of the I/S distinction, this chapter will attempt to reestablish Peirce's (1931–1958) distinction as the foundation for an adequate semiotic analysis of the ad system. It will demonstrate that the key insights of these researchers are supported and deepened when the I/S distinction is affirmed. And it will outline a research program that builds upon that distinction and various important insights of Scott and McQuarrie and Mick.

Do Icons Exist?

Scott's critique of traditional research on visual persuasion has helped consumer researchers understand the rich, symbolic complexity of images. However, in hypercorrecting one very real problem—undercutting the simplistic belief that images are nothing but a copy of their referents—Scott creates the obverse problem, fostering the less simplistic but still mistaken belief that all images are merely symbols, that the relationships between images and their referents are, inevitably, arbitrary.

The main plank of Scott's (1994) critique of traditional advertising research is her case against "copy theory," her rejection of the idea that a picture may be "understood to be 'iconic'—that is, pictures simply point to objects or experiences in the empirical world" and are "passively absorbed" (256). This understanding, which Scott attributes, probably correctly, to most previous researchers on visual persuasion, minimizes the complexity of the image and oversimplifies its potential effects. As the alternative, Scott promotes the view that images are symbols. Following her most important source, Goodman (1976), she suggests that pictures are entirely constituted, like other symbols, by a set of conventions. They do not involve imitation. The concept of imitation, *mimesis,* is merely a conceit of the Western artistic tradition, not a fundamental element of pictorial representation. Believing in it is a form of ethnocentrism. Pictures are "unavoidably artifactual" (Scott 1994, 260), not different, fundamentally, from such prototypical symbols as words and numbers. And "because visuals are convention based, all pictures must be interpreted according to learned patterns—just like reading words or recognizing numbers" (269). As evidence for her position Scott notes, among other things, that photographs—a kind of image that might be held to be especially iconic—differ from direct visual experience in being stationary, monocular, two-dimensional, and more panoramic. Taken altogether, these claims add up to an assertion that the I/S distinction is illusory. In Scott's view, icons, in Peirce's (1931–1958) sense, do not exist. All images are symbols.

In defending Peirce's icon concept, the brief response one might make to Scott's photography argument is that it assumes what it seeks to disprove—the commensurability of photographic images and ordinary experience—for it focuses on ways in which photographs systematically differ from ordinary visual experience. Consequently, instead of showing that there are no iconic images, Scott's catalog of deviations merely indicate that icons may be plotted on a continuum anchored on one end by symbols that do not resemble their referents and on the other by virtual reality that may be indistinguishable from its referent. On this continuum, a photograph is more iconic than an abstract painting, a movie more iconic than a photograph, a 3D movie more iconic than a regular movie, and virtual reality more iconic than a 3D movie precisely because, in each case, the former, unlike the latter, does not deviate from ordinary experience on some dimension Scott identifies. Thus, implicitly, even in Scott's critique of icons, the phenomenology of ordinary visual experience is a standard against which the iconicity of images, or lack thereof, is measured.

Scott's argument against copy theory and iconicity has other facets, but almost every facet is addressed and rebutted by Paul Messaris in Visual "Literacy": Image, Mind, and Reality (1994). Messaris, citing various empirical studies, shows that there is no great disconnect, as the symbol theorists assert, between art and reality. Many of our responses to art and our strategies for making sense of art are identical to our responses to the visual field we confront in reality. The phenomenology of ordinary experience is reflected, for example, in such pictorial conventions as the relationship between magnitude and distance and the implication that objects higher in the frame are further away. Moreover, first-time adult viewers of pictures learn almost instantaneously to match pictures with a wide variety of referents. "Nowhere do we get any evidence of a need for the kind of lengthy, repeated instruction that is prerequisite for the understanding of a genuinely arbitrary system of signification such as language" (Messaris 1994, 61). Messaris's arguments are buttressed by research indicating that direct perception of a thing and indirect, iconic perception produce similar physiological effects and are processed by the same physiological machinery (Levin and Simons 2000).

Scott casts her argument in an *either/or* form: advertising visuals are either simple icons as traditionally assumed by persuasion researchers who have implicitly subscribed to copy theory (and if so these images may be processed simply and directly) or they are symbols (and, thus, are complex human artifacts that resonate on multiple social and cultural dimensions). In her close readings of particular ads, she demonstrates that advertising visuals do resonate on multiple dimensions. It seems to follow that images are symbols, not icons. But a *both/and* analysis that preserves the I/S distinction is more empirically sound and, at the same time, more fully discloses the complex, layered nature of images. Indeed, paradoxically, Scott's main point (that images are rich and variable in their range of meanings) is strengthened if her main supporting argument (her critique of copy theory) is rejected.

So let us be clear. A sign is an icon to the degree that it imitates its referent. At the speculative logical limit—for example, the holodeck in *Star Trek: TNG*—the prototypical sign and its referent become indistinguishable except for their spatial location. Conversely, a sign is a symbol to the degree that it is related to its referent arbitrarily. At its logical limit—a non-onomatopoetic word—nothing but social convention links the prototypical symbol to its referent. This difference has immense consequences for the social production and use of icons and symbols.

Because they resemble their referents, the essential meaning of an icon may be inferred from the sign itself. This explains why no lengthy instruction is needed for a viewer to recognize the basic meaning of an iconic sign. With little or no instruction in the conventions of Chinese art, a European can easily identify the referents of pictures painted by a Chinese artist—a horse, a ship, a tree. Consequently, no feedback loop for the harmonization of intended and received meaning is required for the production and consumption of iconic signs. The sign may be encoded in China and decoded in Europe with shared understanding being a function of the resemblance between icon and referent that is apparent to both the artist and the viewer of the picture.

Because they do not resemble their referents, the meaning of prototypical symbols cannot be inferred from the sign itself. A European who hears the Chinese words *yìpí mǎ, yìsōu chuan, yìkē shù* will have no idea what they signify absent involvement in an elaborate social process through which shared understanding of the conventional meaning of these symbols is achieved. Humpty Dumpty was wrong to assert in *Alice in Wonderland*, "When I use a word, it means just what I choose it to mean—neither more nor less" (Carroll 1960, 269). There can be no private language, so Humpty Dumpty's private intensions are not dispositive. Unlike icons, a prototypical symbol such as a word can have communicative value only if there is quite specific social agreement on what it signifies.

Paradoxically, because social agreement facilitated by feedback mechanisms is essential for symbols to have any meaning and is inessential for icons, the intended meaning of a symbol, which is arbitrarily related to its referent, will normally be more tightly specified than the meaning of an icon, which has a facial link to its referent. Early filmmakers were surprised by this difference. They expected the intended meaning of images in a film to be as apparent to the audience as the intended meaning of words in the script. But beyond surface denotation, images proved to be less determinate in their meaning than words. Kuleshov demonstrated this experimentally by combining the same screenshot of the face of Ivan Mozzhukhin, a famous Russian actor, with three different adjacent shots: a bowl of soup, a woman, and a child's coffin. Viewers of the three sequences believed, respectively, that Mozzhukhin was expressing hunger, sexual desire, and grief, though, of course, his facial expression did not change. Since in film production, there is no elaborate feedback loop between filmmaker and audience that can harmonize intended and received meanings, the meaning of the images beyond their obvious denotation is likely to be underdetermined and, thus, highly sensitive to context effects.

In affirming the context sensitivity of images and their rich meaning potential, I am reaffirming the essential point of Scott's 1994 manifesto. But progress in understanding how images produce these complex effects will require a clear understanding of what an iconic image is and how it signifies. And in her argument, Scott mixes valid assertions about image richness with an invalid rejection of mimesis. I will focus here not on abstract images but on the kind of representational images that predominate in advertising and that Scott used as examples in her article. Images of this kind always copy, in one way or another, the phenomenology of ordinary visual experience. In a word, they are always icons that imitate a real (or, occasionally, an imaginary) referent.

All representational images are icons. But many icons are also symbols. If in addition to its mimetic relationship to a referent, the thing pictured has, by social agreement, certain arbitrary meanings, it will be both an icon and a symbol. For example, a bald eagle icon will always have a mimetic relationship with its referent animal and, in an ad, it might signify mimetically fierceness, wildness, and unspoiled nature since most eagles are in fact fierce, wild, and found in unspoiled natural settings. But in some ads, the eagle may also, by arbitrary convention, symbolically signify the United States or the Boy Scouts. One reason why most ad images are rhetorically rich is because the things pictured in the ad have both literal/iconic and arbitrary/symbolic dimensions of meaning. We will more fully understand that rhetorical richness if we acknowledge both the iconic and the symbolic aspects of the sign.

The principle weakness of Scott's analysis is that it misidentifies the locus of the oversimplification it is correcting. The principle mistake of the researchers Scott criticizes is not that they think images copy reality. It is that they do not recognize the complex rhetoric that can be implicit in objects and their arrangement, whether the objects occur in images or in reality. This is evident from one of Scott's examples, a Clinique ad featuring a realistic photo of a glass of mineral water, garnished with a slice of lime, in which cheek base and an open tube of Clinique lipstick are submerged amid the ice cubes. Scott reads this ad, plausibly, as a visual simile that implicitly asserts: "Clinique's new summer line of makeup is as refreshing as a tall glass of soda with a twist" (Scott 1994, 254). Presumably, the meaning would be largely unchanged if Clinique were to use this same collection of artifacts as a place setting in a meeting with retail buyers or as a counter display in a department store. Likewise, the image of a politician standing in front of a large American flag while surrounded by police and firefighters has similar rhetorical force whether it appears en vivo at a rally or iconically in a television ad. To sum up, not only is the I/S distinction valid, but it can and should be an integral part of the nuanced understanding of images that Scott has so forcefully urged.

Does the I/S Distinction Have Scientific Value?

Let us now briefly consider and respond to an argument in McQuarrie and Mick's (2003) seminal article on visual rhetorical figures that, though different in kind, may be similar in effect to Scott's. Unsurprisingly, since Mick (1986) originally introduced the distinction in consumer research, McQuarrie and Mick do not question whether icons and symbols can be distinguished conceptually. But they do suggest that the distinction may not matter: "In short, at the level of scientific theory, whether something is visual or verbal, pictorial or auditory, may be of little consequence. At the extremes, perhaps 'visual' is only an Aristotelian category, a pre-scientific idea that, while intuitively clear, is not actually linked to distinct causal processes of the sort featured in scientific theory" (216). After reviewing differences that exist between the visual (iconic) and verbal (symbolic) modes of persuasion—for example, the facts that images are processed more immediately and involuntarily than words and that visual assertions are more tacit and memorable than verbal assertions—they recapitulate their original view: "On balance, we are skeptical that distinguishing visual persuasion as a separate category of persuasion attempts rests on much more than an intuitively appealing Aristotelian categorization, convenient for quick communication but not particularly fruitful for building a scientific theory" (41).

In suggesting that images are more likely than words to evoke an involuntary response under conditions of minimal attention and that visual persuasion is more memorable, more tacit and, thus, less counterargued than verbal persuasion, Mc-Quarrie and Mick have identified differences of great practical importance. In the field, as they themselves note, advertising generally receives limited attention. And advertisers are certainly interested in enhancing memory while minimizing counterargumentation. It would seem to follow that the distinction between visual and verbal persuasion will be theoretically, scientifically, and practically important if these different effects can be plausibly linked to features inherent in icons and symbols. And, in fact, a plausible link can be made.

As Peirce (1931–1958) makes the distinction, the fundamental difference between an icon and a symbol is that the icon is similar to its referent in a multiplicity of specific ways whereas the symbol is related only by a convention that is entirely arbitrary. This difference bears directly on the kinds of cognitive effects the two classes of stimuli may be expected to have. Images will tend to elicit an immediate and quite specific cognition. Even relatively abstract images of an automobile will be specified with respect to the general kind of model; that is, whether it be a convertible, station wagon, or sedan. And in the case of the prototypical icon with its high degree of correspondence to its referent, all the specifics of make, model, year, color, and condition can be grasped almost instantaneously. In an icon, quite particular attributes of the referent must be specified to constitute a recognizable gestalt. Without some minimal level of detail, the gestalt cannot exist. So the immediate and involuntary perception of detailed information is an inherent feature of icons.

A symbol is not subject to this specificity limitation. Using a symbol such as the word *automobile,* one may grasp a broad concept that is devoid of any specifics. The arbitrariness of the symbol's relationship to its referent means that the sign itself cannot hint at the referent's particular features. Those must be indicated by a subsequent and—if there is any degree of detail—lengthy set of additional modifying symbols. Nor is the situation much changed when one begins with symbols lower on the ladder of abstraction, for example, *a dark green 1994 Toyota Corolla four-door sedan with standard hubcaps and a gray interior.* To approximate the information in a picture—specifying the car's condition and context and the particular point of view, and so on—one might still have to use the proverbial thousand words. And as reader-response theorists have made clear (Iser 1978), those details must be absorbed and integrated through reading—an unavoidably linear and temporal process. This process is inherently less immediate than the cognition of an icon, and it must be voluntary since cognizing the information requires a willed commitment of time to read the description. So response differences McQuarrie and Mick identify can be plausibly related to distinctive causal attributes of icons and symbols.

Turning to the issue of counterargumentation, while it is true that a picture may take a thousand words, it is equally true that a word may take a thousand pictures. (Imagine trying to communicate the meaning of the word *reification*—or even the word *reliable*—exclusively through the use of pictures.) The moderator of this interaction is the abstractness of the idea being communicated. Pictures (icons) communicate concrete detail more efficiently than words (symbols) because they concretely signify at multiple points of contact with their referent. However, that very concreteness makes it difficult to clearly assert with a picture an abstract idea or a purely formal logical relation. Consequently, the propositional content of an icon, if any, will almost always be underdetermined and obscurely tacit (Tulving 1983, 43). One may feel no strong impulse to logically counterargue a claim that may or may not have been made (Edell and Staelin 1983; Kardes 1988).

This lack of counterargumentation may benefit advertisers, but the benefit will be attenuated by the weakness of iconic assertions. To deploy strong arguments, advertisers will generally have to use symbols—the distinctive capacity of words to put abstract ideas in a sequence ordered by a formal logic. And those less ambiguous verbal assertions may tend to evoke counterargumentation. So here again, the distinction between images and words, icons and symbols, would appear to be causally related to the persuasiveness of a communication and, thus, be a legitimate component of a scientific theory of persuasion.

Making Visual Persuasion Research Scientific

In the wake of Scott's manifesto, acknowledgment of the rich complexity of images and willingness to engage that complexity should be a threshold credential of a bona fide visual-persuasion researcher. Yet, the question that must ultimately be answered is not how images can mean so many different things. It is why and how they ordinarily limit understanding in a given context to some subset of specific meanings among a potentially infinite set. What qualities of an image and of a mind interact to evoke similar understanding and similar responses in different people who see a particular image? Though mind and image surely interact to limit the play of meaning, given our comparatively well-developed understanding of the human system and limited understanding of the ad system, the pressing question is what qualities define the ad system and how these qualities shape and limit our understanding of images.

Put somewhat differently, the most important task necessary for the development of a science of visual persuasion is the specification of relevant ad-system variables and the development of notation that precisely measures degrees of variation in those variables. Music may provide a good example of what is needed. The variables in play in the production of music have been so well specified over the years and are so well captured by musical notation that performers can quite closely replicate earlier performances they have never heard merely by following the performance instructions that are embodied in a score. Indeed, the performance dimensions are so well specified that, through a purely mechanical process, a machine can give a creditable performance of a song. It is arguable that a fully developed science of visual persuasion will not exist until ad-system notation is sufficiently developed that two independent teams can create ads that are very nearly identical in appearance by following a script coded not in ordinary language but in a generally applicable, nomologically integrated ad-system notation.

The development of this notation would involve a shift in the study of visual rhetoric from a primary reliance on structural corroboration to a primary reliance on multiplicative corroboration (Pepper 1970). Structural corroboration is a function of the agreement of fact with fact. It is most persuasive when a great intellect brings many apparently unrelated pieces of information together to support a conclusion and the gestalt "clicks" for others, convincing them that the conclusion is valid. Multiplicative corroboration is a function of the agreement of person with person. It is most persuasive when everyone comes to the same conclusion because the observation is so simple, for example, when a scientist, student, rat, and machine all note and identically record the fact that a reagent has turned yellow or a pointer has moved to a location of interest on a dial. The high level of agreement of person with person is possible because the dimension being measured is so tightly specified that the value on that dimension is apparent to all observers, even an observer with the naivete of a machine. In the study of visual rhetoric, the scientific impulse is to resolve surface variation into combinations of values on well-defined metadimensions. It is to make explicit the underlying logic of the click. The distinction between symbols and icons and the deep structural relationship of referents to their iconic representations are likely to play a key role in the development of ad-system notation that makes a multiplicatively corroborable description of ad system possible.

In her analysis of visual rhetoric in advertising, Scott is the great intellect. She uses theories from the humanities, especially art history and literary theory, to read ads within the frame of her overarching concept of artistic style. Her readings click, but being the particular insights of a distinctively well-trained observer, they do not contribute much to the development of the practical expertise in applied everyday visual persuasion that Malkewitz, Wright, and Friestad (2003) call for. McQuarrie and Mick note this fact and their own displacement in the direction of multiplicative corroboration as follows:

> [The] distinction between the approach of Scott and . . . our work . . . concerns the level of systemization applied to the visual element. The global and subtle character of . . . artistic style, in the hands of a skilled analyst such as Scott, allows for a deep and complex reading of how pictures [persuade]. The problem, of course, is that apprehending and interpreting stylistic characteristics of this sort depend so heavily on the ability and skill of the interpreter. Our own approach to visual rhetoric, shaped by the semiotic tradition, is . . . more analytic and systematic in its focus on particular sign structures . . . and not so dependent on the interpretive and scholarly abilities of the analyst. (2003, 195)

The semiotic tradition they apply leads McQuarrie and Mick to identify a deep structural distinction between two broad classes of visual rhetorical figures, schemes (which exhibit an overcoded degree of regularity in surface features such as sound) and tropes (which exhibit an undercoded degree of deviation at the deeper, semantic level of the code). These deep structural characteristics are manifested in many different concrete expressions of the underlying scheme or trope form, with the various concrete executions of the form producing effects that are similar to those of other members of the sign class. Because the forms are quite tightly specified (especially schemes), intercoder reliability in the identification of schemes and tropes is likely to be quite high, much higher than it would be if coders were asked to classify ads as executions of one or another of Scott's artistic styles. Indeed, that most naive of observers, the computer, could be programmed to identify schematic features such as assonance and rhyme in a verbal text. The mechanical identification of schemes in a visual text would be much more problematic. But in any case, McQuarrie and Mick's analysis is an example of visual rhetorical science that does represent practical expertise in applied everyday visual persuasion.

A study displaced still further in the direction of multiplicative corroboration and scientific notation is Larsen, Luna, and Peracchio's (2004) analysis of camera angles, camera cuts, and camera movement. These researchers develop an integrated notation that is applicable to every iconic ad execution and that is a sufficiently naive observation that it could be coded or executed by machine. This study suggests that the normative orientation of an object relative to a viewer is usually the object position that puts the viewer at right angles to the object's longest axis. Thus, if a human being were the focal object, the normative orientation would be the pose usually shown in a child's stick figure drawing where face, trunk, arms, and legs are all fully visible. The normative position relative to a box of cereal would be on an axis at right angles to the height and width but in line with depth. Position of the camera relative to that normative orientation is then defined on three axes, x, y, and z. If the camera (in the case of icons) or viewer (in the case of reality) is two feet to the left of the box of cereal on the horizontal x-axis, three feet above the box on the vertical y-axis, and four feet from the box on the saggital z-axis, the position would be coded 2 : 3 : 4. The point of view for any object shown in any iconic image or viewed in reality may be coded in this way. And changes in the point of view have been shown to affect persuasion (Kraft 1987; Meyers-Levy and Peracchio 1992).

Another formal attribute of the ad system, camera cuts, is nomologically related to and builds upon the definition of point of view. For full specification, it requires the addition of a fourth dimension, time, coded as t. Camera cuts can be spatial, temporal, or spatiotemporal. A spatial camera cut occurs when the point of view suddenly shifts from one position, $x : y : z_1$ at t_1 to a nonadjacent position $x : y : z_2$ still at t_1 without passing through intervening space. For example, point of view shifts suddenly from showing the front of a box of cereal seen from the right side of a dining room table to showing the back of the same box seen from the left side of the same table. A temporal camera cut (jump cut) occurs when the camera stays in position $x : y : z$ but time jumps from moment t_1 to nonadjacent moment t_2. For example, a woman sits in her kitchen about to dip her spoon into a bowlful of cereal, then following a cut, sits in the same place before a now empty bowl with a smile on her face. A spatiotemporal cut is a hybrid of the other two executions, for the point of view changes from one shot to the next both temporally and spatially, for example, shifting from $x : y : z_1$ at t_1 to $x : y : z_2$ at t_2. For example, a young man eats a bowl of cereal as he sits by a campfire with a lake in the background, then following a cut, sits in a school cafeteria surrounded by friends but again eating a bowl of cereal. Research suggests that camera cuts such as these affect the persuasiveness of ad executions (Heft and Blondal 1987; Kraft 1986; Larsen, Wright, and Hergert 2004).

At first glance, these descriptions of camera cuts might seem to support Scott's assertion that the phenomenology of image perception and the phenomenology of ordinary experience are incommensurate. When the point of view shifts instantaneously from position $x : y : z_1$ to $x : y : z_2$ without passing through intervening space, a spatial ellipsis, a gap in space, is created and experienced by the viewer. When there is a temporal camera cut that shifts from t_1 to nonadjacent time t_2, a temporal ellipsis occurs. Neither kind of ellipsis ever occurs in reality, so in that respect, icon-mediated experience differs in a fundamental way from reality.

However, as film theorist Christian Metz (1974) and literary theorist Gerard Genette (1980) have shown, the referent (in this case, the reality being shown in the ad), has a deep structural relationship with all possible montage representations of that reality. In other words, all possible camera positions and the spatial or temporal magnitude of all possible ellipses can be defined and measured by reference to the action being filmed. Likewise, degrees of distortion introduced by camera filters or even animation can be precisely defined as degrees of deviation from the normal appearance of the original action. This relationship between the reality being portrayed and iconic portrayals of that reality is a nearly perfect analog of a semiotic distinction that has proved to be very fruitful in linguistics—the relationship between the deep structure and surface structure of sentences in transformational grammar. And the foundation of this deep-structure/surface-structure relationship is the recognition that icons imitate a referent with varying (and measurable) degrees of deviation.

By adding another dimension, rate of movement, coded r, to the three spatial dimensions and the one temporal dimension already defined, Larsen, Luna, and Peracchio (2004) rigorously define the range of possible camera movements relative to a focal object. To define the motion path of a camera moving from $x : y : z_1$ to $x : y : z_2$, the x, y, and z values must each be expressed as a function of t and r in the formula $x = rt + k$, where x is the terminal position of the camera on the x-axis, r is the rate of movement, t is the time spent moving, and k is the initial position on the x-axis. This is the familiar *distance = rate × time* calculation. The camera motions this formula measures have been shown to affect responses to a visual stimulus (Kipper 1986).

A Research Program

The starting place for developing a strong research program in visual rhetoric is to acknowledge the general validity of structurally corroborated readings of ad rhetoric and concepts such as artistic style. The persuasiveness of these concepts and readings demonstrates that the play of meaning is not infinite, that interpretation and response are constrained by features of the ad stimulus and of the human mind. The challenge, then, for the visual rhetorical scientist, is to identify the semiotic and psychological metasystems that undergird the shared intuition that such readings are valid. One plausible terminus of the research program would be to reach a point where an expert like Scott could score an ad on the degree to which it embodies a particular artistic style, after which quantitative techniques could be used to determine the contribution of various well-specified formal attributes to the achievement of that style. Given the current state of our ad-system knowledge and the richness of Scott's readings, we are a long way from reaching that terminus.

Getting from here to there will require work on identifying ad-form variables at all levels of the sign system. Much remains to be done at the most basic level of the visual sign system, the level analogous to phonology in linguistics. The Larsen, Luna, and Peracchio (1994) study is pitched at that level. It illustrates the development of an integrated model in which each new dimension is added seamlessly to existing variables and each new dimension equips the model to describe another layer of image complexity.

Thus, given its initial three spatial dimensions, $x : y : z$, the model could specify only a single stationary camera position. Adding the time variable, t, equipped the model to specify the discontinuous spatial and temporal shifts typical of a more complex ad. Adding the rate variable, r, made it possible to model the $x : y : z$ positions of the still more complex patterns of a moving camera.

This model nonetheless has major limitations. It models camera motion but not the motion of the focal object, an important deficit. New dimensions need to be added so that movements of the focal object can be modeled, for it is likely that some responses to an icon will be a function of the interacting motions of the focal object and the camera. Visual persuasion researchers might explore the applicability of notation used in dance or theater for modeling focal object movements, especially when the focus is on a human being. A notation suitable for dance or theater might equip the model to account, as well, for multiple focal objects and their positions relative to each other. At present, the Larsen, Luna, and Peracchio model can handle only a single focal object, a serious limitation.

Though its variables are well defined and the model has obvious utility, the McQuarrie and Mick taxonomy of rhetorical figures is less tightly defined than the Larsen, Luna, and Peracchio model of points of view. The lower degree of specification (in particular with respect to tropes) is not surprising and is not a relative weakness because visual figures are more complex phenomena than point of view. Phillips and McQuarrie (2004) have added other valid dimensions to the McQuarrie and Mick model, but full specification of the kinds of tropes will probably require a major advance in our understanding of the semantic metasystem, for tropes vary primarily in the kinds of semantic deviation they manifest. The semantic metasystem is the semiotic mother lode. The greatest advances in the scientific understanding of the ad system are likely to flow from deeper understanding of how sememes combine to make well-formed and ill-formed, interesting and uninteresting constellations of objects and meanings. The work of Chafe (1970) and his successors may provide a foundation upon which consumer researchers with an interest in visual rhetoric may build as they engage in this essential research task.

The ultimate objective of visual rhetorical science must be to achieve a grand unification theory that melds the human and ad systems in a single tightly integrated and fully specified semiotic/psychological system. Immanuel Kant gave us good reason to think that such a system is achievable when he resolved Hume's induction problem by suggesting that the world we experience must necessarily mirror the structure of the mind through which we know it. Building on Kant's insight, it would seem to follow that, if the icon/symbol distinction is as important as I have argued in this article, it should be replicated in the structure of the mind. Indeed, it seems to be so replicated in the distinction between episodic and semantic memory.

In Tulving's formulation, episodic memory "is a system that receives and stores information about temporally dated episodes and events, and temporal-spatial relations among them" (1983, 21). The contents of episodic memory are specific, often detailed recollections of event sequences. Episodic memories are personal, unique, and inevitably linked to a space/time context. In contrast, semantic memory is the categorical memory that stores organized, abstract knowledge about the world. The contents of semantic memory are concepts or ideas; and semantic knowledge is communal, broadly applicable, and abstracted from particular times and places.

Across these and other dimensions Tulving discusses, the distinction between the two kinds of memory tracks almost perfectly with the distinction between icons and symbols. The relationship between an episodic memory and its referent is closely analogous to the relationship between an icon and its referent. The referent motivates both the memory and the icon in a multiplicity of specific ways. Indeed, the memories of specific icon-mediated experiences would be stored in episodic memory. Thus, icons might be thought of as a kind of externalized and tangible episodic memory. Likewise, the relationship between a semantic memory and its referent is closely analogous to a symbol's relationship to its generalized, nonspecific referent. So a symbol, too—for example, a written word—might be viewed as a kind of externalized semantic concept.

Conclusion

Researchers interested in developing an understanding of what visual rhetoric is and how it persuades are just now beginning to give images the attention they so richly deserve. Scott and McQuarrie and Mick have taken the lead in redirecting consumer research onto a path that will surely lead to substantial practical expertise in applied everyday visual persuasion, but not immediately. The essential task of adequately describing the ad system has just begun. At this early stage—as indeed, at every stage—advances in understanding are mostly likely to follow if one critiques and builds upon research with substantial theoretical scope and precise application across a broad spectrum of concrete phenomena. This is what I have attempted to do in reaffirming the distinction between icons and symbols in dialog with the especially strong visual persuasion research of Scott and McQuarrie and Mick.

References

Carroll, Lewis. 1960. *The Annotated Alice.* New York: Meridian.
Chafe, Wallace L. 1970. *Meaning and the Structure of Language.* Chicago: University of Chicago Press.
Childers, Terry L., and Michael J. Houston. 1984. "Conditions for a Picture-Superiority Effect on Consumer Memory." *Journal of Consumer Research* 11 (September): 643–654.
Edell, Julie A., and Richard Staelin. 1983 "The Information Processing of Pictures and Print Advertisements." *Journal of Consumer Research* 10 (June): 45–61.
Genette, Gérard. 1980. *Narrative Discourse: An Essay in Method.* Ithaca, NY: Cornell University Press.
Goodman, Nelson. 1976. *Languages of Art.* Indianapolis, IN: Hackett.
Heft, Harry, and Ragnar Blondal. 1987. "The Influence of Cutting Rate on the Evaluation of Affective Content of Film." *Empirical Studies of the Arts* 5 (1): 1–14.
Heidegger, Martin. 1962. *Being and Time.* New York: Harper and Row.
Iser, Wolfgang. 1978. The *Act of Reading: A Theory of Aesthetic Response.* Baltimore, MD: Johns Hopkins University Press.
Kardes, Frank R. 1988. "Spontaneous Inference Processes in Advertising: The Effects of Conclusion Omission and Involvement on Persuasion." *Journal of Consumer Research* 15 (September): 225–233.

Kenney, Keith, and Linda M. Scott. 2003. "A Review of the Visual Rhetoric." In *Persuasive Imagery: A Consumer Response Perspective,* ed. Linda M. Scott and Rajeev Batra, 17–56. Mahwah, NJ: Erlbaum.

Kipper, Philip. 1986. "Television Camera Movement as a Source of Perceptual Information." *Journal of Broadcasting & Electronic Media* 30: 295–307.

Kraft, Robert N. 1986. "The Role of Cutting in the Evaluation and Retention of Film." *Journal of Experimental Psychology: Learning, Memory and Cognition* 12: 155–163.

———. 1987. "The Influence of Camera Angle on Comprehension and Retention of Pictorial Events." *Memory and Cognition* 15 (July): 291–307.

Larsen, Val; David Luna; and Laura A. Peracchio. 2004. "Points of View and Pieces of Time: A Taxonomy of Image Attributes." *Journal of Consumer Research* 31 (June): 102–111.

———; Newell D. Wright; and Thomas Robert Hergert. 2004. "Advertising Montage: Two Theoretical Perspectives." *Psychology and Marketing* 21 (January): 1–15.

Levin, Daniel T., and Daniel J. Simons. 2000. "Perceiving Stability in a Changing World: Combining Shots and Integrating Views in Motion Pictures and the Real World." *Media Psychology* 2: 357–380.

Malkewitz, Kevin; Peter Wright; and Marian Friestad. 2003. "Persuasion by Design: The State of Expertise on Visual Influence Tactics." In *Persuasive Imagery: A Consumer Response Perspective,* ed. Linda M. Scott and Rajeev Batra, 3–15. Mahwah, NJ: Erlbaum.

McQuarrie, Edward F., and David Glen Mick. 1996. "Figures of Rhetoric in Advertising Language." *Journal of Consumer Research* 22 (March): 424–438.

———, and ———. 1999. "Visual Rhetoric in Advertising: Text-Interpretive, Experimental, and Reader-Response Analyses." *Journal of Consumer Research* 26 (June): 37–54.

———, and ———. 2003. "The Contribution of Semiotic and Rhetorical Perspectives to the Explanation of Visual Persuasion." In *Persuasive Imagery: A Consumer Response Perspective,* ed. Linda M. Scott and Rajeev Batra, 191–221. Mahwah, NJ: Erlbaum.

Messaris, Paul. 1994. *Visual "Literacy": Image, Mind, and Reality,* Boulder, CO: Westview Press.

Metz, Christian. 1974. *Film Language: A Semiotics of the Cinema.* Chicago: University of Chicago Press.

Meyers-Levy, Joan, and Laura A. Peracchio. 1992. "Getting an Angle in Advertising: The Effect of Camera Angle on Product Evaluation." *Journal of Marketing Research* 29 (November): 454–461.

Mick, David Glen. 1986. "Consumer Research and Semiotics: Exploring the Morphology of Signs, Symbols, and Significance." *Journal of Consumer Research* 13 (September): 196–213.

Peirce, Charles Sanders. 1931–1958. *Collected Papers,* ed. Charles Hartshorne, Paul Weiss, and Arthur W. Burks. Cambridge, MA: Harvard University Press.

Pepper, Stephen C. 1970. *World Hypotheses.* Berkley: University of California Press.

Phillips, Barbara J., and Edward F. McQuarrie. 2004. "Beyond Visual Metaphor: A New Typology of Visual Rhetoric in Advertising." *Marketing Theory* 4 (1/2): 113–136.

Scott, Linda M. 1994. "Images in Advertising: The Need for a Theory of Visual Rhetoric." *Journal of Consumer Research* 21 (September): 252–273.

Tulving, Endel. 1983. *Elements of Episodic Memory.* Oxford: Clarendon Press.

Part II

The Black Box

Understanding the Cognitive Processing of Rhetoric

5

A Model of the Cognitive and Emotional Processing of Rhetorical Works in Advertising

Bruce A. Huhmann

Chapter Summary

This chapter develops an extensive model of the processing of rhetorical works (i.e., figurative language and visual rhetoric). The model synthesizes two theories— experimental aesthetics, which has explained the processing of creative works (e.g., art, geometric shapes, music, and product designs), and the resource-matching perspective, which holds that processing approaches optimization when resource demand matches the resources that an audience is willing and able to make available. The model's combination of these two theories clarifies phenomena (e.g., the Wundt curve or the components of resource demand) that are otherwise unaccounted for. Further, the model subsumes previous research on advertising rhetoric into a single unified explanation. Additionally, extending the resource-matching perspective to encompass emotional appeals expands the scope of advertising rhetoric research into the unexplored emotional component of rhetorical works. This model should also make important contributions to the literature by suggesting theoretically supported hypotheses for future research.

This chapter develops a comprehensive model of the processing effect of rhetorical works. The model presented in Figure 5.1 is theoretically based in experimental aesthetics and the resource-matching perspective. It combines these two theories of cognitive processing in a new way to develop hypotheses about how structural properties of rhetoric influence processing. Although not tested here, the model's value lies in positing theory-based relationships that can be empirically tested. Support for many of the model's individual links can also be derived from the prior research reviewed in this chapter. As such, the model subsumes various mechanisms previously shown to influence processing outcomes of rhetorical works.

All the model's factors are interrelated and each will be explained individually by the chapter's end. First, advertising rhetoric will be briefly introduced. Second, the theoretical basis for the model will be reviewed. Third, each of its structural properties (i.e., complexity, novelty, conflict, and emotional appeal) will be discussed, followed by the resultant processing motivation factors (i.e., meaning openness, resource demand, and hedonic value) and processing outcomes (i.e., orienting response, interpretation, memory, and persuasion). Finally, individual differences that moderate the relationships between processing motivation factors and processing outcomes will be presented.

Types of Rhetorical Works in Advertising

A *rhetorical work* is any visual or verbal communication that applies rhetorical principles to enhance audience processing or persuasion. Common advertising examples are rhetorical figures in headlines or copy (Huhmann, Mothersbaugh, and Franke 1999, 2002; McQuarrie and Mick 1996; Mothersbaugh, Huhmann, and Franke 2002; Tom and Eves 1999) and visual rhetoric (McQuarrie and Mick 1999; Phillips 2000; Phillips and McQuarrie 2004). Rhetorical works are distinguished from *nonfigurative works,* which express literal meanings in typical, expected patterns of elements. For example, one Subaru ad contained the rhetorical headline, "Clings to a surface so well you'll swear you have superpowers." A nonfigurative headline for this same ad might have been "The new Subaru has the traction and control of all-wheel drive."

Much of the research on advertising rhetoric is based on McQuarrie and Mick's (1996) seminal work. Their taxonomy categorized nineteen verbal rhetorical figures found in a pilot study. Table 5.1 presents a more exhaustive list of rhetorical figures developed after consulting and synthesizing additional sources of advertising rhetoric (e.g., Huhmann, Mothersbaugh, and Franke 1999, 2002; Leech 1966; Mothersbaugh, Huhmann, and Franke 2002; Nelson and Hitchon 1999; Pandya 1977; Tanaka 1994).

The taxonomy distinguishes between schemes and tropes. *Schemes* alter the arrangements of *elements* (e.g., sounds, words, clauses, lines, shapes, colors, images, or symbols) to create repeating (i.e., repetition schemes) or reversed patterns (i.e., reversal schemes). For example, the anaphora in a Relpax® ad headline "A tough migraine needs a tough migraine medicine" creates a pattern by repeating the words "a tough migraine." Alternatively, the transposition in a Glucerna® ad headline uses a mirror-image pattern of word order, "Diabetes. Either you control it, or it controls you." While the taxonomy presented in Table 5.1 is primarily concerned with verbal rhetoric, the rhetorical operations can be applied to visual rhetoric (e.g.,

Table 5.1

Expanded Taxonomy of Rhetorical Figures

Rhetorical operation	Figure definition
Repetition schemes	• *Rhyme* repeats sounds at ends of words/phrases (e.g., "We all *adore a* Kia-*Ora*.").
	• *Alliteration/chime* repeats the same consonant sound in the initial position in three or more subsequent words or the majority of the words with alliteration (e.g., "*B*rown *B*ag *B*onus from Dole.") or in the key words with chime (e.g., "*F*ight Your *F*ear. Introducing *F*osamax.").
	• *Assonance* repeats vowel sounds within a majority of the words in a phrase or sentence (e.g., "S*a*m's h*a*s Cr*a*b *A*pples" or Program flea control's "*O*ne d*o*se. *O*nce a m*o*nth.").
	• *Anaphora* repeats the same first word or phrase (e.g., Naturalistics cosmetics' "*Natural* Beauty. *Natural* Ingredients. *Natural* Glow." or Ford Mustang's "*It runs* quick. *It runs* deep.").
	• *Epiphora* repeats the last word(s) (e.g., "Did You Know Gentle Naturals® *Care* / Is Always Effective *Care?*" or Home Pride's "You don't have to butter *it*, jam *it*, or toast *it* to taste *it*.").
	• *Epanalepsis/chiasmus* ends with the same word(s) with which it began (e.g., Bud Dry's "*Why* ask *why?*" or Alpha's "*Your first computer* dealer is just as important as *your first computer*.").
	• *Anadiplosis/epizeuxis* starts a clause or phrase with the last word(s) of the prior clause or phrase (e.g., "Kids & *Fashion*®. *Fashion* for kids from Oilily." or "Now . . . 'facial *soft—Soft*-Weave.").
	• *Polyptoton* uses different forms of the same root word in the same sense (e.g., Armstrong tires' "The *fat* get *fatter*" or Downy fabric softener ball's "*Catch* the ball that *catches* the rinse cycle.").
	• *Parallelism/isocolon/parison* uses parallel construction in similar length phrases that often repeat a number of words (e.g., Silentite windows' "*The beauty you crave—The comfort you want*" or Carnation Evaporated Milk's "*Delicious enough for parties. Simple enough for every day!*").
Reversal schemes	• *Transposition/antimetabole* reverses the word structure of a phrase in another phrase (e.g., Scouting for All's "*All for one and one for all*," or "As long as *Firestone keeps thinking about people, people will keep thinking about Firestone*.").
	• *Antithesis* contrasts opposite or counterpoised words, often in parallel structure (e.g., Gerber Baby Powder's "You can put it *anywhere* and it won't go *everywhere*," or Lady Speed Stick's "Protects you like a *man*, treats you like a *woman*.").
	• *Hyperbaton/anastrophe* reverses the usual word order within a sentence or phrase for emphasis (e.g., "Next time, buy a *bigger car* and *less expensive*," or "Hamm's—a *beer refreshing*.").

(continued)

Table 5.1 *(continued)*

Rhetorical operation	Figure definition
Substitution tropes	• *Hyperbole* deliberately exaggerates for emphasis (e.g., "—ate PowerBar®—*finished grueling 10k 12 miles ago*," or "*A howitzer with windshield wipers.* The new Buick Skylark Gran Sport*.*"). • *Euphemism* substitutes a softer, milder, less direct word or phrase for a more course, harsh, or unpleasant one (e.g., Carefree's "I want that *fresh feeling* every day," or ScotTissue's "I had *a dreadful experience* last winter—that started with *impure toilet tissue.*"). • *Rhetorical question/hypophora* asks a question for effect (e.g., to assert or deny a claim) rather than to receive information. An answer follows with hypophora (e.g., "Doesn't your family deserve the best? Of course they do. That's why Eggland's Best should be the only egg for them."), but not with rhetorical question (e.g., Charmin's "Looking for a more gentle touch?"). • *Epanorthosis* makes a claim to call that claim into doubt (e.g., Campbell's "A lighter, authentic-tasting risotto prepared by a grandmother from Sicily. Ok, Boise."). • *Ellipsis/aposiopesis* deliberately omit words. The omission is readily implied by the context with ellipsis (e.g., "57 varieties are made by Heinz, only 5 by Hunts."), but the audience must discover or self-generate missing information that is not readily implied with aposiopesis. Often aposiopesis is used to impress the audience with a vague hint at something unmentionable or too awesome to put into words (e.g., "Soup from a can is okay for lunch, but. . . ."). • *Metonymy* designates an object by something closely associated with it—a particular instance, property, characteristic, or association (e.g., Coca-Cola's "The *pause* that refreshes" or "PLJ cares so naturally for your *beauty!*"). • *Synecdoche* substitutes a part for a whole (e.g., "blossoms" for flowers), the material for the product (e.g., "tins" for canned goods), a particular for a general category (e.g., "bread" for food), or a general category for a particular (e.g., "creatures" for spiders). Examples: USA Funds' "We offer a *helping hand* to students and parents. . . ." or Toyota's "They're being built in *your backyard.*" • *Onomatopoeia* substitutes words that convey a sound for descriptive words (e.g., Mazda's "*Zoom-Zoom*" or Dunlop golf balls' "They *click.*" or Noxzema's "*Boom. Buzz. Ahhh.*"). • *Anthimeria* substitutes one part of speech for another (e.g., Movado Eliro watch's "*Gift* him with a thinner, more elegant model to wear at your wedding. . . ."). • *Periphrasis* substitutes a proper noun for a related characteristic or a descriptive word for a proper noun (e.g., "If you've got the wheel . . . we've got *B.F. Goodrich,*" or "Be a *Pepper.* Drink Dr. Pepper." or Kellogg's Corn Flakes' "A plateful of *health.*").

Table 5.1 *(continued)*

Rhetorical operation	Figure definition
	• *Idiom* substitutes a particular, common phrase for a culturally invariant meaning. The meaning does not derive from the individual words but the combination of words forming that phrase (e.g., Blue Water Network's "Is Toyota a *wolf in sheep's clothing?"*)
Destabilization tropes	• *Metaphor* compares two unlike things to imply that the qualities of the second object should be attributed to the first object, even though these qualities are not literally applicable (e.g., Schiff vitamins "Your body is *a living engine,"* or "STP is *cough medicine* for your car.").
	• *Simile* makes an explicit comparison using "like" or "as" to attribute connotations and meanings of one object to another (e.g., PlayStation's "To him, it's *like a dozen long-stemmed roses,"* "Camel is as good *as the sea is wide,"* or Canadian Tire's "Give *like Santa.* Save *like Scrooge.*").
	• *Personification* attributes human qualities to an inanimate object (e.g., "Now when Pyrex Ware *finishes work, it dresses for dinner,"* Chevrolet Equinox's "Form *makes sweet love to* function," or Pond's body lotion's "Make your face *jealous.*")
	• *Synesthesia* uses an experience from one of our five senses to describe something from a different sense (e.g., Kent cigarettes' "*Brighten* up your *taste!"* or Cover Girl Lipstick's "*Color* me *soft.*").
	• *Allusion* refers to persons, places, myths, songs, and so on that the audience will recognize. Unlike resonance (see below), it does not require the ad visual to create an alternate meaning (e.g., FTD holiday flower selections' "*Let heaven and nature sing*" or "Similac's "He's not getting all the nutrition he needs, and it's not because *the dish ran away with the spoon.*").
	• *Parody* mimics the language, style, or ideas of another for comic or satiric effect (e.g., PMS Escape dietary supplement's "*No males were harmed in the testing of this product*" or "*Do you,* Canada Dry's Sparkling Water, *promise to* sparkle, bubble and stay zestful, *till* last sip *do you part?*").
	• *Homonym puns* use a word that has different meanings (e.g., Nature Made Herbs' "Are you *happy* with your St. John's Wort?" or Fisher Peanuts' "Who's the *nut* that left out the MSG?").
	• *Antanaclasis puns* repeat a single word, but with different meanings each time (e.g., Rogaine's "For every woman *growing* anxious about thinning hair, there are thousands *growing* it back," or "People on the *go* . . . *Go* for Coke.").
	• *Syllepsis puns* changes a word's meaning as it modifies different words or clauses (e.g., Toyota Tercel's "If you're *itching* to own a new car, scratch here," or "*Breeze* through the summer with an Emerson Electric window fan.").
	• *Paronomasis puns* use words that sound alike but are different in meaning (e.g., "All *Maid*-Rite menu items are *made* to order," Quaker Oats' "*Waist* not. Want not," or Wigler's Bakery's "Look deep within *our ryes.*").

(continued)

Table 5.1 *(continued)*

Rhetorical operation	Figure definition
	• *Loud puns* alter a cliché or common phrase's meaning by the obvious substitution of another word (e.g., Honda Odyssey's "Home is where the *Honda* is," or Kellogg's Smart Start cereal's "*Breakfast* is as *breakfast* does.").
	• *Resonance* is a verbo-pictorial pun that alters a cliché or common phrase's meaning by juxtaposing it with an image (e.g., Pepto-Bismol's "*Recommended for dog bites*" with a picture of a half-eaten hot dog or "*Hit the bar for lunch*" with a picture of a Balance nutrition bar.).
	• *Paradox* appears to be contradictory, but contains some truth (e.g., Oldsmobile Alero's "Only by *hugging the road tightly* can one truly *let go*," or McDonald's Breakfast Bagel's "Even with the *hole*, it's a *complete* breakfast.").
	• *Oxymoron* uses two seemingly contradictory terms together (e.g., "Kidorable makes the *ordinary extraordinary*" or "Chateau Victoria Hotel is a world of *casual elegance*.").
	• *Irony* implies the opposite of what is said through a mismatch between the words used and either the communicator's character or the nature of the subject (e.g., "Sure you could live without Yellow Pages [or without newspapers or automobiles or clocks]" or Winston's "Forget flowers. Say it by putting the seat down.").
	• *Litotes* intensifies an idea or implies the contrary through exaggerated understatement (e.g., Peter Island Hotel's "Peter Island *offers nothing*," or Hockey Canada's "Relax, It's *Just a Game*.").

McQuarrie and Mick [1999] present a visual repetition scheme in which the dark curves of a model's eyelashes are echoed in her sable hat and coat). The syntactic patterns of elements in schemes should add emphasis to main elements in the pattern. *Tropes* have literally false meanings, from which the intended meaning must be interpreted through simple substitution of intended for literal meaning (i.e., *substitution tropes*) or deciphered through greater cognitive effort (i.e., *destabilization tropes*). To interpret a substitution trope, one must replace what was uttered with what was meant. The hyperbole headline "Healthy Choice® Savory Selections™. So full of flavor it'll make your mustard jealous," encourages one to search the ad for taste information to substitute for an obvious exaggeration. On the other hand, the intended meaning of destabilization tropes is initially unclear. One must work to decipher it or choose between multiple meanings. For example, the paradox headline in an Oscillo™ ad "A flu medicine that makes you feel better. Even before you take it" at first does not make sense; it seems impossible for medicine to help one feel better before it is used. But the destabilization trope encourages one to find and use the information that Oscillo™ is an all-natural homeopathic medicine to interpret the paradox. A visual destabilization trope is shown in Phillips (2000); a toothpaste ad has a pictorial metaphor of a string of pearls in the shape of a smile. One should conclude that the toothpaste would make one's teeth pearly white. Table

5.1 presents additional advertising examples for the rhetorical figures categorized as repetition/reversal schemes or substitution/destabilization tropes.

Although processing differences based on this taxonomy have been supported (Huhmann, Mothersbaugh, and Franke 1999, 2002; McQuarrie and Mick 1996, 2003; Mothersbaugh, Huhmann, and Franke 2002), the underlying mechanism of artful deviance may be oversimplified. It is based on the venerable literal-primacy view (e.g., Beardsley 1962; Hungerland 1958), in which a rhetorical work deliberately deviates from ordinary usage. Other theoretical rationales and mechanisms have also been proposed and empirically supported. These hold that rhetorical works create (1) puzzles that persuade as solving them elicits pleasure (Bowers and Osborn 1966; Tanaka 1994), (2) meaning uncertainty that engages one to the degree that counterarguments and source derogations are reduced to the benefit of persuasion (Sopory and Dillard 2002), and (3) increased elabora-tion to link the elements used with persuasion dependent upon the valence of the elaboration (e.g., Hitchon 1991). Anomalies also suggest that more underlies rhetorical work processing. Compared with nonfigurative works, some rhetori-cal works lead to no difference or a decrease in attention or persuasion (e.g., Ahluwalia and Burnkrant 2004; Mitchell, Badzinski, and Pawlowski 1994) or processing effects inconsistent with measured artful deviance (Mothersbaugh, Huhmann, and Franke 2002).

A Comprehensive Model to Explain the Effects
of a Rhetorical Work on Processing

To accommodate the richness of rhetorical works, a comprehensive model of the underlying mechanisms and their effects on processing was developed that syn-thesized prior research on rhetorical work processing and the theoretical precepts of experimental aesthetics and the resource-matching perspective (Figure 5.1). While use of experimental aesthetics in marketing is in its infancy (Veryzer and Hutchinson 1998), it has long attempted to explain how creative works motivate processing and communicate information based upon their structural properties (Berlyne 1960, 1971, 1974; Crozier 1974; Day 1972; Fechner 1876; Wohlwill 1975; Wundt 1874). This chapter creates a unique extension of experimental aes-thetics theory by incorporating the resource-matching perspective and applies it to processing of rhetorical works.

Experimental aesthetics research has consistently observed a nonmonotonic function (i.e., an inverted U-shaped relationship or Wundt curve) between process-ing performance and structural properties, but without a satisfactory theoretical rational (e.g., Berlyne 1960, 1971, 1974; Wohlwill 1975; Wundt 1874). The model proposes that the resource-matching perspective (cf. Anand and Sternthal 1990; Huhmann 2003; Larsen, Luna, and Peracchio 2004; Peracchio and Meyers-Levy 1997) explains this observed nonmonotonic relationship. The resource-matching perspective predicts that processing is optimized when one's available resources

Figure 5.1 **Model of the Cognitive and Emotional Processing of Rhetorical Works**

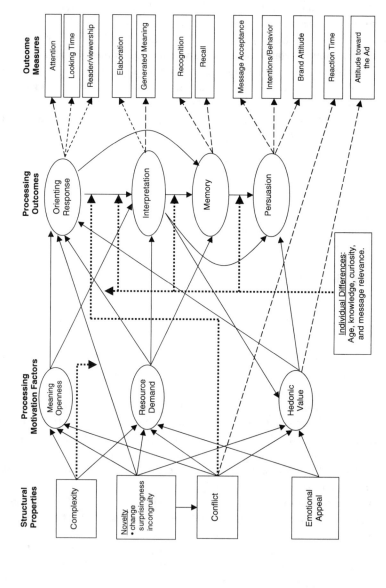

Note: Solid lines are direct links. Dotted lines are moderators. Dashed lines link to variable measures.

match resource demand. An alternative occurs when a stimulus's resource demand is greater than available resources; in this case, one is overwhelmed to the detriment of processing. For example, when no ad headline eased interpretation of a complex visual metaphor, comprehension suffered compared with when an ad had such a headline (Phillips 2000). A third outcome occurs when resource demand is insufficient to fully engage available resources; in this case, the extra resources may be devoted to counterarguments, source derogations, or some other cognitive task to the detriment of processing. For example, ads with lower resource-demand nonfigurative headlines lead to more counterarguments than ads with higher demand trope headlines (McQuarrie and Mick 1992).

Structural Properties Created by the Elements of a Rhetorical Work

Within each rhetorical work, certain structural properties are perceived—complexity, novelty, conflict, and emotional appeal. Experimental aesthetics often referred to structural properties as collative variables because individuals had to collate or compare the stimulus to other stimuli either nearby or stored in memory to determine its relative complexity, novelty, etc. Although communicators assemble elements (e.g., sounds, words, shapes, or images) to inform or persuade, individual perceptions of structural properties arising from the use of these elements drives processing. A rhetorical work can seem more complex, novel, conflict inducing, or emotion-laden to one person than to another or to the same person at different times, or on subsequent exposures.

Complexity

Complexity refers to the variety or diversity in a rhetorical work. Complexity increases with the number of elements, element dissimilarity, the number of forms each element can take, the irregularity of element arrangement, or the difficulty in grouping elements into patterns or units (Berlyne 1960, 1974). Even a nonfigurative work can be complex (e.g., risk information in direct-to-consumer pharmaceutical ads). But rhetorical works should typically be more complex than nonfigurative works, and tropes should be more complex than schemes.

Schemes reduce complexity by grouping elements into repeated or reversed patterns (a.k.a., *unity in diversity* by Berlyne 1960; Veryzer and Hutchinson 1998). Distributional or correlational redundancy also groups elements. With distributional redundancy, some elements occur more frequently than others. For example, repetition schemes with identical elements in multiple locations (e.g., the word "she" in an S. & H. ad headline "She's smart! She's thrifty! She saves"). On the other hand, correlational redundancy creates interdependencies and relationships between elements (Berlyne 1974). For example, the antithesis in a Heinz ad "Ordinary Things. Extraordinary Taste" creates correlational redundancy through the oppositional relationship between the terms "ordinary" and "extraordinary." Schemes are more likely to reduce complexity by featuring distributional or correlational redundancy than tropes.

Destabilization tropes should be more complex than substitution tropes, because destabilization tropes often have more possible meanings and greater dissimilarity between elements. Multiple meanings for "accent" (one from the advertised brand, Nature's Accents®, and one from the French girl shown leaning in for a kiss) are present in the homonym pun "Charm with an accent." A pictorial metaphor in Forceville (1996) asks one to relate dissimilar elements as an automobile is shown with life preservers in the place of Dunlop tires. Applied to the taxonomy in Table 5.1, the model predicts that complexity would increase from repetition schemes to reversal schemes to substitution tropes to destabilization tropes.

Novelty

Novelty decreases when a rhetorical work has been encountered before or recently. Something can be novel in total or recent experience. It can also be absolutely novel with elements that have never before been experienced or relatively novel with some familiar and some novel elements. Familiarity and/or prototypicality (i.e., the perceived degree of category representiveness or commonness) lower novelty. Novelty can be accompanied by one or more subfactors (i.e., change, surprisingness, and incongruity). The frequent co-occurrence of novelty and its subfactors makes it difficult to isolate their effects on processing (Berlyne 1960).

Change involves movement that occurs during exposure. The extent and rate of change, as well as the range of variability, should have a direct impact on orienting response (i.e., exploration or attention) as shown in Figure 5.1 (Berlyne 1960, 1971). Although television and Internet examples of rhetorical works in advertising have yet to be investigated, a visual medium allowing change could create schemes or tropes that present elements sequentially, morph from one element to another, or alter an element as the visual field pans away and back. For example, a Tuborg beer commercial sequentially changes a woman across the pub in stages from plain to gorgeous between each shot of a man drinking beer. One's interest is engaged by the repeated changes in one element of this visual metaphor of beer as a magnifier of attractiveness.

Surprisingness occurs when an element differs from the elements that preceded it in simultaneous or successive element pairings within a work. The degree of surprisingness should be directly related to the number of times that elements co-occur before a violation occurs. Low surprisingness occurs when expectations based on what has come before in the work are confirmed (Berlyne 1974). For example, a Nike television commercial featuring Bo Jackson used an anaphora scheme to first form expectations by following the repeated initial phrase "Bo knows . . ." with something that Bo Jackson could do. The commercial began, "Bo knows football. Bo knows baseball. Bo knows basketball." Surprisingness should occur when Bo

Didley says to Bo Jackson, whose guitar playing leaves much to be desired, "Bo, you don't know Didley."

Whereas surprisingness is perceived when a work induces an expectation and later contradicts it, *incongruity* is perceived when a rhetorical work contradicts expectations based on general experience. Some components of the rhetorical work are similar to what has previously been experienced to trigger expectations, but other elements violate the expectation (Berlyne 1960). General experience has created norms that good communication is informative, true, relevant to the topic, and clear/concise—the incongruity of a rhetorical work is created through violation of these norms (cf. Grice 1989; Mothersbaugh, Huhmann, and Franke 2002; Sperber and Wilson 2004). Schemes yield surface-level incongruity, which violates the clear/concise norm (i.e., Grice's maxim of manner). The S. & H. ad headline mentioned earlier would be more concise if it were "She is smart, thrifty, and saves!" Similarly, "Hamm's—a *beer refreshing*" would be clearer if written "Hamm's is a refreshing beer." These syntactic violations of typical, everyday good communication norms create the surface-level incongruity of schemes. Tropes yield semantic incongruity, which violates the informative, true and/or relevant norms (i.e., Grice's maxims of quantity, quality, and/or relation). One of these violations is the impossible statement made by a trope in a Max Factor ad, " . . . wrap her in fragrance. . . ." Extent-of-processing research has confirmed that tropes are more incongruous than schemes and that the different types of incongruity (i.e., surface-level and semantic) have additive effects (Mothersbaugh, Huhmann, and Franke 2002).

A rhetorical work moves along a continuum from absolute novelty to absolute familiarity in three stages. In the first stage, one initially encounters a rhetorical work. At this point, it should be seen as most surprising and/or incongruous, and its meaning should be most uncertain (i.e., meaning openness will be highest). Orienting response (i.e., exploration or focusing one's senses upon a stimulus) will be the greatest at this stage, but perhaps not comprehension (i.e., successful interpretation of the intended meaning). In the second stage, one has previously encountered a rhetorical work. Thus, surprisingness, incongruity, and meaning openness should not be as high. As surprisingness, incongruity, and meaning openness decline, orienting response is reduced; however, likelihood of interpreting a trope's intended meaning or a scheme's object of focus increases as each repetition affords a greater opportunity to process. More successful interpretation of intended meaning should improve persuasion. The rate of decline should depend on a rhetorical work's other structural properties (e.g., its complexity and conflict) and the characteristics of the audience (e.g., stimulus-seeking tendencies). In the third stage, one is so familiar with the rhetorical work that it should be viewed as typical or common. Surprisingness, incongruity, and meaning openness should, therefore, be low or nonexistent. Orienting response should also be low as one becomes habituated to or bored with processing the rhetorical work. Successful interpretation of intended meaning should be highly probable, but the power of the rhetorical work to persuade should have declined as one begins ignoring the work. A common example of this third stage is the dead metaphor (Beardsley 1962), which will be discussed further in the section on meaning openness.

Past research supports the three stages of novelty. With only one presentation, rhetorical works are rated as more novel than nonfigurative works (Nelson and Hitchon 1999). Novelty should decline as rhetorical work is repeated, which should indirectly reduce persuasion. Repeated rhetorical works have been found to be less persuasive than single presentations (Ahluwalia and Burnkrant 2004; Gladney and Rittenburg 2005; Sopory and Dillard 2002).

Conflict

Conflict occurs when one has two or more competing responses to a rhetorical work or experiences ambivalence. Berlyne (1960) posited that the degree of conflict increased as (1) competing response tendencies neared equal strength, (2) the number of competing responses increased, or (3) the absolute strength of the competing responses rose. The opposite of conflict is harmony. Tropes should increase conflict, whereas schemes should reduce conflict, because schemes can focus awareness or emphasize certain elements of a rhetorical work (Bower and Bolton 1969; Faber 1996; Rubin and Wallace 1989). In fact, schemes can focus awareness to such a degree that they can distract from negative or deceptive information. Mothersbaugh, Huhmann, and Franke (2002) found that scheme headlines featuring positive brand information distracted people from weak or negative brand information in the ad copy. But when ad copy contained strong brand arguments consistent with the positive brand information in scheme headlines, emphasis was focused on it to the degree that valence of message thoughts and brand attitude received a significant boost. Furthermore, the emphasis of one scheme, rhyme, has been found to increase truthfulness perceptions over equivalent, equally comprehensible nonfigurative statements (McGlone and Tofighbakhsh 2000). Alternatively, tropes create conflict between literal and nonliteral meanings or divide focus. Confronting a literally false trope generates cognitive tension or conflict and a desire to reduce the conflict. If one can self-generate a nonliteral meaning to interpret the trope, conflict dissipates. Thus, the more novel a trope is, the greater the conflict because one has less experience to guide the choice between competing responses or meanings. In support of this Flor and Hadar (2005) found that more familiar metaphors generated less conflict than more novel metaphors.

Conflict and its resolution can influence hedonic value. If the resolution of literal falsehood is too difficult or impossible, frustration results. This frustration should negatively impact hedonic value. If the resolution is too simple, boredom or antagonism may be generated. This boredom or antagonism should also negatively impact hedonic value. However, successful resolution of a trope by deciphering its nonliteral meaning can be pleasurable. This has been called the pleasure of the text (e.g., Tanaka 1994). This pleasure should positively impact hedonic value. The focused emphasis or harmony of a scheme should increase positive hedonic value as well (Berlyne 1960, 1974).

The most sensitive and easy-to-measure result of conflict is longer reaction times (Berlyne 1960). Although conflict was not the theoretical explanation, much metaphor research in cognitive and experimental psychology has investigated reaction time differences in the comprehension of literal versus metaphorical utterances (for a review of these studies, see Flor and Hadar [2005] and Hoffman and Kemper [1987]). Consistent with this model's predictions, the experiments suggest that people search for information to resolve the conflict created by a metaphor. Only when context information (e.g., in a paragraph or ad copy) was provided, did metaphorical and literal statements have similar processing times, according to Hoffman and Kemper's (1987) review. Mothersbaugh, Huhmann, and Franke (2002) also found that brand-relevant tropes in ads increased processing of brand information. The lack of context information to resolve trope-elicited conflict may explain reaction time differences for trope versus nonfigurative works presented in isolation (Forceville 1996; Kreuz and Link 2002).

Emotional Appeal

Rhetorical works can include positive (e.g., joy, warmth, humor, etc.) or negative (e.g., fear, guilt, shame, regret, shock, etc.) emotional appeals. Emotional appeals should contribute to hedonic value with positive emotional appeals increasing hedonic value, but negative emotional appeals decreasing hedonic value. Also, emotional appeals should affect resource demand and, through resource demand, processing. Thus, a negative emotional appeal should increase resource demand as its strength increases. The rising resource demand increases processing until the negative appeal's strength pushes resource demand beyond one's capacity to handle it. Schemes' emphasis-enhancing nature should increase the strength of emotional appeals in schemes. For example, if a fear appeal image is emphasized through a visual repetition scheme highlighting a fearful image in a TV commercial, the fear appeal should be stronger than if the fearful image was not repeated. A Honey Maid cracker ad uses anaphora in the headline "Twice the whole grain. Twice the smiles," and a visual repetition of smiling children eating Honey Maid crackers. The warmth appeal should be stronger than if the headline had been "Twice the whole grain. More smiles," and only one smiling child were shown.

Processing Motivation Factors

Unlike the structural properties that are more closely allied with how the elements (i.e., sounds, words, images, etc.) in a rhetorical work are used, the processing motivation factors cannot be specifically linked to a single element itself. Nor do they exist in the rhetorical work itself. Instead, the processing motivation factors arise within the person exposed to the rhetorical work in response to a combination of structural properties, the person's prior experience with the rhetorical work or with other stimuli, or the person's ability to successfully interpret the rhetorical work. These factors include meaning openness, resource demand, and hedonic value.

Meaning Openness

Meaning openness is uncertainty/ambiguity regarding a rhetorical work's interpretation due to novelty, complexity, or conflict among multiple competing interpretations. Novelty can increase meaning openness. Since one has no way of knowing what will come next in a highly novel, changing, surprising, or incongruous rhetorical work, meaning is unclear. Complexity can increase meaning openness (e.g., a Nissan Xterra ad shows an "X =" sign formed of many planks and boards; however, the number of elements (i.e., planks and boards) is so large that it is at first unclear what this visual element is). In regard to conflict, meaning openness can range from disjunctive, in which multiple mutually exclusive meanings vie for selection as the intended meaning, to conjunctive, in which all competing meanings appear appropriate and, therefore, intended. Meaning openness increases as the range of possible meanings (or polysemy) increases. It is greatest when an interpretation is equally likely to be seen as correct or incorrect.

Meaning openness should be greater for rhetorical than nonfigurative works. Thus, nonfigurative works have been found to encourage automatic processing, whereas rhetorical works encourage effortful processing directed at information to end meaning openness (Huhmann, Mothersbaugh, and Franke 1999, 2002; Mothersbaugh, Huhmann, and Franke 2002; Nelson and Hitchon 1999). Tropes often activate more of the structural properties and, hence, have a greater propensity for meaning openness than schemes or nonfigurative works. However, some tropes are low in meaning openness (e.g., dead metaphors and idioms). Dead metaphors have been used so often that they no longer elicit meaning openness. For example, when a Sony camcorder ad headline says "Holding on to your memories . . ." it is a dead metaphor because "holding a memory" means "storing traces of past events" has been used so often that neither the literal (i.e., literally "holding") nor any other meanings are likely to be activated. Idioms are language-specific combinations of words that cannot be understood from the meaning of the individual words forming a phrase. For example, a pro-environment ad headline asks "Is Toyota a wolf in sheep's clothing?" with a specific meaning of "pretending to be something other than what one truly is." Meaning openness is low because dead metaphors and idioms lack a conflict between competing meanings. Schemes and nonfigurative works can generate meaning openness if they are perceived as high in one or more of the contributing structural properties. This differs from the semiotics-based view (e.g., Eco 1976; McQuarrie and Mick 1992, 1996) that tropes are open to interpretation due to undercoding, whereas schemes are closed to alternative interpretations because the intended meaning is overcoded (i.e., redundant information reinforces the intended meaning). While schemes can reinforce or emphasize a particular interpretation by emphasizing certain aspects of a work, redundancy does not eliminate alternative meanings or meaning ambiguity. For example, the epiphora headline "Did You Know Gentle Naturals® *Care* / Is Always Effective *Care?*" emphasizes "care," but meaning openness could still arise from experience with the brand, or lack thereof, conflict between connotations or denotations of "care," or individual differences. A nonfigurative work can also elicit meaning openness (e.g., complex legalistic disclaimers or unfamiliar technical information or terms). Thus, a scheme or nonfigurative work that does not appear complex or novel can still generate meaning openness.

Resource Demand

The resource-matching perspective holds that processing approaches optimization the closer the match between a stimulus's resource demand and the resources that one has the motivation, opportunity, and ability to make available. Thus, a nonmonotonic (inverted-U) function for processing peaks at the point where resource demand equals available resources. Obviously, each person differs in his/her available resources due to individual differences in variables that affect motivation, opportunity, and ability (to be discussed later).

Resource demand is related to cognitive load in that it is the amount of resources required to successfully process a stimulus. However, cognitive load does not take into account the resource demand generated by emotional appeals or content. To date, applications of the resource-matching perspective have also ignored emotional appeals as a source of resource demand (e.g., Anand and Sternthal 1990; Huhmann 2003; Larsen, Luna, and Peracchio 2004; Peracchio and Meyers-Levy 1997). However, emotional content has been found to increase resource demand (Schwarz and Clore 2007). Most people have a greater capacity to handle positive emotion appeals than negative ones; thus, the function's peak should be higher and shifted right for positive compared with negative emotional appeals. When one is overwhelmed by a negative emotion (e.g., through ad context or through an externally or internally generated emotional state), one should avoid even weak negative emotional appeals. At other times, strong emotional appeals are processed when one has available emotional capacity due to an individual trait or a state of emotional nonarousal.

In addition to emotion, the other structural properties should also contribute to resource demand. More complex rhetorical works should increase resource demand as one struggles with greater numbers, dissimilarity, numerous forms, irregularity arrangements, or grouping difficulty of elements. Novelty should increase resource demand because new connections to link elements must be discerned with unfamiliar, unexpected, incongruous, surprising, or changing combinations of elements. As conflict increases, resource demand should also increase as one toils with competing responses or meanings. The structural properties should have an additive effect on resource demand. Thus, a rhetorical work that is novel and complex should demand more resources than one that is only novel, ceteris paribus.

Hedonic Value

Hedonic value is the degree of intrinsic pleasure elicited by a rhetorical work. Positive hedonic value occurs when something is pleasurable or rewarding in itself, not because it is related to or communicates about something else (Berlyne 1974). Thus, a rhetorical work in an ad from another time or culture may be pleasing, even if one does not know what is being advertised. Hedonic value may be increased through a beautiful pattern or arrangement of elements in a scheme or a unique, clever way of indirectly communicating in a trope. Also, hedonic value can be increased when an unpleasant, aversive reaction or emotion arises, then is subsequently removed. For example, the negative response to an image may be defused by resonance in an ad headline or voiceover (McQuarrie and Mick 1992). If a rhetorical work engenders conflict that is challenging, but resolvable, then one should derive pleasure from successfully resolving it (Izard 1977; McQuarrie and Mick 1999; Tanaka 1994). Successful resolution of an aversive reaction or conflict should increase hedonic value more than if the aversive response or conflict is too easy or too difficult to successfully resolve. When resolution is too easy, one will likely become bored and view the rhetorical work as tiresome, which should decrease hedonic value. For example, an ad headline that overtly interprets a visual metaphor reduces its hedonic value (Phillips 2000). Unsuccessful resolution should also decrease hedonic value as one becomes upset or frustrated. One should desire to approach rhetorical works eliciting positive hedonic value and desire to avoid rhetorical works eliciting negative hedonic value. The hedonic value associated with an ad's rhetorical work should also be an important component of attitude toward the ad.

Processing Outcomes Affected by Structural Properties or Processing Motivation Factors

The goal behind including rhetorical works in ads is to influence processing to the benefit of the advertised brand. The model proposes that the structural properties of a rhetoric work and the processing motivation factors experienced by consumers will influence the processing outcomes of orienting response, interpretation, memory, and persuasion. Each processing outcome will now be reviewed along with possible outcome measures.

Orienting Response

Orienting response focuses one's senses upon a rhetorical work. Orienting response has also been called stimulus selection or exploratory behavior. Orienting response should increase with meaning openness as one seeks information to help choose a particular meaning. Orienting response should increase with resource demand. This has empirical support as well as the prediction that, when choosing between two works, one will be more likely to orient toward the more resource-demanding one

(Berlyne 1971; Frisby 1995). Hedonic value should also directly affect orienting response. Hedonic value-related survey items, such as enjoying or liking something, have been found to be important antecedents of orienting response (Izard 1977).

Habituation decreases orienting response as a novel work is repeated (Ben-Shakhar et al. 2000; Berlyne 1960). In advertising, habituation is called "wearout." Complexity should moderate the direct relationship between novelty and orienting response such that a repeated rhetorical work will wear out more slowly the greater its complexity. A series of experiments with paintings and abstract patterns suggests support for this moderating effect (Berlyne 1971). Wearout should be reversible if a rhetorical work is superficially changed (Ben-Shakhar et al. 2000).

Orienting response can be measured as attention, looking time, or readership/ viewership. Compared with nonfigurative works, rhetorical works lead to greater attention (Ahluwalia and Burnkrant 2004; Swasy and Munch 1985), longer looking time (Huhmann, Mothersbaugh, and Franke 1999), and greater ad copy readership (Huhmann, Mothersbaugh, and Franke 1999, 2002; Mothersbaugh, Huhmann, and Franke 2002).

Orienting response is greater with tropes than schemes (Huhmann, Mothersbaugh, and Franke 2002). Also, tropes and schemes differ in the focus of the orienting response. The two types of orienting responses are specific and diversive (Berlyne 1960). A specific orienting response is a detailed investigation of a stimulus to acquire new information. Tropes encourage this specific focus on information that reduces meaning openness and resolves conflict to the exclusion of other information. A diversive orienting response occurs when one explores many aspects of a stimulus without regard for seeking information but instead for amusement or stimulation seeking. Schemes encourage this more general, diversive orienting response that is not directed at particular information, but toward all aspects of an ad (Mothersbaugh, Huhmann, and Franke 2002).

Interpretation

Interpretation is the process of deciphering a rhetorical work's intended meaning (i.e., the meaning that the communicator wanted to convey). Interpretations often, but not always, will be the intended meaning (Forceville 1996). As resource demand and meaning openness increase, interpretation difficulty should increase from nonfigurative works to repetition schemes to reversal schemes to substitution tropes to destabilization tropes. Comprehension is successfully interpreting the intended meaning. When one is unable to interpret a work, the resultant bewilderment, frustration, or confusion should decrease hedonic value. When one generates a meaning for a rhetorical work, but not the intended one, it is miscomprehension, which is another form of failed interpretation. Unlike bewilderment, miscomprehension should only decrease hedonic value if the incorrect generated meaning is negative or negatively reflects on the ad or brand. Otherwise, hedonic value should be unaffected, because one does not realize that one has miscomprehended a work.

However, miscomprehension can go unchecked and decrease persuasion because advertisers typically lack a direct feedback loop to correct misinterpretations.

Given the literal falseness of tropes and emphasis-directing nature of schemes, a rhetorical work can encourage deception without making literal deceptive statements (Faber 1996; McGlone and Tofighbakhsh 2000). For example, the simile in "Similac Advance® can help develop a baby's immune system like breast milk" could lead to the conclusion that Similac is as good as breastfeeding. Also, although Wal-Mart's ad slogan "Always the low price. Always" is not literally deceptive (it refers to their everyday low price strategy), the epanalepsis scheme emphasizing "always" could direct consumers to conclude that Wal-Mart always has lower prices than competitors.

Tropes and schemes should differ in interpretation based on differences in orienting response and resource demand. The specific orienting response of a trope should increase the likelihood of comprehending the intended meaning when an ad includes information to resolve meaning openness (and decrease it when such information is absent). The diversive orienting response of a scheme could reduce the likelihood of comprehending the intended meaning; however, this is moderated by a scheme's ability to reduce conflict by directing emphasis. Thus, diversive orienting response will only negatively affect interpretation when a scheme does not direct emphasis to elements that aid successful interpretation. Since resource demand motivates processing (Mothersbaugh, Huhmann, and Franke 2002), higher resource-demand rhetorical works (e.g., destabilization tropes) should be more successfully interpreted up to the point where resource demand exceeds available resources; after this point interpretation will suffer. Metaphors have often been found to enhance comprehension compared with nonfigurative statements (Marschark and Hunt 1985). However, compared with nonfigurative works, interpretation of a visual or verbal metaphor was impaired when subjects were asked to evaluate eight ads (Mitchell, Badzinski, and Pawlowski 1994).

The interpretation process can be measured through message elaboration or generated meaning. Compared with nonfigurative works, rhetorical works lead to greater message elaboration—more cognitive responses (Mothersbaugh, Huhmann, and Franke 2002; Nelson and Hitchon 1999) and greater numbers of and more favorably valenced message-related thoughts (Ahluwalia and Burnkrant 2004, Hitchon 1991; Mothersbaugh, Huhmann, and Franke 2002). Generated meaning can be measured by having subjects (1) indicate which of two possible meanings is correct; the intended one or another believable, but incorrect meaning (McQuarrie and Mick 1999) or (2) self-generate a rhetorical work's meaning and then code these as denoting the intended meaning or not using independent judges (Mothersbaugh, Huhmann, and Franke 2002).

Rhetorical works transmit four types of information. Communicators are primarily concerned with whether or not the audience comprehended the intended semantic meaning. But a rhetorical work also conveys syntactic, expressive, and cultural information, which collectively are called aesthetic information (Berlyne

1974). Aesthetic information differentiates a rhetorical from a nonfigurative work. In nonfigurative works, semantic information dominates. Schemes also communicate syntactic information (i.e., similarities, contrasts, and other surface-level relationships that create unity or order among the elements) to emphasize certain semantic information. Tropes communicate primarily through aesthetic information, while requiring the audience to generate semantic information through successful interpretation. Expressive information reveals the author's values, attitudes, beliefs, psychological processes, personality, and background. Cultural information allows one to learn more about the culture or subculture (e.g., its values, norms, gender roles, rituals, etc.) in which a rhetorical work originated through the elements chosen (e.g., words, sounds, or images) or inferences based on the work as a whole (e.g., those outside the culture could infer from PlayStation's simile "To him, it's *like a dozen long-stemmed roses*" that roses are a preferred gift among American women).

Memory

Interpretations, either the comprehension of intended meaning or a miscomprehension, can be stored in long-term memory to use during ad processing or later evaluation of a brand. Memory is often measured by recall and recognition. These are also common proxies for the antecedents of memory. Nonfigurative works, tropes, and schemes should have differential effects on memory based on resource matching, specific versus diversive orienting response, and mnemonics. Memory should increase up to the point where resource demand exceeds available resources. Thus, memory has been found to be better for the more resource-demanding rhetorical works than nonfigurative works in terms of better-aided recall (McQuarrie and Mick 2003), unaided recall (Bushman and Wells 2001), and higher Gallup & Robinson brand-recall scores (Tom and Eves 1999). When resource demand exceeds available resources, memory suffers. At times, more complex stimuli have been found to be more difficult to recognize or recall (Berlyne 1960; Lowrey 1998, 2006). Thus, destabilization tropes should be less memorable when resource demand is too high. But when resource demand does not exceed available resources, a trope's specific orienting response should improve recall for the message's gist (e.g., brand information or copy points) although not necessarily its form. Thus, brand recall was better with metaphorical than nonfigurative copy (Gray and Snyder 1989), message argument recall was better with rhetorical question than nonfigurative headlines (Ahluwalia and Burnkrant 2004), and key ad message point recall was better with rhetorical than nonfigurative works, and with tropes than schemes (McQuarrie and Mick 1992, 2003). However, memory for message form should be greater with schemes, because of mnemonics, which creates harmony by reducing conflict and decreases complexity through unified, regular patterns of elements. This has been shown with assonance and rhyme (Bower and Bolton 1969; Rubin and Wallace 1989).

Persuasion

Persuasion is a function of interpretation (partially mediated by memory) and hedonic value. Even if one does not remember a rhetorical work, its interpretation should impact persuasion (e.g., sleeper effects, mere exposure). But memorability should strengthen the effect. Persuasion can be measured through brand attitude, message acceptance, or intentions/behavior. Even though the audience may comprehend the intended meaning and experience positive hedonic value, persuasion is not guaranteed (for enhancing/limiting conditions, see Larson 2004). But rhetorical works should enhance persuasion over nonfigurative works with similar semantic information. Compared with nonfigurative works, rhetorical works improve message acceptance (Bushman and Wells 2001), behavioral intentions (Gladney and Rittenburg 2005; Tom and Eves 1999), brand attitudes (Hitchon 1997), and attitude change (Bowers and Osborn 1966).

Schemes and tropes differentially affect persuasion, due to the orienting response focus. Mothersbaugh, Huhmann, and Franke (2002) found no significant difference in brand attitude when nonfigurative headlines introduced weak or strong argument copy; however, there was a difference with scheme headlines and an even larger difference with trope headlines. Yet, if resource demand exceeds resource availability then persuasion should be impaired, especially for high resource-demand tropes. Lowrey (1998) found that syntactic simplicity (i.e., affirmative statements, active voice, and right-branching structure) lead to more favorable brand attitudes for strong than weak argument copy, whereas syntactic complexity (i.e., negations, passive voice, left-branching structure) led to a less favorable brand attitude for strong arguments than weak ones. However, the level of involvement moderated these relationships.

Individual Difference Variables That Make
Fewer or More Resources Available

Based on the resource-matching perspective, the model predicts that available resources moderate the direction and strength of resource demand's impact on processing outcomes (i.e., orienting response, interpretation, memory, and persuasion). The nonmonotonic function implies that moderate levels of resource demand tend to work best. But individual differences can shift the curve's peak up or down, left or right (i.e., peaks at a point of lesser or greater resource demand, respectively). Although people differ in their reactions to structural properties, research shows that reactions are relatively consistent and the function remains similarly shaped (Berlyne 1974; Crozier 1974). Some individual differences that should alter either resource demand or available resources include age, prior knowledge, curiosity, and message relevance.

Age Differences

Since resources available for processing take time to mature and then decline with age, lower resource-demand rhetorical works should be better processed by the young and the aged, whereas higher resource rhetorical works should be better processed by those in the prime resource availability years. Thus, age should shift the nonmonotonic function as suggested by age and complexity studies and the developmental psychology of metaphor. In terms of shape complexity, Wohlwill (1975) found that complexity monotonically increased orienting response and attitudes for sixth graders, but first graders had a flatter gradient for the orienting response–complexity relationship (i.e., near the function's plateau) and a nonmonotonic relationship between complexity and attitude. Huhmann (2003) found nonmonotonic functions between visual complexity and recall of banner ad images for four age groups. The curves were shifted to the right (i.e., recall peaks with more complex images) for prime resource-availability age groups (sixteen to fifty), but shifted to the left (recall peaks with less complex images) for younger (under fifteen) and older (over fifty-one) groups. Metaphors are increasingly liked in comparison with nonfigurative works as children grow to maturity, regardless of reading ability (Pickens, Pollio, and Pollio 1985; Silberstein et al. 1982). Preschoolers better recall nonfigurative stories than rhyming ones, whereas adults better recall rhyming versions (Hayes 1999).

Prior Knowledge

Prior knowledge should influence the processing effectiveness of rhetorical works. Prior knowledge includes (1) cultural knowledge, which is the degree of knowledge about a society's symbols, values, traditions, conventions, interpretive lens, and other culture-based components of communication; (2) persuasion knowledge, which is the degree of knowledge about the techniques used by advertisers to persuade audiences; (3) product category expertise; and (4) brand familiarity, which is the degree of knowledge about the brand, its features/benefits, its brand personality, and how it is typically promoted based on experience.

A lack of *cultural knowledge* increases resource demand by increasing (1) novelty, since even a culture's idioms and dead metaphors are new to one who has not heard them before; and (2) conflict and meaning openness, which makes interpretation more difficult. Lack of cultural knowledge should shift the resource-matching function so that it peaks at a point of less resource demand. Whereas a visual scheme and a nonfigurative work led to similar attitudes, McQuarrie and Mick's (1999) subjects with cultural knowledge had large differences in attitude toward the ad between a visual trope and a nonfigurative work, but those lacking cultural knowledge did not. The greater resource demand of tropes likely led to resource demand exceeding available resources for those lacking cultural knowledge; thus, processing suffered. Mothersbaugh, Huhmann, and Franke (2002) also found that those lacking cultural knowledge were not able to handle the increased resource demands of verbal rhetorical figures, and processing suffered.

Persuasion knowledge (PK), or knowledge of and ability to perceive persuasive tactics such as rhetoric, should increase efficient use of available resources to handle resource demand. Thus, the function should be flatter and shifted to the right. Predictions for PK effects could be drawn from the effects of expert knowledge with other stimuli. Crozier (1974) found that as musical scale uncertainty increased, experts (i.e., music majors) and nonexperts (i.e., nonmusic majors) had similar-shaped curves relating uncertainty to orienting response and attitude, but the experts' attention to and liking of music peaked at point of greater uncertainty than that of nonexperts. However, the ability to detect persuasive techniques may invoke a schemer's schema, which could negatively impact persuasion (Wright 1986). For example, a PK-shifted function could account for Ahluwalia and Burnkrant's (2004) findings that PK was inversely related to the degree of persuasion with a rhetorical question and that high PK subjects relied more on source derogation or bolstering in their evaluations. Because PK shifts the function's peak, a rhetorical question that was at the optimal resource demand for low PK subjects was insufficient to match the resources available to high PK subjects, leaving extra resources to consider the source.

Product category expertise is knowledge specific to the domain of a particular product category (e.g., automobiles). As such, it should enhance interpretation through familiarity with domain-specific terms, concepts, and technologies. Thus, it would shift the resource-matching function to peak at a point of greater resource demand for those with product category expertise.

Brand familiarity should be inversely related to resource demand for a rhetorical work containing brand information, because the brand itself is novel (e.g., because they must also learn what Kia-Ora is, resource demand should be greater for those lacking brand familiarity in "We all adore a Kia-Ora"). Familiarity should also aid interpretation by leading to more accurate audience assumptions of the communicator's intentions in creating a work (cf. Gibbs 2001).

Diversive Versus Specific Epistemic Curiosity

Experimental aesthetics distinguishes between two curiosity traits—diversive and specific. Diversive curiosity corresponds with need for cognition in the marketing and psychology literature. It intrinsically motivates a diversive orienting response to investigate a wide range of elements and a desire to learn for the enjoyment of learning. The higher one's diversive curiosity, the greater the available resources one should be willing to devote to processing, which would shift the nonmonotonic function to the right. In support of this prediction, Brennan and Bahn (2006) showed that salient extended metaphors in ads led to fewer counterarguments and more favorable attitudes toward the ad and brand than did meaning-equivalent nonfigurative works with higher, but not lower, need for cognition subjects. On the other hand, specific curiosity is enduring involvement with a particular issue or product. It should motivate specific orienting response toward information related to that issue or product (Berlyne 1960; Day 1972; Litman and Spielberger 2003). Greater specific curiosity should also motivate one to make more resources available, so that the processing function peaks at a point of greater resource demand. For example, Lowrey (2006) found that subjects with higher specific curiosity in regard to a product exhibited greater product category, brand, and message element recall than those with lower specific curiosity when exposed to a complex TV commercial script.

Message Relevance or Ad Message Involvement

Message relevance influences the intensity and direction of processing. *Intensity* is the degree of effort devoted to processing. Higher intensity should motivate one to make more resources available. This shifts the nonmonotonic function to the right. In support of this prediction, when combined with high resource-demand extensive ad copy, higher resource-demand schemes led to less processing than nonfigurative works under conditions of low message relevance; however, under high message relevance, schemes led to more processing than nonfigurative works (Huhmann, Mothersbaugh, and Franke 2002). *Direction* is one's processing goal, either non-brand or brand processing. A nonbrand-processing goal can distract one from the ad's brand information toward other stimuli, either within or outside of the ad. With both a brand-processing goal and the resource demand of a brand-relevant rhetorical work matching available resources, processing outcomes should be better than with either a nonbrand-processing goal or a mismatch between resource demand and availability. For example, when a rhetorical work's resource demand exceeds available resources, one will avoid processing brand information, as occurred in the extensive copy-scheme condition under low message relevance in Huhmann, Mothersbaugh, and Franke (2002).

Conclusions and Future Research

This chapter's primary contribution is that it subsumes previous findings and mechanisms used to explain how advertising rhetoric is processed into a comprehensive theory-rich model of the processing of rhetorical works. Rhetorical works include figurative language or visuals. The model extends experimental aesthetics to incorporate the resource-matching perspective. Experimental aesthetics theory has been successfully applied to processing other creative works, such as fine art, music, architecture, museum displays, and product design (Berlyne 1960, 1971, 1974; Crozier 1974; Veryzer and Hutchinson 1998). However, its theoretical precepts backed by strong experimental support are an excellent basis for modeling rhetorical-work processing. The resource-matching perspective posits that a match between resource demand and available resources optimizes processing. Thus, processing performance is nonmonotically related to resource demand. Individual differences shift the processing-resource demand function's peak but not the nonmonotonic relationship. Another contribution is the extension of the resource-matching perspective to include emotional as well as cognitive processing. Processing should be optimized when strength of an emotional appeal matches one's available capacity to handle emotion.

Increasingly, consumers are multitasking during ad exposure (Pilotta et al. 2004). Thus, fewer resources are available for ad processing. The model contributes a theory-based solution to this problem by predicting that resource demand motivates orienting response (i.e., exploration or attention). To increase resource demand, advertisers should rely more on rhetorical works, especially more resource-demanding destabilization tropes, and make interpretation more challenging by decreasing informative context. One study of forty-five years of magazine advertising indicates that many advertisers are following this strategy (Phillips and McQuarrie 2002). However, this strategy limits the brand information in an ad. Thus, this strategy should be more effective with (1) established products than new ones, because benefit and feature information is often crucial to persuade consumers to try new products, whereas ads for established products often serve a reminder or brand-building role; and (2) convenience products than search products, because consumers prefer and will process more brand information for search products than convenience products (Franke, Huhmann, and Mothersbaugh 2004; Mothersbaugh, Huhmann, and Franke 2007).

Another contribution of the model is its delineation of processing differences between schemes and tropes. Schemes, which organize elements into repeating or reversed patterns, should lower complexity through unifying elements and lower conflict by emphasizing certain elements. However, schemes encourage a diverse orienting response divided over peripheral and brand-relevant ad aspects. This could harm brand information acquisition or even interpretation of the scheme if it does not emphasize the right elements. Tropes should be more incongruous than schemes, because tropes can violate more norms, or Grice's (1989) maxims. Tropes encourage specific orienting responses directed at information that will resolve the greater meaning openness that stems from the greater incongruity, complexity, and conflict typical of tropes.

A final contribution of the model is its ability to suggest many theory-based avenues for future research. The following are some possible studies to test hypotheses derived from the model.

First, the model extends the resource-matching perspective to include emotional as well as cognitive processing. Available resources to handle an emotion-laden stimulus's resource demand might be measured by one's emotional intelligence or ability to manage emotional information (Taute 2005). Future research should verify this extension's validity.

Second, Figure 5.1 shows four main structural properties. Future research should determine whether all four influence the processing of rhetorical works as well as whether any other structural properties need to be considered.

Third, future research should help develop or validate existing measures of each structural property in the context of rhetorical works. Researchers applying the model would benefit from either measuring perceptions of or controlling the level of these structural properties. In addition, because perceptions of the structural properties are some antecedents of the higher-order processing motivation factors (e.g., meaning opening, resource demand, and hedonic value), measures of these processing motivation factors may also prove more useful.

Fourth, the model predicts lower conflict for schemes than tropes, because schemes can emphasize certain elements. However, an alternative view (cf. Cohen 1966) suggests that schemes should increase conflict via form–content conflict. Form–content conflict arises as the form of schemes imposes similarity on elements that are unrelated in terms of content or meanings. This conflict would have to be resolved by determining why the communicator chose to relate semantically dissimilar elements. Future research needs to test these competing views.

Fifth, the model posits that meaning openness arises from perceptions of complexity, novelty, and conflict. Thus, schemes, tropes, or even nonfigurative works can generate meaning openness. This differs from the semiotic view (Eco 1976; McQuarrie and Mick 1992, 1996) in which tropes are open in meaning due to undercoding, whereas schemes are overcoded (i.e., redundant information removes meaning openness). These competing views should be tested.

Sixth, future research should investigate the consequences of nonbrand-relevant rhetorical works in advertising. The rhetorical works studied in prior ad-processing research have been brand-relevant (e.g., Huhmann, Mothersbaugh, and Franke 1999, 2002; McQuarrie and Mick 1992, 1999, 2003; Mothersbaugh, Huhmann, and Franke 2002; Nelson and Hitchon 1999). For example, in Huhmann, Mothersbaugh, and Franke (2002), the rhetorical ad headlines all referred to a benefit of using the brand. Nonbrand-relevant (i.e., unrelated to the advertised brand) rhetorical works should increase resource demand (e.g., by increasing surprisingness, incongruity, and conflict between brand message and the rhetorical work). This should benefit persuasion if the audience would otherwise have had excess available resources that would have been devoted to counterarguments and source derogations. Also, nonbrand-relevant schemes should be more useful than nonbrand-relevant tropes, because schemes encourage a diversive orienting response, which would motivate exploration of all aspects of the ad, including brand information, whereas tropes encourage a specific orienting response to find information that will help decipher the trope's meaning or determine why it was used in the ad. Consumers exposed to a nonbrand-relevant trope should be distracted from brand processing and frustrated in linking the trope to the ad, both of which should harm persuasion. Further, the impact of individual differences in diversive versus specific curiosity on the processing should be investigated. Specific curiosity about the issue or product advertised should moderate the negative effect of a nonbrand-relevant trope on processing outcomes.

Although media effects are outside the model, future research should study rhetorical works in media that include audio-visual modalities or allow for image change (e.g., TV, cinema, or Internet ads). First, researchers should determine whether existing rhetorical taxonomies based on print ads (e.g., McQuarrie and Mick 1996; Phillips and McQuarrie 2004) could be generalized to ads in audio-visual or visual movement/change media. Some attributes are unique to the visual modality as research has begun to confirm (Larsen, Luna, and Peracchio 2004). Next, experimental research should examine media differences in rhetorical work processing. Given differences in resource demand, the model predicts that higher resource-demand rhetorical works (e.g., tropes) will perform better in self-paced media (e.g., print) and lower resource-demand rhetorical works (e.g., schemes) will perform better in externally paced media (e.g., radio, television) due to better matches with available resources (cf. Mothersbaugh, Huhmann, and Franke 2002). Processing differences may also arise between single modality (audio- or visual-only) and audio-visual media. Audio-visual media can present information simultaneously; so, one modality could present a rhetorical work while the other presents context information that resolves a trope's conflict or that a scheme can emphasize. This should increase persuasion in comparison with a single modality presentation.

In conclusion, the model of the processing of rhetorical works should prove of great value as a source of theory and ideas for researchers who study the rhetorical works frequently encountered in advertising. However, it could be equally applied to the processing of rhetorical works used in politics, literature, film, or art. It synthesizes two theoretical traditions with strong empirical support—experimental aesthetics and resource matching. Also, it expands the scope of research into rhetorical works to include emotional as well as cognitive variables.

References

Ahluwalia, Rohini, and Robert E. Burnkrant. 2004. "Answering Questions about Questions: A Persuasion Knowledge Perspective for Understanding the Effects of Rhetorical Questions." *Journal of Consumer Research* 31 (June): 26–42.

Anand, Punam, and Brian Sternthal. 1990. "Ease of Message Processing as a Moderator of Repetition Effects in Advertising." *Journal of Marketing Research* 27 (August): 345–353.

Beardsley, Monroe C. 1962. "The Metaphorical Twist." *Philosophy and Phenomenological Research* 22 (March): 293–307.

Ben-Shakhar, Gershon; Itamar Gati; Naomi Ben-Bassat; and Galit Sniper. 2000. "Orienting Response Reinstatement and Dishabituation: The Effects of Substituting, Adding and Deleting Components of Nonsignificant Stimuli." *Psychophysiology* 37: 102–110.

Berlyne, Daniel E. 1960. *Conflict, Arousal, and Curiosity.* New York: McGraw-Hill.

———. 1971. *Aesthetics and Psychobiology.* New York: Appleton.

———. 1974. "The New Experimental Aesthetics." In *Studies in the New Experimental Aesthetics: Steps Toward an Objective Psychology of Aesthetic Appreciation,* ed. Daniel E. Berlyne, 1–25. Washington, DC: Hemisphere.

Bower, Gordon H., and Laura S. Bolton. 1969. "Why Are Rhymes Easier to Learn?" *Journal of Experimental Psychology* 82 (December): 453–461.

Bowers, John Waite, and Michael M. Osborn. 1966. "Attitudinal Effects of Selected Types of Concluding Metaphors in Persuasive Speeches." *Speech Monographs* 33 (2): 147–155.

Brennan, Ian, and Kenneth D. Bahn. 2006. "Literal versus Extended Symbolic Messages and Advertising Effectiveness: The Moderating Role of Need for Cognition." *Psychology & Marketing* 23 (April): 273–295.

Bushman, Brad J., and Gary L. Wells. 2001. "Narrative Impressions of Literature: The Availability Bias and the Corrective Properties of Meta-Analytic Approaches." *Personality and Social Psychology Bulletin* 27 (September): 1123–1130.

Cohen, Jean. 1966. *Structure du Language Poétique.* Paris: Flammarion.

Crozier, J.B. 1974. "Verbal and Exploratory Responses to Sound Sequences Varying in Uncertainty Level." In *Studies in the New Experimental Aesthetics: Steps Toward an Objective Psychology of Aesthetic Appreciation,* ed. Daniel E. Berlyne, 27–90. Washington, DC: Hemisphere.

Day, Hy I. 1972. "Curiosity and Willingness to Become Involved." *Psychological Reports* 30 (June): 807–814.

Eco, Umberto. 1976. *A Theory of Semiotics.* Bloomington: Indiana University Press.

Faber, M.D. 1996. "The Pleasures of Music: A Psychoanalytic Note." *Psychoanalytic Review* 83 (June): 419–434.

Fechner, G.T. 1876. *Vorschule der Ästhetik.* Leipzig: Breitkopf und Härtel.

Flor, Michael, and Uri Hadar. 2005. "The Production of Metaphoric Expressions in Spontaneous Speech: A Controlled-Setting Experiment." *Metaphor and Symbol* 20 (1): 1–34.

Forceville, Charles. 1996. *Pictorial Metaphor in Advertising.* New York: Routledge.

Franke, George R.; Bruce A. Huhmann; and David L. Mothersbaugh. 2004. "Information Content and Consumer Readership of Print Ads: A Comparison of Search and Experience Products." *Journal of the Academy of Marketing Science* 32 (Winter): 20–31.

Frisby, Cynthia. 1995. "Don't Zip That Ad! Exploring the Effects of Need for Arousal and Ad Content on Television Commercial Viewing Time." In *The Proceedings of the 1995 Conference of the American Academy of Advertising,* ed. Charles S. Madden, 116–117. Waco, TX: Baylor University.

Gibbs, Raymond W. Jr. 2001. "Authorial Intentions in Text Understanding." *Discourse Processes* 32 (1): 73–80.

Gladney, George Albert, and Terry L. Rittenburg. 2005. "Euphemistic Text Affects Attitudes, Behavior." *Newspaper Research Journal* 26 (Winter): 28–41.

Gray, Stephanie A., and Rita Snyder. 1989. "Metaphor in Advertising: Effects on Memory." In *Proceedings of the Society for Consumer Psychology,* ed. Meryl P. Gardner, 85–87. Washington, DC: American Psychological Association.

Grice, Herbert Paul. 1989. *Studies in the Way of Words.* Cambridge, MA: Harvard University Press.

Hayes, Donald S. 1999. "Young Children's Exposure to Rhyming and Nonrhyming Stories: A Structural Analysis of Recall." *Journal of Genetic Psychology* 160 (3): 280–293.

Hitchon, Jacqueline C. 1991. "Effects of Metaphorical vs. Literal Headlines on Advertising Persuasion." In *Advances in Consumer Research,* vol. 18, ed. Rebecca H. Holman and Michael Solomon, 752–753. Provo, UT: Association for Consumer Research.

———. 1997. "The Locus of Metaphorical Persuasion: An Empirical Test." *Journalism and Mass Communication Quarterly* 74 (Spring): 55–68.

Hoffman, Robert R., and Susan Kemper. 1987. "What Could Reaction-Time Studies Be Telling Us About Metaphorical Comprehension?" *Metaphor and Symbolic Activity* 2 (3): 149–186.

Huhmann, Bruce A. 2003. "Visual Complexity in Banner Ads: The Role of Color, Photography, and Animation." *Visual Communication Quarterly* 10 (Summer): 10–17.

————; David L. Mothersbaugh; and George R. Franke. 1999. "Figurative Language Effects on Ad Readership and Processing: An Experimental Investigation." In *Proceedings of the 1999 Winter Conference of the Society for Consumer Psychology,* ed. Madhu Viswanathan, Larry Compeau, and Manoj Hastak, 153–154. St. Petersburg, FL: Society for Consumer Psychology.

————; ————; and ————. 2002. "Rhetorical Figures in Headings and Their Effect on Text Processing: The Moderating Role of Information Relevance and Text Length." *IEEE Transactions on Professional Communication* 45 (September): 157–169.

Hungerland, Isabel. 1958. *Poetic Discourse.* Berkeley: University of California Press.

Izard, Carroll E. 1977. *Human Emotions.* New York: Plenum.

Kreuz, Roger J., and Kristin E. Link. 2002. "Assymetries in the Use of Verbal Irony." *Journal of Language and Social Psychology* 21 (June): 127–143.

Larson, Charles U. 2004. *Persuasion: Reception and Responsibility.* Belmont, CA: Wadsworth.

Larson, Val; David Luna; and Laura A. Peracchio. 2004. "Points of View and Pieces of Time: A Taxonomy of Image Attributes." *Journal of Consumer Research* 31 (June): 102–111.

Leech, Geoffrey N. 1966. *English in Advertising: A Linguistic Study of Advertising in Great Britain.* London: Longman.

Litman, Jordan A., and Charles D. Spielberger. 2003. "Measuring Epistemic Curiosity and Its Diversive and Specific Components." *Journal of Personality Assessment* 80 (1): 75–86.

Lowrey, Tina M. 1998. "The Effects of Syntactic Complexity on Advertising Persuasiveness." *Journal of Consumer Psychology* 7 (2): 187–206.

————. 2006. "The Relationship Between Script Complexity and Commercial Memorability." *Journal of Advertising* 35 (Fall): 7–15.

Marschark, Marc, and R. Reed Hunt. 1985. "On Memory for Metaphor." *Memory and Cognition* 13 (September): 413–424.

McGlone, Matthew S., and Jessica Tofighbakhsh. 2000. "Birds of a Feather Flock Conjointly? Rhyme as Reason in Aphorisms." *Psychological Science* 11 (September): 424–428.

McQuarrie, Edward F., and David Glen Mick. 1992. "On Resonance: A Critical Pluralistic Inquiry into Advertising Rhetoric." *Journal of Consumer Research* 19 (September): 180–197.

————, and ————. 1996. "Figures of Rhetoric in Advertising Language." *Journal of Consumer Research* 22 (March): 424–438.

————, and ————. 1999. "Visual Rhetoric in Advertising: Text-Interpretive, Experimental, and Reader-Response Analyses." *Journal of Consumer Research* 26 (June): 37–54.

————, and ————. 2003. "Visual and Verbal Rhetorical Figures under Directed Processing versus Incidental Exposure to Advertising." *Journal of Consumer Research* 29 (March): 579–587.

Mitchell, Nancy A.; Diane M. Badzinski; and Donna R. Pawlowski. 1994. "The Use of Metaphors as Vivid Stimuli to Enhance Comprehension and Recall of Print Advertisements." In *Proceedings of the 1994 Conference of the American Academy of Advertising,* ed. Karen Whitehill King, 198–205. Athens: University of Georgia.

Mothersbaugh, David L.; Bruce A. Huhmann; and George R. Franke. 2002. "Combinatory and Separative Effects of Rhetorical Figures on Consumers' Effort and Focus in Ad Processing." *Journal of Consumer Research* 28 (March): 589–602.

————; ————; and ————. 2007. "Product Category Differences in Rhetorical Figure Usage." Working paper.

Nelson, Michelle R., and Jacqueline C. Hitchon. 1999. "Loud Tastes, Colored Fragrances, and Scented Sounds: How and When to Mix the Senses in Persuasive Communications." *Journalism and Mass Communication Quarterly* 76 (Summer): 354–372.

Pandya, Indubala H. 1977. *English Language in Advertising: A Linguistic Study of Indian Press Advertising.* Delhi: Ajanta.

Peracchio, Laura A., and Joan Meyers-Levy. 1997. "Evaluating Persuasion-Enhancing Techniques from a Resource-Matching Perspective." *Journal of Consumer Research* 24 (September): 178–191.

Phillips, Barbara J. 2000. "The Impact of Verbal Anchoring on Consumer Response to Image Ads." *Journal of Advertising* 29 (1): 15–24.

———, and Edward F. McQuarrie. 2002. "The Development, Change, and Transformation of Rhetorical Style in Magazine Advertisements 1954–1999." *Journal of Advertising* 31 (4): 1–13.

———, and ———. 2004. "Beyond Visual Metaphor: A New Typology of Visual Rhetoric." *Marketing Theory* 4 (1/2): 113–136.

Pickens, James D.; Marilyn R. Pollio; and Howard R. Pollio. 1985. "A Developmental Analysis of Metaphoric Competence and Reading." In *The Ubiquity of Metaphor: Metaphor in Language and Thought,* ed. Wolf Paprotte and Rene Dirven, 481–523. Amsterdam: John Benjamins.

Pilotta, Joseph J.; Don E. Schultz; Gary Drenik; and Philip Rist. 2004. "Simultaneous Media Usage: A Critical Consumer Orientation to Media Planning" *Journal of Consumer Behaviour* 3 (3): 285–292.

Rubin, David C., and Wanda T. Wallace. 1989. "Rhyme and Reason: Analysis of Dual Retrieval Cues." *Journal of Experimental Psychology: Learning, Memory, and Cognition* 15 (July): 698–709.

Schwarz, Norbert, and Gerald L. Clore. 2007. "Feelings and Phenomenal Experiences." In *Social Psychology. Handbook of Basic Principles,* 2d ed., ed. Arie W. Kruglanski and E. Tony Higgins, 385–407. New York: Guilford.

Silberstein, Lisa; Howard Gardner; Erin Phelps; and Ellen Winner. 1982. "Autumn Leaves and Old Photographs: The Development of Metaphor Preferences." *Journal of Experimental Child Psychology* 34 (August): 135–150.

Sopory, Pradeep, and James Price Dillard. 2002. "The Persuasive Effects of Metaphor: A Meta-Analysis." *Human Communication Research* 28 (July): 382–419.

Sperber, Dan, and Deirdre Wilson. 2004. "Relevance Theory." In *The Handbook of Pragmatics,* ed. Laurence R. Horn and Gregory Ward, 607–632. Oxford: Blackwell.

Swasy, John L., and James M. Munch. 1985. "Examining Target Receiver Elaborations: Rhetorical Question Effects on Source Processing and Persuasion." *Journal of Consumer Research* 11 (March): 877–886.

Tanaka, Keiko. 1994. *Advertising Language: A Pragmatic Approach to Advertisements in Britain and Japan.* London: Routledge.

Taute, Harry A. 2005. *Responses to Emotional Appeals: Cognitive or Emotional Control?* Unpublished doctoral dissertation, New Mexico State University, Las Cruces.

Tom, Gail, and Anmarie Eves. 1999. "The Use of Rhetorical Devices in Advertising." *Journal of Advertising Research* 39 (July/August): 39–43.

Veryzer, Robert W., and J. Wesley Hutchinson. 1998. "The Influence of Unity and Prototypicality on Aesthetic Responses to New Product Designs." *Journal of Consumer Research* 24 (March): 374–394.

Wohlwill, Joachim F. 1975. "Children's Voluntary Exploration and Preference for Tactually Presented Nonsense Shapes Differing in Complexity." *Journal of Experimental Child Psychology* 20 (August): 159–167.

Wright, Peter. 1986. "Schemer's Schema: Consumer's Intuitive Theories about Marketers' Influence Tactics." In *Advances in Consumer Research,* vol. 13, ed. Richard Lutz, 1–3. Provo, UT: Association for Consumer Research.

Wundt, Wilhelm M. 1874. *Grundzüge der Physiologischen Psychologie.* Leipzig: Engelmann.

6

The Dark Side of Openness for Consumer Response

Paul Ketelaar, Marnix S. van Gisbergen, and Johannes W.J. Beentjes

Chapter Summary

The study presented in this chapter aims at providing the foundation for future research examining the potential negative results of open ads. In past decades there has been a shift toward ads with less guidance toward a specific interpretation. Different terms have been used to denote these ads—for instance, complex image ads, implicit ads, ambiguous ads, and undercoded ads. Open ads have the common characteristic that consumers are not manifestly directed toward a certain interpretation. We formulate five antecedents that render an ad more open: presence of a prominent visual, presence of rhetorical figures, absence of the product, absence of verbal anchoring, and a low level of brand anchoring. We distinguish four categories of open ads: riddle ads, story ads, issue ads, and aesthetic ads. Although the literature generally stresses positive outcomes of openness on consumer reactions, five experiments show preliminary support for the arguments stressing a possible dark side of openness for consumer response. We have found negative effects of openness on interpretation, attitude toward the ad and the brand, and null-effects on attention and recall.

□ □ □ □

During past decades, a growing share of advertisements has become "open"; that is, they provide little guidance toward a specific interpretation (van Gisbergen, Ketelaar, and Beentjes 2004). For example, a Dutch travel company advertises with people sitting in the water on the edge of a waterfall, without giving any comment

Figure 6.1 **Open Ads for Travel Company** (left) **and Deodorant** (right)

Sources: Left: Advertising Post, Amsterdam, 1995; Right: Lowe Lintas, São Paulo, 2000.

about this peculiar situation, except for the caption: "What is your story?" (Figure 6.1). Another example is a print ad for a deodorant: the consumer has to figure out why a nun is pictured with a clothespin on her nose (Figure 6.1; even nuns can not resist the scent, without assistance). Verbal copy that explains how this picture is related to the product or brand is missing; hence the advertisement does not explicitly guide the consumer toward a specific interpretation.

Why would advertisers want to increase the amount of openness in an ad, presuming that an increase in openness is not accidental but intended? Some advertisers and trend watchers claim that visual media increasingly dominate society. Consumers who have grown up with visual media may be expected to make sense of visuals without the help of verbal copy. In addition, the trend toward openness might be explained on the basis that some advertisers expect open ads to be more effective. One argument is that less-open ads, in which the message is spelled out, may cause irritation among the present generation of ad-wise consumers who might feel that their intelligence is being underestimated. Advertisers may hope that openness in ads not only reduces irritation but also increases ad appreciation when the search for meaning is rewarded. Another argument is that, because of the increased cognitive effort that consumers spend on these ads when searching for an interpretation, they devote more attention to the ads, they have better retention, and they do not engage in counterargumentation so readily (Berger 2001; Leiss, Kline, and Jhally 1990; McQuarrie and Mick 1992; Phillips 2000).

In semiotics, the term "openness" was used by Eco (1979) to differentiate between various "texts." Various researchers have transferred this concept from semiotics to advertising. Previous research has highlighted the positive outcomes obtained by open ads, while ignoring or downplaying the negative outcomes. Our chapter aims at laying the foundation for future research examining the potential negative results of using open ads.

Opera Aperta

In his book, *The Open Work*, originally published as *Opera aperta* in 1962, Eco (1989) proposes the concepts of "openness" and "open work." To illustrate the concept of openness, Eco uses examples of open and closed texts and works, not only from art and literature such as the writings of James Joyce but also from popular culture such as James Bond novels and comic books. Eco uses the term "works" as well as "texts" when explaining openness. He explains that works turn into texts when the reader is about to use and interpret them. Eco characterizes open texts in two ways. First, a text is open when the "product" itself is unfinished. Eco refers to these products as "works in movement." This is the case when the product is made in collaboration with the reader—for instance, when a musician is free to choose how long to hold a note. Hence, the musical performance is never the same. Second, a text, although completed, is labeled open "on account of its susceptibility to countless different interpretations" (Eco 1979, 49). In this latter sense, Eco explains openness in two ways.

On the one hand, Eco describes openness as something intended by the author. An open text proposes a range of interpretative possibilities and, therefore, allows a number of possible readings. In open texts, the author wants the reader to have several choices of how to interpret the text. This means that open texts leave more initiative and freedom for readers to create their own interpretations. On the other hand, Eco explains openness in terms of possible effects on the reader. Confronted with an open work, the reader has to participate actively in the interpretation process. Eco uses several terms to describe the different possibilities a reader has to interpret a text, such as different interpretations (Eco 1979, 49), meanings (51), solutions (52), (emotional) responses (62), or readings (63). For instance, when discussing medieval poetics, he writes, "The reader of the text knows that every sentence and every trope is open to a multiplicity of meanings" (51). It is left to readers to choose their own point of view, their own guidelines and associations in order to create a certain interpretation. Readers, therefore, can create different interpretations of the same text.

According to Eco, the interpretation of a text should be seen as the cooperation between a reader and the text itself. To create an interpretation, readers use their own frame of reference, but at the same time they have to follow guidelines imposed by the text's lexical and syntactical structure. Hence, Eco argues that the amount of openness is affected by the reader as well as by the text. Readers are free to choose their own interpretations but only within a range of possible meanings that is determined by the interplay of both the readers' and the work's features. The terms open and closed should, therefore, be interpreted as illustrating the reciprocal relations between the work and the interpreter.

The difference between an open and a closed text is described in terms of its aim. Unlike an open text, a closed text aims to predetermine a reader's interpretations and allows far less choice in the interpretation process. Eco reasons that the author can close a text by foreseeing a "model reader"; that is, a reader who is able to interpret the text as intended by the author. In other words, the author has to make sure that the addressed reader shares the author's "codes." Such closed texts intend to elicit an expected interpretation, and are "pulling the reader along a predetermined path" (Eco 1979, 8). For instance, texts with a practical function, such as road signs or instructions, demand obviousness and need to be interpreted "univocally," without any possibility of misunderstanding or of individual multiple interpretations. Eco views these examples as closed forms of communication.

Eco argues that the theoretical concepts "open texts" and "closed texts" must be seen as the abstract ends on a continuum (texts with one meaning versus texts with an infinite number of possible meanings) rather than as a dichotomy. We should therefore regard texts not as open or closed, but rather as "more open" or "more closed."

Openness in Advertising

In order to illustrate the concept of openness in mass media texts, Eco analyzed contemporary advertising for brands such as Volkswagen, Camay (soap), and Knorr (soup), concluding that "Every [advertising] message only repeats what the listener already expected and already knew" because consumers are aware of the ideology of consumption and persuasion behind advertising (Bondanella 1997, 77). Some open texts, such as music, can be regarded as unfinished texts; the author seems less concerned about how readers use the text or about the interpretations that readers infer from the text (Eco 1979). In contrast, advertisements always communicate two central messages: (a) this is an ad for brand x, and (b) this ad conveys a *positive* claim about that brand (Tanaka 1992). According to the persuasion knowledge model of Friestad and Wright (1994), and the ideas of several authors (Forceville 1996; McQuarrie and Mick 1996; Mick 1992; Phillips 1997; Warlaumont 1995), consumers are aware of these goals and adjust their expectations of advertising messages accordingly, thus reducing their potential openness: "The very fact that we know that what we see is an ad . . . considerably helps shape our expectations about what it will communicate" (Forceville 1996, 67). Therefore, the sheer insertion of a brand in a picture limits the interpretation of that picture.

The openness of advertisements is restricted not only by the expectations of consumers but also by the intentions of the advertisers. Advertisers do not try to reach the maximum of openness that some artists attempt with their aesthetic works such as paintings or music.

Because of the apparent usefulness of the concept of openness, several advertising researchers transferred this concept from semiotics to advertising. Remarkably, some researchers have used the label "open" whereas others have employed the label "closed" to characterize the same type of ad, although all authors refer to Eco's description of openness. In line with Eco, we will use the term "open ad" to refer to ads that provide relatively little guidance toward an interpretation, whereas ads that provide relatively strong guidance will be called "closed." Even though no ads exist that are completely open or closed, ads can differ in their amount of openness or guidance toward a certain interpretation.

Several terms in advertising research are related to openness (i.e., "ambiguous ads," "image ads," "indirect ads," "implicit ads," "polysemic ads," "unframed ads," "abstract ads," "undercoded ads," "visual absurdity in ads," and "complex ads"). Although not synonymous, all of these terms are highly related to the concept of openness because they imply less guidance toward an intended interpretation, and indicate that research on the effects of openness in advertising is more broadly studied than the studies that explicitly refer to openness. These related studies helped us to formulate certain characteristics that render an ad more open: presence of a prominent visual, presence of rhetorical figures, absence of the product and of verbal anchoring, and a low level of brand anchoring.

Characteristics of Open Advertisements

In this section, we discuss characteristics of ads that may contribute to an increase of openness. Although we are aware that it is not possible to predict the actual amount of guidance a consumer experiences, "we can identify the textual characteristics that make polysemic readings possible" (Fiske 1987, 394). We will argue that openness may be affected by the combination of the following characteristics: (a) presence of a prominent visual, (b) presence of undercoded rhetorical figures, (c) absence of verbal anchoring, (d) absence of the product, and (e) low brand anchoring. An ad does not have to contain all five characteristics to be experienced as open.

Presence of a Prominent Visual

Although photos may include details that can reduce openness, the presence of a prominent visual is more likely to indicate openness of an ad. Several researchers have pointed out that images may be open to a multitude of interpretations (e.g., Barthes 1977; Eco 1979; McQuarrie and Phillips 2005). Besides the term "open," McQuarrie and Phillips (2005), used the term "indirect" to describe pictures that may be open to multiple interpretations. According to Eco, messages in pictures are often more open to multiple interpretations than similar messages in words. This, of course, does not mean that verbal copy is not susceptible to different interpretations.

However, as Messaris notes, whereas verbal language contains words and structures that can be used to make explicit connections or causalities (e.g., "because of" or "due to"), visual images lack such "an explicit syntax for expressing analogies, contrasts, causal claims, and other kinds of propositions" (Messaris 1997, xi). Hence, several researchers (Messaris 1997; Moriarty 1996) argue that visuals are more indeterminate and more open to viewer's interpretations than verbal copy: "Attempts to express arguments through the images themselves in either TV or print ads must necessarily fall short of complete explicitness" (Messaris 1997, xviii). When two elements are placed in one visual their causality is always suggested, whereas in verbal language this causality can be made more explicit because it can be spelled out (Messaris 1992). Moreover, most pictures in ads contain cues ("open communication codes") that can be interpreted in different ways (Moriarty 1996).

Although visuals have the ability to indicate openness in an ad, they also differ in their effect on openness. Certain types of images, such as nonrealistic or absurd images, are more likely to indicate openness than others. For instance, the meaning that "a spoiler is available for this vehicle" is easily portrayed with a closed visual—one simply shows a photo of the car with a spoiler on it. However, other less straightforward meanings are more difficult to portray. Arias-Bolzmann, Chakraborty, and Mowen (2000) studied visual absurdity in ads. They describe visually absurd ads as illogical, ambiguous, and open to different interpretations.

Presence of Undercoded Rhetorical Figures

Some authors describe rhetorical figures as artful deviations from expectations (e.g., McQuarrie and Mick 1996, 2003a; Phillips and McQuarrie 2004) that suggest several meanings (McQuarrie and Mick 1996). Because rhetorical figures are susceptible to different interpretations, they indicate openness. However, rhetorical figures can differ in their guidance toward these alternative meanings (Stern 1989). Several researchers have tried to categorize rhetorical figures in advertisements (e.g., McQuarrie and Mick 1996, 2003b; Phillips and McQuarrie 2004). These categorizations suggest that the presence of certain types of rhetorical figures in advertisements is likely to indicate openness.

McQuarrie and Mick (1996, 2003b) categorize rhetorical figures into tropes and schemes. They claim that schemes (such as a rhyme or antithesis) are excessively ordered and overcoded, and that tropes (e.g., metaphor, irony, and pun) are disordered and undercoded.

Schemes are "overcomplete" and superficial, because they contain redundant information and instructions about how consumers should interpret them. Tropes are incomplete, lack closure, and can be interpreted in different ways (McQuarrie and Mick 1996, 2003b). McQuarrie and Mick (1996, 2003b) distinguish between substitution tropes (such as hyperbole and metonym) and destabilization tropes (such as metaphors and puns). When advertisers use substitution tropes they say something other than what they mean, whereas when they use destabilization tropes they mean more than what they say, creating parallel meanings without making explicit which of these meanings is intended. Hence, tropes indicate openness in advertisements.

Another categorization of rhetorical figures is provided by Phillips and McQuarrie (2004). They focus on visual instead of verbal rhetorical figures. Phillips and McQuarrie differentiate visual rhetorical figures according to their visual structure (arrangement of visual figure elements) and meaning operation (instructions for inference). They claim that the visual structure dimension affects the amount of complexity (processing demands) and that the meaning operation affects the amount of experienced ambiguity (number of possible interpretations). Whereas visual structures can be arrayed according to their degree of complexity, meaning operations can be arrayed according to their degree of richness. Richness refers to the degree and range of processing opportunity afforded by the various meaning operations. An operation is richer if the instructions for interpretation that it provides allow for a larger number of alternative responses, which increases perceived openness. According to the authors, richness is thus a matter of ambiguity, not in the negative sense of opacity or confusion, but in the positive sense of multiplicity and polysemy. The typology suggests that visual rhetorical figures range "from relatively simple and readily interpretable figures to highly complex figures open to a wide range of interpretations" (Phillips and McQuarrie 2004, 127). Hence, the typology created by Phillips and McQuarrie indicates that ads with visual rhetorical figures are more open than ads without visual rhetorical figures, and that the amount of openness is affected by the type of visual rhetorical figure present in the ad.

Absence of Verbal Anchoring

In most ads, visuals are accompanied by verbal copy that guides the reader in the identification and interpretation of the visual elements, a technique called "verbal anchoring" (Barthes 1977). Every verbal element (e.g., the headline or body copy) may constrain the interpretation of an image: "The text directs the reader among various signifiers of the image, causes him to avoid some and receive others . . . it remote-controls him toward a meaning chosen in advance (Barthes 1977, 37–38). Other authors put the same idea in different words. According to Hall (1997), verbal anchoring directs consumers' attention to meaningful parts in the image and instructs consumers concerning how the image must be read. Phillips (2000) argues that verbal anchoring helps consumers to interpret the message in the ad, guiding the reader toward the visual's "presumably intended interpretation" (Forceville 1996, 75). In doing so, verbal anchoring reduces the openness of a pictorial in an ad. Consequently, when verbal anchoring is absent, consumers have more options for choosing an interpretation, which indicates openness in an ad.

Although Barthes describes anchoring in terms of verbal copy that explains the interpretation of the image, it is not always the image that needs to be "anchored" (Forceville 1996). An image can also be used to anchor ambiguous verbal copy (Chandler 2002) or a puzzling caption (Dyer 1982; Forceville 1996). However, for print ads it is probably more common that verbal copy is used to anchor an image (Chandler 2002). The concept of verbal anchoring is also used to explain the relationship between verbal copy and rhetorical figures. For instance, Phillips (2000) uses the term "verbal anchoring" when the meaning of a rhetorical figure in the picture or headline is spelled out in literal terms in the body copy.

In the advertising literature, different terms are used to describe anchoring or the idea that verbal copy can be used to interpret the image. Several authors (Dingena 1994; Edell and Staelin 1983) use the term "verbal reference point" or "verbal labeling" to depict verbal copy that gives direction to the interpretation of the image in an ad. The same authors use the term "framing" to describe the correspondence of visual and verbal messages in advertising. In framed pictures, the message in the visual is restated in the verbal copy.

Absence of the Product

Absence of the advertised product also indicates openness in an ad. When the product features are not verbally described or visually depicted, the ad becomes more susceptible to different interpretations (Barthes 1977; Loef 2002; Phillips 1997). "In advertising, the exclusion of products . . . gives subjects the impression that they are free to produce a meaning for themselves" (Williamson 1978, 71). Depiction or description of the product guides the interpretation of the ad. For instance, the image of a sports car with all of its features signifying speed (e.g., aerodynamic design, spoiler, big exhaust pipe) makes it more obvious to consumers that the car is fast, even to consumers who are not familiar with the car or brand. The ad becomes more susceptible to different interpretations when the product is absent. Because consumers use product information to interpret advertising images, absence of the product in the ad can be characterized as absence of product anchoring. Consumers use product schemas that contain information about attributes of a product class as a whole to infer interpretations (Loef 2002). For instance, consumers are aware that car ads often address safety, and this product schema directs the interpretation of the ad.

Low Brand Anchoring

Whether in the form of a logo, verbal copy, or picture, most ads contain some reference to a brand. Without the brand, it is difficult to recognize the text as an ad (except for those ads that advertise a product class as a whole, or "teaser ads" that postpone brand presence). A brand restricts the openness of a text, because it makes consumers aware that positive claims about a certain product are being communicated. Moreover, just as we argued with respect to the advertised product, brand associations or brand schemas can affect the amount of guidance toward a certain interpretation as well. Several researchers claim that brand information helps consumers to understand the ad's message because the brand provides a context for interpreting the ad and guides the reader toward meaningful elements in it (Curlo and Chamblee 1998; Forceville 1996; MacInnis and Jaworski 1989; Warlaumont 1995). Brand schemas or associations represent consumers' knowledge about brands, such as knowledge about brand benefits and drawbacks, about the image of a brand, about its users, and how the brand is po-

Figure 6.2   **Cartoon Used in Car Ad**

Source: Remu Asatsu, Madrid, 1993.

sitioned relative to other brands within a product category (Loef 2002). Consumers can use the emotions, beliefs, and values that they have learned to associate with certain brands to create interpretations of an open ad. This process may be referred to as brand anchoring.

Consider, for instance, the image used in an ad for Mitsubishi (see Figure 6.2). Once the consumer is aware that a car is being advertised, the image may guide the reader toward the message that the car is fast (the cartoon character is hit by a car because the car was so fast, that he had no time to leave the road) or that the car has a silent engine (the cartoon character is hit because he could not hear the car). Both interpretations of the image seem plausible. However, when the image is accompanied by a brand that is strongly associated with speed (for instance Porsche) or silence (for instance Toyota Prius), it is likely that consumers will infer an interpretation associated either with speed or silence. In this sense, the brand anchors the image because it suggests how the image must be read. Consumers who are not able to form an interpretation based on visual or verbal elements in the ad may even create an interpretation exclusively based on brand associations (Forceville 1996; MacInnis and Jaworski 1989). In sum, an ad for a brand that already evokes strong associations is likely to decrease openness. On the other hand, ads for new or fictitious brands are often used in experiments, and these brands will obviously lack strong associations, suggesting that these ads will be more open.

Variety of Open Ads

Open ads have in common that they provide little guidance toward an interpretation. However, openness in print ads is manifested in different ways, possibly related to different advertising goals. We have examined a large number of ads that appeared on face value to be open, collected over a period of five years from Dutch magazines, advertising yearbooks (e.g., *Art Directors Annual* and *Advertising Annual*), and

Figure 6.3 **Riddle Ads for Eye Curl** (left) **and Car** (right)

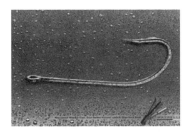 

Sources: Left: McCann-Erickson, Rio de Janeiro, 2001; Right: DDB, London Ltd, 2000.

online magazine databases (e.g., *Lürzer's Int'l Archive*). We selected those ads that best met the aspects of openness in ads mentioned in the previous section. We were able to divide the majority of these ads into four different, although not mutually exclusive, categories: riddle ads, story ads, issue ads, and aesthetic ads.

The riddle ad (Figure 6.3) contains a hidden interpretation reflecting the advertiser's intention. The verbal or visual elements in the ad create a puzzle. The hidden interpretation is the solution of the riddle that the consumer must discover. Whereas various elements in the ad seem unrelated to the advertised brand, they always point the way to a certain solution (McQuarrie and Mick 1996; Toncar and Munch 2001). The ad invites and challenges consumers to solve the riddle and discover the intended interpretation. Although the riddle ad does not explicitly guide consumers toward an intended interpretation, the advertiser wants consumers to know that the ad contains a concrete (intended) interpretation.[1] Riddle ads are similar to rhetorical figure ads studied by several advertising researchers (e.g. McQuarrie and Mick 1996; Phillips 2000; Toncar and Munch 2001).

The story ad (Figure 6.4) shows only part of a story or event. The story ad in Eco's (1979) terms, has an open narrative structure because it does not guide toward a specific ending. Because just a part of the story is shown, as in a movie with an open end, the ad gives rise to questions such as: What is happening here? How does this story end? How did it start? Consumers are challenged to make up their own story. Although the ad suggests certain outcomes, the story ad leaves room for the consumer to imagine various possible outcomes. Consumers must create part of the story on the basis of the advertised product and their personal experience and fantasy. Because the story ad leaves room for several narrative possibilities, it is susceptible to a multitude of possible interpretations.[2]

The issue ad (Figure 6.5) communicates messages that are not related to the product that is advertised, and in so doing reduces the guidance toward a specific interpretation. The issue ad breaks with the "overcoded rule" (Eco 1979) that an ad has to communicate something about the product advertised. Instead, the issue

Figure 6.4 **Story Ads for Shoes** (left) **and Backpacks** (right)

Sources: Left: Stempels & Oster, Amsterdam, 1999; Right: Satisfaction, Brussels, 1998.

ad invites the consumer to think and form an opinion about an important political, social or philosophical matter. Often, this message is communicated in an indirect manner, using shocking and taboo-breaking images. The campaigns for Benetton are good examples of issue ads. Issue ads have previously been studied under the heading "provocative ads" by Vezina and Paul (1997).

The aesthetic ad (Figure 6.6) is intended as art to look at, from which consumers should derive feelings of aesthetic pleasure. Compared with the other open-ad types, the aesthetic ad is less intended to invite consumers to construct a desired interpretation. The aesthetic ad, often seen for fashion and perfume products, resembles open texts such as poetry and music. The ad does not create the feelings of tension and the need to create an interpretation as much as in other open-ad types.

Alleged Positive and Negative Effects of Openness

The effects that have been attributed to openness may be divided into three positive and three negative effects. First, openness is said to be a device for ad-makers to retain *attention* (Arias-Bolzmann, Chakraborty, and Mowen 2000; Macinnis, Moorman, and Jaworski 1991; McQuarrie and Mick 1992; Morgan and Reichert 1999; Mothersbaugh, Huhmann, and Franke 2002; Peracchio and Meyers-Levy 1994; Phillips and McQuarrie 2004; Toncar and Munch 2001; Warlaumont 1995, 1997). Open ads may sustain consumers' attention for several reasons: (1) open ads are experienced as relatively difficult to interpret; (2) openness is experienced

Figure 6.5   **Issue Ads for Clothing** (left) **and Jeans** (right)

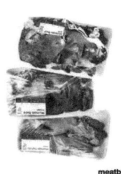

Sources: Left: Benetton, Intern, Mailand, 1991; Right: Blink hardcore supplies BV, 1999.

as relatively incongruent with expectations of advertising; (3) openness increases uncertainty about the accuracy of the created interpretation; and (4) openness makes consumers pay attention to the brand because they need to know about it in order to create an interpretation.

Second, openness is regarded as capable of stimulating *recall* of (elements in) the ad (Arias-Bolzmann, Chakraborty, and Mowen 2000; Childers and Houston 1984; McQuarrie and Mick 1992, 1999, 2003b; Mothersbaugh, Huhmann, and Franke 2002; Phillips 2003; Phillips and McQuarrie 2004; Tanaka 1992; Toncar and Munch 2001). The arguments for a positive effect of openness on attention also apply to the effect of openness on recall. Previous research has shown that (elements in) open ads are better recalled or recognized than (elements in) closed ads. In these studies openness was indicated by the presence of rhetorical figures (Gail and Eves 1999; McQuarrie and Mick 1992, 2003b; Toncar and Munch 2001).

Third, openness might positively affect the *attitude toward the ad* (A_{ad}) (Barthes 1977; Eco 1979; Kardes 1988; McQuarrie and Mick 1992, 1999, 2003a, 2003b; Mick 1992; Perracchio and Meyers-Levy 1994; Petty and Cacioppo 1996; Phillips 2000; Phillips and McQuarrie 2004; Sawyer and Howard 1991; Tanaka 1992; Toncar and Munch 2001; Warlaumont 1995). Openness in ads may lead to a relatively positive A_{ad} (1) when consumers experience pleasure in searching for an interpretation, (2) when consumers consider finding a plausible interpretation as a reward, (3) when consumers experience openness as pleasantly incongruent with their expectations of advertising, (4) when consumers view openness as an intelligent form of communication that they appreciate, and (5) when openness decreases counterargumentation. Three studies, conducted by McQuarrie and Mick (1992, 1999, 2003b), indicated that openness results in a more positive A_{ad}.

In addition to positive effects, openness is said to have negative effects. First,

Figure 6.6   **Aesthetic Ads for Clothing** (left) **and Perfume** (right)

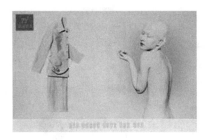 

Source: Pickl, Munich, 1998.

in contrast to authors who claim the opposite, others expect that openness may decrease *attention* because consumers are likely to avoid investing cognitive effort in ads (Chamblee, Thomas, and Soldow 1993; Franzen 1997). Yet another claim is that openness does not yield any effect on attention, because consumers are not motivated to devote attention to persuasive messages in general (Kroeber-Riel and Esch 2000; Messaris 1997; Peracchio and Meyers-Levy 1994; Toncar and Munch 2001; Warlaumont 1995, 1997). Indeed, the only study that addressed the effect of openness on consumers' attention to ads found that openness had no effect on viewing time (McQuarrie and Mick 1992).

Second, openness might negatively affect *interpretation.* When openness decreases consumers' willingness to invest mental effort, they are less likely to create any interpretation. And even when consumers do decide to elaborate upon open ads, there is a risk that they cannot create a plausible interpretation, because they experience open ads as difficult to interpret. Several researchers (e.g., Kardes 1988; Mick and Politi 1989) argued that openness increases the chance that consumers do not create the intended interpretation. Previous research suggests that openness negatively affects the creation of any interpretation (Dingena 1994; Warlaumont 1995), as well as the creation of the intended interpretation (Morgan and Reichert 1999; Phillips 1997). Moreover, openness might favor the creation of alternative interpretations across consumers that are not intended by the ad-makers (Barthes 1977; Eco 1979; Forceville 1996; McQuarrie and Mick 1996; Mick 1992; Mick and Politi 1989; Morgan and Reichert 1999; Phillips 1997, 2003; Sperber and Wilson 1986; Warlaumont 1995) because consumers must decide for themselves which characteristics in the ad are relevant to the product and brand (McQuarrie and Phillips 2005; Phillips and McQuarrie 2004; Phillips 2003). "Interpretation diversity" points to the occurrence of one or more alternative interpretations next to the intended interpretation. Although some researchers view diversity of interpretations positively, it can be a negative outcome in advertising where most advertisers want to communicate one obvious message. These notions are corroborated by the results of three studies (Forceville 1996;

Mick and Politi 1989; Phillips 1997), showing that openness leads to different interpretations across consumers.

Third, unlike the authors who argue that openness may lead to a positive *attitude toward the ad,* others expect that a negative effect is more likely (Dingena 1994; Franzen 1997; Kardes 1988; McQuarrie 1989; McQuarrie and Mick 1999, 2003a; McQuarrie and Phillips 2005; Mick 1992; Nelson and Hitchon 1995; Perrachio and Meyers-Levy 1994; Phillips 2000, 2003; Phillips and McQuarrie 2004; Sawyer and Howard 1991; Toncar and Munch 2001; Warlaumont 1995). Openness might affect A_{ad} negatively (1) when consumers experience difficulty creating an interpretation, (2) when consumers are not able to create an interpretation, and (3) when consumers are uncertain whether the created interpretation is the one intended by the ad-maker. Two studies, conducted by Phillips (2000) and Warlaumont (1995), showed a negative effect of openness on A_{ad}. In these studies, openness was realized by the absence of verbal anchoring.

Finally, it seems likely that the individual consumer's *need for cognition* interacts with the effect of openness on attention, recall, interpretation, and attitude toward the ad. Need for cognition refers to the tendency to engage in and derive pleasure from effortful cognitive activities. Because consumers have to spend more energy to interpret an open ad than a closed ad, one might expect that openness has different effects on consumers with different degrees of need for cognition. More precisely, consumers with a high need for cognition might (a) recall open ads better than closed ones (b) hold a more positive attitude toward (open) ads, and (c) be better able to interpret (open) ads than consumers with a low need for cognition.

Effects of Openness

In order to investigate the alleged effects of openness in ads on consumers, we carried out a series of five experiments, focusing on the effects of open riddle ads. In this section we summarize the designs of the experiments, and provide preliminary conclusions about the effects of openness and the moderating effects of need for cognition (for a more detailed report, see Ketelaar and Van Gisbergen 2006).

No Effect of Openness on Attention

In Experiments 1, 2, and 3, we explored the effect of openness on consumers' attention toward ads. In *Experiment 1,* we investigated whether open ads command more attention than their closed counterparts. The typical forced-exposure paradigm used in laboratory experiments did not seem to provide a very suitable test of any of our contentions about openness and attention. We therefore simulated natural viewing conditions by using the advanced infrared eye-tracking equipment of the company Verify. We measured the attention of 216 participants who browsed through a general audience magazine that contained three test ads: two car ads and one whiskey ad. For each ad we made two conditions: one without a headline and another with a headline that provided the reader with moderate guidance toward the intended interpretation.

Experiment 2 replicated Experiment 1, and extended it by measuring attention not only to the ad as a whole but also attention specifically directed at the brand, and by establishing the effect of openness on ad recall and product recall. We also established whether "need for cognition" plays a role in the effect of openness on attention and recall. This study addressed the possibility that the presence of headlines in Experiment 1 might have been responsible for the fact that the closed ads received more attention than the open ones. Therefore, Experiment 2 had four conditions (instead of two) for each of the four selected car ads. We manipulated the level of openness by inserting headlines that differed in the amount of verbal anchoring, creating low and moderate verbal-guidance conditions, and by altering the visuals, creating a low and a moderate visual-guidance condition. A total of 425 participants representative of the Dutch population participated in the study. We used the same eye-tracking device to measure attention as was used in Experiment 1, and added an indirect-recall task in which participants had to identify the ad and the product when pixilated images of the ads were shown.

In *Experiment 3* consumers' attention was measured for a large number of open ($n = 99$) and closed ads ($n = 97$) in order to generalize the findings of Experiment 2. Each of these ads was tested among 114 participants within a single-exposure design that involved various cluttered magazines containing several interesting articles and numerous filler ads. These ads were not systematically manipulated as in Experiments 1 and 2, but selected from the database of Verify at face value.

The results show that openness does not influence consumers' attention toward ads. Our findings do not support the notion that open ads hold attention better than closed ones (e.g., Morgan and Reichert 1999; Mothersbaugh, Huhmann, and Franke 2002; Peracchio and Meyers-Levy 1994; Phillips and McQuarrie 2004; Toncar and Munch 2001; Warlaumont 1995, 1997), or that openness decreases attention duration (Chamblee, Thomas, and Soldow 1993; Franzen 1997). Instead, our experiments strengthened the finding of McQuarrie and Mick (1992), that openness has no beneficial or detrimental effects on consumers' attention toward ads. Open ads retain attention for as long—or rather as short—a time as closed ones do, which corroborates the notion that consumers are not motivated to devote their attention to ads in general because they know they are dealing with persuasive messages (Kroeber-Riel and Esch 2000; Messaris 1997; Peracchio and Meyers-Levy 1994; Toncar and Munch 2001; Warlaumont 1995, 1997).

Our conclusion that open ads do not differ from closed ones in their capacity to hold consumers' attention is convincing for two reasons. First, we used a research situation that approached normal circumstances in that: (a) participants were not instructed to look at ads; (b) the experimental ads strongly resembled real ads; (c) consumers could browse through magazines at their own pace; (d) the selected magazines were existing magazines that contained ads as well as editorial content; and (e) we used unobtrusive and precise equipment, an infrared eye-tracking instrument, to determine whether openness affected attention to the ad or brand. Second, the finding that openness does not influence attention seems very robust as this result showed up in two experiments where we compared small numbers of systematically manipulated open and closed ads (Experiments 1 and 2) as well as in an experiment where we compared large numbers of open and closed ads (Experiment 3). Therefore, the absence of differences in attention duration between open and closed ads seems not restricted to manipulated experimental ads, but characterizes a larger population of ads situated on a broad part of the openness continuum.

No Effect of Openness on Recall of the Ad, Yet a Positive Effect on Product Recall

In Experiment 2 we determined recall of the ad and recall of the advertised product, and concluded that the open strategy does not increase recall of the ad, but does increase recall of the product. The central notion behind the arguments for and against an effect of openness on recall is that openness stimulates a high level of cognitive elaboration that, in turn, improves recall. Although several researchers expect a positive effect of openness on recall of (elements in) the ad (Arias-Bolzmann, Chakraborty, and Mowen 2000; Childers and Houston 1984; McQuarrie and Mick 1992, 1999, 2003b; Mothersbaugh, Huhmann, and Franke 2002; Phillips 2003; Phillips and McQuarrie 2004; Tanaka 1992; Toncar and Munch 2001), we found no beneficial effects of openness on recall of the ad. However, we did find a positive effect of openness on recall of the product. Consumers remembered the product advertised in the open versions of the ads better than when it was included in the closed versions. This result extends previous research findings showing a positive effect of openness (ads that contained rhetorical figures) on recall of brands, product claims, and verbal copy (Gail and Eves 1999; McQuarrie and Mick 1992; Toncar and Munch 2001). Improved recall of the advertised product in open ads is a remarkable result, because the product was never depicted in the ads that we used in our experiments and, therefore, had to be inferred from the brand. Perhaps the open versions yielded better recall of the product because participants tried to infer the product in order to be able to plausibly interpret the open ads.

Negative Effect of Openness on Creating an Interpretation

In *Experiment 4* we determined whether openness influenced consumers' ability to create an interpretation, to create the intended interpretation, and to create alternative interpretations besides the one intended. First-year students at the Institute for the Car Branch and Management in Driebergen, the Netherlands, participated in the experiment ($n = 148$). In comparison with average consumers, they were more motivated and able to interpret ads. For three car ads, open and closed conditions were created by adding headlines that differed in the amount of guidance toward an interpretation.

In *Experiment 5* we reexamined the effects of openness on interpretation among a sample of 957 consumers representative of the Dutch population. We selected four car ads and two ads for mobile phones, for which we created three conditions differing in amount of anchoring: an ad without a headline, one with a moderately guiding headline, and one with a highly guiding headline.

Both experiments suggested that openness not only increased the number of consumers who were unable to create an interpretation, but also decreased the number of consumers who created the intended interpretation. These conclusions corroborate the notions of advertising researchers (Kardes 1988; Mick and Politi 1989) and are in line with previous research findings (Dingena 1994; Morgan and Reichert 1999; Phillips 1997; Warlaumont 1995). Moreover, our findings indicated an increase in the diversity of interpretations across consumers, for most open ads, supporting the notions of several researchers (Barthes 1977; Eco 1979; Forceville 1996; McQuarrie and Mick 1996; Mick 1992; Mick and Politi 1989; Phillips 1997; Sperber and Wilson 1986; Warlaumont 1995) and corroborating the results of three studies (Forceville 1996; Mick and Politi 1989; Phillips 1997).

Negative Effect of Openness on Attitude Toward the Ad and the Brand

In addition to the impact on interpretation, Experiments 4 and 5 determined the effect of openness on A_{ad}. We found consumers' attitudes to be more negative toward open ads than toward closed ads. Beforehand, the possible effect of openness on A_{ad} was unclear, because prior research of McQuarrie and Mick (1992, 1999, 2003b) showed positive effects of openness on A_{ad}, whereas Phillips (2000) and Warlaumont (1995) revealed negative effects of openness. This raises the question of why we found a predominantly negative effect of openness on A_{ad}. A plausible explanation involves differences in the selection and manipulation of the experimental ads. The open ads that we selected provided little guidance. In contrast, in the studies that showed a positive effect of openness on A_{ad}, the closed as well as the open conditions contained a headline that guided consumers toward the intended interpretation. Due to this guiding headline, the visual tropes in the open-ad conditions were probably not considered to be a necessary information source to create an interpretation. Because the tropes implicitly communicated the same message, as did the guiding headline, they may have elicited feelings of pleasure, thus increasing A_{ad}. Hence, the negative attitudinal effects of openness in our studies seem attributable to a lack of guidance.

In addition to the negative effect on attitude toward the ad, we found that openness affects A_{br} negatively. This finding is no surprise, because research has shown that A_{br} is strongly related to A_{ad} (e.g., Heath and Gaeth 1994).

To gain more insight into the causes of the negative effect of openness on A_{ad}, in Experiment 5 we examined three reasons why openness might affect consumers' attitudes toward open ads. Openness might affect A_{ad} negatively because consumers (a) are not able to interpret open ads, (b) experience difficulty interpreting open ads, and (c) are uncertain whether their interpretation coincides with the intended one.

First, as expected, and corroborating the notions of several researchers (Kardes 1988; Mick 1992; McQuarrie and Mick 1992, 1999, 2003a; Peracchio and Meyers-Levy 1994; Phillips 2000; Tanaka 1992), our experiments showed that *not being able to create an interpretation* relates negatively to A_{ad}. This is a negative effect for openness as more consumers were unable to interpret open ads than closed ads.

Second, we found support for the argument that *the difficulty that consumers experience when they interpret open ads* negatively mediates the effect of openness on A_{ad}. Confirming the notions of several authors (Franzen 1997; Phillips 2003; Phillips and McQuarrie 2004; Toncar and Munch 2001; Warlaumont 1995) and consistent with research performed by McQuarrie and Mick (1992) and Phillips (2000), our results showed a more negative A_{ad} when participants experienced more difficulty in creating an interpretation, which was more the case for open ads than for closed ads. This result contradicts the notion that consumers experience pleasure when searching for an interpretation (McQuarrie and Mick 1992; Phillips and McQuarrie 2004).

In order to test the argument that the eventual discovery of a satisfactory interpretation might relate to a positive A_{ad} (McQuarrie and Mick 1992, 1999; Peracchio and Meyers-Levy 1994; Phillips 2000; Phillips and McQuarrie 2004; Sawyer and Howard 1991; Tanaka 1992; Toncar and Munch 2001; Warlaumont 1995), we limited our analysis of the mediating effect of "interpretation difficulty" on A_{ad} to those participants who were able to interpret open ads. Confirming the finding of van Mulken, van Enschot, and Hoeken (2005), the negative relation of openness with A_{ad} did not change into a positive relation, but only changed in strength, becoming less negative. Even when participants were able to interpret the open ad, A_{ad} was lower than for closed ads that were easier to understand.

Last, confirming our expectation, *experienced "interpretation uncertainty"* was negatively related to A_{ad}. Consumers were more uncertain about the intended interpretation when exposed to open ads than to closed ads, a finding that corroborated the notion of McQuarrie and Mick (2003a). Because participants were more uncertain whether they had reached the interpretation intended by the ad-maker with open ads than with closed ones, their appreciation of the ad was lower. This finding confirms Peracchio and Meyers-Levy's (1994) argument that when ambiguous (i.e., open) ads do not allow consumers to verify their created interpretations, a negative effect on A_{ad} can be expected.

No Moderating Effects of Need for Cognition

In Experiments 2, 4, and 5, we examined the moderating role of need for cognition on attention, recall, A_{ad}, and interpretation. We assumed that consumers with a high

Figure 6.7 **Model: Antecedents and Consequences of Openness**

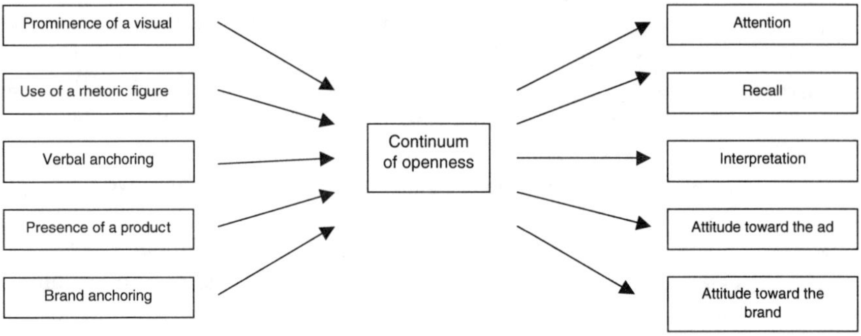

need for cognition would spend more viewing time on open ads than on closed ads because they feel the urge and desire to create an interpretation. For the same reason, we expected that consumers with a high need for cognition would recall the advertised products in open ads better than the advertised products in closed ads. Our findings revealed that this was not the case. Open ads still have negative outcomes even for people who like to think a lot. It is possible that need for cognition does not have a moderating role on the effects of openness in advertising in general because consumers do not want to invest effort in commercial messages in general.

Implications

Openness is an attractive and useful concept for research in the field of persuasive communication. It seems a fruitful term to describe a dimension connecting several advertising studies determining the effects of different kinds of ads, and it provides a theoretical framework that makes sense of the results reported in a wide variety of studies on advertising effects. These studies, using a large variety of terms to denote open ads, are conceptually connected by the common dimension of openness. The results of these related studies may be interpreted in terms of the effects of openness. We have described these effects in terms of guidance: that is, a more open ad provides less guidance toward a certain interpretation than a more closed ad does. Therefore, the concept of openness relates to the central goal of persuasive communication, namely, to communicate certain commercial messages. Finally, openness has proved to be a suitable concept to be operationalized for empirical research because our manipulation checks have shown that consumers are able to distinguish between ads with regard to their level of openness.

Although previous authors have stressed the positive effects of openness, we may cautiously conclude that our exploration of the consequences of openness has yielded negative consequences of openness.

Figure 6.7 provides a diagram containing the antecedents and consequences of openness. The structural elements that contribute to openness are aligned on the left part of the diagram, with the continuum of openness in the middle. The outcomes of openness are aligned on the right including consumer responses such as attention, memory, interpretation, A_{ad}, and A_{br}.

We recommend that future research focus more on the impact of the combination of the structural elements that contribute to the outcomes of openness. In particular, the influence of the brand on the experience of openness of consumers should be considered.

We already discussed that brands may differ in their ability to anchor interpretations because consumers have different perceptions of brands. Future research might assess whether the brand plays a role in guiding consumers toward a certain interpretation, by using different car brands in the same open ad Figure 6.7. The ad's image may guide the reader toward the message that the car is fast or that the car has a silent engine. When a pretest shows that consumers generally associate the brand "Toyota Prius" with "a silent car" and associate the brand "Subaru Impreza" with "a fast car," one would expect that the number of elicited interpretations that relate to "silence" and "speed" would differ according to the brand depicted in the ad. The expectations that (a) brands can guide the reader toward an interpretation, which we call "brand anchoring," and that (b) brands differ in their ability to guide the consumer toward a specific interpretation of an (open) ad have not yet been empirically examined.

One final remark concerns the use of fictitious brands in open-ad related research (e.g., Martin, Lang, and Wong 2003; McQuarrie and Mick 1999; McQuarrie and Phillips 2005; Peracchio and Meyers-Levy 1994; Phillips 1997, 2000; Toncar and Munch 2001). Advertising scholars should consider how this form of low brand anchoring could affect experienced openness.

Considering its clear negative effects and the large amounts of money involved in the advertising business, an open-ad strategy seems a risky undertaking.

Notes

1. The intended interpretation of the ad on the left is: "Use Maybelline waterproof wonder curl and guys will get completely hooked on you." The intended interpretation of the ad on the right is: "Like a beetle, this new Volkswagen has the power of a turbo engine."

2. A possible interpretation of the left ad for Dr. Adams shoes: A train is approaching a lady who got stuck with her Dr. Adams shoe between the rails. The lady faces a dilemma: although the train is approaching rapidly, she will not just step out of the shoe because she is too attached to the shoe. A possible interpretation of the right ad for Eastpak is that Eastpak produces backpacks and bags that amply outlive their owners.

References

Arias-Bolzmann, Leopoldo; Goutam Chakraborty; and John C. Mowen. 2000. "Effects of Absurdity in Advertising: The Moderating Role of Product Category Attitude and the Mediating Role of Cognitive Responses." *Journal of Advertising* 29: 35–49.

Barthes, Roland. 1977. *Image Music Text*. New York: Hill and Wang.

Berger, Warren. 2001. *Advertising Today*. New York: Phaidon Press.

Bondanella, Peter E. 1997. *Umberto Eco and the Open Text: Semiotics, Fiction, Popular Culture*. Cambridge: Cambridge University Press.

Chamblee, Robert; Robert F. Gilmore; Gloria Thomas; and Gary F. Soldow. 1993. "When Copy Complexity Can Help Ad Readership." *Journal of Advertising* Research 33: 23–28.

Chandler, Daniel. 2002. *Semiotics: The Basics*. London: Routledge.

Childers, Terry L., and Michael J. Houston. 1984. "Conditions for a Picture-Superiority Effect on Consumer Memory." *Journal of Consumer Research* 11: 643–654.

Curlo, Eleanora, and Robert Chamblee. 1998. "Ad Processing and Persuasion: The Role of Brand Identification." *Psychology and Marketing* 1998: 279–299.

Dingena, Marian. 1994. *The Creation of Meaning in Advertising: Interaction of Figurative Advertising and Individual Differences in Processing Styles*. Amsterdam: Thesis.

Dyer, Gillian. 1982. *Advertising as Communication*. London: Methuen.

Eco, Umberto. 1979. *The Role of the Reader: Explorations in the Semiotics of Texts*. London: Indiana University Press.

Eco, Umberto. 1989. *The Open Work*. Cambridge, Massachusetts: Harvard University Press.

Edell, Julie A., and Richard Staelin. 1983. "The Information Processing of Pictures in Print Advertisements." *Journal of Consumer Research* 10 (June): 45–61.

Fiske, John. 1987. *Television Culture*. London: Methuen.

Forceville, Charles J. 1996. *Pictorial Metaphor in Advertising*. New York: Routledge.

Franzen, Giep. 1997. *Advertising Effectiveness. Findings from Empirical Research*, 2d ed. Oxfordshire, UK: Admap.

Friestad, Marian, and Peter Wright. 1994. "The Persuasion Knowledge Model: How People Cope with Persuasion Attempts." *Journal of Consumer Research* 21: 1–31.

Gail, Tom, and Annmarie Eves. 1999. "The Use of Rhetorical Devices in Advertising." *Journal of Advertising Research* 39: 39–41.

Hall, Stuart. 1997. "Representation: Cultural Representations and Signifying Practices." London: Sage.

Heath, Timothy B., and Gary J. Gaeth. 1994. "Theory and Method in the Study of Ad and Brand Attitudes: Toward a Systemic Model." In *Attention, Attitude, and Affect in Response to Advertising*, ed. Eddie M. Clark, Timothy W. Brock, and David W. Stewart, 125–148. Hillsdale, NJ: Erlbaum.

Kardes, Frank R. 1988. "Spontaneous Inference Processing in Advertising: The Effects of Conclusion Omission and Involvement on Persuasion." *Journal of Consumer Research* 15: 225–223.

Ketelaar, Paul E., and Marnix S. Van Gisbergen. 2006. "Openness in Advertising: Occurrence and Effects of Open Advertisements in Magazines." Unpublished doctoral dissertation, Radboud University Nijmegen, the Netherlands.

Kroeber-Riel, Werner, and Franz R. Esch. 2000. *Strategie und Technik der Werbung: verhaltungswissenschaftliche Ansatze*. Stuttgart: Kohlhammer.

Leiss, William; Stephen Kline; and Sut Jhally. 1990. *Social Communication in Advertising: Persons, Products, and Images of Well-Being*, 2d ed. New York: Methuen.

Loef, Joost. 2002. "Incongruity between Ads and Consumer Expectations of Advertising." Amsterdam: Thela Thesis.

MacInnis, Deborah J., and Bernard J. Jaworski. 1989. "Information Processing from Advertisements: Toward an Integrative Framework." *Journal of Marketing* 53: 1–23.

———; Christine Moorman; and Bernard J. Jaworski. 1991. "Enhancing and Measuring Consumers' Motivation, Opportunity, and Ability to Process Brand Information From Ads." *Journal of Marketing* 55 (October): 32–53.

Martin, Brett A.S.; Bodo Lang; and Stephanie Wong. 2003. "Conclusion Explicitness in Advertising: The Moderating Role of Need for Cognition (NFC) and Argument Quality (AQ) on Persuasion." *Journal of Advertising* 32: 57–66.

McQuarrie, Edward, F. 1989. "Advertising Resonance: A Semiological Perspective." In *Interpretive Consumer Research,* ed. Elizabeth C. Hirschman, 97–114. Provo, UT: Association for Consumer Research.

———, and David Glen Mick. 1992. "On Resonance: A Critical Pluralistic Inquiry into Advertising Rhetoric." *Journal of Consumer Research* 19 (September): 180–197.

———, and ———. 1996. "Figures of Rhetoric in Advertising Language." *Journal of Consumer Research* 22 (March): 424–438.

———, and ———. 1999. "Visual Rhetoric in Advertising: Text-Interpretive, Experimental, and Reader-Response Analyses." *Journal of Consumer Research* 26 (June): 37–54.

———, and ———. 2003a. "The Contribution of Semiotic and Rhetorical Perspectives to the Explanation of Visual Persuasion in Advertising." In *Persuasive Imagery: A Consumer Response Perspective,* ed. Linda M. Scott and Rajeev Batra, 191–221. Mahwah, NJ: Erlbaum.

———, and ———. 2003b. "Visual and Verbal Rhetorical Figures under Direct Processing versus Incidental Exposure to Advertising." *Journal of Consumer Research* 29 (March): 579–587.

———, and Barbara J. Phillips. 2005. "Indirect Persuasion in Advertising: How Consumers Process Metaphors Presented in Pictures and Words." *Journal of Advertising* 34: 7–20.

Messaris, Paul. 1992. " Visual Manipulation: Visual Means of Affecting Responses to Images." *Communication* 13: 181–195.

———. 1997. *Visual Persuasion: The Role of Images in Advertising.* London: Sage.

Mick, David Glen. 1992. "Levels of Subjective Comprehension in Advertising Processing and Their Relations to Ad Perceptions, Attitudes, and Memory." *Journal of Consumer Research* 18: 411–424.

———, and Laura Politi. 1989. "Consumers' Interpretations of Advertising Imagery: A Visit to the Hell of Connotation." In *Interpretive Consumer Research,* ed. Elizabeth C. Hirschman, 85–96. Provo, UT: Association for Consumer Research.

Morgan, Susan E., and Tom Reichert. 1999. "The Message Is in the Metaphor: Assessing the Comprehension of Metaphors in Advertisements." *Journal of Advertising* 28: 1–11.

Moriarty, Sandra E. 1996. "Abduction: A Theory of Visual Interpretation." *Communication Theory* 6: 167–187.

Mothersbaugh, David L.; Bruce A. Huhmann; and George R. Franke. 2002. "Combinatory and Separative Effects of Rhetorical Figures on Consumers' Effort and Focus in Ad Processing. *Journal of Consumer Research* 28: 589–602.

Nelson, Michelle R., and Jacqueline C. Hitchon. 1995. "Theory of Synesthesia Applied to Persuasion in Print Advertising Headlines." *Journalism and Mass Communication Quarterly* 72: 346–360.

Peracchio, Laura A., and Joan Meyers-Levy. 1994. "How Ambiguous Cropped Objects in Ad Photos Can Affect Product Evaluations." *Journal of Consumer Research* 21 (June): 190–204.

Petty, Richard E., and John T. Cacioppo. 1996. *Attitudes & Persuasion: Classic & Contemporary Approaches.* Boulder, CO: Westview Press.

Phillips, Barbara J. 1997. "Thinking into It: Consumer Interpretation of Complex Advertising Images." *Journal of Advertising* 26 (2): 77–87.

———. 2000. "The Impact of Verbal Anchoring on Consumer Response to Image Ads." *Journal of Advertising* 29 (1): 15–24.

———. 2003. "Understanding Visual Metaphor in Advertising." In *Persuasive Imagery: A Consumer Response Perspective,* ed. Linda M. Scott and Rajeev Batra, 297–310. Mahwah, NJ: Erlbaum.

————, and Edward F. McQuarrie. 2004. "Beyond Visual Metaphor: A New Typology of Visual Rhetoric in Advertising." *Marketing Theory* 4 (1/2): 113–136.

Sawyer, Alan G., and Daniel J. Howard. 1991. "The Effects of Omitting Conclusions in Advertisements to Low and Moderately Involved Audiences." *Journal of Marketing Research* 28: 467–476.

Sperber, Dan, and Deirdre Wilson. 1986. *Relevance: Communication and Cognition.* Oxford: Blackwell.

Stern, Barbara B. 1989. "Literary Explication: A Methodology for Consumer Research." In *Interpretive Consumer Research*, ed. Elizabeth C. Hirschman, 48–59. Provo, UT: Association for Consumer Research.

Tanaka, Keiko. 1992. "The Pun in Advertising: A Pragmatic Approach." *Lingua* 87: 91–102.

Toncar, Mark, and James Munch. 2001. "Consumer Response to Tropes in Print Advertising." *Journal of Advertising* 30 (1): 55–65.

van Gisbergen, Marnix S.; Paul E. Ketelaar; and Hans Beentjes. 2004. "Changes in Advertising Language? A Content Analysis of Magazine Advertisements in 1980 and 2000." In *Content and Media Factors in Advertising,* ed. Peter Neijens, C. Hess, B. van den Putte, and E. Smith, 51–61. Amsterdam: Het Spinhuis.

van Mulken, Margot J.P.; Renske van Enschot; and Hans Hoeken. 2005. "Levels of Implicitness in Magazine Advertisements: An Experimental Study into the Relationship between Complexity and Appreciation in Magazine Advertisements." *Information Design Journal and Document Design* 13 (2): 155–164.

Vezina, Richard, and Olivia Paul. 1997. "Provocation in Advertising: A Conceptualization and Empirical Assessment." *International Journal of Research in Marketing* 14 (2): 177–192.

Warlaumont, Hazel. 1995. "Advertising Images: From Persuasion to Polysemy." *Journal of Current Issues and Research in Advertising* 17 (Spring): 19–31.

————. 1997. "Appropriating Reality: Consumers' Perceptions of Schema-inconsistent Advertising." *Journalism & Mass Communication Quarterly* 74: 39–54.

Williamson, Judith. 1978. *Decoding Advertisements: Ideology and Meaning in Advertising.* London: Boyars.

7

Inspecting the Unexpected

Schema and the Processing of Visual Deviations

Mark A. Callister and Lesa A. Stern

Chapter Summary

A growing trend in print advertising involves violating expectations to draw consumer attention to products that may otherwise hold little interest. The purposes of this chapter are first, to better understand how visual imagery functions in relation to expectations—in doing so we merge concepts from message incongruity and visual rhetoric literature—and second, to review schema-based sources of expectations commonly used in print advertising. We review ad, product, brand, cultural, reality-deviating, and media-vehicle–based sources of schemas. We argue that a visual can both set and violate schema expectations and may violate multiple schemas in an ad execution.

Exposed to some 3,000 advertisements each day, we live amid a deluge of ad messages (Bower 2002). In print advertising, research indicates these advertisements have steadily become more visual over the past century (Phillips and McQuarrie 2002; Pollay 1985). Although it is difficult to escape this unremitting flood of commercial persuasion, we learn to attend to those relatively few ads that have some personal interest or relevance. However, there is a growing trend in print advertising to insert visual images that are novel, startling, jolting, or incongruent in hopes of sweeping us into ads for products or services that may otherwise hold little interest. Many of these visuals go beyond merely attracting attention; they also show an ability to motivate people to elaborate more fully on message elements. Even when visuals are not tied to extrinsic or intrinsic sources of personal relevance for a viewer, a novel or startling visual can draw immediate attention (Celsi and Olson 1988).

Explanations for this effect may vary, but the inclusion of visuals that are incongruent with or deviate from established expectations may offer some insights. As Scott (1990) observes, we approach or frame an ad much as we do a novel, symphony, or sculpture—with a set of expectations that are derived from our culture and mediated by experiences. These expectations arise from prior knowledge structures, or schema (Bobrow and Norman 1975), related to our experiences with advertising, products, brands, object relationships, depictions, and the like. According to Scott (1994b), advertisers recognize that consumers eventually become bored with many advertising conventions and strategies, and will therefore search out new ways of "luring readers into listening to their appeals" (464). One way to "lure" readers is to violate consumer schema, whether through the visual or verbal portions of an ad. Such violations abound in print ads today and are often referred to as *schema incongruity* (Sujan, Bettman, and Sujan 1986). As Zaltman (1997) reminds us, our mental models, knowledge, beliefs, and expectations are crucial for us to explore and understand in our study of advertising messages.

However, the relationship between visuals and viewer expectations is complex and elusive. A close inspection of shifts in conceptual definitions featured in message incongruity literature points to, yet does not adequately discuss, the possibility that visual images in print ads can either *create* or *violate* schema expectations. Yet, beyond these two functions, there is still an additional possibility that a carefully crafted visual can simultaneously serve both functions, *creator* and *violator* of expectations, within a single ad execution. As violator of expectations, the image potentially draws the viewer into an ad, motivating the reader to reconcile the incongruity. As creator, the image triggers related schema and opens the way for additional ad elements (headlines, other visuals, etc.) to violate the invoked schema.

In studying visual imagery in the role of *violator,* consumer behavior researchers typically instruct subjects to evaluate the expectancy of the visual in relationship to some other ad element (e.g., headline), resulting in a fixed classification (based on aggregate evaluations) as either *congruent* or *incongruent.* However, subjects may not invoke a single schema when viewing visual imagery, but may in fact draw upon multiple schemas in processing a given ad. Like the impact of a firework carrying more than one explosive charge, a visual may flare and flare again in a single ad execution as consumers work through ad elements, applying relevant schema as they go. Therefore, a visual that violates multiple schema may prove a useful advertising strategy in gaining and sustaining attention, and thus worthy of closer examination. For instance, Mothersbaugh, Huhmann, and Franke (2002) found incremental processing gains when they combined, or layered, *verbal* figures (in the form of schemes and tropes) into single ad executions. In other words, when unique mechanisms, such as a trope (e.g., metaphor, pun, etc.) is combined with a scheme (e.g., rhyme, alliteration, etc.), greater processing results than is the case when redundant mechanisms (e.g., a trope is combined with another trope) are layered together. Exploring the possibility of schema layering among *visual* elements may result in incremental processing gains and attitudinal responses. However, before this type of research can be conducted, a fuller understanding of relevant schemas that can potentially guide advertisers in employing such visuals must be explored.

Two related areas of research in visual persuasion, *message incongruity* and *visual rhetoric,* have made important contributions to our understanding of the nature and impact of schema incongruity. The purpose of this article is first, to better understand how visual imagery functions in relation to expectations—in doing so we review and merge relevant concepts from message incongruity and visual rhetoric literature; and second, to closely review the sources of schema-based expectations commonly used in processing print advertising—here we propose additional sources and highlight ones that have not been fully explored. The intent in creating such a taxonomy of schema-based expectations is to provide useful insights into how schema violations and the possibility of layering such violations can arouse greater interest in ads and motivate more elaborate processing of ad elements. A consumer may judge a given visual image as both congruent and incongruent depending on the schema applied. Similarly, a visual may violate multiple schemas in a given print ad execution. The multilayering of schema and fluctuating judgments of schema (in)congruity have not been adequately explored in advertising research and can have important implications for advertising practice. The proposed taxonomy is not exhaustive, but attempts to identify those schema-based violations most relevant to processing visual imagery in print advertising.

Message Incongruity

In the area of message incongruity, consumer behavior researchers examine the incongruity that emerges as verbal and visual ad elements interact. This interaction between elements often results in gaining attention and more elaborative forms of information processing. Initially, research in message incongruity examined one type of schema violation wherein visual images violated expectations established in the ad's theme contained in the headline (Heckler and Childers 1992). Later, researchers shifted to a more picture-based source of expectation, violated by the headline (Lee 2000; Stafford, Walker, and Blasko 1996). While such shifts in conceptual definitions reflected the particular research interests of the researchers, a fuller appreciation of the relationship of visual imagery to schema violations was not adequately explored.

Theme-Based Incongruities

Studies in message incongruity typically draw upon Heckler and Childers's (1992) two-dimensional conceptualization of incongruity: *relevancy* and *expectancy.* *Relevancy* generally refers to the degree to which material in an ad pertains or contributes to the theme or primary message. *Expectancy* refers to the degree to which a piece of information falls into a predetermined pattern or structure evoked by the theme. Incongruity researchers have drawn upon the conceptual and operational clarity offered in the "theme-based" approach (Areni and Cox 1994; Callister 2000; Heckler and Childers 1992; Lee 2000; Lee and Mason 1999).

To illustrate the use of theme-based expectations, Heckler and Childers (1992) offer the example of an ad for airline travel with a theme of "seating comfort" appearing in the headline. One ad features a man reclining comfortably in the airplane while a second ad replaces the man with an elephant. The picture of the reclining man in the first ad might be considered both *relevant* to the theme of seating comfort and *expected* for airline ads containing such a theme. For incongruity research, a visual image that is considered both relevant and expected is considered "congruent." The relaxed elephant in the second ad, on the other hand, is certainly *relevant* to the theme of seating comfort, but perhaps *unexpected* (one might not expect to see a seated elephant in an airline ad touting comfort), and forms the "incongruent" condition, sometimes referred to as "moderately incongruent" (Stafford, Walker, and Blasko 1996). A final type of incongruity, sometimes referred to as "extreme incongruity" (Ibid. 1996) and closely associated with "absurdity" (Arias-Bolzman, Chakraborty, and Mowen 2000), is considered *irrelevant* and *unexpected*. This type of incongruity is typically not examined given its nonsensical nature, such as a robot standing in the aisle of the airplane.

As illustrated, the concept of "theme" is central to both expectancy and relevancy dimensions. For expectancy, the theme activates schema from which the expectancy of a visual is judged. For relevancy, visuals are judged according to their ability to contribute to the identification of the theme. The theme of the ad is created through the headline or product-attribute statements.

The focus on theme and its relationship to stored knowledge originates from research in social cognition and verbal discourse. Heckler and Childers (1992) found a rich source of theoretical and conceptual guidance from research in social cognition. Responding to the lack of clear conceptual distinctions in incongruity terminology found in consumer and marketing research, these researchers found greater clarity in the works of Hastie (1980, 1981) and Srull and his colleagues (Srull 1981; Srull, Lichtenstein, and Rothbart 1985; Srull and Wyer 1989). In this research domain, subjects are typically provided with personality descriptions of people followed by behaviors that are either congruent or incongruent with the newly formed expectations.

Heckler and Childers (1992) apply incongruity concepts from person-perception literature to advertising perceptions, arguing that consumers will likely, over time, possess expectations for certain brands and products similar to behavioral expectations of people. To further the conceptual development of incongruence, they also draw on the concept of "themes" originating from studies in verbal discourse. The theme is the focus of a story to which the plot is directed (Thorndyke 1977). The concept of theme finds application in person-perception literature when one views a personality trait as a theme. For instance, learning that a very religious friend was caught stealing might be similar to seeing a Chevy Blazer atop a lighthouse in a truck ad promoting a theme of security and safety. The religiosity of the friend becomes the theme, and knowledge of the theme sets expectations by which the criminal act is judged as incongruent. Similarly, repeated exposure to truck ads with a theme of "security" sets expectations from which the odd image of a perched truck is similarly judged as incongruent.

Verbal messages may activate expectations from which the visual is judged when the ads contain prominent headlines or product attributes that attract initial attention and clearly establish a theme, and when consumers have well-developed schema based on different possible themes for a given product type. However, for many ads, given the increased prominence of visuals, a theme-based approach may not be applicable. Arguably, a startling image can draw attention away from a prominent headline. In such cases, the visual may create an expectation for what might appear in the headline.

Moving Beyond Theme to Picture-Based Incongruities

The picture portion of an ad often functions as an "advance organizer" that cues the receiver to the content of the advertisement's message (Houston, Childers, and Heckler 1987), thereby creating an expectation for what the copy portion will contain. Interestingly, although Heckler and Childers (1992) manipulate incongruence through visuals that violate theme-based expectations in a later study, they agree with their earlier study (Houston, Childers, and Heckler 1987) that visual images are usually the element initially processed in a print ad and that pictures typically create the initial expectancy for processing the other ad elements.

Perhaps recognizing the conceptual limitations of a theme-based approach, Stafford, Walker, and Blasko (1996) modify Heckler and Childer's definition of expectancy to one that adopts a picture-based accounting of incongruence and expectancy. *Expectancy* becomes "the degree to which the headline fits the pattern or structure evoked by the *visual portion* [italics added] of the advertisement" (Stafford, Walker, and Blasko 1996, 57). For Stafford, Walker, and Blasko, the reliance on "theme" is relaxed. In operationalizing the incongruent (unexpected, relevant) condition, the researchers create an ad featuring a muddy cyclist racing down a mountain trail and a headline that reads "Good Clean Fun." Rather than a theme creating an expectation for the visual, the visual creates the expectation for the theme or headline.

Message incongruity research, therefore, has studied visual images as either *violators* (as in theme-based) or *creators* (picture-based) of expectations. The possibility of a given visual in an ad performing both functions, however, is not entertained in this line of research.

Further, incongruity research has focused almost exclusively on the interaction between the visual and verbal elements of ads in creating incongruence, without full consideration of the relationships that exist between visuals. Embedding images into incongruent visual contexts is a popular strategy among advertisers and warrants closer examination.

To illustrate visual-visual incongruence and a visual's ability to function as violator and source of expectations, recall the example of the traveling elephant. The elephant will be considered incongruent in the visual context of an airplane regardless of whether or not the theme is processed first or even if the theme is processed at all. Moreover, note how the image of the elephant is able to both violate (people sit in airplane seats) and create (the theme should focus on comfort and space) expectations.

Visual Rhetoric

We now turn to visual rhetoric, the other line of research that has made important contributions to the study of visuals and incongruity. Rhetorical studies of visual imagery in advertising examine incongruent visuals known as visual figures. From this line of research, we have come to understand the rhetorical capabilities and properties of visual figures as well as how these figures impact important consumer processing and outcome measures (McQuarrie and Mick 1992, 1996, 1999, 2003; McQuarrie and Phillips 2005; Phillips 1997; Phillips and McQuarrie 2004; Scott 1994a).

This research largely ignores conceptual and operational definitions used in incongruity literature, opting instead for a more broadly defined conceptualization. For these researchers, visuals that function as rhetorical figures are considered "artful deviations" that represent a "swerve from expectations" (McQuarrie and Mick 2003; see also McQuarrie and Mick 1996) and that conform to a template that is independent of the specific content asserted in an ad (McQuarrie and Mick 1999). By *artful,* a rhetorical figure is considered aesthetic in the sense that the viewer of the text finds pleasure in the multiple meanings proposed by the visual and in the opportunity to play with those meanings and interpretations (McQuarrie and Mick 2003). As for *deviation,* McQuarrie and Mick link the term to "what consumer researchers might have called incongruity" (1996, 426). McQuarrie and Phillips reinforce this connection, noting that artful deviations are "incongruities that both require resolution and point the way to resolution" (2005, 8). In Phillips's (1997) study of pictorial metaphors, she refers to the "incongruity" of the visual contained in her treatment ad.

Similar to incongruity research, rhetorical figures can vary in degree of deviation or incongruity. Both lines of research virtually dismiss the extreme cases of incongruity, which combine unexpected and irrelevant figures as nonsensical or absurd. Lee and Mason's (1999) research suggests that while this type of figure increases recall of the ad, it does so in an undesirable manner—it produces negative attitudes toward the ad and brand. Most research, however, focuses almost exclusively on the unexpected yet relevant (Heckler and Childers 1992; McQuarrie and Mick 1996). The dimension of unexpectedness, for rhetorical researchers, is further distinguished by McQuarrie and Mick's (1999) *gradient of deviation* wherein visual *schemes* deviate from expectations with their excessive regularity (e.g., visual rhymes, etc.), while visual *tropes* experience greater deviation with their irregularity in usage (e.g., visual metaphors or puns). The deviations expressed by the irregularity of visual tropes and excessive regularity of visual schemes mark an important contribution by rhetorical theorists. For these researchers, the ability of visuals to deviate does not depend on a departure from a theme, as in incongruity research, but from the unconventional usage of the visual.

In the context of advertising, therefore, the source of expectations from the rhetorical perspective comes from the consumers' past experience with the functions and depictions of visuals in ads. Phillips and McQuarrie's (2002) content analysis of print ads shows an increase over the past half century in the use of visual figures such as tropes. The appearance of these visual tropes and the multiple meanings that they engender, represent breaks from conventional uses of visuals.

While practitioners have come to appreciate the figurative capabilities of visuals, advertising and marketing researchers have been slow to recognize these properties (Scott 1994a). Traditionally, researchers have been guilty of limiting the role of visual imagery in commercial persuasion to merely creating affect or displaying the features of a product (Ibid.). As Scott asserts, however, visuals in advertising are not just reflections of reality or simple peripheral or affective cues that demonstrate product attributes. She notes that "pictures are . . . symbolic artifacts constructed from the conventions of a particular culture" that are capable of "declaration, comparison, and other kinds of symbolic statements" (Ibid. 252).

McQuarrie and Mick further champion this position, explaining that pictures are and can be "fragmented, combined, or altered for rhetorical purposes" (1996, 436). Like rhetorical linguistic figures, therefore, visual figures can violate the conventional use of signs or texts. Consider print ads for Orbit White, a gum that whitens teeth. Each ad features a person whose head and face are covered by an oddly styled lampshade intended to shield others from the bright light emanating from a whitened smile. The rendered visual is probably startling to most consumers. Consumers accustomed to advertisements that merely display products or more specifically to the way that gum advertisements typically feature the product, may find a person wearing a lampshade rather unconventional and strange. They understand that Orbit White will not literally produce a blinding smile, but that a type of humorous exaggeration or visual hyperbole emphasizes the product's ability to whiten teeth.

The definition of "artful deviation" is not restricted to conventions created solely through experience with advertising executions. A deviation from conventions can, given the broadness of the rhetorical definition, refer to departures from the way that consumers typically encounter visual images from their own personal experiences. A person wearing a lampshade, for instance, is unconventional whether embedded in a magazine ad or viewed in a family photo album.

A distinction bears mentioning at this point. Visual rhetorical figures require a reinterpretation of the image in order to resolve the incongruity. However, not all incongruous visuals involve visual rhetoric. Visuals with intended literal interpretations can also garner attention and encourage reconciliation through the process of deviation or incongruity. For example, a recent MasterCard ad features a smiling man cooking in a feminine-style apron. Many would consider these elements incongruent, yet this would not be defined as an artful deviation in the sense that a figurative reinterpretation is required. For the consumer whose curiosity was piqued, the incongruent image of the apron-clad man will motivate further elaboration.

Schema-Based Deviations

From message incongruity research, we learn that a visual can deviate from theme-based expectations or create expectations concerning the content of the verbal text. From visual rhetoric we learn that visuals can contain rhetorical properties, and just as linguistic figures of speech deviate from conventional usage, so too can visual images. Rhetorical theorists have also opened up the possibility of multiple visual figures appearing in a single ad, referred to as "layering." But can a single visual be judged as both congruent and incongruent by the same viewer? What about the possibility of a visual becoming more or less (in)congruent as the consumer elaborates on ad content? Can a given visual experience a "layering" of sorts where a consumer activates multiple schema, any one of which might render different judgments of (in)congruity? Does this layering increase the attractive power of a visual? What impact does it have on elaboration and recall?

Answering these questions requires a more thoughtful analysis of the schema involved in judgments of incongruity. From incongruity research, the potential for a visual to violate multiple expectations is not discussed, and from the conceptual framework of the rhetorical literature, the possibility is allowed, but not fully specified. Understanding schema incongruity and the ability to activate multiple schemas require a clear taxonomy of the types of schema relevant to advertising visuals. Understanding relevant schemas that possibly underlie advertising visuals gives practitioners and researchers increased ability to select or create visuals that generate more potent incongruities. Executing such ad designs can be accomplished with a clearer eye toward what visuals might increase the attractive power of an ad and direct consumers toward reconciling the incongruities in ways that further advance the information processing objectives of advertisers.

As a prelude to the discussion, let us return to the earlier example of the airline ad carrying the theme of comfort and space. Imagine that through the use of computer graphics advertisers create a reclining elephant that immediately grabs attention. What consumer expectation did this image violate? Perhaps the elephant looks so lifelike that to the consumer he appears to be actually sitting in an airline seat. Perhaps the elephant's unique posture or business suit deviates from the consumer's experience in viewing elephants at a zoo or circus. Or what about the possibility that the viewer spends considerable time flying, making the traveling elephant even more odd. If the traveler is familiar with airline ads, perhaps this travel ad represents a shift in style. Perhaps the elephant is always featured in a business suit, but in this particular ad he sports a Hawaiian shirt. If the travel magazine usually features very traditional, conservative ads, the subscriber may find the strange image even more surprising. Imagine that the ad includes a large headline reading "An airline with adequate *trunk* space . . ." from which the consumer judges the expectedness of an elephant—or if viewed first, the elephant creates expectations about the headline. Finally, perhaps the answer to the question "What consumer expectation did this image violate?" is not found in any one of the above answers, but in a combination of these potential sources from which incongruity judgments are made.

This section reviews literature from disparate studies that address sources relevant to schema-based expectations commonly used in processing print advertising, while proposing additional sources or highlighting ones that have not been fully explored. This taxonomy is not exhaustive, but represents primary schema relevant to process-ing visual imagery in print ads. The schemas proposed include *ad, product, brand, cultural, reality-deviating,* and *vehicle-media*–based sources of schemas.

Ad Schema

Schematic structures often result from repeated experience within a domain; in the context of advertising, the repetitive nature and the regularities of advertising (e.g., redundant semantic, physical, and structural features) provide support that ad-related schema exist (Stoltman 1991). Ad schema reflect the strategies and tactics used by advertisers and the constituent elements of an ad schema might contain expectations regarding the characters, visual objects, execution structures, appeals, camera movement, auditory devices, and the props and scenery contained in advertising.

With the aid of computer graphics software, advertisers can easily move, alter, combine, color, and distort images to maximize their uniqueness and visual intrigue. Although they do not expressly label it as such, Phillips and McQuarrie (2004) offer the example of an ad schema in an ad for Tide liquid laundry detergent. The ad shows billowing clouds and blue sky contained inside a measuring cup. The authors note that the ad deviates from the more realistic depictions of products and typical users found in conventional ads. Within the context of print advertising, consumers will have expectations about the way that products are usually featured. The billowing clouds in a measuring cup may deviate from such expectations, creating a visual incongruity in the mind of the consumer.

Another example of an ad schema is found in a Briggs & Stratton ad for a home generator system. The entire ad is black, empty space except for a small font text at the bottom of the ad and the Briggs & Stratton logo. The absence of any visual elements and the enormity of empty space are startling. The unexpectedness of the ad's execution lies in the ad schema for the conventional inclusion of visuals or more dominant text. The headline reads, "Don't get caught with your lights down." The black background is certainly relevant to a theme of safety in the event of a power failure and the need for having a generator, but unexpected in terms of a possible ad schema.

Phillips and McQuarrie (2002) provide another example of an ad schema. The authors found that advertisers historically provided within an ad headline or body copy the interpretation of an ad's rhetorical figures, referred to as "verbal anchoring" (Phillips 2000). The historical prevalence of verbal anchoring establishes expectations that the ad's copy will explain the rhetorical figure. However, Phillips and McQuarrie (2002) note a decrease in the use of verbal anchoring in recent years. Consumers who continue to have expectations that an ad with a visual figure will contain a verbal anchor may find the absence of such anchoring unexpected.

The measuring cup in the Tide ad illustrates the dual function of visuals as both "violator" and "creator" of expectations. The sky and clouds in a measuring cup *violate* an ad schema, and as a visual metaphor, the measuring cup *creates* an expectation that a verbal anchor will be provided.

Product Schema

Product-related schemas exist at many different levels (Goodstein 1993) and at a basic level they are organized around product types (Goodstein, Moore, and Cours 1992). These product schemas are recognized by both consumers and the ad agencies that create them. One advertising agency president stated that his company's goal was to "make commercials that are unique relative to others in the product class" (Goodstein 1993, 89). Once advertisers identify these product schemas, they can capitalize on them, perhaps inserting a visual that may not typically appear in that genre of product ads. Thus, in advertisements, regularities may exist within a product category that creates expectations for the consumers. For instance, in the product category of skin cleansers and acne treatments, the common ad executions invariably feature models with clear, healthy complexions or the "Before and After" photos. A recent ad by Clearasil Ultra shows a fully spotted Dalmatian dog at "Day 1," and then that same dog with only a few black spots at "Day 3." Dalmatians losing their spots certainly catch viewer attention, but the knowledge that this is an ad for skin cleansers creates an additional violation of expectations for what is typically featured in ads for this product type.

Heckler and Childers's theme-based model of incongruity is perhaps best included in the product schema type. For example, when the authors discuss the seated elephant in the airplane, they argue that subjects link that visual image to other picture elements stored within their memory network "for this ad's product class" (1992, 479). Some advertisers might take out the verbal theme altogether and allow for the visual alone to communicate the theme, as rhetorical researchers have argued. This brings up an interesting possibility. If consumers do indeed draw upon theme-based expectations, then, given the rhetorical capabilities of visuals, a visual, such as the "unspotting" of a Dalmatian, can both create an expectation and then violate it. The Dalmatian losing her spots, therefore, violates our experience with Dalmatians' spots, yet also creates an expectation that this ad will most likely advertise a product for dogs. The realization that this ad deals with facial cleansing would most likely add to the viewers' surprise.

Brand Schema

Print ads entitled "Welcome to Condom Country," launched by the AIDS Committee of Toronto, depict rugged men in western gear on horseback leaning over to kiss each other. These ads have obvious allusion to "Marlboro Country" and the Marlboro man. The mimicking of the classic cigarette ads, however, is a strategy that underscores the power of brand schema as well as product schema. For most viewers of the ads, the scenery, horses, and cowboys certainly evoke a brand schema, but the kissing men violate the schema, deviating from the way that the Marlboro Man is usually depicted.

Brand schemas focus on the expectations that arise when people perceive regularities or patterns in ad executions for particular brands (Callister and Stern 2002). Since incongruity research typically uses fictive brands in its experimental ads, brand schema violations have not been adequately examined in advertising research. While fictional brand names are an important and necessary means of controlling extraneous sources of error arising from subjects' experience with actual brands, such fictional names inadvertently obscure an important source of schema violation. Advertisers often follow a format in which certain ad elements reappear as a defining feature of the ad campaign. The possible elements could include almost anything: a tag line, a character, event, object, or situation. Alden, Mukherjee, and Hoyer note, "Some brands (e.g., Miller Lite, Energizer, Pepsi, MetLife, and Little Caesar's) have acquired a reputation for airing humorous television advertisements. As such, consumers could have a prior expectation for humor when they watch ads for these particular brands" (2000, 12). A serious advertisement for these products may constitute a violation for some viewers. Repeated viewing of ads for brands that carry recurring elements will invariably result in a brand schema, as in the famous vodka bottle formations in Absolut ads or the lampshade in Orbit White ads.

Brand schema, like any schema, are susceptible to change with repeated exposures to patterned content. Interestingly, what was once deemed unexpected, with time, can become expected. Bottle formations and lampshades become part of the brand schema. The absence of such items in subsequent ads can create an incongruity or deviation, perhaps generating just as much attention as when they first appeared in the Absolut and Orbit White ads, respectively. McQuarrie and Mick (2003) write of "frozen" metaphors where figures (visual or verbal) become clichés. The figures cease to function as figures because they no longer reach a threshold for a deviation to occur (e.g., a tire that "hugs the road"). A visual initially judged as incongruent (whether a figure or nonfigure), therefore, can become frozen or expected through repeated use. However, the "frozen" figure can become "unfrozen" or incongruent once more through its absence in subsequent ads for that brand. A recent Orbit Gum ad featuring a young woman's arm covered with bees as she holds up the product while working in her garden is certainly eye-catching, not only because of the bees but also because of the absence of the lampshade.

Cultural Schema

Cultural experiences provide another source of expectations. People learn to interpret ads according to cultural rules, and these ad interpretations may be affected by all of the different cultural groups to which one belongs (Bhat, Thomas, Wardlow 1998; Phillips 1997; Scott 1994b). Examples of cultural influences include gender, religion, ethnicity, and social identity. Scott (1994b) refers to these cultural groups as "interpretive communities" where people come to process information differently based on their cultural orientations. In advertising studies, researchers often make the assumption of a homogenous audience that comes to process ads in ways similar to those intended by the advertisers. In reality, consumers' unique cultural conventions underlie their different responses to visuals.

The function of cultural schema, as conceptualized here, differs somewhat from that in other studies examining the role of culture in information processing and consumer evaluations: the cultural knowledge required to reconcile an incongruous visual. Cultural schema are based more on experience with what symbols in a culture are typically used to communicate certain messages, and less so with the knowledge required to interpret the symbols. Although in name, Luna, Peracchio, and de Juan's (2003) concept of *cultural congruity* seems similar to a cultural schema, their conceptualization deals more with issues of relevancy (are the text and/or graphics on a Web site congruent with or relevant to the culture of the bilingual viewer of the Web site) and not expectancy, the latter of which is key to schema violations. Scott (1994b) and Phillips (1997) focus on how ad, product, and *cultural knowledge* allow consumers to ascribe meanings to ads, referred to as *implicatures*. The function of a cultural schema as defined here is not in the creation of an implicature, but in the creation of expectations for what symbols are conventionally used to communicate certain messages in a given culture.

As an example, consider a recent V8 vegetable juice ad featuring a young college student sprawled face down on the floor of his messy dorm room wearing only his underwear and baseball cap. Stacked high behind the unconscious student is a pyramid of dented V8 cans and other empty cans are strewn about him on the floor. The ad does not contain copy. The visual story is reminiscent of a binge-drinking episode, sans alcoholic beverages. Those within the interpretive community of the American culture might connect the scene with binging and the resulting loss of control. The apparent message is that V8 is so addictive, you cannot stop drinking it. Perhaps those unfamiliar with binge drinking on American college campuses may still register a deviation from their own personal experience with how much beverage most people can drink, but those familiar with the concerns, tragedies, and sorrows surrounding binge drinking among young people may experience an additional deviation. V8's use of this negatively charged issue as a referent or frame for their message is unexpected and startling. A message of addiction might have involved a more expected and arguably more appropriate association or juxtaposition such as with chocolate or other "addictive" foods.

Contrast V8's possible violation of a cultural schema with that found in a recent Dr. Pepper commercial. The commercial shows a young man whose love for his girlfriend is so strong he is willing to do anything for her: he folds her laundry, goes with her to yoga classes, and buys feminine hygiene products for her (a Dr. Pepper always in his hand). But when his girlfriend attempts to share his Dr. Pepper, he flees into the night with his rescued Dr. Pepper in hand. One might argue that while his specific reaction was unexpected, advertisers' use of hyperbole in our culture is not. The V8 example, however, is unexpected, both in our personal experience with the volume of consumed drinks and in the decision to use binge drinking as the vehicle to deliver a message. A deviation based on a cultural schema, therefore, is achieved when the consumer perceives that the choice of a visual to convey a given message falls outside the culturally expected consideration set of possible visuals that are typically used to convey such messages.

As a further example, consider one of the complex advertising images used in Phillips (1997). An ad for a fictive brand, Sport Athletic Clothing, attempts to communicate an image of tough, strong, durable fabric. A consumer's cultural consideration set for communicating toughness in clothing might include the images of or references to rocks, cowboys, football or hockey players, tigers, and so on. These expected images or references are more broad and general than a product schema, involving expectations about messages across contexts. The Sport Athletic Clothing ad uses the image of a spoon and a cereal bowl filled with milk and nails. Although most subjects will draw upon cultural knowledge of the saying "He eats nails for breakfast" in interpreting the message, the initial reaction to a paired association of a bowl of milk and nails with sports athletic clothing as a means of communicating the strong and durable nature of the fabric, compared with more culturally common associations, may be perceived as incongruent.

Reality-Deviating Schema

Drawing on our experiences with how people and physical objects are perceived or function in the real world, we may see an ad with visuals that deviate from reality. Consider two recent Tyson Food ads. One ad features a woman rowing a canoe while pulling a man in a parasail. A second ad shows a young boy on the elementary school playground rings, with arms fully extended outward and body bent in a pike position, with the perfect form of an Olympic gymnast. In both ads the headline reads, "Powered by Tyson" and the body copy asks "Have you had your protein today?" Although the related images represent clear departures from reality, the realistic rendering of the images creates intriguing, albeit bizarre, scenes.

The reality-deviating schema is similar to what Pezdek et al. (1989) describe as schema people hold for scenes that appear in ads. These authors maintain that people are very accurate in distinguishing scenes they have seen before from those they have not seen. Moreover, the perception and cognition of scenes are largely schema guided (Pezdek et al. 1989) and the perception of contextualized objects pervades consumers' everyday experiences (Kleine and Kernan 1991). For instance, a recent print ad for Dodge shows a truck pulling oversized, 7,000 pound barbells across a beach. Barbells judged incongruent based on size and use may also be judged by the same consumer as incongruent based on their personal schema for what typically appears within the scene or context of a beach. Therefore, a simplistic image of a truck pulling a barbell is incongruent, but the incongruity deepens in richness as additional contextual elements are added.

Returning to the barbell example, a consumer may not have the knowledge to judge the expectedness of a Dodge pulling oversized barbells in an ad, product, or cultural context, but as mentioned, a deviation most likely registered. The consumer's own personal experience with barbells allowed her to see the oversized set as a departure from a schema. No experience unique to her cultural background or experience with advertising of that particular product class was required. One of the respondents in Phillips (1997) provides an example of the personal schema relating to the bowl of nails: "I think it sparks my curiosity, because you don't have nails for a meal. I want to know what it is supposed to mean or symbolize" (80). This student has drawn upon a personal schema in judging the image as incongruent.

Media Vehicle Schema

A *media vehicle* is a single media publication, such as the *Chicago Tribune*, eBay, NPR, or *Time*. With magazines, advertisers will often feature advertisements in a select set of media vehicles that attract their specific target audiences. Frequent readers of *Golf Digest*, for instance, will note recurrences of advertisements for certain product types and brands and the visual images that usually accompany them. These recurrences create expectations that we refer to as *media-vehicle schema*. In Callister and Stern, for instance, one participant described this schema when he wrote:

> I don't read magazines for older people like *Reader's Digest* or *Business World*. I read ones more targeted to my age group like *Rolling Stone, SI,* or *Maxim*. The images in those magazines are more odd or push the limit, particularly clothing or cologne [ads], like showing skin. In the other magazines, they might have some of the clever ads, but given the products they are trying to push in those magazines, they will be more traditional and not push the norm. (2002, 10)

A colleague recently noted an EDS ad appearing in the *Economist* that features a bolt cutter. The ad stood out for this individual because, "it deviates from the type of ad typically featured in the magazine." In another example, high-speed SBC Yahoo features an ad in a gaming magazine with an innocent looking ten-year-old girl who stares expressionless into the camera. The headline reads, "SARAH JOHNSON WANTS TO DESTROY YOU. Are you tough enough for the world of online gaming?" The image of a little girl in a male- and teen-targeted magazine is surprising. In sum, people expect to see ads for products, brands, or types of visual images that are consistent with the nature and readership of that particular magazine.

Layering of Schema

Violating a single schema has been shown to attract attention. Therefore, a visual that violates multiple schemas may prove a useful advertising strategy. An understanding of relevant schemas can guide advertisers in creating visuals that carry additional power to attract and motivate consumers to further engage an ad text. An example of this layering effect is provided by Callister and Stern (2002), who showed subjects a series of unaltered print ads and asked them to verbally describe what they were focusing their attention on. Subjects provided accompanying thoughts as they viewed each ad. One respondent provides an example of the layering effect as she viewed an Absolut ad in which Victorian-styled, bright lavender luggage shaped in the form of the Absolut bottle are stacked next to a departing train. Surprisingly, she was not very familiar with Absolut ads, but was immediately drawn to the luggage. After initially thinking the luggage was the train's smokestack, she realized it was shaped like a bottle. Attempting to understand why the luggage was shaped as such, she was further surprised that the ad provided no information to help her understand what it meant. At that point, the respondent stated, "My Mother has an old hat box like that where she puts her hat or wig." She noted, however, that her mother's old-fashioned luggage was not of such bright colors. The stacked luggage *violated* her personal schema three times—the mistaken smokestack, formation of a bottle, and the bright colors. The luggage also created the expectation that the ad would include a verbal anchor, an example of her ad schema. For most other subjects familiar with Absolut ads, however, the stacked luggage in the form of a bottle and lack of verbal anchoring might be judged "expected" from the standpoint of a brand schema. However, the luggage may still have generated some intrigue from a reality-deviating-schema standpoint.

A recent "Got Milk" ad provides a wonderful example of multiple layering. The advertisers capitalize on the butterfly-like resemblance of human pelvic bones to provide the strange, even haunting image of pelvic bones ascending upward against a contrasting black background. The viewer's initial impression is that these are indeed butterflies, but closer scrutiny brings the realization that these are human bones. The copy reads, "Because it's not so beautiful that half of all women over 50 suffer an osteoporotic fracture. Got Milk?" Pelvic bones fluttering upward like butterflies certainly violate a reality-deviation schema. Showing bones in a milk ad may not be considered unexpected. However, for Got Milk ads, the replacement of the milk-mustached celebrity with pelvic bones is unexpected.

Aside from layering, these examples also highlight how a given visual can be both incongruent and congruent in the same ad execution, depending on what schemas are applied. For example, Callister and Stern (2002) note one student's comment after seeing a VW ad where the bottom half of a backpacker's pack is the back section of VW, carefully spliced into the image both in form and color using computer graphics: "The combination [of car and backpack] surprised me, but the idea did not. The idea of a 'morphed' advertisement seems to be popular lately." In other words, the image is incongruent with his reality-deviating schema, but congruent with his ad schema.

Conclusion

Exploring schema-based incongruities is an important area of research in our age of visually dominated advertising. Given the prominence of visual material in advertising communication, it is not surprising that visual imagery in print ads has drawn much attention in recent years. Researchers and advertisers alike seek to understand how visuals operate in an ever increasingly complex, rich, and vibrant advertising landscape. This article has sought to uncover part of the attractive and elaborative influences contained in the employment of certain visual ad elements. From research in message incongruity and rhetoric, we learn that consumers have expectations upon which they judge ad elements. Visuals can be designed and employed in ways that both set and trigger expectations, often motivating consumers to reconcile the incongruities and search for additional meanings. Patterns emerging from consumers' ad, product, brand, cultural, and personal experiences shape perceptions and create expectations upon which visuals are judged or used. Consumers may solicit any number of these patterned experiences in understanding visual images, creating a layering of sorts that involves multiple expectations. Deviating from more than one source of expectations may possibly deepen the impact of a visual.

Future Research

Research into message incongruity draws primarily from the experimental tradition. While this research tradition provides strong causal analysis and theoretical specifications, consumer responses tend to be impoverished (McQuarrie and Mick 1999). With a more balanced approach that also uses qualitative methods of inquiry, researchers can gain additional insights into how readers actually process visual incongruities. Evidence shows that individuals—due to unique backgrounds, motives, experiences, and expectations—will process ad content differentially (Bhat, Leigh, and Wardlow 1998; Mick and Buhl 1992). In the past decade, more attention has been given to how real people, engaging actual advertising stimuli, interpret these ads (Hirschman and Thompson 1997; McQuarrie and Mick 1999; Mick and Buhl 1992; Phillips 1997; Scott 1994a, 1994b). Rhetorical researchers have successfully used qualitative methods in studying consumer responses to visual rhetoric (McQuarrie and Mick 1992, 1999; Phillips 1997).

Interpretation-oriented research often uses some form of a reader-response approach, producing rich descriptions of individual responses to advertising stimuli. A reader-response approach attempts to "show how a text works with the probable knowledge, expectations, or motives of the reader" (Scott 1994b, 463). This approach begins with observation of the phenomenon of interest as it actually occurs, focusing on a consumer's experience with ad elements, suggesting that people approach advertisements with a host of cultural, social, group, and individual predispositions that affect how they read and interpret an ad. Such an approach may open our understanding of the types and nature of schema-related expectations that consumers have of visual imagery in print ads. Interpretive approaches may also discover whether certain schemas are typically activated earlier in the viewing processes compared with other schema that may require greater elaboration or interpretation of ad elements before judgments of expectedness can be made. For instance, are reality-deviating schemas more readily retrieved and activated during initial exposure than perhaps product or cultural schemas?

Experimental studies can play a critical role in examining the impact of schema layering on information processing and attitudinal outcome measures. For instance, consumer processing and responses may be differentially affected by the number or type of incongruities requiring reconciliation that a visual excites. As noted previously, Mothersbaugh, Huhmann, and Franke (2002) found incremental processing gains when they combined, or layered, *verbal* figures into single ad executions. The gains were achieved when the combined rhetorical figures were unique in that they "differ[ed] with respect to the underlying mechanisms driving their incongruity" (591). Exploring the possibility of schema layering among *visual* elements may also result in incremental processing gains and attitudinal responses, especially if the layered schema types are unique or different from one another. Thus, the butterfly-like depiction of ascending pelvic bones in the "Got Milk" ad, for instance, may generate additional processing because of the unique violations to reality-deviating and brand (treated as a brand, although the campaign is supported by a consortium of milk producers) schemas.

Experimental studies may also vary the size and placement of headlines relative to visual elements to determine the degree to which the visual is processed first. The order in which ad elements are processed will impact the order in which schema are activated, which in turn can affect the direction and outcome of subsequent information processing.

Future research may also focus on consumer characteristics affecting message incongruity processing. This area of research might help researchers and practitioners understand how different consumer audiences recognize and reconcile incongruities. For instance, does the level of visual literacy or competency influence consumers' ability to identify varying types and numbers of schema-based violations? Other characteristics such as involvement, need for cognition, tolerance for ambiguity, and cultural competency may provide fruitful areas of research in the role of visual imagery in message incongruity. Similarly, individual differences in the ability or motivation to process metaphors and visuals (Burroughs and Mick 2004) may be more closely investigated.

References

Alden, Dana L.; Ashesh Mukherjee; and Wayne D. Hoyer. 2000. "The Effects of Incongruity, Surprise, and Positive Moderators on Perceived Humor in Television Advertising." *Journal of Advertising* 29 (Summer): 1–15.

Arias-Bolzmann, Leopoldo; Goutam Chakraborty; and John C. Mowen. 2000. "Effects of Absurdity in Advertising: The Moderating Role of Product Category Attitude and the Mediating Role of Cognitive Responses." *Journal of Advertising* 29 (Spring): 35–49.

Areni, Charles S., and K. Chris Cox. 1994. "The Persuasive Effects of Evaluation, Expectancy and Relevancy Dimensions of Incongruent Visual and Verbal Information." *Advances in Consumer Research* 21: 337–342.

Bhat, Subodh; Thomas W. Leigh; and Daniel L. Wardlow. 1998. "The Effect of Consumer Prejudices on Ad Processing: Heterosexual Consumers' Responses to Homosexual Imagery in Ads." *Journal of Advertising* 27 (Winter): 9–28.

Bobrow, Daniel G., and Norman, Donal A. 1975. "Some Principles of Memory Schemata." In *Representation and Understanding: Studies in Cognitive Science,* ed. Daniel G. Bobrow and Allan M. Collins, 131–149. New York: Academic Press.

Bower, M. 2002. Advertising Educational Foundation. Personal interview, March 13.

Burroughs, James E., and David Glen Mick. 2004. "Exploring Antecedents and Consequences of Consumer Creativity in a Problem-Solving Context." *Journal of Consumer Research* 31 (September): 402–411.

Callister, Mark. 2000. "Relevancy and Expectancy: Incongruence's Effect on High- and Low-Involvement Consumers' Processing of Ad Information." Paper presented at the National Communication Association Conference, Seattle, Washington, November 9–11.

———, and Lesa A. Stern. 2002. "Inspecting the Unexpected in Print Ads." Paper presented at the National Communication Association Conference, New Orleans, Louisiana, November 21–23.

Celsi, Richard L., and Jerry C. Olson. 1988. "The Role of Involvement in Attention and Comprehension Processes." *Journal of Consumer Research* 15 (September): 210–224.

Goodstein, Ronald C. 1993. "Category-Based Applications and Extensions in Advertising: Motivating More Extensive Ad Processing," *Journal of Consumer Research* 20 (June): 87–99.

———; Marian Chapman Moore; and Deborah A. Cours. 1992. "Exploring Advertising Schema: A Multi-Method Investigation." Paper presented at the American Marketing Association Winter Educators' Conference, San Antonio, Texas, February 18–22.

Hastie, Reid. 1980. "Memory for Information Which Confirms or Contradicts a General Impression." In *Person Memory: The Cognitive Basis of Social Perception,* ed. Reid Hastie et al., 155–177. Hillsdale, NJ: Erlbaum.

———. 1981. "Schematic Principles in Human Memory." In *Social Cognition: The Ontario Symposium,* vol. 1, ed. E. Higgins et al., 39–88. Hillsdale, NJ: Erlbaum.

Heckler, Susan E., and Terry L. Childers. 1992. "The Role of Expectancy and Relevancy in Memory for Verbal and Visual Information: What Is Incongruency?" *Journal of Consumer Research* 18 (March): 475–492.

Hirschman, Elizabeth. C., and Craig. J. Thompson. 1997. "Why Media Matter: Toward a Richer Understanding of Consumers' Relationships with Advertising and Mass Media." *Journal of Advertising* 26 (Spring): 43–60.

Houston, Michael J.; Terry L. Childers; and Susan E. Heckler. 1987. "Picture-Word Consistency and the Elaborative Processing of Advertisements." *Journal of Marketing Research* 24 (November): 359–369.

Kleine, Robert E. III, and Jerome B. Kernan. 1991. "Contextual Influence on the Meanings Ascribed to Ordinary Consumption Objects." *Journal of Consumer Research* 18 (December): 311–324.

Lee, Yih Hwai. 2000. "Manipulating Ad Message Involvement Through Information Expectancy: Effects on Attitude Evaluation and Confidence." *Journal of Advertising* 29 (Summer): 29–41.

———, and Charlotte Mason. 1999. "Responses to Information Incongruency in Advertising: The Role of Expectancy, Relevancy, and Humor." *Journal of Consumer Research* 26 (September): 156–169.

Luna, David; Laura A. Peracchio; and Maria Dolores de Juan. 2003. "The Impact of Language and Congruity on Persuasion in Multicultural E-Marketing." *Journal of Consumer Psychology* 13 (1/2): 41–50.

McQuarrie, Edward F., and David Glen Mick. 1992. "On Resonance: A Critical Pluralistic Perspective." *Journal of Consumer Research* 19 (September): 180–197.

———, and ———. 1996. "Figures of Rhetoric in Advertising Language." *Journal of Consumer Research* 22 (March): 424–438.

———, and ———. 1999. "Visual Rhetoric in Advertising: Text-Interpretive, Experimental, and Reader-Response Analyses." *Journal of Consumer Research* 26 (June): 37–54.

———, and ———. 2003. "Visual and Verbal Rhetorical Figures Under Directed Processing versus Incidental Exposure to Advertising." *Journal of Consumer Research* 29 (March): 579–587.

———, and Barbara J. Phillips. 2005. "Indirect Persuasion in Advertising: How Consumers Process Metaphors Presented in Pictures and Words." *Journal of Advertising* 34 (2): 7–21.

Mick, David Glen, and Claus Buhl. 1992. "A Meaning-Based Model of Advertising Experiences." *Journal of Consumer Research* 19 (December): 317–338.

Mothersbaugh, David L.; Bruce A. Huhmann; and George R. Franke. 2002. "Combinatory and Separative Effects of Rhetorical Figures on Consumers' Effort and Focus in Ad Processing." *Journal of Consumer Research* 28 (March): 589–602.

Pezdek, Kathy; Tony Whetstone; Kirk Reynolds; Nusha Askari; and Thomas Dougherty. 1989. "Memory for Real-World Scenes: The Role of Consistency with Schema Expectations." *Journal of Experimental Psychology* 15 (4): 587–595.

Phillips, Barbara J. 1997. "Thinking into It: Consumer Interpretation of Complex Advertising Images." *Journal of Advertising* 26 (2): 77–87.

———. 2000. "The Impact of Verbal Anchoring on Consumer Response to Image Ads." *Journal of Advertising* 29 (1): 15–24.

———, and Edward F. McQuarrie. 2002. "The Development, Change, and Transformation of Rhetorical Style in Magazine Advertisements, 1954–1999." *Journal of Advertising* 31 (4): 1–13.

———, and ———. 2004. "Beyond Visual Metaphor: A New Typology of Visual Rhetoric in Advertising." *Marketing Theory* 4 (1/2): 113–136.

Pollay, R.W. 1985. "The Subsidizing Sizzle: A Descriptive History of Print Advertising 1900–1980." *Journal of Marketing* 48: 24–37.

Scott, Linda M. 1990. "Understanding Jingles and Needledrop: A Rhetorical Approach to Music in Advertising." *Journal of Consumer Research* 17 (September): 223–236.

———. 1994a. "Images in Advertising: The Need for a Theory of Visual Rhetoric." *Journal of Consumer Research* 21 (September): 252–273.

———. 1994b. "Bridge From Text to Mind: Adaptation of Reader-Response Theory." *Journal of Consumer Research* 21 (December): 461–480.

Srull, Thomas K. 1981. "Person Memory: Some Tests of Associative Storage and Retrieval Models." *Journal of Experimental Psychology: Human Learning and Memory* 7: 440–463.

————; Meryl Lichtenstein; and Myron Rothbart.1985. "Associative Storage and Retrieval Processes in Person Memory." *Journal of Experimental Psychology: Learning, Memory, and Cognition* 11 (2): 316–345.

————, and Robert S. Wyer Jr. 1989. "Person Memory and Judgment." *Psychological Review* 96 (1): 58–83.

Stafford, Edwin. R.; Beth A. Walker; and Vincent J. Blasko. 1996. "Headline-Visual Consistency in Print Advertisements: Effects on Processing and Evaluation." *Advances in Consumer Research* 23 (1): 56–62.

Stoltman, Jeffrey J. 1991. "Advertising Effectiveness: The Role of Advertising Schemas." In *Marketing Theory and Applications,* vol. 2, ed. Terry L. Childers, 317–318. Chicago: American Marketing Association.

Sujan, Mita; James R. Bettman; and Harish Sujan. 1986. "Effects of Consumer Expectations on Information Processing in Selling Encounters." *Journal of Marketing Research* 23 (November): 346–352.

Thorndyke, Perry. 1977. "Cognitive Structures in Comprehension and Memory of Narrative Discourse." *Cognitive Psychology* 9 (1): 77–110.

Zaltman, Gerald. 1997. "Rethinking Market Research: Putting People Back In." *Journal of Marketing Research* 34 (November): 424–437.

Part III

The Gift Box

Examining the Structure of Style

8

The Case for a Complexity Continuum

Tina M. Lowrey

Chapter Summary

Research on the effects of complexity in an advertising context has yielded seemingly contradictory findings. Rather than being problematic, however, the results from previous research can be reconciled by placing each set of findings along a complexity continuum based on textual factors, the advertising medium, and individual difference variables. The purpose of this chapter is to explain the interactive effects of respondent characteristics, the medium, and the message itself in determining the ultimate impact of the message, allowing for a more thorough understanding of how complexity operates.

Common wisdom for copywriters is that advertising copy should be kept relatively simple (otherwise known as KISS, or "keep it simple, stupid"). Obviously, the level of simplicity required will depend on the target market, but in general, writers strive to increase readability levels of their advertising copy by avoiding lengthy and/or complicated words, reducing sentence length, and using the active voice. However, despite the intuitive obviousness of this dictum, it is worth asking whether it yields the desired results. In other words, does writing simple copy always enhance either the memory for or persuasiveness of advertising relative to more complex copy?

Several recent articles have provided evidence that the effects of complexity are actually more complicated than previously thought. In many instances, research has shown that advertising written at higher levels of complexity are better recalled and liked better than are ads written at lower levels of complexity (Chamblee et al. 1993; Macklin, Bruvold, and Shea 1985; but see also Meeds and Bradley 2007).

Thus, "keep it simple, stupid" may not always be the best policy for copywriters. There are a variety of factors that can moderate the effects of complexity. When should copy be kept as simple as possible and when is it advisable to write at a more complex level? To quote an anonymous reviewer, "Studying message complexity has turned out to be, well, complex."

Unfortunately, past research on complexity effects in an advertising context has yielded seemingly contradictory findings in attempting to answer these questions. Some research has shown positive effects of complexity, but others have shown negative effects of complexity. As just one example, Lowrey (1998) showed that complexity can enhance attitudes, but Chebat et al. (2003) found the opposite.

The purpose of this chapter is to provide a framework that can reconcile these conflicting findings. This framework is based on a complexity continuum that takes into consideration a variety of factors, including the reading level and overall length of the copy, the advertising medium, and individual differences of respondents. This continuum ranges from simpler passages of text, through moderate passages, to more complex passages. The complexity continuum is used to examine recent research findings on the effects of complexity on memory and persuasion in an advertising context. As will be shown presently, complexity effects show a clear, nonlinear pattern. Specifically, very high levels of complexity are detrimental to both memory and persuasion measures, but at lower levels of complexity, very simple text can also be detrimental. At moderate levels of complexity, the complexity of the text interacts with a variety of extratextual factors to determine memory for and attitudes toward advertising.

In this chapter I argue that discussing the effects of complexity in terms of textual factors alone overlooks what really goes on when individuals encounter advertising messages. Complexity effects actually occur within the individual. For example, an individual encounters text that is either simple or not for the individual to process. Although the text is a key determinant of how easy the processing will be, characteristics of the individual (e.g., cognitive processing abilities and/or motivation) and the situation (e.g., time pressure due to the advertising medium) contribute as well. Thus, the same exact text presented to two different individuals in two different situations may yield very different results.

The remainder of the chapter is structured as follows. First, I discuss textual factors that contribute to message complexity, including word difficulty, syntax, and message length. These factors dictate the initial placement of messages on the complexity continuum. I then briefly review other factors that may inhibit or enhance message processing, including the advertising medium and individual difference variables. These factors can cause shifts along the complexity continuum in either direction. Next, I discuss five separate complexity articles, and place each along the complexity continuum in an effort to understand the "big picture" of all of the results combined. I conclude the chapter with a summary and directions for future research in this area.

Contributing Factors to Message Complexity

Both textual factors and "extratextual" factors can impact how difficult a message is to process. The basic textual factors addressed here include word difficulty, syntax (sentence structure), and the overall length of the message. Extratextual factors include the advertising medium (e.g., print versus broadcast) and those individual difference variables most likely to impact motivation and ability to process information, including age, education level, and motivational state.

Textual Factors

There are several factors that contribute to the complexity of any passage of text, but the two major contributors are vocabulary and syntax. Both the specific words selected and how the words are strung together into sentences can impact message complexity, and thus impact the initial placement of texts along the complexity continuum. Indeed, these two factors are the primary contributors to common measures of text complexity. In addition, although the impact of overall text length has not been thoroughly addressed in previous research, this factor will be included in an effort to be as theoretically inclusive as possible in formulating the complexity continuum.

The words used in a passage of text may be short, single-syllable words that first-graders can easily understand (e.g., cat) or multisyllabic, obscure terms that only college graduates with a sophisticated vocabulary would use (e.g., tautological). In addition, words may be those that use everyday language or those that are technical terms specific to a particular industry. With respect to syntax, or how these words are strung together into sentences, sentences can range from very simple (e.g., one clause written in the active voice with no negation) to very complex (e.g., several clauses written in the passive voice with negation). For example, "Most doctors recommend caffeine-free beverages for their sleep-deprived patients" is easier to process than "For their sleep-deprived patients, beverages with no caffeine are recommended by most doctors." How syntactic complexity is assessed, however, differs across readability measures.

Assessing Text Complexity

Word difficulty and syntactic complexity are typically combined when assessing the reading level of any given passage of text. For example, the two most commonly used measures of readability, the Flesch Reading Ease formula (Flesch 1951) and the Gunning Fog index (Gunning 1968), combine assessments of word difficulty and sentence difficulty. The Flesch formula computes the average number of syllables per 100 words (to assess word difficulty) and the average number of words per sentence (to assess sentence difficulty). These two measures are then combined to provide a single index of overall complexity (ranging from 0 to 100, with higher numbers indicating greater readability). The Fog index counts the number of words

Figure 8.1   **Initial Placement on the Complexity Continuum**

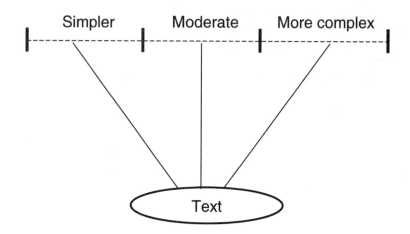

Note: Based on Flesch formula, Fog index, or assessment of word difficulty, syntactic complexity, and/or copy length.

and the number of sentences to calculate average sentence length (based on the assumption that longer sentences are more difficult to process). In addition, words with three or more syllables are counted to assess word difficulty. A Fog score is indexed to grade in school. That is, an index of 5 indicates fifth-grade material, whereas an index of 17 would indicate material suitable for a college graduate.

Other measures have been developed in response to criticisms of these measures, but both the Flesch formula and the Fog index correlate highly with these newer measures and are generally simpler to administer. Thus, both Flesch and Fog are commonly used to assess the readability of print materials (Bogert 1985; Metoyer-Duran 1993; Olson 1984) and the "listenability" of text presented in broadcast contexts (Allen 1952; Denbow 1975; Fang 1966–1967; Lowrey 2006a).

Overall Text Length

For the purposes of this chapter, the two textual factors that contribute to the Flesch and Fog indices (word difficulty and syntactic complexity) will be the primary determinants of where specific passages of text should be initially placed along the complexity continuum (see Figure 8.1).

However, another textual factor that may contribute to complexity is overall length of the text, although I have found no published research that has addressed this issue. On the one hand, neither the Flesch nor Fog indices include overall length of a passage of text, implying that overall length is not a contributor to complexity. On the other hand, Denbow (1975) pointed out the need to investigate longer passages of text (in a nonmarketing context), suggesting that longer passages might make the text more complex. Thus, in order to be as thorough as possible, the overall lengths of the various stimuli used will be presented in addition to word difficulty and syntactic complexity.

Extratextual Factors

In addition to factors inherent to the message itself, there are factors external to the message that can impact message complexity. Rather than contributing directly to complexity, however, it is more appropriate to view these factors as those that increase or decrease the effects of complexity, thus causing shifts along the complexity continuum. Two of the most important factors in an advertising context are the medium in which the message appears and individual difference variables in information processing. Although there are a variety of advertising media, the most basic dichotomy is print versus broadcast, which differ in obvious ways. Broadcast media are externally paced (i.e., the viewer/listener does not control the pace of message delivery), whereas most print media are self-paced (with the exception of some transit advertising). Individual difference variables related to information processing include age, education level, and motivational state, all of which have implications for message processing.

Advertising Medium

Some media may contribute to processing constraints more than others, making text more difficult to process. For example, for externally paced media such as radio and television, complexity effects may be magnified, causing shifts to the more complex end of the complexity continuum (see Figure 8.2). This is due to the fleeting nature and speed of presentation of the message that is out of the perceiver's control. Conversely, in self-paced media such as magazines and newspapers, the fact that an individual can read the message slowly and repeatedly should minimize the effects of complexity, causing shifts to the simpler end of the complexity continuum. It is well documented that consumers have limited abilities when it comes to processing advertising information, and that ads presented via broadcast media are generally more difficult to process than ads presented via print media (Bettman 1979; Webb 1979).

Individual Difference Variables

Although many variables have the potential to impact the effects of complexity, age, education level, and motivational state seem the most important factors to consider. These factors have been shown to affect the ability or motivation to process information in a variety of contexts.

164

Figure 8.2　**How Extratextual Factors Shift Placement on the Complexity Continuum**

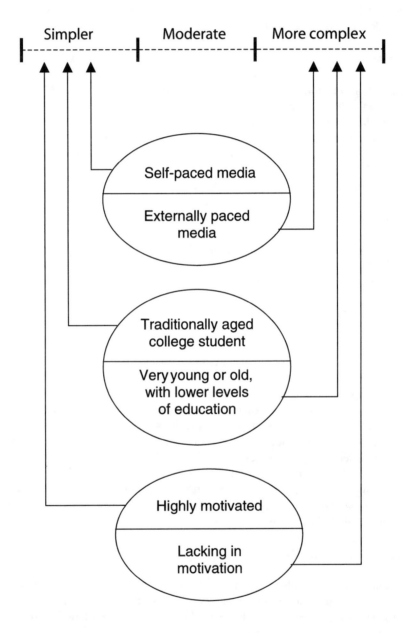

Age. Many researchers have documented how aging affects the processing of information, both in general (Cohen and Faulkner 1983; Denney 1982; Hartley and Anderson 1983; Salthouse 1985; Wright 1981) and in a consumer context (Cole and Gaeth 1990; French and Crask 1977; John and Cole 1986; Phillips and Sternthal 1977; Stephens 1981). Most children have processing abilities lower than those of most adults, regardless of presentation format. However, older adults have a more difficult time processing information than do younger adults in any presentation format, and this is particularly true for broadcast media (Johnson and Cobb-Walgren 1994; Stephens 1981).

Education Level. This factor, although important, presents operational problems. First, the Fog index is linked directly to educational level (recall that a Fog index of 5 indicates material suitable for fifth-graders and a Fog index of 17 indicates material suitable for college graduates). Thus, it becomes somewhat circular to argue that education level is an individual difference variable that can inhibit or enhance message processing. Add to this issue the fact that, at least for children, education level is directly tied to age, and the picture becomes murkier still. However, in comparing adults of the same age, education level does need to be taken into account. Therefore, it is an essential factor to consider in any development of a framework such as the complexity continuum, especially for the purposes of comparing across articles that have yielded seemingly contradictory results.

Motivation. Numerous studies have shown that greater motivation leads to greater elaboration. This is true whether the motivation is induced by the situation (Houston and Rothschild 1978), is induced by the product category in a consumer context (Laurent and Kapferer 1985; Zaichkowsky 1985), or is a trait characteristic of the individual, such as need for cognition (Cacioppo and Petty 1982). An example of situational motivation is if an individual happened to be in the market for the product being advertised in the experimental stimuli (e.g., someone preparing to buy a new car). An example of involvement with the product category is an individual who is "chronically" interested in the product (e.g., car enthusiasts). An example of a trait characteristic related to motivation to process information is need for cognition, a trait that indicates the degree to which an individual enjoys activities that require cognitive effort (e.g., crossword puzzles). Because those who are more motivated tend to elaborate more fully on messages to which they are exposed than those who are less motivated, they tend to encounter fewer processing difficulties despite potential processing constraints such as message complexity (Petty and Cacioppo 1986).

The Interaction Between Textual Factors and Extratextual Factors

Extratextual factors such as the advertising medium and individual difference variables, rather than being primary contributors to the complexity continuum, serve as "shifters" along the complexity continuum. That is, whereas textual factors cause initial placement along the complexity continuum, the other two factors (medium and individual differences) can shift the text in either direction (again, see Figure 8.2). For example, when exposed to a complex TV commercial, processing difficulties might arise, shifting the complexity of the message to the more complex end of the complexity continuum. However, if one is highly motivated to process, the effects of complexity may be less severe, thus shifting the complexity of the message to the simpler end of the complexity continuum.

It should be noted that the extratextual factors basically deal with ability and motivation to process messages. Many theories have outlined the potential impact of ability and motivational factors on information processing (Craik and Lockhart 1972; Petty and Cacioppo 1986). Although there are differences between Craik and Lockhart's levels of processing framework and Petty and Cacioppo's Elaboration Likelihood Model, they agree that ability and motivation to process are both critical factors in message processing.

To summarize, whether an ad appears in print or via broadcast has implications for processing capabilities. Similarly, age can impact an individual's ability to process (with younger children and older adults having lower levels of ability, in general). Higher education levels tend to increase processing abilities. Motivation to process can be situational or inherent in an individual (whether it stems from involvement with a particular product category or is a trait characteristic). Regardless of the source of the motivation, high levels of motivation enhance message processing and low levels hinder processing. Ability and motivation factors can also interact with one another.

Summary of Contributing Factors to the Complexity Continuum

Seven factors that influence complexity have been identified. Two textual factors (word difficulty and syntax) are viewed as primary contributors to complexity, and cause initial placement of a given message on the complexity continuum. In addition, overall text length may contribute to complexity and thus play a role in initial placement on the continuum. Four extratextual factors (the advertising medium, age, education level, and motivation) can lessen or magnify the effects of complexity, causing shifts along the complexity continuum in either direction.

In the following section, I review five recent articles that deal with the effects of complexity on memory for and attitudes toward advertising. At first glance, these articles yield conflicting findings. However, as I will show, these seemingly conflicting findings can be reconciled when viewed in the context of the complexity continuum.

Recent Advertising Complexity Research

For each article to be reviewed, an overview of the study design will be presented first, followed by the results. For initial placement along the complexity continuum based on textual factors, complex stimuli reading levels (including word difficulty and syntactic complexity) and overall copy length will be assessed. In addition, the advertising medium, average age and education level of the participants, and motivation (when measured) will be reviewed to determine how each set of studies might shift along the complexity continuum based on extratextual factors. The major findings will also be contrasted and compared (for an overview of each article, see Table 8.1).

Article One: Lowrey (1998)

These three experiments were among the first to look at how complexity impacts memory for and the persuasiveness of print and TV advertising. In Experiment 1, participants from a general population sample were exposed to a TV commercial written at a moderate level of complexity. The copy consisted of five sentences of approximately forty-eight words, written at moderate Flesch levels. The simple version was written in the active voice and contained no negations. The complex version was written in the passive voice and contained negations. This manipulation of complexity was very subtle, yet the two versions did vary in terms of their readability scores. In Experiments 2 and 3, college students were exposed to the same copy, but in a magazine context. In Experiment 1, it was not possible to measure motivation, but in Experiments 2 and 3, motivation was measured. Complexity reduced memory measures for both TV and print, and led to less favorable attitudes in a print context for those low in motivation to process. However, this was not true for those who were highly motivated to process. In fact, complexity actually enhanced the attitudes of high involvement participants.

For initial placement of the copy, given that both versions were written at moderate Flesch levels, the textual factors place it in the middle of the complexity continuum (see Figure 8.3).

For extratextual factors, the first experiment was conducted in a TV context (field study), with participants ranging in age from eighteen to sixty-five and education level averaging some high school. Motivation was not measured. Experiments 2 and 3 were conducted in a print context (lab study) with participants who were traditionally aged college students (eighteen to twenty-five). Motivation was measured. The medium causes a shift toward the simpler end of the complexity continuum for print, and toward the more complex end of the complexity continuum for TV. Keep in mind that participants in Experiments 2 and 3 were college students exposed to moderate level copy in the two print experiments, some of whom were highly motivated to process (which causes a shift to the simpler end of the complexity continuum), but participants in Experiment 1 came from a general population sample (which causes a shift to the more complex end of the complexity continuum, due to the lower education levels and the higher average age of participants—see Figure 8.3).

Table 8.1

Textual and Extratextual Factors Analyzed in Each Article

Article	Text Complexity	Medium	Age	Education
Bradley and Meeds (2002)	Simpler (1 sentence of 5 words with 1 [or 2] transformations)	Print	18–25	High
Chebat et al. (2003)	More complex (2–7 sentences of 66 words at Fog college level)	Print	18–65	Moderate
Lowrey (1998)				
Experiment 1	Moderate (5 sentences of 48 words at moderate Flesch levels)	TV	18–65	Moderate
Experiments 2 and 3	Moderate (5 sentences of 48 words at moderate Flesch levels)	Print	18–25	High
Lowrey (2006a)				
Study 1	Moderate (5 sentences at moderate Flesch levels)	TV	18–65	Moderate
Experiment 2	Moderate (5 sentences at moderate Flesch levels)	Print	18–25	High
Lowrey (2006b)	More complex (600–900 words at Fog college level)	Print	18–25	High

Figure 8.3   **Initial Placement of Complex Texts in Past Research with Resulting Shift Due to Extratextual Factors**

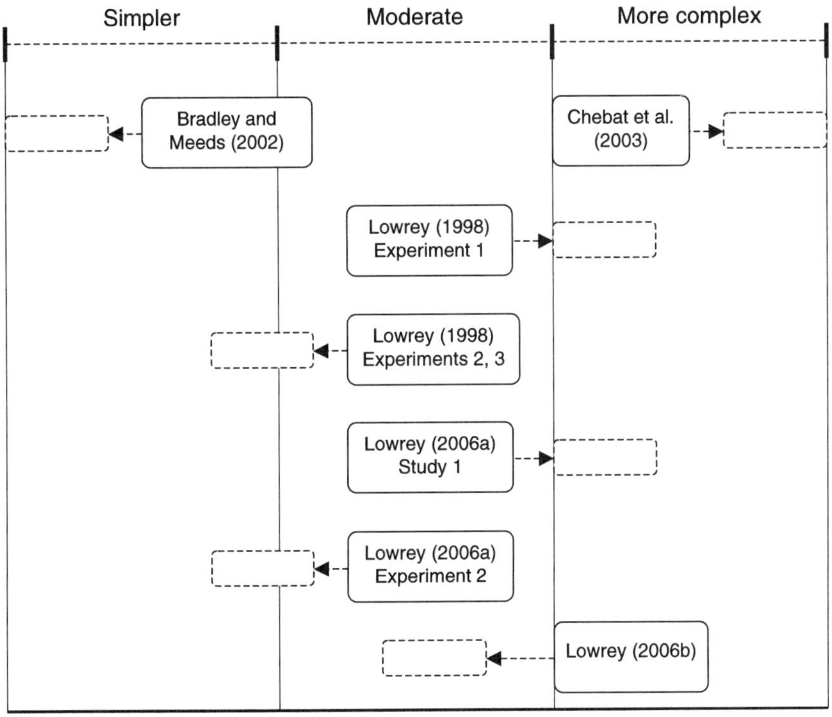

Article Two: Bradley and Meeds (2002)

In this experiment college students read a slogan (rather than a block of ad copy) in a print context. All slogans were one sentence consisting of five words. Complexity was manipulated by making either one or two transformations to a kernel sentence (the simplest utterance). For example, the kernel sentence "Comtech accurately reproduces your thoughts," which is written in the active voice, was changed by one transformation to the passive voice, "Your thoughts are accurately reproduced by Comtech." As with Lowrey (1998), this was a subtle, yet successful manipulation of complexity. Motivation was measured. Complexity did not affect comprehension (with the exception of the recognition measure, which was lower for all participants exposed to complex slogans). However, complexity did enhance recall and attitudes toward the ad. The findings did not differ as a function of the motivation level of the participants.

For initial placement, this type of text is at the simpler end of the complexity continuum (although reading level cannot be computed for single sentences—see

Figure 8.3). For extratextual factors, the medium was print and participants were traditionally aged college students, both of which cause shifts to the simpler end of the continuum as well. Bradley and Meeds found that the effects of syntactic complexity on a variety of measures occurred regardless of motivation level.

Whereas Bradley and Meeds' results might seem, at first glance, to directly contradict the findings in Lowrey (1998), the stimuli used in the two studies were quite different. Not only is the text already at the simpler end of the complexity continuum, the combination of a print medium with college students as participants should cause an even further shift toward the simplest end of the complexity continuum (see Figure 8.3). That is, the combination of high cognitive ability with relatively easy-to-process stimuli presented in a self-paced medium made for a very simple task, resulting in no effects based on motivation to process.

Article Three: Chebat et al. (2003)

In this study, participants from a general population sample were exposed to print advertising that differed in terms of Fog readability levels. The ad copy ranged from two to seven sentences in length (with a constant word count of sixty-six—one contributor to complexity in the Fog index is sentence length), with the complex version written at college level. Thus, the stimuli differed both from Bradley and Meeds' (in terms of word count and sentence length, reading level differences were undetermined) and from Lowrey's (primarily in terms of reading level—word count and sentence length were similar). Motivation was measured. Complexity had a strong negative impact on memory and persuasion measures, and these effects occurred regardless of motivation level.

Initial placement based on textual factors is at the more complex end of the complexity continuum (see Figure 8.3). For extratextual factors, although the medium was print, the use of older, less educated participants would cause a further shift to the more complex end of the continuum.

The strong negative impact of complexity on both memory and persuasion measures, regardless of level of motivation, can be explained with the complexity continuum. Whereas Bradley and Meeds (2002) found no complexity differences as a function of motivation, and Lowrey (1998) found complexity differences primarily for those low in involvement, Chebat et al. (2003) found that complexity impaired both memory and persuasion *regardless* of level of motivation. The print medium context was used in all three articles. However, in Chebat et al. participants were not traditionally aged college students, as was the case in both Bradley and Meeds and in Experiments 2 and 3 of Lowrey. Although in Chebat et al., the text is already on the more complex end of the complexity continuum, the combination of lower education level and higher age causes an even further shift toward the most complex end of the complexity continuum, making already more difficult, college material potentially even more difficult for their participants (see Figure 8.3). That is, the combination of lower cognitive ability with relatively difficult stimuli made for a very difficult task, resulting in complexity-induced processing impairment, regardless of level of motivation.

Article Four: Lowrey (2006a)

This set of studies extended my previous research in a TV context. In Study 1, participants from a general population sample were exposed to a variety of TV commercials, with scripts averaging five sentences in length and complex scripts written at moderate Flesch levels. This secondary data set (which did not include a measure of motivation) was provided by a research firm. In Experiment 2, college students were exposed to two of the scripts in a print context. Specifically, two scripts for one product that varied sufficiently in terms of the Flesch formula were selected from the sample of scripts used in the first study (the two scripts had Flesch scores of "easy" versus "more difficult"). Motivation was measured. As with Lowrey (1998), complexity had negative effects on memory measures for both TV and print. However, these relations were again moderated by level of motivation in Experiment 2. For those who were highly motivated to process, complexity actually enhanced memory measures.

For initial placement based on textual factors alone, the complex scripts belong in the middle of the complexity continuum (see Figure 8.3). For extratextual factors, in the first study, the broadcast context shifts the scripts to the more complex end of the complexity continuum. In addition, in the first study, the use of older, less educated participants also requires a further shift to the more complex end of the complexity continuum. This is not the case with the second experiment, in which college students were participants. Ability to process was also enhanced in the second experiment by using a print medium. In addition, motivation to process caused complexity effects to weaken, as would be expected. All of these extratextual factors cause shifts to the simpler end of the complexity continuum (see Figure 8.3).

Negative effects of complexity on memory were found in both studies, but these relations were moderated by motivation in the second experiment. As with Lowrey (1998), those who had enhanced processing capabilities and higher motivation to process were positively impacted by complexity, whereas those with lower motivation were negatively affected. In addition, those who had decreased processing capabilities due to the broadcast medium, higher age, and lower education, showed negative effects of complexity similar to those obtained in the first experiment of Lowrey (1998) and by Chebat et al. (2003).

Article Five: Lowrey (2006b)

The final article to be reviewed involves an experiment conducted in a direct marketing context in order to investigate the contribution of overall text length to the complexity continuum. College students were exposed to one of four versions of a direct mail piece that systematically varied length and complexity (i.e., short/ moderate complexity, short/complex, long/moderate complexity, long/complex). Short versions had 600–650 words and were just over one page in length, whereas long versions had 850–900 words and were just over two pages long. Moderately complex versions of the stimuli had high school-level Fog indices, whereas complex versions had college-level Fog indices. Motivation was measured. There was no effect of overall text length on intentions to order the product. Complexity had a positive main effect on order intentions, but this effect was qualified by an interaction with motivation. Specifically, the positive effect of complexity on order intentions held only for those who were highly motivated.

Initial placement based on textual factors is at the more complex end of the complexity continuum (see Figure 8.3). For extratextual factors, the medium was print and participants were traditionally aged college students, some of whom were highly motivated to process. All of the extratextual factors cause shifts from the more complex end to the middle of the continuum (see Figure 8.3). The results replicate both Lowrey (1998, 2006a), suggesting that for those with high cognitive ability and motivation to process, moderate complexity can enhance memory for and the persuasiveness of advertising. The levels of complexity used in this experiment are consistent with previous work in this area, with the complex versions similar to material used in Chebat et al. (2003). It was initially difficult to decide whether the length of the stimuli should cause an initial placement further toward the most complex end of the complexity continuum, as the number of words far exceeded those found in previous stimuli. However, the results indicate that length was not an issue (i.e., there was no main effect for length in this experiment). The nature of the participants (college students, some of whom were motivated to process) may have negated the effects of length. Moreover, although length did not have an effect in this particular experiment, it is possible that the stimuli did not differ sufficiently on this construct to tease out any impact. Additional research is needed to fully address this issue.

Integration of the Results from the Five Articles Reviewed

By comparing and contrasting across the findings from the five articles reviewed in this chapter, one can see a fairly strong pattern emerging (see Figure 8.3). At simpler levels, complexity enhances memory and persuasion. At more complex levels, complexity impairs these processes. It is in the moderate, middle portion of the complexity continuum where extratextual factors interact with complexity to affect memory and persuasion.

Bradley and Meeds (2002) is an example of research conducted at simpler levels of the complexity continuum, and they found that complexity enhanced a variety of measures in an experiment that exposed college students to fairly simple copy (one-sentence slogans) in a print context. Results did not differ as a result of motivation to process. Given the nature of their stimuli, the medium, and their participants (i.e., high cognitive ability), it appears that the overall task was relatively simple and did not require high degrees of motivation to perform.

Chebat et al. (2003) is an example of research conducted at more complex levels of the complexity continuum, and they found strong negative effects of complexity in a study that exposed participants from a general population sample to fairly complex copy (written at college level) in a print context. Again, however, results did not differ as a result of motivation to process. Given the nature of their stimuli and their participants (i.e., lower cognitive abilities), it appears the overall task was quite difficult to perform, despite the medium, resulting in impaired processing regardless of motivation level.

It is only in the set of experiments and studies reported in Lowrey (1998, 2006a, 2006b) that motivation interacts with complexity, and then only in the print context with college students. Stimuli were typically of moderate complexity (with the exception of those used in 2006b). Still, for participants with lower cognitive abilities exposed to the stimuli in TV contexts, complexity impaired processing. Only for college students exposed to print stimuli did motivation interact with complexity. Specifically, for those highly motivated to process, complexity did not have negative effects on processing. On the contrary, complexity actually enhanced memory for and attitudes toward the various stimuli.

Summary

Once one has taken into consideration inherent textual factors, the advertising medium, and individual difference variables, one can clearly see that the various sets of results obtained in past research are complementary to one another and validate the complexity continuum as a logical framework for positioning advertising complexity research. The important issue is the recognition that complexity effects *occur in the individual.* Yet we often overlook this and focus solely on the manipulated complexity of a given text. Whereas this is often useful for determining specific effects within an experiment, it ignores how complexity operates in natural settings. Consequently, the overall conclusions drawn from these various articles, if taken in isolation, may be misleading if one does not take into account the fact that extratextual factors influence movement along the complexity continuum in either direction from the objectively determined initial placement. This is particularly important given that the effects of complexity are not linear. Rather, the optimal range appears to be at moderate levels.

Thus, the complexity continuum makes two equally important and related contributions to the study of complexity in an advertising context. First, it is imperative that extratextual factors are taken into account when assessing the effects of complexity based on textual factors. That is, different media and different participant types can lead to very different results even when the same textual stimuli are used. Indeed, the shifted placements shown in Figure 8.3 for Lowrey (1998, 2006a) show direct evidence of this phenomenon. Second, both textual and extratextual factors interact with one other in complicated ways. Although researchers in this area have begun to investigate some of these interactions, much remains to be done.

Discussion

This chapter has provided several insights to those interested in complexity effects in an advertising context. First, previous research on the effects of complexity in an advertising context has focused on very short messages. The exception is the fifth article reported here, which is the first experiment to investigate whether length has any impact on complexity in general (with no support for such a contention). Overall length of the message does not seem to be a contributing factor for placement along the complexity continuum (at least for college students), although additional research may be warranted. It is possible that the manipulation of length in Lowrey (2006b) was insufficient to capture the potential impact of overall text length on complexity. Second, although both complexity and involvement seem to exert main effects on advertising persuasiveness in many of the articles covered here, it is the interaction between the two that is most interesting. Thus, higher complexity for those highly involved with the message actually enhances attitudes (within a moderate range of complexity, that is).

Obviously, it is not advisable to conclude from this chapter that specific complexity levels used in the various stimuli reported would be applicable to more generalized audiences. Indeed, that is one of the very premises of the complexity continuum—that individual difference variables such as age, education level, and motivation to process can shift complexity effects in either direction, as can the advertising medium. Thus, many of these stimuli might be too difficult for the general public to comfortably process. Further research is required to determine optimal levels for specific types of audiences, both in terms of medium and in terms of individual differences.

It should be noted here that the complexity continuum is entirely consistent with resource matching theory (Anand and Sternthal 1990). That is, when resources available to process a message match the resources required to process the message, persuasion will be most successful (see also McQuarrie and Mick 1996; Peracchio and Meyers-Levy 1997). Thus, textual factors (and perhaps also the medium) could be viewed as major contributors to the resources required, whereas individual difference variables could be viewed as contributors to the resources available.

Given that motivation is one factor that clearly moderates the effects of complexity, more research should be conducted to determine exactly how and when it exerts its effects, along with other factors that may impact such effects. Chebat et al.'s (2003) study of ability factors is a good example of an area that should be investigated more thoroughly. The effect of the advertising medium is another area ripe for future exploration. Despite findings in a broadcast context (Lowrey 1998, 2006a), much more remains to be done in order to understand the difference between externally paced and self-paced media. In addition, beyond the dichotomy of traditional broadcast and print media lies Internet advertising, which has the potential for a more complicated set of effects on processing. The Internet allows for a mixture of self-paced information search within a site, combined with externally paced pop-up advertising at intermittent intervals. In addition, Liu and Shrum (2003) suggest that the degree of interactivity, which can be viewed as a potential contributor to complexity, may also play a role. Thus, theorizing about how this medium's special characteristics may impact the processing of text could be quite complex.

Another important factor to be considered in future research is the impact of additional textual factors that may contribute to or magnify the effects of complexity. Two of the articles reviewed in this chapter focused solely on syntactic complexity (Bradley and Meeds 2002; Lowrey 1998), whereas the other three investigated readability in a more general manner (Chebat et al. 2003 and Lowrey 2006b with the Fog index; Lowrey 2006a with the Flesch formula). The latter three articles go beyond syntactic complexity to include word difficulty in assessing overall complexity. Additional research might investigate how complexity is affected by other textual factors, such as puns and wordplay, the use of simile and metaphor, and other linguistic variables that might impact initial placements of text on the complexity continuum and/or cause shifts along the continuum in either direction.

In addition to verbal text elements, future research should take into consideration the impact of visual elements of the text. A number of studies have investigated the effects of font selection on advertising effectiveness (Doyle and Bottomley 2006; Henderson and Cote 1998; Henderson, Giese, and Cote 2004; McCarthy and Mothersbaugh 2002), but not in the context of contributing to (or alleviating) the overall complexity of a given passage of text. For example, to what extent could a simpler font style assist in the processing of more complicated messages? To my knowledge, this question has not yet been addressed.

The study of additional visual elements that are not textual is another area to be investigated. Copy layout decisions may contribute to textual processing difficulties (this obviously has to do with the placement of text, but is not strictly textual in nature). Finally, future research should address how the verbal/textual elements of an advertisement might interact with completely nontextual, visual elements (such as illustrations or photographs). Phillips and McQuarrie (2004, 116) have posited a typology of visual complexity that would be a useful starting point for the complicated task of investigating how verbal complexity and visual complexity interact with one another.

It is clear that much more needs to be done to address these issues. Research that provides additional insights into how other textual factors contribute to complexity is needed. So too are experimental designs that include potential extratextual moderators of the impact of complexity on advertising persuasiveness. It is hoped that this chapter will be a starting point for researchers to continue to investigate how complexity exerts its effects along the complexity continuum.

References

Allen, William. 1952. "Readability of Instructional Film Commentary." *Journal of Applied Psychology* 36 (June): 164–168.

Anand, Punam, and Brian Sternthal. 1990. "Ease of Message Processing as a Moderator of Repetition Effects in Advertising." *Journal of Marketing Research* 27 (August): 345–353.

Bettman, James R. 1979. *An Information Processing Theory of Consumer Choice.* Reading, MA: Addison-Wesley.

Bogert, Judith. 1985. "In Defense of the Fog Index." *Bulletin* 48 (June): 9–11.

Bradley, Samuel D., and Robert Meeds. 2002. "Surface-structure Transformations and Advertising Slogans: The Case for Moderate Syntactic Complexity." *Psychology & Marketing* 19 (July–August): 595–619.

Cacioppo, John T., and Richard E. Petty. 1982. "The Need for Cognition." *Journal of Personality and Social Psychology* 42 (January): 116–131.

Chamblee, Robert; Robert Gilmore; Gloria Thomas; and Gary Soldow. 1993. "When Copy Complexity Can Help Ad Readership." *Journal of Advertising* 33 (May–June): 23–28.

Chebat, Jean-Charles; Claire Gelinas-Chebat; Sabrina Hombourger; and Arch G. Woodside. 2003. "Testing Consumers' Motivation and Linguistic Ability as Moderators of Advertising Readability." *Psychology & Marketing* 20 (July): 599–624.

Cohen, Gillian, and Dorothy Faulkner. 1983. "Age Differences in Performance on Two Information Processing Tasks: Strategy Selection and Processing Efficiency." *Journal of Gerontology* 38 (4): 447–454.

Cole, Catherine A., and Gary J. Gaeth. 1990. "Cognitive and Age-related Differences in the Ability to Use Nutritional Information in a Complex Environment." *Journal of Marketing Research* 27 (2): 175–184.

Craik, Fergus I.M., and Robert S. Lockhart. 1972. "Levels of Processing: A Framework for Memory Research." *Journal of Verbal Learning and Verbal Behavior* 11: 671–684.

Denbow, Carl J. 1975. "Listenability and Readability: An Experimental Investigation." *Journalism Quarterly* 52 (2): 285–290.

Denney, Nancy Wadsworth. 1982. "Aging and Cognitive Changes." In *Handbook of Developmental Psychology,* ed. Benjamin B. Wolman, 807–827. Englewood Cliffs, NJ: Prentice Hall.

Doyle, John R., and Paul A. Bottomley. 2006. "Dressed for the Occasion: Font-Product Congruity in the Perception of Logotype." *Journal of Consumer Psychology* 16 (2): 112–123.

Fang, Irving E. 1966–1967. "The 'Easy Listening Formula.'" *Journal of Broadcasting* 11 (Winter): 63–68.

Flesch, Rudolph. 1951. *How to Test Readability.* New York: Harper and Brothers.

French, Warren A., and Melvin R. Crask. 1977. "The Credibility of Media Advertising for the Elderly." In *Contemporary Marketing Thought,* ed. Barnett A. Greenberg and Danny N. Bellinger, 74–77. Chicago: American Marketing Association.

Gunning, Robert. 1968. *The Technique of Clear Writing.* New York: McGraw-Hill.

Hartley, Alan A., and Joan Wilson Anderson. 1983. "Task Complexity and Problem-solving Performance in Younger and Older Adults." *Journal of Gerontology* 38 (1): 72–77.

Henderson, Pamela W., and Joseph A. Cote. 1998. "Guidelines for Selecting or Modifying Logos." *Journal of Marketing* 62 (April): 14–30.

———, Joan L. Giese; and Joseph A. Cote. 2004. "Impression Management Using Typeface Design." *Journal of Marketing* 68 (October): 60–72.

Houston, Michael J., and Michael L. Rothschild. 1978. "Conceptual and Methodological Perspectives on Involvement." In *1978 Educators' Proceedings,* ed. S. Jain, 184–187. Chicago: American Marketing Association.

John, Deborah Roedder, and Catherine A. Cole. 1986. "Age Differences in Information Processing: Understanding Deficits in Young and Elderly Consumers." *Journal of Consumer Research* 13 (3): 297–315.

Johnson, Rose L., and Cathy J. Cobb-Walgren. 1994. "Aging and the Problem of Television Clutter." *Journal of Advertising Research* 34 (4): 54–62.

Laurent, Gilles, and Jean-Noel Kapferer. 1985. "Measuring Consumer Involvement Profiles." *Journal of Marketing Research* 22 (1): 41–53.

Liu, Yuping, and L.J. Shrum. 2003. "What Is Interactivity and Is It Always Such a Good Thing? Implications of Definition, Person, and Situation for the Influence of Interactivity on Advertising Effectiveness." *Journal of Advertising* 31 (4): 53–64.

Lowrey, Tina M. 1998. "The Effects of Syntactic Complexity on Advertising Persuasiveness." *Journal of Consumer Psychology* 7 (2): 187–206.

———. 2006a. "The Relation Between Script Complexity and Commercial Memorability." *Journal of Advertising* 35 (Fall): 7–15.

———. 2006b. "Moderate Copy Complexity Enhances the Persuasiveness of Direct Mail." Unpublished manuscript, University of Texas at San Antonio.

Macklin, M. Carole; Norman T. Bruvold; and Caroly Lynn Shea. 1985. "Is It Always as Simple as 'Keep It Simple!'?" *Journal of Advertising* 14 (4): 28–35.

McCarthy, Michael S., and David L. Mothersbaugh. 2002. "Effects of Typographic Factors in Advertising-Based Persuasion: A General Model and Initial Empirical Tests." *Psychology & Marketing* 19 (7–8): 663–691.

McQuarrie, Edward F., and David Glen Mick. 1996. "Figures of Rhetoric in Advertising Language." *Journal of Consumer Research* 22 (March): 424–438.

Meeds, Robert, and Samuel D. Bradley. 2007. "The Role of the Sentence and Its Importance in Marketing Communications." In *Psycholinguistic Phenomena in Marketing Communications,* ed. Tina M. Lowrey, 103–118. Mahwah, NJ: Erlbaum.

Metoyer-Duran, Cheryl. 1993. "The Readability of Published, Accepted, and Rejected Papers Appearing in *College & Research Libraries." College & Research Libraries* November: 517–526.

Olson, Arthur V. 1984. *Readability Formulas—Fact or Fiction.* Washington, DC: U.S. Department of Education.

Peracchio, Laura A., and Joan Meyers-Levy. 1997. "Evaluating Persuasion-Enhancing Techniques from a Resource-Matching Perspective." *Journal of Consumer Research* 24 (September): 178–191.

Petty, Richard E., and John T. Cacioppo. 1986. *Communication and Persuasion: Central and Peripheral Routes to Attitude Change.* New York: Springer-Verlag.

Phillips, Barbara J., and Edward F. McQuarrie. 2004. "Beyond Visual Metaphor: A New Typology of Visual Rhetoric in Advertising." *Marketing Theory* 4 (1/2): 113–136.

Phillips, Lynn W., and Brian Sternthal. 1977. "Age Differences in Information Processing: A Perspective on the Aged Consumer." *Journal of Marketing Research* 14 (4): 444–447.

Salthouse, Timothy A. 1985. *A Theory of Cognitive Aging.* Amsterdam: North-Holland.

Stephens, Nancy. 1981. "Media Usage and Media Attitude Change with Age and with Time." *Journal of Advertising* 10 (1): 38–47.

Webb, Peter H. 1979. "Consumer Initial Processing in a Difficult Media Environment." *Journal of Consumer Research* 6 (4): 225–236.

Wright, Ruth E. 1981. "Aging, Divided Attention, and Processing Capacity." *Journal of Gerontology* 36 (5): 605–614.

Zaichkowsky, Judith Lynne. 1985. "Measuring the Involvement Construct." *Journal of Consumer Research* 12 (3): 616–618.

9

Pictorial and Multimodal Metaphor in Commercials

Charles Forceville

Chapter Summary

Deploying metaphor is an attractive and efficient way for advertisers to make positive claims for their products, brands, or services. For a long time, metaphor studies focused almost exclusively on language, but over the past fifteen years the concept of pictorial (or visual) metaphor has been fairly well developed, particularly in the realm of print advertising and billboards. Metaphors, however, also occur in commercials. Their occurrence in moving images is more complex than in static ones, both because the two parts of a metaphor ("target" and "source") need not occur simultaneously and because music and sound, too, might play a role in the identification and interpretation of metaphor. These factors necessitate a theoretical shift from pictorial to multimodal metaphor. This chapter discusses nine case studies of commercials containing pictorial and multimodal metaphors with the aim to define, and speculate about the effects of, the various parameters that play a role in the way they can occur. The last section discusses how the effect of these parameters can be tested in empirical research.

Advertisers' perennial task is to make positive claims for brands, products, and services, in the hope that these will induce prospective consumers to consider, buy, and use them. These claims must always be pitched in a limited space or time slot. Moreover, the message should attract attention, and ideally stick in people's memories, for instance by being humorous, or beautiful, or intriguing. This latter requirement is particularly important given that competition for audience attention, via an ever-broadening variety of media, is fierce. One way to meet this requirement is to deploy a good metaphor.

For me, as a humanities scholar interested in multimodal rhetoric, more specifically in its metaphorical dimensions, the omnipresence of metaphors in advertisements was in fact the reason to start concentrating on the genre of advertising in the first place: advertising provides a rich source of examples within short, complete texts, within a genre flaunting the clear-cut message "Buy me!" (Forceville 1994, 1996). Advertising is thus a goldmine for furthering the theory of pictorial and multimodal metaphor. For present purposes I will somewhat reverse priorities, and reflect on how metaphor theory can be used in both the production and analysis of advertising (in the spirit of Mick and Politi 1989; Phillips 2003; Scott 1994; and Wiggin and Miller 2003). Moreover, I shift focus from the approach adopted in Forceville (1996) by concentrating on pictorial and multimodal metaphor in commercials rather than in print ads and billboards, discussing some of the dimensions that govern metaphorizing in *moving* images. The structure of this chapter is as follows: after a brief introduction of verbal metaphor, I define and explain the concepts of pictorial and multimodal metaphor. Subsequently, nine case studies of pictorial and multimodal metaphor in commercials are described in order to extract pertinent parameters for the study of this trope. After a more general discussion of these parameters, the concluding section provides a list of issues that require further theoretical and empirical investigation.

Metaphor: Preliminaries

Lakoff and Johnson's "The essence of metaphor is understanding and experiencing one kind of thing in terms of another" (Lakoff and Johnson 1980, 5) captures three important aspects of this trope: (1) metaphor involves no less and no more than two domains; (2) one of the domains pertains to the topic about which something is predicated (in line with cognitive linguistics practice here called the "target"), while the other domain pertains to the predication (the "source"). Target and source are, in principle, irreversible; and (3) a metaphor is not necessarily verbal in nature.

Construing and interpreting a phenomenon as a metaphor requires at least the following actions from recipients. They must:

1. conclude that two phenomena, which, in the given context, belong to different categories, are presented as somehow being "one" thing;
2. assess which of the two phenomena is the target and which is the source. The requirement that target and source are distinguishable means that it is clear that the metaphor is "about" one of the things, not about the other thing;
3. decide which facts and connotations adhering to the source domain (the sum total of which Max Black, referring to Aristotle, calls "endoxa" [1979, 29]), can be mapped onto the target domain;
4. make appropriate adjustments to optimize the match between target and source.

The last two requirements pertain to the interpretation of the metaphor, which boils down to determining which characteristic(s) of the source domain is/are "transferred" (the literal translation of Greek *meta-pherein*) to the target. When, as often happens in advertising, the target coincides with the product, the interpretation of the metaphor is equivalent to listing the positive qualities or associations claimed for the product. By contrast, when the target coincides with the to-be-disparaged product of competitors, interpretation amounts to searching for negative qualities that can be mapped from source to target.

For purposes of analysis, a metaphor can be verbally rendered as NOUN A IS NOUN B. (The convention to use small capitals to signal the conceptual level of metaphors was introduced by Lakoff and Johnson [1980] and has been broadly adopted by cognitive linguists and by journals such as *Metaphor and Symbol*.) An important difference between the Lakoffian conceptual metaphor theory and Black's interaction theory is that the former takes for granted that most metaphors are manifestations of underlying, conceptual metaphors (see also Lakoff and Turner 1989), whereas Black stresses that metaphor can create ad hoc similarity between a target and a source. It is not necessary here to resolve this difference in emphasis (although Lakoff and Turner may overstate their case, see Forceville [2006]). What matters here is that metaphors in advertising, particularly good ones, are typically *experienced* as surprising, creative couplings of target and source.

A useful concept pertaining to metaphor that Black develops is "resonance." Black calls metaphors resonant when they "support a high degree of implicative elaboration" (1979, 27). That is, a metaphor is resonant if it allows for a rich array of mappings from source to target. Shakespeare's "the world is a stage" is resonant because it allows for many mappings (actors become people; major protagonists become people that matter, contrasting to those having nonspeaking parts; a plot becomes a person's development or destiny in life, etc.). Similarly, in the poem "Laying a lawn," Craig Raine consistently explores the metaphor SLABS OF GRASS ARE BOOKS, and by teasing out many mappings from source to target he demonstrates the metaphor to be highly resonant (Raine 1979). Another resonant poetic metaphor is the famous one in which John Donne's speaking persona compares himself to one leg of a pair of compasses, and the beloved lady he must leave behind when he goes on his travels to the other leg (in "Valediction: Forbidden Mourning"). By contrast, imagine Maureen tells her friend Ellen that "Jodocus is an ass," the intended mapping from "ass" to "Jodocus" being "stupidity"—no more and no less. Since not much gets mapped, the metaphor is not very resonant. The resonance of metaphors usually resides in the fact that it is the source's internal structure, not just a series of isolated features, that is "co-mapped" to the target (Gentner and Markman [1997] discuss this phenomenon in terms of "aligned structure"). Moreover, we should not forget that metaphors are best interpreted by analyzing them in context (the rest of the poem, speech, article, picture, film, commercial), and by taking cognizance of which audience is to be addressed. As Aristotle already pointed out, "the persuasive is persuasive to *someone*" (Aristotle 1991, 41; emphasis added), which means among other things that the intended mappings from a metaphor's source domain need to be commensurate with the envisaged audience's "endoxa."

It is also important to emphasize that Black delimitates "metaphor" in a precise and narrow sense. Some other authors listing and analyzing what Tversky calls "figures of depiction" (2001, 86) use the word "metaphor" in the all-inclusive sense of "trope" and thus as including rhetorical figures such as metonymy, litotes, hyperbole, meiosis, and many others (e.g., Kennedy 1982; Whittock [1990] also takes a broader view; see Forceville [1996, 53ff.] for discussion).

A last preliminary remark: The interpretive decisions involved in assessing that a metaphor is to be construed in the first place, and given that assessment, how this is to be done, are governed—like any other message—by the presumption of relevance, as developed by Sperber and Wilson (1995), which is based on the Gricean claim that "an essential feature of most human communication is the expression and recognition of intentions" (Wilson and Sperber 2004, 607; see also Clark 1996; Gibbs 1999; Tomasello 2003). What constitutes relevance is highly situation-dependent. A stimulus (here: a commercial) is used at a particular moment, in a particular place (say, the Netherlands, or North Holland, or Amsterdam; or Canada, or Saskatchewan, or Saskatoon) for a more or less specific audience (say, prospective car buyers, or children, or hedonists, or people with a lot of money to invest). In short, as Sperber and Wilson emphasize, relevance is always relevance to an individual (1995, 142; for applications of relevance theory to mass-communicative messages, see Forceville [1996, ch. 5; 2005a]; Yus forthcoming). Advertisers, whose messages are very expensive, are acutely aware of this, and try hard to be optimally relevant to the consumers they consider to constitute their target audience.

Pictorial and Multimodal Metaphors in Commercials

Adequate uptake of a metaphor occurring in advertising requires first of all that the product or brand be recognized. Typically, the identification of the product is ensured by simply depicting it. If the product has an immediately recognizable unique design (say, the British–French Concorde airplane, or the Rietveld chair) or logo (for instance the Nike "swoosh" or Heineken beer's red star), depiction alone may suffice for recognition. This recognition may be restricted to a certain country, region, subculture, or community, and is thus by no means necessarily universal. To aid identification, the product type and name is often conveyed verbally, via the name of the product (service, brand), as well as visually. But there is no reason why a product, service or brand should not be identified by means of a sound or a tune as well. In the Netherlands various brands (such as Hema supermarkets, C-1000 supermarkets, Nationale Nederlanden insurance company, and Randstad temporary job agency) through sustained marketing campaigns associate tunes or sound effects with their brands, thus creating "audio logos" that connote the brand as uniquely as do the visual logos. And people all over the world are familiar with

Microsoft's welcoming tune on the computer. In theory, an audio logo could thus also fill the "target domain" slot of a metaphor.

The source domain of a metaphor no less than the target domain must be recognized for what it is; and, moreover, evoke the "right" kind of mappable features. What is the "right" kind of mappable features in an advertising metaphor? Unlike in artistic metaphors (cf. Carroll 1994, 1996; Forceville 2002, 2005b; Whittock 1990), in advertising metaphors this is always relatively clear-cut. Everything in an advertisement or commercial—including any metaphor in it—obeys one central convention of the genre: it is meant to evoke positive feelings toward the product, service, or brand promoted (Forceville 1996, 104). This assumption governs consumers' search for mappable features in a metaphor—even though they may flippantly entertain subversive interpretations for the sheer fun of it, or as a means to protest the ideology of consumerism in general, as happens in many Adbuster creations. But using metaphors (and other tropes) always involves the risk of subversive, against-the-grain interpretations (for examples, see Forceville 1996, ch. 7).

In Forceville (1994, 1996, 2000, 2005c) a model was developed for the analysis of pictorial metaphor in static (print and billboard) advertisements. On the basis of how target and source were represented, the following prototypes were distinguished, whereby it should be realized that in practice many specimens share features of two or more types:

(1) *Hybrid metaphor* (originally called MP2). The metaphorical identity relationship is conveyed visually by conflating target and source into a single, "impossible" gestalt. An example is found in a governmentally sponsored ad featuring the earth whose upper half is a burning candle. The ad draws upon the viewer's knowledge that a candle's energy is nonrenewable to warn against exhausting the earth's energy resources (Forceville 1996, figure 6.11).

(2) *Contextual metaphor* (originally called MP1). The target of the metaphor is placed in a visual context that forces or invites the viewer to evoke the identity of the source, which is itself not pictured. For instance, a beer bottle is put in a champagne cooler to elicit the metaphor BEER IS CHAMPAGNE, with "high quality" or "drunk at festive occasions" among the associations that can be mapped from source to target (Forceville 1996, figure 6.4).

(3) *Pictorial simile.* A target and a source are saliently juxtaposed. That is, both target and source are represented, the similarity between them created by one or more visual traits (color, posture, size, texture . . .) they share. An example is an ad for swimwear in which a girl with a tight-fitting bathing suit is diving, apparently in midair. Next to her, a dolphin is seen diving in the same curved position, while the similarity between them is further reinforced by the fact that the dolphin's back fin is subtly echoed in the girl's mop of protruding wet hair. The viewer may consider the skin of the dolphin a mappable feature ("the bathing suit fits the girl as smoothly as a dolphin's skin"), but in principle any positive *endoxa* associated with the dolphin may be co-mapped, such as the animal's intelligence, or apparent cheerfulness (Forceville 1996, figure 6.17).

(4) *Integrated metaphor* (a type first suggested, though not so named, by van Rompay [2005, ch. 3]). A target can be shown in a posture or position such that it conveys the source visually without (partially) representing it or suggesting it due to visual context. An example is the Philips Senseo coffee machine, which has been designed in such a way that it appears to resemble a servant or butler. The mappable feature could then be "always being at the user's disposal" or "showing respect to the user by modestly bowing" (Forceville, Hekkert, and Tan 2006, figure 4).

But nonverbal metaphors can also occur in commercials. This shift in focus to *moving* images considerably broadens the ways in which a metaphor can be presented, and includes the following:

1. Thanks to the stylistic opportunities open to the medium of film—for example, montage of shots, camera angles, camera movement, as well as their interactions—the repertoire of techniques by which similarity between a metaphorical target and source can be conveyed visually is increased.

2. Commercials do not necessarily present or suggest the metaphor's target and source simultaneously: it is possible to convey a target and source *after* one another.

3. Commercials need not, like static advertisements, be restricted to pictures and written language (logos being an intriguing intermediate category), but can deploy other modes of communication.

In fact, metaphors in commercials draw usually on more than one mode of communication. These modes include at least the following: (1) visuals; (2) written language; (3) spoken language; (4) nonverbal sound; (5) music. This subdivision allows for a rough twofold distinction into monomodal and multimodal metaphors. The former are metaphors whose target and source are conveyed in the same mode; the latter are metaphors whose target and source are conveyed, entirely or partly, in different modes (for more discussion on "modes," see Forceville [2006, forthcoming a]). The verbal metaphors that until recently were the only type of metaphor systematically studied are thus monomodal metaphors, and so are purely pictorial metaphors. But outside of language, metaphorical targets and sources are often cued in more than one mode simultaneously, which makes it sometimes difficult to decide whether a metaphor is monomodal or multimodal. For instance, if a target is signaled visually, and a source is signaled visually *and* verbally, should the metaphor be labeled "monomodal" or "multimodal"? The decision is somewhat arbitrary. It seems wise to see the two as extremes on a continuum rather than as two distinct types. A metaphor, then, will be considered to belong to the monomodal (for instance, pictorial) extreme of the continuum if both target and source are cued in one mode, and one mode only (for instance, both visually). It will be classified as typically multimodal if target and source are cued entirely in two different modes (for instance, the target visually and the source verbally). In practice, however, many specimens are somewhere in between these extremes.

184

Figure 9.1 **Brand Beer. Man descending into a wine cellar** (still).

Figure 9.2 **Brand Beer. The bottle from the "wine rack" turns out to be a beer bottle** (still).

Examples of Metaphors in Commercials

Nine commercials (unless otherwise indicated: all screened on Dutch TV, with translations by the author) that all invite a metaphorical reading will now be described and analyzed. The goal of this discussion is to pave the way for identifying pertinent dimensions governing pictorial and multimodal metaphors in this genre.

Example 1. Brand Beer: Pictorial Metaphor
of the Contextual-Cum-Simile Type

A man descends into a wine cellar that contains bottles lying flat in racks (Figure 9.1). He carefully extracts a bottle from what appears to be a wine rack; but after a few seconds it transpires that the rack was actually a horizontally lying beer crate, with the name "Brand" on it (Figure 9.2). The initial misreading is reinforced by the voice-over, which praises the drink as "rich and refined. Brightly colored. Refined and with a full taste. With a fresh, slightly bitter aftertaste"—all reminiscent of "winespeak" (Caballero et al. 2006, Caballero forthcoming). The metaphor BEER IS WINE borrows the positive associations of wine: social prestige, a quality drink, something for connoisseurs (for another Brand commercial exploiting the same metaphor, see Forceville [2007]). The metaphor in this commercial has elements of both the contextual type (the cellar-as-typical-location-to-store-wine) and the simile type (the wine bottles that are visible in the cellar, and to which the beer bottles are thus implicitly compared).

Example 2. Guhl Shampoo: Pictorial Metaphor
of the Contextual-Cum-Simile Type

In each of the commercials in the series, the first shot is a static medium—close-ups of an attractive female model with what initially looks like an incredibly spectacular hairdo. When the camera begins to move, the viewer realizes that the "hair" was in fact a feature of the natural environment (a tree or a shrub) in which the woman was standing. The metaphor that the viewer is invited to construe is thus HAIR IS TREE/SHRUB, with "naturalness" presumably being the feature mappable from the natural phenomenon to "hair." Given that viewers are aware that advertisers make positive claims for their products, they will infer that, in turn, the hair's "naturalness" is aided by Guhl shampoo. The metaphor is a pictorial one inasmuch as its target and source are both rendered in the visual mode. It displays features both of the contextual type (the tree/shrub-behind-the-woman's-head) and the simile type (the tree as the object that the hair is compared to once the camera has moved and thus shifted perspective).

Example 3. Bavaria Beer: Pictorial Metaphor
of the Contextual Type

This commercial, broadcast in the Olympic year 2004, features Gianni Romme, who at the time was a successful speed skater. A voice-over tells us, "Bavaria wants to conquer Holland this autumn with Bavaria Hooghe Bock. That's why we invoked the help of Brabant-born speed fiend Gianni Romme. He set out to take this robust high-ferment beer to the high North." In a sequence of shots we see Romme running a demanding race, allegedly across the country from the south in the province of Brabant to the northernmost village in the province of Frisia, Moddergat, with a bottle of Hooghe Bock Bavaria beer held high in his right hand (Figures 9.3 and 9.4). It is this salient posture of Romme's, in combination with the running, that invites a metaphorical construal, since it is strongly reminiscent of the posture of the runners that take the Olympic torch from Olympia in Greece to the location hosting the Olympic games that year, resulting in the metaphor BAVARIA BEER IS OLYMPIC TORCH. The metaphor rests on the tongue-in-cheek suggestion that the beer, too, is "needed" in the place where Romme takes it: the Northern hamlet Moddergat. The mappings to be construed thus can be any positive connotation adhering to "carrying the Olympic torch" that are translatable to qualifying Bavaria beer—ranging from "glory" or "event-launching" to "being a necessity." The idea that all these high-minded qualifications should be seen as playfully over-the-top does not detract from their pertinence. The Bavaria beer commercial clearly belongs to the contextual type, since it is the visual context (Romme's posture and running) that supplies the source (Olympic torch).

Example 4. Palm Beer: Pictorial Metaphor
of the Simile Type

This beer commercial begins with a close-up of a bottle being snapped open. It is followed by a series of close-ups of the beer being poured into a glass (brown beer, white foam, flowing movements), crosscut with and sometimes superimposed by (Figure 9.5) shots of a sturdy brown horse, its white mane waving in the wind. A tune with nonsense text ("Pa-da-pa-pam") suggestively plays on the brand's name. The brand's logo, a Belgian horse, is visible several times on the beer-filled glass (Figure 9.6). The final voice-over says, "Belgian opulence since 1947," while this text simultaneously appears onscreen in the last shot. PALM BEER IS A BELGIAN HORSE is the metaphor that can be construed, with the Belgian horse's healthy color and strength among the mappable features—the latter presumably translating in the target domain into alcoholic strength. The crosscutting between beer and horse makes this a simile, although the occasional superimposition of the two provides a faint hint of the hybrid type.

Figure 9.3   **Bavaria Beer. Gianni Romme cheered on by spectators** (still).

Figure 9.4   **Bavaria Beer. Gianni Romme, passing other runners in his cross-country race** (still).

188

Figure 9.5 **Palm Beer. Glass of beer and horse superimposed** (still).

Figure 9.6 **Palm Beer. Glass of Palm Beer with horse logo** (still).

Figure 9.7   **Sun Dishwasher Powder. "Tulips" in a vase** (still).

Example 5. Sun Dishwasher Powder: Pictorial Metaphor of the Integrated-Cum-Contextual Type

A number of wine glasses, resembling tulips, stand in a vase-like container. Some of them "droop" (Figure 9.7). GLASSES ARE TULIPS is thus the central metaphor. The voice-over informs the viewer that new Sun protects against corrosion. Since it is the use of Sun that enhances the glasses' "health," the implied metaphor is something like SUN IS FLOWER FERTILIZER or SUN IS SUNLIGHT. The Sun dishwasher powder metaphor required the manipulation of the glasses (they had to be suggestive of "drooping" to make them resemble tulips in need of strengthening), and hence exemplifies the integrated type, but since the presence of the vase also helps identify the glasses as tulips, it displays an aspect of the contextual type as well.

Example 6. Peugeot Cars: Pictorial Metaphor of the Simile Type

A silver-colored car is seen driving fast alongside a beautifully designed modern train, also silver-colored, in an otherwise empty desert landscape. The relationship between car and train is further emphasized by a shot in which we see the train mirrored in the side of the car. It is hinted that they are racing against each other. The alarms of a railroad crossing become audible. An aerial shot reveals that the road and the railway track do not run parallel but cross each other. At the railway crossing, the train has to give way to the car. A voice-over concludes, "The new Peugeot 406 Coupé . . . You feel better in a Peugeot." The latter text coincides with its written version in the very last shot, which also displays the Peugeot logo. We are invited, though not forced, to construe the metaphor PEUGEOT CAR IS TRAIN, with as possible candidates for mapping: state-of-the-art design, riding comfort—and whatever other good feelings the train evokes in the viewer. The Peugeot commercial is a straightforward example of a simile: both target and source are depicted in their entirety.

Example 7. Aegon Insurance: Multimodal Metaphor with Visual Target and Verbal (Written) Source

The commercial, accompanied by "heroic" music, begins by showing eight horses, apparently drawing a wagon, approaching the viewer from the distance, in a desert (the Mojave Desert, California, personal communication, Jan Driessen at Aegon). In a fast montage sequence we then see the horses in close-ups, a chain snaps, we hear whinnying, and one of the horses breaks loose and escapes from the constrictions of the eight-in-hand (Figure 9.8). It shakes off its harness (Figure 9.9), rears up, and enjoying its newfound liberty runs alone in a spacious, sunlit landscape. Only in the very last shot is the audience given any verbal information, in the form of two consecutively appearing phrases: "Think Free. . . . Think Aegon insurance." Combining the visual information of the line-breaking horse with the verbal imperative to the prospective insurance-taker that he/she should not, somehow, feel constricted or imprisoned, the resulting metaphor can be verbalized as INSURANCE-TAKER IS HORSE THAT IS/BREAKS FREE. Since there is no further verbal information that steers the interpretation of the metaphor in the form of verbal anchoring or relay (Barthes 1986), it is up to the viewer to fill in the details of the metaphor. After all, the commercial does not tell us in what the "freedom" of the (prospective) Aegon client resides. Does he or she have an unusually wide-ranging choice from various types of insurance policies? Is it easy to terminate an insurance policy if it no longer satisfies the needs of the client? Or does the company more generically indicate that it sees the client as an individual, with specific needs that are catered for by considering personal circumstances rather than forcing him/her into the straitjacket of a uniform insurance policy? All of these interpretations are commensurate with the metaphor, allowing for a degree of individual variation in the potential meaning perceived by the viewer. (Sometimes, of course, other expressions of the marketing campaign—for instance in print advertisements, billboards, radio commercials—steer or reinforce certain interpretations over others.) The metaphor is truly a multimodal metaphor inasmuch as the verbal information is indispensable for cuing the metaphor's

Figure 9.8 **Aegon Insurance. A horse breaks loose from an eight-in-hand** (still).

Figure 9.9 **Aegon Insurance. The horse gets rid of its harness** (still).

target domain ("client"); deletion of the verbal text would altogether eliminate the metaphor. (Note that while in Forceville [1996] I discussed this as a subtype of pictorial metaphor, I now consider it a subtype of multimodal metaphor, albeit that here it is, unusually, the metaphor's source [the horse] that is depicted, and the target [the prospective client] that is verbally cued).

Example 8. Senseo Coffee Machine: Multimodal Metaphor Involving Visual Target and Sonic and Musical Source

In this commercial (also discussed in Forceville [forthcoming b]; I owe the example to Paul Victor), we first see a series of extreme close-ups of what must be some high-tech machine. We hear the familiar first notes of Steppenwolf's "Born to be Wild," made even more famous by the opening sequence of the film *Easy Rider,* followed by the sounds of a kick-starting motorbike. A series of texts is superimposed over the images: "Designed with a vision" . . . "Designed with passion" . . . "Turns each moment into a sensation . . . that pleases all the senses." By now we are confident that this must be a commercial for some brand of motorbike. But at the end of the commercial, we see a shot of the Senseo coffee machine, so we realize we have been tricked: the motorbike domain is to be construed as the source domain of a metaphor: COFFEE MACHINE IS MOTORBIKE. The voice-over enthuses, "Senseo, sensational cup of coffee," while the last superimposed text runs, "Three years old and already a legend—at least in the kitchen." Obviously, the metaphor in this commercial is cued both aurally and visually. With the sound switched off, we would have inferred that the close-ups portrayed a machine. Since coffee machines are literally machines, this awareness would not have triggered a metaphor. It is the combination of the pop song and the motorbike noises that evoke the source domain of motorbiking. One transferable feature is presumably the revolutionary design of the *Easy Rider* bikes; another is the legendary status of the biker film. But the music also evokes other connotations: leading an exciting life, freedom, being different. In Black's terminology, then, the metaphor is resonant, since it allows for many mappings. Of course not every viewer will come up with exactly the same mappings. Indeed, it is one of the strengths of this metaphor (and many others that are deployed in commercials) that it gives viewers a choice to decide which of these qualities associated with Easy-Rider motorbiking they wish to map onto making coffee with a Senseo machine.

Example 9. IKEA Lamps: Multimodal Metaphor Involving Visual Target and Musical plus Verbal (Spoken) Source (see IKEA 2006)

This Swedish commercial, brought to my attention by Valerie Boswinkel, shows a desk lamp that is unplugged by a woman and thrown out with the garbage, to be replaced by a newer model. The way the old lamp is framed (its upper part is made to look like a head, its posture outside in the rain with the garbage that of a slumping human, whereas the cross-cuts between it and the new lamp, visible through the window, as well as some zooming shots, suggest a jealous point-of-view) as well as lighted, contributes to personifying it. That this is what we are supposed to do is made clear by the surprising climax of this mini-narrative: a man walking past the lamp on the rainy pavement addresses the camera, saying in Scandinavian-accented English, "Many of you feel bad for this lamp. That is because you are crazy. It has no feelings. And the new one is much better." The payoff gives the IKEA logo. The point to be made here is that whereas this could be considered a monomodal metaphor of the pictorial variety, there is no doubt that the slow, sad piano music accompanying the film until the man begins to speak contributes to the personification of the lamp—not because lamps make such music but because we have grown accustomed to this kind of score music in numerous heart-breaking separation scenes in feature films. So although the metaphor could be called a pictorial one, I would claim that the music adds both to the alleged sense of desertion experienced by the lamp and to the speed with which viewers are aware of its personification. Such examples should remind us that although for analytical purposes it will be useful to distinguish between monomodal and multimodal metaphors as prototypes in the sense of Lakoff (1987), in fact there is a continuum between them.

Ways of Creating Similarity in Pictorial and Multimodal Metaphors

There must be a cue for the recipient of a commercial to link one thing metaphorically with something else. If target and source occur in the same mode, some sort of resemblance between them is construed. In verbal metaphors, this is done by equating the two dissimilar phenomena via a nonliteral "is" or "is like" ("Surgeons are butchers"; "Sally is a block of ice") or by using other grammatical constructions that create identity ("The ship plowed through the waves" can be traced back to SEA IS ACRE or SHIP IS PLOW; "The brook smiled," depending on context, can be seen as a manifestation of BROOK IS PERSON or RIPPLING WATER IS SMILING). But in pictorial metaphors there is no simple equivalent to the verbal "is." As we have seen, various forms can be deployed to make an audience aware that a metaphor is to be construed.

It has been suggested that the specific form chosen for an advertising metaphor may have consequences for consumer interpretation and response (Phillips 2003, 301). I agree, and in this section I want to speculate about this claim somewhat further, beginning with the various pictorial types and then shifting to multimodal specimens. Examples 1–6 all count as monomodal metaphors of the pictorial kind on the basis of the fact that both their targets and their sources are cued by visual means. Examples 7–9 are labeled multimodal because target and source are entirely or predominantly signaled in different modes.

Pictorial Metaphors

Hybrid Metaphor

A hybrid metaphor cannot exist as such in the "real" world. For this reason, advertisers may find this an unattractive option for the promotion of a high-profile physical product, as it might seem to have been damaged or manipulated. Hybridization is of course a problem only when the metaphorical target coincides with the product itself. In other situations, this restriction may not apply: for instance, if an advertiser wants to degrade a competitor by means of the metaphor; or if the advertisement does not promote a product, but an idea, as in public-service types of messages; or if the product has no high-profile visual qualities, such as computer software (cf. van den Boomen 2006). I note in passing that in the realm of art, there is no problem with hybrid metaphors: think of numerous science-fiction films that have a humanoid target and an animal- or machine-related source.

Integrated Metaphor

The integrated subtype similarly "changes" the product. Since it requires the target to be bent, folded, or otherwise construed in a manner that evokes the source domain, it may appear as altered or affected, which again may be unappealing to advertisers who want to turn the product into the target of a metaphor. However, if the target of the metaphor does not represent the product itself, but something metonymically related to it, this drawback presumably does not apply. An example in Forceville (1996) that in retrospect has elements of the integrated type (a type not yet identified as such in that study) is an Air France series in which the airline company's tickets have been folded in such a way that they appear as a deck chair, a snowboard, and an Indian headdress, respectively (Forceville 1996, figures 6.6, 6.7, and 6.13). This is possible first of all because of the strong metonymic link between airline companies and something that is unproblematically bendable/foldable: the ticket. Unsurprisingly, the integrated type works excellently with the human body as target domain: shove your right hand under your jacket at chest height and without further ado, metaphorically, you are Napoleon (although you would have to wear a jacket rather than a sweater to achieve the effect); extend your arm in front of your nose and wriggle about with your hand, and there is a fair chance that people would recognize the domain ELEPHANT—which, given the right circumstances, could be the source of a metaphor.

Contextual Metaphor

This type shares with the integrated subtype the characteristic that one of the terms (the source) is not visually represented; the difference is that the identification of the source in the contextual subtype depends on the visual context in which it has been carefully placed, while the integrated type bears in itself the "ghost" presence of the source, irrespective of visual context. In contextual metaphor the location of the target is often crucial, since it helps identify the (absent) source: without the "context" of Romme holding the Bavaria bottle over his head in precisely the way he does, the source domain OLYMPIC TORCH would not have been recognizable; if the model in the Guhl commercial did not stand precisely where she stands, we would not, or not as easily, have been able to metaphorically equate her hairdo with the shrub or tree. Phillips and McQuarrie would rank contextual metaphors under the "replacement" variety of visual structures in advertisements, which they consider as more complex than juxtaposition (the simile metaphor is one manifestation of this structure) and fusion structures (hybrid metaphors would belong to this category) (Phillips and McQuarrie 2004, 116). The authors moreover hypothesize that complex visual structures are better liked (because they require the successful solving of a mini-puzzle) and remembered (because of the cognitive effort invested in solving the puzzle) than less complex structures.

Simile

Since in the simile type both target and source are visually present, there are many other ways besides location to convey or suggest visual resemblance between two phenomena, for instance by using the same color, size, posture, texture, function, drawing style, direction of movement, or framing: the simile in the Peugeot commercial draws on similar function (both car and train are means of transport), color (silver), direction of movement (they "race" parallel to each other).

Multimodal Metaphors

Contrary to a pictorial metaphor—which is a variety of monomodal metaphor—in multimodal metaphor it is not so much resemblance between target and source that triggers metaphorical construal, but the suggestion of their co-referentiality: two somehow incompatible phenomena are presented as a single entity (Carroll [1994, 1996] would call this conjunction "noncompossible"). In print advertisements and billboards the only variety is verbo-pictorial metaphor, where the usual situation is a visual target that is metaphorically transformed by a verbal, written source. We are used to verbal explanations of pictures, in the form of captions or legends, so we tend to take a piece of language accompanying the picture naturally as an explanation of or complement to it. In commercials (as opposed to print ads and billboards, or most Internet banners), the language component can assume spoken as well as written forms. This allows for metaphorical play of the VISUAL TARGET IS VERBAL SOURCE variety (or, less often, vice versa). In the latter case, there is often deictic information ("this," "he," "here") that invites the recipient to understand the verbal information as referring to what is visually salient. But to the degree that a phenomenon can be unambiguously evoked by a specific sound or a musical theme, it could in principle cue a target or source, even single-handedly. In practice, however, both targets and sources are often cued in more than one mode simultaneously, which makes it more difficult to subcategorize multimodal metaphors than pictorial ones. But this leaves intact the central idea: metaphorical identification can be prompted by any salient manner of simultaneous cuing of the two clearly identifiable domains (for more examples as well as discussion of multimodal metaphors, see Forceville [2006, 2007, forthcoming a, b]; see also Forceville 1999).

Degree of Salience of the Metaphor and of Its Mappable Features

When advertisers develop a metaphor as the key device to make a claim for a product, they will probably want to make sure that the audience recognizes the metaphor. Whittock calls salient metaphors "marked metaphors" (1990, 50) and Forceville labels them "explicitly signaled metaphors" (1999, 191–192). Indeed the very fact that often (for more examples, see Forceville 2003) the advertiser playfully misleads the viewer by *first* showing the "thing" that turns out to be the source domain of the metaphor and *then* revealing the target domain (usually the product) strongly suggests that the advertiser alerts us to the need for metaphor construal—otherwise the salient positioning of the thing shown first would make no sense.

But advertisers do not necessarily want to make their metaphors salient; they may want to invite rather than force viewers to construe a metaphor. The juxtaposition typical of the pictorial simile variety is particularly suited to such an invitation: if the object cuing the source domain is not as such an improbable phenomenon to appear in the given context anyway, its presence can be explained on other than metaphorical grounds (namely, as a coincidental or "natural" presence not unlikely to occur in the scene under consideration), so that a metaphor can, but need not, be construed. The Peugeot car and train juxtaposition in example 6, for instance, can in principle also be understood as no more than a race between the car and the train, won by the car. And whereas the train is very saliently and enduringly present in this commercial, the advertisers could have chosen to bestow no such emphasis on it. Car commercials often feature cars riding through beautiful or impressive scenery. When, as in a Dutch 2006 commercial for Cadillac, the car crosses a futuristically designed bridge, viewers may simply interpret, subconsciously, that bridges are likely occurrences on road journeys, but they may also construe a metaphor CAR IS FUTURISTIC BRIDGE, with "state-of-the-art design" as a mappable feature. The reason why the construal of a metaphor is not compulsory here is that the presence of the source is realistically motivated.

Of course in the case of advertising (unlike in an artistic feature film), it may be undesirable to be subtle in this respect. Note that the fewer contextual elements are pictorially present in a visual representation, the more attention is drawn to any remaining element. Consequently, a metaphor producer who wants to be subtle can "camouflage" a source domain in the pictorial context—with the risk that people will not recognize it as such. Conversely, getting rid of any potentially distracting context will highlight metaphors of the simile type. In addition, there is usually *some* cuing of similarity to enable a metaphorical interpretation: whether in color, size, posture, position, texture, positioning, or any combination of these strategies. It is to be noted, however, that even when a metaphor is saliently presented, there is often some sort of (quasi) realistic motivation for the source's occurrence in the commercial: in the Brand beer commercial, wine bottles are indeed often kept in cellars—just as beer crates are; and in the Palm beer commercial the Belgian horse is a live-action version of the logo of the beer brand.

The metaphor is not only to be recognized as such; it is also to be interpreted, although in practice the two phases are difficult to separate. The interpretation of a metaphor pertains to the selection of one or more features in the source domain that are mapped onto the target domain. Which features a recipient deems pertinent will depend on a number of factors. The fact that the footage under consideration here belongs to the genre of advertising means that viewers aware of the genre conventions know that if the target of the metaphor is the product advertised, they are to look for positive mappable features in the source domain. Usually, the source evokes certain "endoxa" even when presented out of context, but the way the source is visually presented, accompanied by music or sounds will further strengthen these. It is up to the advertiser to determine whether the mappable connotations (strength, cuteness, beauty, speed, caution, safety, state-of-the-art design . . .) are to be explicitized. Verbalizing mappable features—in a voice-over, a monologue or dialogue, or a written and/or spoken payoff at the end of the commercial—is the most explicit way of conveying them. Such explicitness presumably reduces the risk that the metaphor is misunderstood. On the other hand, the advertiser may decide that it is more challenging for viewers, or for certain groups of viewers, to abstain from such verbal explicitization, so that they have to solve the metaphorical puzzle themselves. Moreover, refraining from verbalizing mappable features gives room to individual viewers to come up with their own choice of mappable features, thus "customizing" the metaphor. Another factor that plays a role in the choice of mappable features is the knowledge about, and attitude toward, the source domain that viewers have. Knowledge of, and love for, horses may influence and refine the interpretation of the Aegon and Palm commercials discussed above. Indeed, given that animals are favorite source domains to characterize products, the like or dislike for them appears to influence appreciation of the metaphor—and hence presumably of the product (Forceville, Hilscher, and Cupchik in preparation).

Metaphor and Other Tropes

A metaphor in a commercial may be its structuring element; that is, the central claim of a commercial about the product may hinge on the metaphor, but this is not necessarily the case. A metaphor may also be a fleeting element, used in addition to, claims made by other means. In a 2006 Dutch commercial for Miele washing machines, a blue piece of clothing twirls in a washing machine to briefly suggest it is a cloud, or a wave, with as implied mapping probably "naturalness" (of course, in praise of the machine), but if this metaphor is consciously or subconsciously picked up at all, it is presumably entertained for a few seconds at most. In fact, in these latter cases, it may be argued that we are shifting from metaphor to "mere" pleasurable resemblance.

There is no reason why other tropes should not occur in advertising just as well as metaphor, but it is not at all clear that these various tropes all "behave" in the same way as metaphor in the narrow sense defined by Black (1979). As argued above, in order to ensure that the concept of metaphor does not become vacuous because of an indiscriminate application of the label to anything that appears nonliteral, *and* in order to preserve the kinship of pictorial and multimodal metaphor with their far better-theorized verbal sister, metaphors need to be distinguished from other tropes. As in the study of verbal rhetoric (e.g., Gibbs 1993), it is crucial that different tropes, both their perceptual manifestations and their potential effects, are studied in their own right, and that both similarities and differences are conscientiously charted. The revived interest within cognitive linguistics for metonymy (Barcelona 2000; Dirven and Pörings 2002) deserves to be extended to multimodal representations as well. The characteristic difference between metaphor and metonymy is that the former presents something belonging in one domain or category in terms of something from another domain or category, whereas the latter presents something in one domain in terms of something else from the same domain; the part for the whole—synecdoche—is the best-known variant of metonymy. Inasmuch as any advertiser must make a choice about which quality or qualities to emphasize in a product (price, color, availability, design, prestige . . .), metonymies reveal rhetorical strategies, and are thus worthy of consistent study. But though it is useful and helpful to be guided by tropes developed in verbal rhetoric, we must not be blinded by the limitations of this heuristic. There is no guarantee that each and every trope from classic verbal rhetoric has a pictorial or multimodal counterpart, while, conversely, it is certainly possible that there are audiovisual phenomena that deserve the name of "trope" without having an equivalent in verbal rhetoric. Work on figures of depiction—and indeed on figures in multimodal representations—outside of metaphor has still hardly been embarked on. An exception is Teng and Sun (2002), who present proposals for "pictorial oxymoron" and "pictorial grouping." Another pertinent trope is the visual or verbo-visual pun, in which some phenomenon is both A *and* B, rather than A *in terms of* B, as in metaphor. This is a common occurrence in advertising, which often promotes products as being multifunctional. A car is both a sporty car and a family car, say, and a snack is both tasty and healthy. Abed discusses visual puns, defining them as using "one or more symbols (picture and/or text) to suggest two meanings or two different sets of associations" (1994, 46). He empirically investigates verbo-visual puns, finding that after an eight-week interval subjects significantly better remembered them than either their nonpun alternatives or the distracter items. Phillips and McQuarrie (2004) propose a typology in which one parameter is the complexity of nonliteral visual structures, and the other is its richness, and present testable hypotheses for the assessment of these structures' impact on viewers. All of the above, however, focus on visual structures in static images. The current chapter has attempted to identify pertinent parameters in one type of "figure," metaphor, in representations that differ both in constituting *moving* images and in drawing on sound, music, and spoken language as well as on visuals and written language. Theorizing in this more complex type of texts has hardly begun. A promising genre for studying pictorial and multimodal tropes is animation. Wells (1998) mentions ten "narrative strategies" (metamorphosis, condensation, synecdoche, symbolism and metaphor, fabrication, associative relations, sound, acting and performance, choreography, and penetration), which partly overlap with what in literary studies are called tropes. They are in need, however, of far more precise definition and theorization.

Finally, to further complicate matters, more than one trope can occur in a single advertisement. Indeed, it is difficult to take the metaphor in the Bavaria commercial completely seriously, nor are we meant to do so. Arguably, the tongue-in-cheek character of this commercial could be discussed in terms of irony, or anticlimax, or hyperbole (Kennedy 1982, 594). The same holds for the personification in the IKEA example. So apparently, two tropes can coincide in a single commercial.

Further Research

To conclude, I will rephrase as questions the parameters that have been identified as playing a role in the construal of multimodal metaphors in commercials. These questions may in turn lead the way to operationalization in experimental research. Since it is increasingly easy to digitalize and then manipulate pictures and moving images (with computer programs such as Photoshop and Adobe Premiere), it should be feasible to design experiments in which commercials are presented with one variable changed: Elimination of sound, music, spoken language, written language, and visuals reveal their relative importance for metaphor identification and interpretation. Moreover, manipulating modes helps clarify to what extent the metaphors are transferable from one medium to another without extensive adaptation, for instance from film to radio or print advertising—an important issue in the design of an advertising campaign.

How are viewers alerted that a metaphor must or may be construed in the first place, that is, how do they know that one thing (the "target") is presented in terms of a thing from another category (the "source")? The identification of the metaphor requires first of all, the recognition of target and source, and second, their ad hoc conjoining. Target and source can each be represented visually, sonically, musically, or verbally (in spoken or written form)—or in a combination of these modes. Their conjoining is triggered by salient similarity (in the case of pictorial or other monomodal metaphors) or by simultaneous occurrence (in the case of multimodal metaphors). An important area for further research is thus in what mode(s) a target and a source are cued. The use of sound or music without lyrics to (help) cue a source domain, for instance, is probably more subtle than the use of language, while it can no less effectively be deployed to strategically connect the commercials in a campaign straddling different media (TV and cinema advertising, radio, viral advertising on the Internet).

What general target categories can we distinguish in commercials? We can distinguish the following situations:

1. A target coincides with the product advertised (Brand, Bavaria, Palm, Peugeot, and Senseo) or is metonymically related to the product advertised (the hairdo in the Guhl commercial is the target, for which the shampoo is used; the glasses in the Sun commercial, for which the dishwasher powder is used).
2. A target is antonymically related to the product advertised (in the IKEA commercial, the target domain does not correspond to the product promoted, the new IKEA lamp, but to the old, discarded lamp—whether a competitor's or an older IKEA model that is ready to be replaced).
3. A target is related neither to the product nor to its competitor. The metaphor in the Aegon commercial has the (prospective) client, addressed by the imperative "Think Aegon." The Aegon commercial happens to be also the only one among the nine case studies promoting a service (insurance policies) rather than a tangible, easily visualizable product. It may well be that metaphors promoting services "behave" differently than those promoting products.

Future research will have to reveal whether there are systematic correspondences between these categories and pictorial metaphor subtypes (contextual, hybrid, integrated, simile).

What mode(s) is/are used to trigger features that can be mapped from source to target? A source domain evokes facts and connotations (Aristotle's "endoxa"), some of which are pertinent for the metaphor's interpretation. Given commercials' genre convention that positive connotations are mapped from source to target if the target coincides with the product (and negative ones if the target refers to a competitor's product), the pertinent "endoxa" are necessarily positive and negative, respectively. Inasmuch as language allows for the most explicit conveying of features, it is, from the advertisers' point of view, the most reliable mode to communicate them; but by the same token, such explicitness is probably experienced as less complex (as defined in Phillips and McQuarrie 2004), and therefore less challenging and pleasurable than when these features are suggested via other modes: visuals, sound, music, because the latter allow viewers to solve the mini-puzzle themselves. I propose that, ceteris paribus, the explicitness of the source domain's mappable features decreases as follows: language → visuals → nonverbal sound → music without text. A source domain verging toward the implicit extreme of the continuum will, I suspect, moreover evoke stronger emotion-related mappings.

At what stage is the metaphor identified and interpreted? In a discussion of verbal metaphor, Gibbs (1994, 114–118) distinguishes various stages of metaphor uptake and interpretation. This issue is no less pertinent to pictorial and multimodal metaphors. In commercials, metaphor processing ranges from milliseconds to, say, the entire period during which they are broadcast (some viewers may require repeated viewings to "get" the metaphor). One element that facilitates or impedes recognition and comprehension is the time it takes before both target and source have been recognized as such. An advertiser can tease the viewer for instance by presenting the source before the target, making the viewer wonder what product is being advertised. Among the case studies in this chapter this happens in the Aegon commercial as well as in the Brand one, and this appears to be a recurrent feature of metaphors in commercials (for more examples, see Forceville 2003, 2007, forthcoming b). The viewers' assessment of what the mappable feature(s) is(are) may also gradually unfold in the course of the commercial. I propose, for instance, that the viewer of the Aegon commercial identifies features of the horse such as "wild," "beautiful," and "unruly" on the basis of the visuals and the music alone. In the last shot, the verbal text and the logo not only reveal the identity of the advertiser and the nature of the target but also capture the various visual features under the label "free." The advertiser thus ensures that viewers are given one mappable feature explicitly; but that does not need to keep them, on the basis of the visuals, from entertaining others as well (this taps into the continuum between strong and weak communication as theorized in Sperber and Wilson [1995]). Put differently, a commercial may initially convey mappable features nonverbally, ending with linguistically explicitizing one or more of these features. The Palm beer commercial provides another example: the expression "Belgian opulence" suggests that "opulence" is one of the features that is to be mapped from horse to beer. On the basis of the visuals or visuals-cum-music alone, this would not have been self-evidently clear. Similarly, the voice-over in the Brand commercial emphasizes the sensory qualities of wine (over, say, its reputation as a prestigious drink) as mappable feature.

   To what extent do pictorial/multimodal metaphors appeal to, or repel, certain (sub)cultural groups in the envisaged audience? Since metaphor interpretation always starts with the *endoxa* evoked by the source domain, it is important for advertisers to ensure that they do not confuse or alienate prospective consumer groups among the audience by the choice of source domain or by the way this source domain is visually, musically, or sonically represented. Maalej (2001), for instance, points out that a Clerget shoe ad in which a man's torso wears a shoe on the spot of the expected tie (i.e., on his chest, see Forceville [1996, figure 6.1, SHOE IS TIE]) might offend a traditional Tunisian-Arabic audience because such an audience would consider a shoe dirty, and hence not wearable on one's chest, while, moreover, country-dwellers might not be familiar with the concept of tie. Similarly, since observant Islamists refrain from drinking alcohol, the source domain wine is relatively unfamiliar to them, so that many, Maalej argues, would mistake a wine glass (Forceville 1996, figure 6.3, SWEETCORN SEEDS ARE WINE) for a soft-drink glass. Research focusing on reception might also focus on systematic differences between (sub)cultural groups with respect to the features mapped from source to target in a given metaphor.

The present chapter has aimed at providing avenues for theorizing and testing pictorial and multimodal metaphor. Clearly, a lot of work remains to be done, with reference to advertising as well as to other genres. Several issues touched upon in this chapter are further explored by contributions in Forceville and Urios-Aparisi (in preparation).

Acknowledgments

The author is indebted to the editors of this volume as well as to Val Larsen. Their comments on an earlier draft have helped improve the argumentative structure of this chapter. They cannot be blamed, of course, for any mistakes or faulty reasoning that have survived their suggestions and advice. Furthermore, thanks are due to the copyright holders for granting permission to reprint shots from the commercials discussed.

References

Abed, Farough. 1994. "Visual Puns as Interactive Illustrations: Their Effects on Recognition Memory." *Metaphor and Symbolic Activity* 9: 45–60.
Aristotle. 1991. *On Rhetoric: A Theory of Civic Discourse,* trans. and ed. George A. Kennedy. New York and Oxford: Oxford University Press.
Barcelona, Antonio. 2000. *Metaphor and Metonymy at the Crossroads: A Cognitive Perspective.* New York: Mouton de Gruyter.
Barthes, Roland. 1986 [1964]. "Rhetoric of the Image." In Barthes, *The Responsibility of Forms,* trans. Richard Howard, 21–40. Oxford: Blackwell.
Black, Max. 1979. "More About Metaphor." In *Metaphor and Thought,* ed. Andrew Ortony, 19–43. Cambridge: Cambridge University Press.
Caballero, Rosario. Forthcoming. "Cutting Across the Senses: Imagery in Winespeak and Audiovisual Promotion." In *Multimodal Metaphor,* ed. Charles Forceville and Eduardo Urios-Aparisi, in preparation. New York: Mouton de Gruyter.
Caballero, Rosario; Ernesto Suarez-Toste; Raquel Segovia; and Teresa de Cuadra. 2006. "Metaphors We Drink By: Figurative Language in Wine Discourse." Paper presented at the Workshop on Research and Applying Metaphor (RaAM) VI conference, University of Leeds, United Kingdom, April 10–13.
Carroll, Noel. 1994. "Visual Metaphor." In *Aspects of Metaphor,* ed. Jaakko Hintikka, 189–218. Dordrecht: Kluwer.
———. 1996. "A Note on Film Metaphor." In Carroll, *Theorizing the Moving Image,* 212–223. Cambridge: Cambridge University Press.
Clark, Herbert H. 1996. *Using Language.* Cambridge: Cambridge University Press.
Dirven, René, and Ralf Pörings. 2002. *Metaphor and Metonymy in Comparison and Contrast.* New York: Mouton de Gruyter.
Forceville, Charles. 1994. "Pictorial Metaphor in Advertisements." *Metaphor and Symbolic Activity* 9: 1–29.
———. 1996. *Pictorial Metaphor in Advertising.* New York: Routledge.

———. 1999. "The Metaphor Colin Is a Child in Ian McEwan's, Harold Pinter's, and Paul Schrader's *The Comfort of Strangers.*" *Metaphor and Symbol* 14: 179–198.

———. 2000. "Compasses, Beauty Queens and other PCs: Pictorial Metaphors in Computer Advertisements." *Hermes, Journal of Linguistics* 24: 31–55.

———. 2002. "The Identification of Target and Source in Pictorial Metaphors." *Journal of Pragmatics* 34: 1–14.

———. 2003. "Bildliche und Multimodale Metaphern in Werbespots." Trans. from English, Dagmar Schmauks. *Zeitschrift für Semiotik* 25: 39–60.

———. 2005a. "Addressing an Audience: Time, Place, and Genre in Peter van Straaten's Calendar Cartoons." *Humor: International Journal of Humor Research* 18: 247–278.

———. 2005b. "Cognitive Linguistics and Multimodal Metaphor." In *Bildwissenschaft: Zwischen Reflektion und Anwendung,* ed. Klaus Sachs-Hombach, 264–284. Cologne: Von Halem.

———. 2005c. "When Is a Pictorial Metaphor?" Lecture 2 in A Course in Pictorial and Multimodal Metaphor. www.chass.utoronto.ca/epc/srb/cyber/cforcevilleout.pdf.

———. 2006. "Non-Verbal and Multimodal Metaphor in a Cognitivist Framework: Agendas for Research." In *Cognitive Linguistics: Current Applications and Future Perspectives,* ed. Gitte Kristiansen, Michel Achard, René Dirven, and Francisco Ruiz de Mendoza Ibàñez, 379–402. New York: Mouton de Gruyter.

———. 2007. "Multimodal Metaphor in Ten Dutch TV Commercials." *Public Journal of Semiotics* 1: 19–51. http://semiotics.ca/.

———. Forthcoming a. "Metaphor in Pictures and Multimodal Representations." In *Cambridge Handbook of Metaphor and Thought,* ed. Ray Gibbs. Cambridge: Cambridge University Press.

———. Forthcoming b. "The Role of Non-Verbal Sound and Music in Multimodal Metaphor." In *Multimodal Metaphor,* ed. Charles Forceville and Eduardo Urios-Aparisi. New York: Mouton de Gruyter.

———; Paul Hekkert; and Ed Tan. 2006. "The Adaptive Value of Metaphors." In *Heuristiken der Literaturwissenschaft. Einladung zu disziplinexternen Perspektiven auf Literatur,* ed. Uta Klein, Katja Mellmann, and Steffanie Metzger, 85–109. Paderborn: Mentis.

———; Michelle Hilscher; and Gerald Cupchik. In preparation. "The Interpretation of Multimodal Metaphors in Dutch Commercials by Dutch and Canadian Subjects."

Forceville, Charles, and Eduardo Urios-Aparisi, eds. In preparation. *Multimodal Metaphor.* New York: Mouton de Gruyter.

Gentner, Dedre, and Arthur Markman. 1997. "Structure Mapping in Analogy and Similarity." *American Psychologist* 52: 45–56.

Gibbs, Raymond W. Jr. 1993. "Process and Products in Making Sense of Tropes." In *Metaphor and Thought,* 2d ed., ed. Andrew Ortony, 252–276. Cambridge: Cambridge University Press.

———. 1994. *The Poetics of the Mind: Figurative Thought, Language, and Understanding.* Cambridge: Cambridge University Press.

———. 1999. *Intentions in the Experience of Meaning.* Cambridge: Cambridge University Press.

IKEA. 2006. www.youtube.com/watch?v=I07xDdFMdgw (accessed May 26, 2007).

Kennedy, John M. 1982. "Metaphor in Pictures." *Perception* 11: 589–605.

Lakoff, George. 1987. *Women, Fire and Dangerous Things: What Categories Reveal About the Mind.* Chicago: University of Chicago Press.

———, and Mark Johnson. 1980. *Metaphors We Live By.* Chicago: University of Chicago Press.

———, and Mark Turner. 1989. *More than Cool Reason: A Field Guide to Poetic Metaphor.* Chicago: University of Chicago Press.

Maalej, Zouhair. 2001. "Processing Pictorial Metaphor in Advertising: A Cross-Cultural Perspective." *Academic Research* 1: 19–42 (Sfax, Tunisia).

Mick, David Glen, and Laura G. Politi. 1989. "Consumers' Interpretations of Advertising Imagery: A Visit to the Hell of Connotation." In *Interpretive Consumer Research,* ed. Elizabeth C. Hirschman, 85–96. Provo, UT: Association for Consumer Research.

Phillips, Barbara J. 2003. "Understanding Visual Metaphor." In *Persuasive Imagery: A Consumer Response Perspective,* ed. Linda M. Scott and Rajeev Batra, 297–310. Mahwah, NJ: Erlbaum.

———, and Edward F. McQuarrie. 2004. "Beyond Visual Metaphor: A New Typology of Visual Rhetoric in Advertising." *Marketing Theory* 4 (1/2): 113–136.

Raine, Craig. 1979. *A Martian Sends a Postcard Home.* Oxford: Oxford University Press.

Scott, Linda M. 1994. "Images in Advertising: The Need for a Theory of Visual Rhetoric." *Journal of Consumer Research* 21 (September): 252–273.

Sperber, Dan, and Deirdre Wilson. 1995. *Relevance: Communication and Cognition,* 2d ed. Oxford: Blackwell.

Teng, Norman Y., and Sewen Sun. 2002. "Grouping, Simile, and Oxymoron in Pictures: A Design-Based Cognitive Approach." *Metaphor and Symbol* 17: 295–316.

Tomasello, Michael. 2003. *Constructing a Language: A Usage-Based Theory of Language Acquisition.* Cambridge, MA: Harvard University Press.

Tversky, Barbara. 2001. "Spatial Schemas in Depictions." In *Spatial Schemas and Abstract Thought,* ed. Merideth Gattis, 79–112. Cambridge, MA: MIT Press/Bradford Book.

van den Boomen, Marianne. 2006. http://vandenboomen.org/blog/?p=83 (accessed May 26, 2007).

van Rompay, Thomas. 2005. "Expressions: Embodiment in the Experience of Design." Ph.D. dissertation, Technische Universiteit Delft, the Netherlands.

Wells, Paul. 1998. *Understanding Animation.* New York: Routledge.

Whittock, Trevor. 1990. *Metaphor and Film.* Cambridge: Cambridge University Press.

Wiggin, Amy A., and Christine M. Miller. 2003. "'Uncle Sam Wants You!' Exploring Verbal-Visual Juxtapositions in Television Advertising." In *Persuasive Imagery: A Consumer Response Perspective,* ed. Linda M. Scott and Rajeev Batra, 267–295. Mahwah, NJ: Erlbaum.

Wilson, Deirdre, and Dan Sperber. 2004. "Relevance Theory." In *The Handbook of Pragmatics,* ed. Laurence R. Horn and Gregory Ward, 607–632. Malden, MA: Blackwell.

Yus, Francisco. Forthcoming. "Towards a Pragmatics of Weblogs." *Quaderns de filologia* (Valencia).

10

Reading Pictures

Understanding the Stylistic Properties of Advertising Images

Kai-Yu Wang and Laura A. Peracchio

Chapter Summary

Although visual images are ubiquitous in advertising, little work has been done to systematically investigate how images are processed. In this chapter, we present a model that describes how ad viewers process visual images. Then, we review a series of studies relevant to the issue of how the stylistic properties (e.g., camera angles and the cropping of images in ads) of ads impact ad viewers' evaluations of ads and products. The purpose of this chapter is to provide a systematic account detailing how the stylistic properties of visual images persuade.

□ □ □ □

It is common practice for print advertisements to include a visual image as a prominent, or even a focal, design element. Guidelines for creating effective print advertising exhort advertisers to employ visual images as a means to attract and convince viewers of an advertisement's and a product's merits (Goodman 2002; Messaris 1997). Andy Goodman (2002, 37) writes that, "As the initial point of interest, the image must also be presented in ways that pull the reader deeper into the ad." Despite the central role visual images play in marketing communications, most marketers select pictures for advertisements based on intuition and personal judgment. Gaining a scholarly conceptualization of and appreciation for how visual images might persuade, or perhaps even inhibit, the persuasion of ad viewers, would seem to be of great benefit to those seeking to understand the impact of advertising on consumers.

Advertising rhetoric pertains to the manner in which ads are designed to persuade and influence consumers (Phillips and McQuarrie 2002). As McQuarrie and Mick

(1996) have observed, the stylistic devices used by advertisers to persuade extend beyond language to include the properties of visual images. McQuarrie and Mick (1999, 51) write, "Today the visual element is understood to be an essential, intricate, meaningful, and culturally imbedded characteristic of contemporary marketing communication." Although much research has focused on the art of using language to persuade, relatively little attention has been devoted to the persuasive power of images and the particular properties of images that impact persuasion.

Systematic consumer research examining the stylistic properties of advertising images provides some insight into how visual images may enhance or detract from consumers' perceptions of the products portrayed in ads. Stylistic properties refer to a variety of factors that impact the manner in which visual material is displayed, such as camera angles, the cropping of images in ads, and the orientation (e.g., vertical, diagonal) of objects displayed in a scene as well as various other production elements (Peracchio and Meyers-Levy 2005). Nascent consumer research concerned with visual images, conducted over the past fifteen years, offers some insights into how the stylistic properties of advertising images may impact ad viewers' reactions to marketing communications.

Many researchers have suggested that visual images communicate concepts that extend beyond the ideas that are overtly depicted in an advertisement. In their research, Phillips and McQuarrie (2002, 2004) develop a visual rhetorical approach to studying and understanding the visual images in advertising that offers insight into how visual images may impact ad evaluations. Phillips and McQuarrie (2004, 114) write, ". . . we assume that advertisers select pictorial elements from a palette; that specific pictorial elements can be linked to particular consumer responses."

Researchers have suggested that visual images often convey semantically meaningful concepts that impact consumer judgments via their stylistic properties (Messaris 1997; Scott 1994; Scott and Batra 2003). Stylistic properties impart descriptive meanings through a learned system of pictorial conventions or analogies that are shared among viewers and often are derived from common observations (Dondis 1993; Kreitler and Kreitler 1972; Messaris 1997; Peracchio and Meyers-Levy 2005). Scott (1994, 253) suggests that stylistic properties of pictures can be thought of as "information in symbolic form—as messages that must be processed cognitively by means of complex combinations of learned pictorial schemata."

As an example, viewers often attribute greater potency and efficacy to objects that are depicted using a particular stylistic device, a low camera angle that seemingly causes the viewer to "look up at" the object depicted in a visual image. This attribution of greater power and performance to such objects may be due to viewers' experiences with those they literally "look up to." For example, young children must look up to view an adult's face. Although the particular concepts conveyed by stylistic properties may vary depending on contextual or even person-specific factors, research suggests that individuals in a given culture often exhibit considerable consensus in the meanings they infer from particular stylistic properties of images (Hatcher 1974; Kreitler and Kreitler 1972).

The notion that fairly predictable concepts can be imparted by stylistic properties and appreciated by viewers proliferates in the scholarly, applied, and popular literature (e.g., Kress and van Leeuwen 1996; Nelson 1973). Consumer researchers have explored related issues, such as how the literal features of visual elements might affect product perceptions (e.g., the softness of a kitten shown in a tissue ad, Mitchell and Olson 1981). More recent research has explored whether, when, and how readily consumers truly discern descriptive concepts from the subtle stylistic properties of ad pictures, what the particular nature of these meanings may be, or whether, once discerned, these meanings can impact persuasion or consumers' perceptions and attitudes toward products (Peracchio and Meyers-Levy 2005).

We begin this chapter by presenting a model that describes how ad viewers process visual images. In developing this model, we explore both cognitive information—processing theory and the study of nonconscious processes. Then, we review a series of empirical investigations examining how the stylistic properties of ads impact consumers' understanding of visual images and perceptions about the products depicted in ads. To begin, we discuss research examining how camera angles commonly used in photographing products for advertising, orientations (e.g., vertical, diagonal) of objects displayed in an image, and visual perspective of an image can impact consumers' product evaluations (Meyers-Levy and Peracchio 1992, 1996; Peracchio and Meyers-Levy 2005). We also explore whether or under what conditions image color may significantly enhance consumers' product attitudes (Meyers-Levy and Peracchio 1995). Next, we examine how the ambiguity created by a cropped or incomplete object in a visual image may impact consumers' attitudes toward and evaluations of products (Peracchio and Meyers-Levy 1994). We then report research exploring how advertisers heighten persuasion by employing particular types of ad layouts (Peracchio and Meyers-Levy 1997). Finally, we examine how these stylistic properties may work in combination to impact ad viewers' perceptions of products. The goal of this approach is to illustrate how the stylistic properties of advertising images influence ad viewers and to begin to provide a systematic account of how the stylistic properties of visual images persuade.

How Do People Process the Stylistic Properties of Advertising Images?

Over the past twenty-five years, research examining the impact of advertising on consumers has adhered largely to the cognitive information-processing approach (Johar, Maheswaran, and Peracchio 2006). This paradigm suggests that consumers process the stylistic properties of advertising images in a conscious and deliberate manner. This cognitive and deliberative processing is thought to consume cognitive resources and to be intentional, controllable, and within the awareness of an individual (Bargh 1996). Alternatively, other research has suggested that nonconscious and nondeliberative efforts may characterize much of consumers' processing of the stylistic properties of advertising images (Johar, Maheswaran, and Peracchio 2006).

In this section, we will begin by discussing the cognitive information—processing approach and what it suggests regarding how consumers process the stylistic properties of ad images. Then, we will explore the impact of nonconscious processes on viewers' perceptions of the stylistic properties of visual images.

Cognitive Information-Processing Paradigm

In the cognitive information-processing paradigm, the elaboration-likelihood model (Petty, Cacioppo, and Schumann 1983) and the resource-matching theory (Anand and Sternthal 1989) have been widely used to explain how viewers process the stylistic properties of ads. The elaboration-likelihood model suggests that there are two routes to persuasion. The central route to persuasion occurs when a consumer is able and motivated to elaborate on the core or central arguments of a marketing message in a more extensive manner (Petty, Cacioppo, and Schumann 1983). By contrast, the peripheral route to persuasion occurs when a consumer relies on surface characteristics of the marketing message, such as the stylistic properties of an advertisement, to form an impression of an advertisement or a product. These surface characteristics are posited to be irrelevant to the message content and are thought to be processed in a less extensive manner.

Resource-matching theory (Anand and Sternthal 1989) presents two core concepts: resources available and resources required for ad processing. Resources available for ad processing refers to the amount of cognitive resources a consumer brings to processing an ad while resources required for ad processing refers to the amount of cognitive resources needed to process an ad. Resource-matching theory suggests that persuasion should be heightened when the supply of cognitive resources ad recipients make available for ad processing matches, rather than either exceeds or falls short of, those required to process an ad.

Meyers-Levy and Peracchio (1995) have crafted an explanation for how the stylistic properties of a visual image impact the persuasiveness of an ad by integrating notions from both the elaboration-likelihood model and resource-matching theory. These researchers have suggested that cognitive resource demands versus availability of cognitive resources underlie the elaboration-likelihood model and help to address how and why this model impacts consumers' processing of the stylistic properties of ads. Meyers-Levy and Peracchio's model explaining how the stylistic properties of ads are processed suggests that a consumers' motivation, ability, and opportunity to engage in more extensive and detailed central processing or in less extensive and more cursory peripheral processing depends on both the cognitive resources the consumer has available for processing and the resource demands imposed by the advertising image and ad context. Their theorizing suggests that the stylistic properties of ad images can represent either cursory, peripheral information or detailed, central information depending upon how these elements are employed in an ad and whether consumers have sufficient cognitive resources available to process them in a more detailed and deliberative manner.

For example, Meyers-Levy and Peracchio (1995) suggest that consumers' processing motivation may moderate the effect of one stylistic property of an advertisement, a full-color versus a black-and-white visual image. When consumers have lower ad-processing motivation, perhaps due to disinterest or preoccupation with other concerns, they generally possess few cognitive resources available for ad processing. In this situation, consumers seem to base their attitudes toward an ad and a product on heuristic cues such as the attractiveness of the ad photo or a product and/or a person shown with the product (Chaiken 1980; Petty, Cacioppo, and Schumann 1983). Such heuristic cues consume few cognitive resources. The use of color in a visual image may also act as a heuristic cue. Full-color ads have been found to be more likeable, to increase the perceived attractiveness of a visual image, and to consume more cognitive resources than black-and-white images (Bohle and Garcia 1986; Click and Stempel 1976; Meyers-Levy and Peracchio 1995). Meyers-Levy and Peracchio (1995) found that products are viewed more favorably when they appear in full-color ad images rather than in black-and-white images when consumers' processing motivation is low. This result seems to occur because the few resources consumers have available for processing the ad are matched to those resources made available for ad processing.

When processing motivation is high, however, consumers are thought to engage in more effortful ad processing (Petty, Cacioppo, and Schumann 1983), allotting a sizable portion of their cognitive resource capacity to processing the ad. Like less motivated consumers, motivated viewers may initially attend to the visual image in an ad and use this as the starting point for processing the ad. Yet, they go beyond this by processing the verbal ad claims extensively and examining specific objects in the ad photo that enable ad-claim substantiation (Meyers-Levy and Peracchio 1995). Thus, these more motivated consumers with greater available cognitive resources process the stylistic properties of the ad, such as color and black-and-white visual images, as well as other elements of the ad including verbal ad claims. The greater resources available to these consumers allow them to go beyond merely processing stylistic properties and to examine other features of the ad. Resource matching occurs when the greater resources highly motivated consumers have available are equivalent to the resources required for processing the ad.

These research findings offer several important inferences regarding how consumers process the stylistic properties of visual images. This research suggests that a single cue such as a full-color ad can be processed either as a substantive resource-consuming "central" cue or as a less resource-demanding "peripheral" cue, depending on a viewer's processing motivation. The implication is that the same cue, the same stylistic property of an ad, can be processed in either a central or peripheral manner. Similarly, in other research, Peracchio and Meyers-Levy (2005) showed that incidental, peripheral cues (i.e., visual stylistic properties) serve somewhat like central arguments by conveying descriptive concepts that people regard as diagnostic. These findings also suggest that the stylistic elements of visual images frame the way consumers process other elements of the ad such as the advertising copy. Thus, even those highly motivated processors who engage in detailed and extensive processing use the stylistic properties of an ad as a starting point for examining an ad and for forming evaluations of the advertisement and of the product.

Nonconscious Processes

More recently, marketing researchers have begun to consider the role of nonconscious processes in understanding how consumers process advertisements and, in particular, the stylistic properties of ads. Automatic processes are typically thought to have several distinguishing features, including a lack of intention, of conscious awareness, and of control, as well as a great deal of efficiency in that they occur without deliberative effort on the part of an individual and are immune to conditions that tax an individual's cognitive resources (Bargh 1996). Consumer researchers have suggested that more research is needed to understand the role of nonconscious processes in processing and forming evaluations of ads and products (Johar, Maheswaran, and Peracchio 2006; Zaltman 2000).

Research on picture processing has shown that people can and do process pictures fairly effortlessly. In this research, pictures seem to be processed in a holistic, automatic manner whereby surface representations are apprehended (Goossens 2003; Nordhielm 2002). This research suggests that visual images, or perhaps even the stylistic properties of images, may elicit an automatic, emotional response. Future research needs to explore whether, under particular conditions, individual stylistic properties of ads are processed in an automatic manner without cognitive effort or the consumption of cognitive resources resulting in an automatic reaction to the ad or product. This topic awaits investigation.

Recent consumer research supports the contention that many consumer psychological processes may have both automatic and conscious components (Raghubir and Krishna 1996; Raghubir and Srivastava 2002; Yorkston and Menon 2004). This research suggests that consumers begin judgment formation in an initial, automatic stage in which they rely upon surface-level cues, for example, the stylistic properties of an ad, to form an initial judgment of an ad or product. Later, in a second stage characterized by deliberative, systematic processing, these initial judgments are updated. This two-stage model of cognition suggests that consumer judgments are formed and framed in an initial automatic stage and then followed by conscious, deliberate processing. This model would seem to be applicable to how consumers may process some of the more straightforward stylistic properties of ads, such as ad color, and it deserves empirical exploration. More broadly, Peracchio and Meyers-Levy (1995) theorized that certain stylistic properties may be discerned and used spontaneously in evaluating product and ads. Future research should pursue and explore the potential application of this two-stage model of cognition to consumers' processing of the stylistic properties of ads.

Other research suggests that not all stylistic properties of ads are processed in an automatic manner. Several studies have shown that people with very low motivation do not discern descriptive concepts of certain stylistic properties of a visual image, such as the orientation of an object in a visual scene, automatically and absent external prompting (Peracchio and Meyers-Levy 2005). Instead, viewers seem to discern descriptive concepts imparted by the stylistic properties of visual images and apply them to featured products provided that two conditions are met: that viewers process the images somewhat extensively and that they are sensitized to the appropriate concept by, for example, verbal ad claims. This research suggests that extracting content-specific, descriptive meaning (e.g., a concept like "high performance") requires time, effort, and processing and is best characterized using a cognitive information-processing model.

The Stylistic Properties of Visual Images

Stylistic properties refer to a variety of factors that impact the manner in which visual material is displayed such as various production elements including camera angle, orientation of objects in a visual scene, visual perspective, cropping or the representation of an incomplete object in a scene, and the use of color. As an example, Figures 10.1 and 10.2 illustrate one particular stylistic property, the orientation of objects in a visual scene. In Figure 10.1, the product featured in the ad, a watch, is vertically oriented while Figure 10.2 presents the same watch in a diagonal orientation. Although this stylistic orientation difference is subtle, research has found that, in general, a vertical orientation conveys greater product potency and power while a diagonal orientation imparts greater dynamism and activity (Peracchio and Meyers-Levy 2005). In the following sections, we will discuss research examining how consumers process several different stylistic properties of visual images as well as how these stylistic properties impact consumers' evaluations of products.

Camera Angle

A commonly held belief among advertisers is that a visual image of a product depicted from a lower versus a higher camera angle will offer different perceptions about the product and impact product assessments. For example, when a product is photographed from a low, upward-looking camera angle, viewers seem to ascribe positive efficacy assessments to the product and often express greater preference for the product. By contrast, when a product is photographed from a high, downward camera angle, it is commonly thought to elicit more negative assessments as viewers seem to look down on the product image. That is, our experience with the natural visual world may give rise to a simple decision rule such that items we visually look up to are viewed positively, and those that we visually look down on are viewed negatively.

Kraft (1987) suggested that these camera-angle effects on judgments might be due to the use of heuristics. Research by Meyers-Levy and Peracchio (1992)

Figure 10.1   **Gordon Watches. An example of a vertical orientation.**

Successful, Confident, and Admired.
A Powerful Statement of Who You Are.

Gordon Watches.

provides empirical evidence for this contention. Previous research has shown that when processing motivation is low, consumers often render product judgments on the basis of experientially derived heuristics that relate to contextual cues, such as the attractiveness of the communicator (Chaiken 1980; Pallak 1983; Petty, Cacioppo, and Schumann 1983). Meyers-Levy and Peracchio (1992) have suggested that people may interpret camera angles heuristically. When processing motivation was extremely low, these researchers found that viewers interpreted camera angle in terms of a simple, experientially derived decision rule that ascribes generally positive characteristics and assessments to objects viewed from low camera angles and negative characteristics and assessments to objects viewed from higher camera angles. Thus, viewers who are not motivated to devote substantial effort to processing seem to believe that objects that are high or above eye level tend to be relatively dominant, powerful, and superior, whereas those that are low or below eye level are subordinate, weak, and inferior.

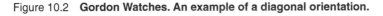
Figure 10.2   **Gordon Watches. An example of a diagonal orientation.**

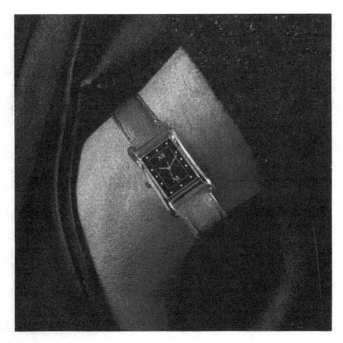

Spirited, Spontaneous, and Expressive. A Provocative Statement of Who You Are.

Gordon Watches.

Much theory and empirical evidence in marketing suggest that when people are highly motivated to process message information in detail, they form judgments by carefully weighing the perceived true merits of the issue or product (Petty, Cacioppo, and Schumann 1983). In their studies, Meyers-Levy and Peracchio (1992) found that camera angle did not appear to affect consumers' judgments of products when respondents were extremely motivated to process an advertisement. Rather, under such conditions, viewers seemed to render judgments on the basis of their assessments of the perceived true merits of the product without any impact of camera angle.

Future research needs to examine the cognitive, or perhaps automatic, processes underlying this research in more detail. Although Meyers-Levy and Peracchio's (1992) findings offer an overarching explanation for how consumers with lower versus higher levels of motivation process camera angles and perhaps other stylistic features of visual images, several different micromediating accounts may explain why these results occur. One possible account might suggest that consumers with lower levels of processing motivation rely upon whatever element, or stylistic property of an ad, is most perceptually salient to form an ad judgment. When camera angle is most salient, it becomes the basis for evaluation. However, when another ad element is more salient, consumers with lower levels of motivation will rely on that element in forming a judgment of an ad. Although the findings of this research indicate that higher motivation consumers render judgments based on a product's true merits, it may be that under certain conditions, perhaps when the inferences offered by a camera angle are relevant to the evaluation of an ad or product, these higher motivation consumers also rely upon camera angle in forming judgments. These and other plausible accounts that offer an explanation for how consumers process camera angles in ad images await investigation.

Also awaiting future inquiry is the possibility that under certain conditions, the heuristic rule observed under low motivation such that consumers prefer products viewed from a low as compared to a high camera angle, may not occur. For example, certain products or images may be prized and positively valued for their diminutive characteristics (i.e., an image of a child or perhaps a technology product for which small size is considered an asset). Images of these products may exhibit a reversed camera-angle effect. Thus, evaluations for such products might be more positive when the camera is angled down rather than up at the product. These important issues pertaining to camera-angle effects should be explored in the future.

Orientation of Objects Within a Visual Scene

Stylistic properties of visual images are thought to convey meaning to consumers through a learned system of pictorial conventions that are shared among consumers within a particular culture and are often grounded in everyday experience (Peracchio and Meyers-Levy 2005). Although the meaning of certain stylistic properties, such as camera angle, may be discerned spontaneously, decoding the meaning of other stylistic properties of pictures may not occur spontaneously. For example, the figures depict a watch displayed in a vertical orientation in Figure 10.1 and a diagonal orientation in Figure 10.2. A vertical orientation within a visual scene is commonly believed to convey power and potency while a diagonal orientation is thought to convey dynamism and activity.

Peracchio and Meyers-Levy (2005) found that the orientation of the watch in the ads depicted in Figures 10.1 and 10.2 impacted respondents' product evaluations when they were prompted to engage in extensive processing of the ad and the ad copy heightened respondents sensitivity to the same concept implied by the vertical or diagonal stylistic property. For example, when respondents were engaged in more extensive ad processing, the vertically oriented product thought to convey power had a positive impact on product evaluations when it was matched with ad copy concerned with the product's potency and power. Conversely, the diagonally oriented product, thought to convey dynamism or activity, positively impacted product evaluations when matched with ad copy that focused on the concepts of dynamism or activity if respondents were prompted to process the ads extensively.

This research suggests that consumers will discern and use certain stylistic properties of visual images in forming product evaluations only when they process an image somewhat extensively and they are sensitized to the appropriate concept by, for example, verbal ad claims. In the absence of either of these conditions, consumers may be insensitive to such concepts. Perhaps this effect occurs because viewers whose extensiveness of processing is extremely high generally may make little use of stylistic properties of visual images. For example, in Meyers-Levy and Peracchio's (1992) research on camera angle, those who were highly motivated, and thus were processing information in a more extensive manner, did not appear to incorporate camera angle in making product evaluations. Instead, such highly motivated consumers were likely to give greater credence to other information, such as ad copy, that tends to be perceived as more substantive and diagnostic than the stylistic properties of visual images.

The idea that stylistic properties of a visual image offer meaning to the ad viewer suggests a number of interesting ideas for future research. Although Peracchio and Meyers-Levy (2005) found that stylistic properties communicated meaning only when the concept they expressed was accessible in memory due to the exposition of the ad copy, situations may exist such that the communication of meaning is immune to moderation from the ad copy or other ad elements. Indeed, suppose that the components of a visual composition were arranged in such a manner that the orientation of the products or other objects in a scene induced a more extreme reaction, perhaps even a reaction at a physiological level. Consumers' spontaneous and perhaps automatic physiological reaction to the composition and the descriptive concepts implied by the composition may impact evaluations even in the absence of other ad elements that activate a particular concept. In the future, research should pursue these and other questions.

Visual Perspective

Advertisers often use self-reference techniques, such as the visual perspective employed in an image, to encourage consumers to relate a product to their own experience in daily life. One particular image-driven self-reference technique, investigated by Meyers-Levy and Peracchio (1996) places the viewer of an ad in the position of the active participant rather than an uninvolved bystander. For example, in this research, two variations of an image were employed in an ad for car insurance. In one ad, the active-participant condition (high self-reference) displayed a photo shot from the driver's position of a car with parts of the interior visible. The observer condition of this car insurance ad (low self-reference) presented a picture shot from outside the car from an observer's point of view.

This research revealed that ads generated favorable product evaluations when the ad photo was shot from an active participant's point of view and the ad copy used third-person wording (he is leaving work). In addition, when the ad photo was shot from an observer's perspective and the ad copy employed second-person wording (you are leaving work), ad viewers reacted in an equally favorable manner. However, when both the ad photo and ad copy employed high self-reference techniques (photo was shot from an active participant's point of view and ad copy employed second-person wording) respondents did not react favorably. Instead, the ads were most effective when a moderate level of self-reference was activated. An extremely low level of self-reference (third-person wording and an observer view) or an extremely high level of self-reference (second-person wording and an active participant view) produced less favorable product evaluations. This research also revealed that these findings only emerged when an ad focused on averting a negative outcome but not when the ad focused on achieving a positive outcome.

These findings would seem to be consistent with the notion of the modified two-factor theory (Anand and Sternthal 1990; Cacioppo and Petty 1979) as they offer an inverted U-shape for the relationship between the level of self-reference and product evaluations. When consumers view the ad photo and ad copy and relate the product to themselves, they appear to process an ad more extensively and to allow themselves greater opportunity to scrutinize and appreciate the ad. Consumers' favorable or supportive thoughts (e.g., "A realistic example of why insurance is necessary for everyone") dominated over negative or counterpersuasive thoughts (e.g., "Who cares about insurance?"). Thus, product evaluations are heightened. However, when multiple self-reference techniques are employed and both the ad photo and ad copy encourage self-reference, elaboration increased to a high level, and consumers generated more unfavorable thoughts or even raised unrelated issues. This may be so because reactance or tedium set in. Respondents might have exhausted their supply of favorable thoughts about the product and started to generate more counterpersuasive or unrelated thoughts. Hence, these thoughts overwhelmed favorable thoughts, causing product evaluations to decline.

Several issues still await investigation and empirical study. One issue of considerable interest would be to investigate the impact of repeated exposure to ads that encourage self-reference. In particular, this research found an inverted U for self-reference only when an ad focused on averting a negative outcome. Ads that offered positive outcomes did not exhibit self-reference effects. It may be that with sufficient repetition, ads that depict a positive outcome produce the same inverted U-shaped pattern of effects observed when ads depicted a negative outcome. That is, the research found that positive outcomes resulted in consumers processing information in a more cursory manner. An increase in repetition may overcome the lack of careful processing people devote to ads featuring positive outcomes, such that eventually consumers might become responsive to prompts that encourage self-reference.

A higher level of repetition may also impact experimental findings when a negative outcome is presented. For ads that portray negative outcomes and that otherwise produce a moderate level of self-reference, repetition results in advertising wearout such that moderate self-reference conditions resemble extremely high self-reference contexts. Repetition, coupled with negative outcomes, may eliminate the inverted-U effects found in Meyers-Levy and Peracchio's (1996).

Another issue awaiting further inquiry is the threshold beyond which an ad that depicts a negative outcome evokes a fear-arousing response, which is likely to terminate processing and, thus, undermine the inverted-U effects that characterize a moderate level of self-reference. Whether appeals that invoke high levels of fear and arousal prompt a desirable, moderate level of self-reference or extreme anxiety and fear remains uncertain.

Color

Full-color and color-highlighted ads are used in advertising because they are thought to attract attention and to heighten persuasion (Meyers-Levy and Peracchio 1995). Color highlighting uses color to selectively highlight certain elements such as the product or the logo in a black-and-white ad. Research by Meyers-Levy and Peracchio (1995) found that when consumers are processing extensively, the attention-getting and persuasive properties of full-color and color-highlighted ads are moderated by the complexity of an ad. Thus, color ads do not always offer superior results. When consumers' process information in a less extensive manner, product attitudes will often be based on simple heuristics associated with superficial cues such as the physical attractiveness of the photo, the product, and/or the product user or spokesperson. Because color is used to enhance the perceived attractiveness of products, Meyers-Levy and Peracchio (1995) found that consumers who are processing information in a less extensive manner are likely to have more favorable product attitudes when ads contain color, either full color or color highlighting, rather than purely black-and-white visual images.

However, when consumers are motivated to process an ad critically and extensively with an eye toward substantiating the ad's assertions, Meyers-Levy and Peracchio (1995) found that color seems to have one of two effects. Color can consume resources by stimulating inferential processing that benefits ad-claim substantiation as colors and objects that are congenial with the ad message are processed. Alternatively, color may undermine ad-claim substantiation by usurping resources that would otherwise have been devoted to processing the ad claims. Whether color enhances or undermines product attitudes depends on the correspondence between the level of resources made available for ad processing and that required to process the ad. When processing motivation is high and ad processing consumes relatively few resources, ads are likely to benefit from the use of color that reinforces the ad copy, for example, when color-highlighting is used to highlight a product and the ad copy is concerned with touting the benefits of the product. Yet, if such processing or ad-claim substantiation is relatively taxing and usurps much of the consumers' cognitive resources, ad and product attitudes do not benefit. Thus, attitudes are likely to be more favorable when ads are simpler and use only black-and-white or when they color highlight only those elements in the ad that are relevant to substantiating the ad claims.

Future research might explore whether other ad elements that, like color, seem to consume cognitive resources by attracting attention and imparting information, also impact ad evaluations in a similar manner. For example, both the size of a product's image and the visual appeal of the product in an ad may have a similar impact on consumers' product evaluations (Meyers-Levy and Peracchio 1995). Future research should examine whether such ad elements enhance product evaluations when consumers are motivated to process and substantiate advertising, when processing or substantiating such advertising consumes a large amount of cognitive resources, and when the resources consumers make available to process and substantiate the advertising are equivalent to those required for ad processing. Future inquiry should assess such predictions.

Cropping

Ads often create visual ambiguity when objects of some relevance to the product featured in the ad appear severely cropped within an ad photo (Aaker 1982). For example, an ad for Hilton Hotels bears several verbal ad claims concerning the quality of the hotel's restaurants and depicts a well-dressed woman holding a cocktail. The woman's face in the ad is severely cropped so that only the portion below her nose is visible. Thus, her face is ambiguous, as it can be interpreted or completed in any number of ways. Research in both the consumer and aesthetics literatures suggests that the ambiguity created by a cropped or incomplete object may prompt people to seek closure by supplying the missing part. In turn, this process of resolving the ambiguity can enhance product evaluations.

In their research, Peracchio and Meyers-Levy (1994) have found that a severely cropped or incomplete object in an ad photo is often viewed as ambiguous, prompting more extensive ad processing as well as a search for closure, which, if successful, elicits positive product evaluations. Moreover, because extensive processing seems to intensify consumers' affective responses (Tesser 1978), the resulting positive effect is relatively extreme, thereby translating into more favorable product evaluations than would occur if the object were uncropped and thus prompted nonextensive processing and no closure.

However, Peracchio and Meyers-Levy (1994) find that object cropping in ads does not always enhance evaluations. This is because the task of mentally completing objects is likely to require substantial cognitive resources that in some instances may exceed the level of resources an individual evokes in processing the ad (Aaker 1982). The findings of this research indicate that only consumers who possess a high level of processing motivation are likely to perceive the ambiguity created by object cropping, be sufficiently motivated to complete the figure, and display elevated product evaluations in response to the cropped object.

Peracchio and Meyers-Levy's (1994) research suggests that cropping-induced ambiguity enhances consumers' product evaluations if the viewer is sufficiently motivated to mentally complete the ambiguous image of the cropped object. However, this enhancement of evaluations will occur only when the object that is cropped is not directly relevant to the ad claims, while the object that is relevant to and reinforces the ad claims remains largely uncropped and thus unambiguous. If motivated viewers encounter an ad containing an ambiguous cropped object that is relevant to but impairs their attempts to substantiate those ad claims, Peracchio and Meyers-Levy (1994) find that cropping-induced ambiguity produces product evaluations that are no more favorable than they would be if no object was cropped. This may be so because if the object that is relevant to substantiating the verbal ad claims is severely cropped and thus ambiguous, ad-claim substantiation is likely to be impaired or limited. As such, the affective advantage that otherwise might be associated with the severely cropped object seems to be offset by intense negative effect spawned by the viewer's unsuccessful attempts to substantiate the verbal ad claims. Thus, object cropping heightens product evaluations only if the object that is severely cropped is not the one that is directly relevant to, and hence potentially serves to, substantiate the verbal ad claims.

A number of issues concerning cropping effects remain to be addressed. First, research needs to investigate whether repeated exposure to ads that depict severely cropped objects will result in typical patterns of advertising wearout. Ads depicting severely cropped objects that are of low relevance to ad claims can be intriguing or involving for the ad viewer. These ads may wear out more slowly than ads with no cropped objects. For example, an ad for Thomasville home furnishings crops images of both a Thomasville bed and a female model such that half of each image is visible to the ad viewer. The two half-images are juxtaposed side by side in the ad prompting the viewer to seek out connections between the two images. Such an ad may wear out more slowly as the viewer attempts to find connections between the two different severely cropped images.

Future research should also investigate whether the effects observed in Peracchio and Meyers-Levy (1994) are robust across varying levels of cropping, for example, moderate versus severe object cropping. If an object of considerable relevance to ad copy is moderately cropped, the cropped object might result in greater processing and perhaps not impede viewers' substantiation of the ad claims. Alternatively, consumers' evaluation of moderately cropped objects may not differ if the cropped object is of high or low relevance to the ad claims.

Finally, future research should examine situations in which object cropping invites negative associations. In particular, if a low relevance object in an ad is cropped and invites negative associations or images when a viewer mentally completes it, how will product evaluations be affected? These and other issues involving object cropping in advertising need to be investigated.

Ad Layout

Advertisers often attempt to heighten product persuasion by employing particular stylistic properties in developing an ad. One such stylistic device involves physically integrating or separating the visual image in an ad and the ad claims. For example, an ad for Clarins self-tanner physically integrates the ad copy with the visual image in the ad. The ad copy in the Clarins ad offers a narrative about the experience a consumer might have walking in "a light, refreshing rain" after using the product featured in the ad. This copy contains a great deal of contextual information about experiencing the advertised product. The visual image in this ad depicts an attractive female model, dressed in white, and walking in the rain. The ad copy in this ad is superimposed over the visual image. Physically integrating this narrative ad copy with the visual image would seem to have heightened the likelihood that the ad viewer will read the ad copy while cross-referencing the visual image.

Peracchio and Meyers-Levy (1997) explored the impact of integrating or physically separating the visual image in an ad and the ad copy. For example, in their research they employed a beer ad that conveyed the product features or benefits in a straightforward and factual manner (e.g., "It's masterfully processed in specially designed hops. And each batch is made using a unique brewing method."). They also tested narrative ad copy for the same beer ad that portrayed the product features by expressing them in a narrative manner and providing much contextual information about the advertised product (e.g., "As a perfectionist, however, he designed his own hops, [and] employed his family-inspired superior brewing methods."). The beer ad employed two ad layouts. In one ad layout the visual image was physically integrated with the ad copy while the second ad layout separated the ad copy from the image.

Consistent with resource-matching theory, Peracchio and Meyers-Levy (1997) found that the type of ad copy used in an ad, along with the physical layout of the ad, could impact the degree to which balance is achieved between the resources one makes available for processing versus those required to process the ad. Persuasion is maximized when a match between resource required and resource available occurs (Anand and Sternthal 1989). Specifically, when viewers encountered an ad in which identification of the product assertions requires substantial resources because they are embedded in contextually rich narrative ad copy, persuasion was greater when the ad copy and ad picture were physically integrated rather than separated. This occurred because the integrated ad layout eased the process of cross-referencing and substantiating the verbal product claims with relevant ad picture elements and reduced the relatively high resource demands imposed by the ad. Thus, the resources viewers needed to process the ad were made commensurate with those available for processing. On the other hand, when motivated viewers received an ad that featured product assertions that required few resources to process because they were presented in to-the-point, factual ad copy, persuasion was greater when the ad copy and ad picture were physically separated and thereby heightened the resources required to cross-reference and visually substantiate the product assertions, as opposed to when these ad components were integrated.

In this research, only motivated viewers responded to physically separating versus integrating the ad copy and visual image used in the ad. These elements had no effect on those viewers with lower motivational levels. Viewers with lower motivation appeared to rely on easily available heuristics or simple decision rules in making their product assessments. In sum, this research suggests that people's ability and motivation (i.e., available resources) to process an ad determine how they form product evaluations. Specifically, under high motivation, viewers generated product evaluations based on "central" information (Petty, Cacioppo, and Schumann 1983) obtained from processing the ad copy and substantiating the ad picture when the resources required for ad processing match those that are available (e.g., narrative ad copy/separated ad layout condition). When the resource demands exceeded or fall short of the resources required, "peripheral" information may dominate the formation of product evaluations.

A number of issues regarding integrating or separating the visual image and copy in an ad remain to be addressed. In Peracchio and Meyers-Levy (1997), ad viewers were exposed to only two ads. This advertising was viewed in isolation, not in a naturalistic print advertising context containing articles as well as an array of advertisements. In the future, researchers should explore the impact of integrating or separating the visual image and copy in an ad within a more typical cluttered advertising.

In addition, future research should also examine the impact of repeated exposure on integrating or separating the visual image and copy in an ad. It might be expected that under higher levels of exposure, respondents who are less motivated might process aspects of the ads beyond the easily accessed heuristic cues. Ad repetition might eliminate the impact of integrating versus separating the visual image and copy for more motivated viewers due to the onset of advertising wearout. Such viewers might tire of the ads and respond to them by generating relatively negative thoughts and product evaluations that reflect such tedium. Finally, in the future, research should identify factors that might qualify the findings of Peracchio and Meyers-Levy (1997). Along these lines, we suspect that if an ad picture were very complex, integrating ad copy with it actually may complicate rather than simplify ad processing. We hope that future research will investigate this and other factors that may moderate our findings.

Processing Multiple Stylistic Properties of Visual Images

Most visual images rely upon a number of stylistic properties including camera angle, color, visual orientation, and cropping. Although the empirical research reported in this chapter describes the impact of individual stylistic properties of a visual image, to date, no empirical work has investigated the impact of multiple stylistic properties of a particular visual image within a single research effort.

Empirical research has yet to investigate the impact or interaction of two or more stylistic properties; for example, the impact of both the camera angle and color of a particular visual image within a single research effort.

The notion that visual images rely upon and integrate multiple stylistic properties raises a number of interesting questions regarding how these properties might be simultaneously or sequentially processed. In particular, how might consumers reconcile the potentially conflicting stylistic properties that are often present in the visual images viewed in ads? And as a corollary to this question, should the stylistic properties of a visual image be selected to convey multiple concepts or should these stylistic properties be designed to converge and convey upon a single concept?

In considering these questions, it may be helpful to conjecture how multiple stylistic properties might interact within a specific ad. For example, in an ad for the action movie *Mission Impossible III,* a visual image of Tom Cruise employs an upward-focused, low camera angle thought to convey power and potency (Meyers-Levy and Peracchio 1992). This visual image of Mr. Cruise also employs soft, muted lighting and color, perhaps negating and certainly conflicting with the power conveyed by the camera angle. As this ad is promoting an action movie, one may wonder if the image of Mr. Cruise would have had greater impact on potential moviegoers if the lighting and color echoed the power and potency conveyed by the camera angle. Alternatively, it may be that by combining two seemingly conflicting stylistic properties in this image of Mr. Cruise and "softening" the impact of the power conveyed by the low camera angle, the image, the ad, and the movie have greater appeal to a wider variety of moviegoers. In this particular case, during 2006, Mr. Cruise's Q score, a measure used to quantify a celebrity's likeability and popularity, dropped from a high of 30 percent to 19 percent due primarily to a decrease in female moviegoers' assessments of Mr. Cruise (Marr 2006). Perhaps softening the visual image of Mr. Cruise had a positive impact on his and *Mission Impossible III*'s appeal among these moviegoers.

Now consider an advertisement for the movie *Superman Returns.* This ad features a visual image of Superman looking down upon the earth. The visual image in this ad employs a high, downward-looking camera angle thought to convey weakness (Meyers-Levy and Peracchio 1992). However, in this ad the high camera angle is matched with a powerful theme, rescuing people in need. In addition to employing a high camera angle, this ad also appears to place the ad viewer in the role of active participant. The ad viewer seems to be looking down upon the earth from the same perspective as Superman. Thus, the ad allows the ad viewer to assume the perspective or the role of Superman. It seems possible that the combination of these two particular stylistic properties, a high camera angle and a visual perspective that places the viewer in the role of active participant, generates a positive reaction from ad viewers. Future research should explore how various combinations of stylistic properties of visual images impact the persuasiveness of both products and advertisements.

Research by Phillips and McQuarrie (2002) may also help to explain how the multiple stylistic properties of a visual image are processed and integrated. In their research, Phillips and McQuarrie (2002) observed a dramatic shift in the way rhetorical figures have been used in advertising. Their exploration of rhetorical style in U.S. magazine advertisements from 1954 to 1999 indicates that more layering of multiple rhetorical figures has been used over time. That is, in earlier ads, advertisers used complex rhetorical figures, such as tropes, alone. Over the study period, the number of ads containing more than one complex rhetorical figure has increased. As suggested by Phillips and McQuarrie (2002, 11), this phenomenon is the result of ". . . a mutual adaptation of advertisers and consumers to a changed advertising environment." Consumers today are more adept and competent with regard to processing advertising. They seek out novel, creative, and interesting advertising. Future research should investigate how advertisers have used multiple stylistic properties in advertising over time. Have advertisers increased their use and layering of multiple stylistic properties in visual images over time?

Furthermore, future research should investigate when and whether multiple stylistic properties may have additive or redundant effects. Previous research indicates that when rhetorical figures are redundant (e.g., multiple schemes), the combination of rhetorical figures generates redundant effects on the extent of processing. However, when different rhetorical figures are unique to one another (e.g., schemes and tropes), the combination of rhetorical figures results in additive effects (Mothersbaugh, Huhmann, and Franke 2002). Similarly, what effects might occur when advertisers combine multiple stylistic properties in advertising? For example, when respondents are engaged in more extensive ad processing, does a high or above eye-level camera angle have a positive impact on vertically oriented objects and yield additive effects? Or do the two aforementioned stylistic properties have redundant effects? These and other issues involving the potential additive or redundant effects of multiple stylistic properties should be explored in the future.

In considering how the various stylistic properties of a visual image might be processed, it is helpful to ponder how each of these stylistic elements individually contributes to the impact of the visual image. As empirical research has yet to explore this issue, it seems appropriate to look outside of marketing and psychology to consider both how the multiple stylistic properties of an image might be processed as well as how to develop a visual image that builds upon and from each of its stylistic properties. Perhaps by considering ideas from new areas, we may develop insight that illuminates our understanding of the stylistic properties of images.

A key technique in Italian cooking is called *insaporire,* literally the process of "making tasty" (Hazen 2004). Marcella Hazen (2004, 15–16) writes, "A crucial step in the making of most Italian dishes, insaporire is what you do to draw out and develop the flavor of a single or several ingredients. . . . There are occasions when you need to insaporire more than one ingredient. In such instances you apply the method successively to each ingredient, thus layering its flavor over that of the ingredient that preceded it. . . . (Insaporire) holds that flavor resides within those ingredients that define a dish, and that the object of cooking anything is to open the way for that flavor to emerge." Perhaps *insaporire* is relevant to understanding how the stylistic properties of a visual image work together or detract from one another in creating a visual image. It would seem that the cultivation of each individual stylistic property and the process of layering each property successively within an image is essential to creating a persuasive visual image. Perhaps, it is this cultivation and layering process that allows a visual image to become more than the sum of its stylistic properties.

Conclusion

Taken together, the results of research examining the stylistic properties of visual images indicate that seemingly subtle features of images have a significant impact on consumers' advertising and product assessments. Future research should continue to examine the various stylistic properties of visual images including dynamic versus static images, the impact of image size within the visual frame, the realistic versus stylized representation of an image, the impact of the visual composition on image processing, and the narrative quality of an image as well as many others. This future research should seek to shed insight into the role that cognitive and implicit processes play in consumers' assessments of visual images and their stylistic properties. Future research should explore how and when implicit and explicit attitudes can exist simultaneously and impact the assessments of the stylistic properties of visual images (Johar, Maheswaran, and Peracchio 2006; Wilson, Lindsey, and Schooler 2000). The exploration of these issues offers the promise of important insights to our understanding of the power of visual images, and from a theoretical perspective, a greater understanding of how these images are processed. The key to crafting persuasive visual images is to gain a theoretical understanding of how consumers process images and to create images based on this conceptualization.

   A cursory reflection upon the stylistic properties of images may lead one to wonder if these properties really offer a significant contribution to the processing of visual images. Our empirical review of research examining the stylistic properties of images would seem to negate this assessment and suggests that these stylistic properties have a powerful impact on consumers' reactions to images and to the products depicted in them. Although theoretical advances in our understanding of the stylistic properties of visual images are evident, much research awaits future investigation. We urge researchers to explore the stylistic properties of visual images. Perhaps by gaining a greater understanding of the stylistic properties of images, we will better comprehend and appreciate the power of the visual image.

> We shall not cease from exploration
> And the end of all our exploring
> Will be to arrive where we started
> And to know the place for the first time
> T.S. Eliot, "Little Gidding"

References

Aaker, David A. 1982. *Advertising Management.* Englewood Cliffs, NJ: Prentice Hall.

Anand, Punam, and Brian Sternthal. 1989. "Strategies for Designing Persuasive Messages: Deductions from the Resource Matching Hypothesis." In *Cognitive and Affective Responses to Advertising,* ed. Patricia Cafferata and Alice Tybout, 135–159. Lexington, MA: Lexington Books.

———, and ———. 1990. "Ease of Message Processing as a Moderator of Repetition Effects in Advertising." *Journal of Marketing Research* 27 (August): 345–353.

Bargh, John A. 1996. "Automaticity in Social Psychology." In *Social Psychology: Handbook of Basic Principles,* ed. E. Tory Higgins and Arie W. Kruglanski, 169–183. New York: Guilford Press.

Bohle, Robert, and Mario Garcia. 1986. "Readers Reactions to Color in Newspapers." Paper presented at the annual meeting of the Association for Education in Journalism and Mass Communication, Norman, Oklahoma, August 3–6.

Cacioppo, John T., and Richard E. Petty. 1979. "Effects of Message Repetition and Position on Cognitive Response, Recall, and Persuasion." *Journal of Personality and Social Psychology* 37 (January): 97–109.

Chaiken, Shelly. 1980. "Heuristic versus Systematic Information Processing and the Use of Source versus Message Cues in Persuasion." *Journal of Personality and Social Psychology* 39 (November): 752–766.

Click, J.W., and Guido H. Stempel III. 1976. "Reader Response to Front Pages with Four-Color Halftones." *Journalism Quarterly* 53 (Winter): 736–738.

Dondis, A. Donis. 1993. *A Primer of Visual Literacy.* Cambridge, MA: MIT Press.

Goodman, Andy. 2002. *Why Bad Ads Happen to Good Causes.* Los Angeles: Cause Communication.

Goossens, Cees. 2003. "Visual Persuasion: Mental Imagery Processing and Emotional Experiences." In *Persuasive Imagery,* ed. Linda M. Scott and Rajeev Batra, 129–138. Mahwah, NJ: Erlbaum.

Hatcher, Evelyn P. 1974. *Visual Metaphors: A Methodological Study in Visual Communication.* Albuquerque: University of New Mexico Press.

Hazen, Marcella. 2004. *Marcella Says.* New York: HarperCollins.

Johar, Gita V.; Durairaj Maheswaran; and Laura A. Peracchio. 2006. "*MAP*ping the Frontiers: Theoretical Advances in Consumer Research on *M*emory, *A*ffect, and *P*ersuasion." *Journal of Consumer Research* 33 (June): 139–149.

Kraft, Robert N. 1987. "The Influence of Camera Angle on Comprehension and Retention of Pictorial Events." *Memory & Cognition* 15 (July): 291–307.

Kreitler, Hans, and Shulamith Kreitler. 1972. *Psychology of the Arts.* Durham, NC: Duke University Press.

Kress, Gunther, and Theo van Leeuwen. 1996. *Reading Images: The Grammar of Visual Design.* London: Routledge.

Marr, Melissa. 2006. "Studio Woos Women Turned Off by Cruise." *Wall Street Journal,* May 1.

McQuarrie, Edward F., and David Glen Mick. 1996. "Figures of Rhetoric in Advertising Language." *Journal of Consumer Research* 22 (March): 424–438.

———, and ———. 1999. "Visual Rhetoric in Advertising: Text-Interpretive, Experimental, and Reader-Response Analysis." *Journal of Consumer Research* 26 (June): 37–54.

Messaris, Paul. 1997. *Visual Persuasion: The Role of Images in Advertising.* Thousand Oaks, CA: Sage.

Meyers-Levy, Joan, and Laura A. Peracchio. 1992. "Getting an Angle in Advertising: The Effect of Camera Angle on Product Evaluations." *Journal of Marketing Research* 29 (November): 454–461.

————, and ————. 1995. "Understanding the Effects of Color: How the Correspondence between Available and Required Resources Affects Attitudes." *Journal of Consumer Research* 22 (September): 121–138.

————, and ————. 1996. "Moderators of the Impact of Self-Reference on Persuasion." *Journal of Consumer Research* 22 (March): 408–423.

Mitchell, Andrew A., and Jerry C. Olson. 1981. "Are Product Attribute Beliefs the Only Mediator of Advertising Effects on Brand Attitude?" *Journal of Marketing Research* 18 (August): 318–332.

Mothersbaugh, David L.; Bruce A. Huhmann; and George R. Franke. 2002. "Combinatory and Separative Effects of Rhetorical Figures on Consumers' Effort and Focus in Ad Processing." *Journal of Consumer Research* 28 (March): 589–602.

Nelson, Roy P. 1973. *The Design of Advertising*. Dubuque, IA: Brown & Benchmark.

Nordhielm, Christie L. 2002. "The Influence of Level of Processing on Advertising Repetition Effects." *Journal of Consumer Research* 29 (December): 371–382.

Pallak, Suzanne R. 1983. "Salience of a Communicator's Physical Attractiveness and Persuasion: A Heuristic versus Systematic Processing Interpretation." *Social Cognition* 2 (Summer): 158–170.

Peracchio, Laura A., and Joan Meyers-Levy. 1994. "How Ambiguous Cropped Objects in Ad Photos Can Affect Product Evaluations." *Journal of Consumer Research* 21 (June): 190–204.

————, and ————. 1997. "Evaluating Persuasion-Enhancing Techniques from a Resource-Matching Perspective." *Journal of Consumer Research* 24 (September): 178–191.

————, and ————. 2005. "Using Stylistic Properties of Ad Pictures to Communicate with Consumers." *Journal of Consumer Research* 32 (June): 29–40.

Petty, Richard E.; John T. Cacioppo; and David Schumann. 1983. "Central and Peripheral Routes to Advertising Effectiveness: The Moderating Role of Involvement." *Journal of Consumer Research* 10 (September): 135–146.

Phillips, Barbara J., and Edward F. McQuarrie. 2002. "The Development, Change, and Transformation of Rhetorical Style in Magazine Advertisements 1954–1999." *Journal of Advertising* 31 (Winter): 1–13.

————, and ————. 2004. "Beyond Visual Metaphor: A New Typology of Visual Rhetoric in Advertising." *Marketing Theory* 4 (1/2): 113–136.

Raghubir, Priya, and Aradhna Krishna. 1996. "As the Crow Flies: Bias in Consumers' Map-Based Distance Judgments." *Journal of Consumer Research* 23 (June): 26–39.

————, and Joydeep Srivastava. 2002. "Effect of Face Value on Product Valuation in Foreign Currencies." *Journal of Consumer Research* 29 (December): 335–347.

Scott, Linda M. 1994. "Images in Advertising: The Need for a Theory of Visual Rhetoric." *Journal of Consumer Research* 21 (September): 252–273.

————, and Rajeev Batra, eds. 2003. *Persuasive Imagery: A Consumer Response Perspective*. Mahwah, NJ: Erlbaum.

Tesser, Abraham. 1978. "Self-Generated Attitude Change." In *Advances in Experimental Social Psychology*, ed. Leonard Berkowitz, 289–338. New York: Academic Press.

Wilson, Timothy D.; Samuel Lindsey; and Tonya Y. Schooler. 2000. "A Model of Dual Attitudes." *Psychological Review* 107 (January): 101–126.

Yorkston, Eric, and Geeta Menon. 2004. "A Sound Idea: Phonetic Effects of Brand Names on Consumer Judgments." *Journal of Consumer Research* 31 (June): 43–51.

Zaltman, Gerald. 2000. "Consumer Researchers: Take a Hike!" *Journal of Consumer Research* 26 (March): 423–428.

11

Classifying Visual Rhetoric

Conceptual and Structural Heuristics

Alfons Maes and Joost Schilperoord

Chapter Summary

This chapter discusses a number of problems and heuristics with regard to iden-tifying and analyzing classes of visual rhetoric in commercial ads. The chapter argues that clear-cut structural and conceptual classes of visual rhetoric do not sufficiently take into account the interpretation subtleties and ambiguities pres-ent in visual rhetoric. We propose a series of heuristic steps needed to define the rhetorical nature of ads and to exploit the structural and conceptual load of visual rhetoric in ads. These heuristics, we contend, will not always result in an unequivo-cal interpretation of visual rhetoric, but will at least explain on what point and why interpretations differ.

Over the past decade, figures of visual rhetoric have attracted a great deal of attention from researchers working in the field of consumer research, communication, and cognitive linguistics. A large number of studies focus on visual rhetoric in relation to persuasion or consumers' responses, with a special focus on visual metaphor (e.g., Forceville 1996; Kenney and Scott 2003; McQuarrie and Mick 1999; Phillips 2003; Scott and Batra 2003; Teng and Sun 2002; Van Mulken, Van Enschot-van Dijk, and Hoeken 2005). Despite large differences in perspective and ambition, all researchers deal in some way with three intimately related aspects of visual rhetoric: the visual design or structure of rhetorical figures (i.e., the form of the message), the meaning operations related to these figures (i.e., the message content), and the pragmatic effects they have on viewers. We will refer to these aspects as the structural, the conceptual, and the pragmatic aspects of visual rhetoric, respectively.

An intriguing aspect in the study of rhetoric in general and visual rhetoric in particular is the continuing quest for a suitable classification of specimens of rhetoric. Since the early days of classical rhetoric, scholars have been trying to define different form-meaning manipulations in language that can be considered rhetorical. Think of the well-known dichotomy between schemes and tropes. More recently, similar attempts can be found to classify types of visual rhetoric, either grafted onto existing classifications for verbal rhetoric (e.g., Durand 1987; Kennedy 1982; McQuarrie and Mick 1999) or starting purely from the visual characteristics of rhetoric (e.g., Forceville 1996; Groupe Mu 1992; Phillips and McQuarrie 2004; Van Mulken 2003).

The aim of this chapter is to contribute to the state of the art of classifying visual rhetoric by discussing a number of problems with regard to identifying and analyzing visual rhetorical figuration. The chapter argues that the fairly clear-cut structural and conceptual classes of visual rhetoric, as they have been put forward thus far, do not sufficiently take into account the interpretation subtleties and ambiguities present in visual rhetoric. This in turn makes these classes an uncertain basis for predicting pragmatic effects or viewers' responses. However, we explicitly do *not* intend to construct a full-fledged new taxonomy. Rather, we want to show that the process of identifying and analyzing visual rhetoric can be turned into a series of steps that represent separate decisions. These decisions can subsequently be guided by heuristics. Our goal in this chapter is to suggest the kind of heuristic questions that are needed and the way they can be underpinned theoretically. We do not think that heuristics always lead to proper results, let alone "correct" ones, but we do believe that heuristics have the virtue of rendering the process of identification and analysis more transparent. Disagreements between different analysts can be traced to the relevant steps within the process and described in terms of the heuristic procedures. Disagreements seem inevitable, but an explicit heuristic procedure may at least explain the disagreements.

In this chapter, first, we briefly define the goals of a taxonomy of visual rhetoric: what do we want a taxonomy to be and to do for us? Second, we review a number of taxonomies of visual rhetoric. Then we discuss interpretation heuristics, enabling us to answer three successive questions of the analytical procedure: (1) Is this ad rhetorical or not? (2) What is the conceptual interpretation of the ad? and (3) What is the structural interpretation of the ad? In the conclusion, we show how the conceptual and structural characteristics discussed in the chapter relate to the pragmatic effects of ads.

Criteria for Evaluating Taxonomies of Visual Rhetoric

As a starting point, we contend that a sound and useful taxonomy enables experts and informed users:

- to decide whether an ad is rhetorical or not (criterion 1),
- to analyze the meaning operations that are involved (criterion 2),

- to analyze the design templates or characteristics that are employed in rhetorical ads (criterion 3), and
- to ground hypotheses concerning viewer's responses to the various conceptual and structural configurations (criterion 4).

The overall goal of an advertisement for a product is to persuade an audience of the product's benefits or positive qualities. Ads attempt to achieve this by attributing certain qualities to the product. This qualification defines the main message of an ad, and it can be represented as a basic propositional message expressing a relation between two entities, the product, *X*, on the one hand, and the quality or qualification, *Y*, on the other (for a similar idea, see, e.g., Durand 1987; van Mulken 2003). The basic propositional message can take various shapes, such as *product X has property Y*, or *product X leads to situation Y*, or *product X is preferred by person Y*, and so on. All such messages can thus be subsumed under the generic conceptual template *product X is somehow related to Y*, or, in a quasi-formal notation: $X \sim Y$.

Starting from this interpretation anchor point, the first taxonomic goal follows straightforwardly: any taxonomy of visual rhetoric should provide users with analytical tools to answer the question whether this basic $X \sim Y$ message is expressed by a visual rhetorical figure or not. If the answer is yes, the taxonomy should subsequently enable users to determine how the rhetorical figure packages the basic propositional message, both structurally and conceptually. Therefore, it should define the structural templates involved as well as the different meaning operations that ultimately result in the basic propositional message. Structural templates define the visual syntax that characterizes figures of visual rhetoric, in particular the way in which the two entities or domains (*X* and *Y*) are visually present in the image. On the conceptual axis, the taxonomy is supposed to define the basic types of meaning operations triggered by a rhetorical figure. A rhetorical figure may invite viewers to associate *X* and *Y*, to compare them, to draw causal, temporal, or other contiguity relations between them, or even to consider them identical. A final criterion for evaluating a taxonomy concerns the extent to which it enables users to deduce testable hypotheses concerning the way viewers will process visual rhetorical figures and how these figures will affect them in terms of ad liking, persuasive impact, perceived complexity, and recall. Hence, the taxonomy should allow for empirical predictions, such as *this structural class of visual rhetoric leads to a better recall of the basic propositional message than that one*, or *this class is better liked or perceived as more complex than that one.*

These four taxonomic goals can also be seen as four criteria for evaluating proposals in this vein. So, before going into them in more detail, we shall discuss a number of recent classification proposals for visual rhetoric, thereby focusing on whether and how they meet these four criteria.

Taxonomies of Visual Rhetoric

Over the past two decades, a number of taxonomies have been proposed for the classification of visual rhetoric. These proposals come in two different types. The first type starts from language-based, classical rhetorical figures such as *rhyme* and *metaphor* and tries to identify the characteristics of visual manifestations of these figures, as can be seen, for example, in Durand (1987) and Kennedy (1982). These proposals typically address questions such as *what does visual rhyme look like? how are visual puns shaped?* and *can we identify visual manifestations of paradoxes?* A prominent example can be found in McQuarrie and Mick (1999). Their proposal exemplifies the kinds of considerations that may lead one to treat visual and verbal figures of rhetoric on a par. McQuarrie and Mick (1996) distinguish visual rhetorical figures by means of the model they had developed earlier for classifying verbal rhetorical figures in advertisements. This is a three-level hierarchical model that distinguishes rhetorical figures in general (level 1), rhetorical mode (level 2), and rhetorical operation (level 3). At level 1, the level relevant to our current discussion, rhetorical figures are defined as "deviations from expectation" (McQuarrie and Mick 1996, 425), which are nonetheless not rejected as nonsensical by readers/viewers. In addition, each figure conforms to a template that is *invariant across contexts* and *contents*. In their 1999 article, McQuarrie and Mick add to these one additional factor: the medium employed to express the rhetorical figure. They reason that it should be possible to vary not only contents and contexts but also the mode of expression independently from the template itself. Therefore, they contend that manifestations of the classical figures of rhetoric ought to be possible. It would then also follow that verbal and visual manifestations can be classified according to the same set of rhetorical distinctions.

Proposals of the second type take the visual rather than the verbal mode as a starting point. Visual manifestations are considered in their own right, and therefore they can be sufficiently classified only by a taxonomy that explicitly focuses on the specifics of the visual modality. Three prominent examples of this classification type are Groupe Mu (1992; van Mulken 2003), Forceville's (1996) theory of visual metaphor, and Phillips and McQuarrie's (2004) taxonomy.

Groupe Mu (1992)

The first proposal was developed by a group of Belgian researchers called "Groupe Mu" (1992; van Mulken 2003). This taxonomy posits two dimensions that are considered unique for the visual modality: object presence (with the values: present or absent) and object connection (values: conjoint or disjoint). Together, they yield a two-by-two crossed taxonomy. The presence dimension covers images in which two objects are present as well as cases in which only one of them is present, but in such a way that the present object triggers the salience of another, absent object. Visual hyperboles are a case in point. They occur if an image depicts an exagger-

Figure 11.1   **Light Cheese Ad (Babybel Light)**

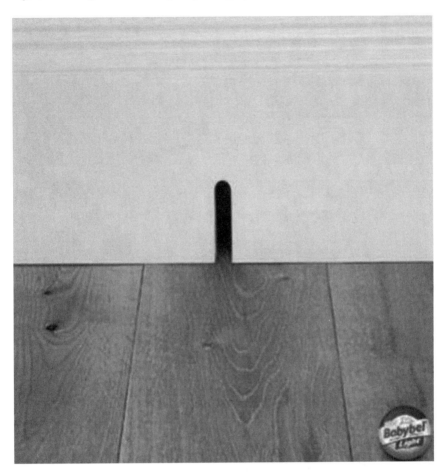

ated object, for example, an oversized object (or the opposite, e.g., the mouse hole in Figure 11.1). Because such deviations can be acknowledged only if one knows the normal size of the object that is shown, the normally sized object may be said to be absent in the image, while at the same time the exaggeration calls it to mind. According to the connection dimension, objects may be conjoint, which means that they are somehow merged to render a hybrid, homospatial object, or disjoint, in which case the objects are simply put next to or above each other.

How does the Groupe Mu proposal relate to the criteria that we discussed in the former section? First, the model has the obvious advantage of simplicity as it distinguishes only four types of visual rhetoric. Furthermore, the model may serve as a basis for deducing hypotheses regarding the perceived complexity of figures that follow from the different dimensional combinations (criterion 4). For example,

Figure 11.2   **Blond Beer Ad (Grolsch)**

absent objects can be considered more complex to process than present objects. In addition, the model enables one to classify visual configurations in their own right, rather than approaching them from the point of view of verbal figurations. This is achieved by explicitly taking into account the structural templates on which visual rhetorical figures are based (criterion 3).

Despite these qualities the model also has serious drawbacks. It is not easily applicable in actual practice, as has been demonstrated in van Mulken (2003). For example, instances of absent–conjoined visual rhetoric are hard to imagine: how can two objects be depicted as conjoined or merged, if one of them is absent? Moreover, the taxonomy has little to say about the conceptual relations that hold between the objects (criterion 2), as it is confined only to the structural features of visual rhetorical figures. Finally, the model seems to presuppose cases of visual rhetorical figuration, rather than truly identifying them (criterion 1).

Forceville (1996)

Forceville's (1996) proposal is specifically designed to analyze visual instances of metaphors and similes rather than visual rhetorical figures in general. Forceville distinguishes four meaning-form classes of visual metaphors (criteria 2 and 3): advertisements in which the two terms are both present but shown separately (which he labels similes), ads containing images in which the two terms are merged (MP2s), ads in which only one of the two terms is present whereas the other one should be inferred from contextual elements (MP1s), and finally, ads in which metaphors are based on visual and verbal triggers (verbo-pictorial metaphors or VPMs).

Unlike the other proposals, Forceville's model explicitly addresses the issue of identification (criterion 1). He claims that we are dealing with an instance of visual metaphor if and only if the following three analytical questions can be satisfactorily answered: (1) What are the two objects? (2) Which one is the source and which one the target object? (3) What attributes and relations are to be transferred from source to target? In terms of the propositional template $X \sim Y$, the first analytical step should thus identify the X and Y objects. If the source and target terms are furthermore identified (question 2), the $X \sim Y$ can be rephrased as an instance of a metaphorical $X = Y$ relation. For example, in Figure 11.2, the two terms to be identified are the product, *Grolsch premium blond beer* and *Marilyn Monroe*. Since an ad is usually about the product, Forceville reasons that this object is the target term and the other one, the source. Hence, step 2 results in X (GROLSCH PREMIUM BLOND) $\sim Y$ (MARILYN MONROE). Step 3 requires interpretation: the viewer should look for those features or attributes linked to the source term that are to be transferred to the target term. For Figure 11.2, the viewer should infer that the (highly salient) property *blond* is the main candidate for transfer. This renders the full interpretation at which the viewer should arrive: "This particular beer is as (prominently) blond as Marilyn Monroe." Note that the deviation from expectation in this particular case lies in the somewhat unusual comparison between the source term and the product. In sum, in terms of the four criteria, Forceville's proposal meets the first three; however, it is silent about the fourth criterion.

Phillips and McQuarrie (2004)

The most recent classification proposal, developed by Phillips and McQuarrie (2004), is the only one that explicitly addresses criterion 4. Their taxonomy is specifically directed at classifying visual figures of rhetoric. The authors contend that "pictures are not speech" (2004, 114) and therefore visual rhetoric cannot be considered as the mere visualization of verbal figures of rhetoric. Consequently, their proposal eliminates classical notions such as metaphor, pun, and rhyme, and also drops the basic distinction between schemes and tropes. The taxonomy combines two dimensions in a crossed model: visual complexity (criterion 3) and meaning operation (criterion 2) and it allows for specific predictions concerning cognitive and emotional responses by viewers, given a particular combination of the structural and conceptual aspect (criterion 4).

Visual structure refers to "the way the two elements that comprise the visual rhetorical figure are physically pictured in the ad" (Phillips and McQuarrie 2004, 116). The model distinguishes three classes, juxtaposition, fusion, and replacement, and the authors claim that all instances of visual rhetoric conform to one of these categories, or a combination of them. Meaning operation refers to "the target or focus of the cognitive processing required to comprehend the picture" (Ibid.). Again, the model distinguishes three types: connection, similarity, and opposition. Meaning operations are viewed as "instructions to consumers that direct their inferences from the arranged elements" (Ibid. 118). Connection is a simple meaning operation, whereas similarity allows one to draw multiple meanings from an image. Finally, if two objects have a relation of opposition their associated meanings are to be contrasted to each other.

The model furthermore accounts for the pragmatic effects of visual rhetoric by relating visual structure and meaning operation to distinct types of cognitive and affective responses. The visual structure dimension is defined as a complexity scale, with images being perceived as more complex as one moves from juxtaposition to fusion to replacement. Increased complexity means an increase in cognitive processes such as cognitive elaboration and recall, but also increased positive attitudes toward the ad (Ibid. 128). Meaning operation is projected on a scale, on which meaning richness increases as one moves from connection to similarity to opposition (Ibid. 120). In turn, this is assumed to lead to increased cognitive elaboration, belief formation, recall, and ad liking.

Phillips and McQuarrie's model does not deal with identifying visual rhetoric (criterion 1). Like the Groupe Mu proposal, the model presupposes rhetorical figuration, rather than identifying it. However, an important asset of the Phillips and McQuarrie model is that it elegantly integrates three of the four criteria we put forth: the matrix is based on a structural and a conceptual dimension and it predicts differences in persuasive impact. Apart from the general prediction that any message containing a figure of rhetoric has greater persuasive impact than ads without figures, the model predicts different grades of complexity and meaning richness

Table 11.1

Comparing Three Taxonomies for Visual Rhetoric

	Groupe Mu	Forceville	Phillips and McQuarrie
Identification	–	+	–
Structural	+/–	+	+
Conceptual	–	+	+
Pragmatic	+/–	–	+

from the upper-left box in the model (juxtaposition–connection) to the lower-right box (replacement–opposition). This naturally calls for empirical validation, which falls outside the scope of this chapter.

Table 11.1 summarizes how the three taxonomies that are typically focused on visual rhetoric deal with the criteria we have put forward.

In the next sections, we discuss heuristics to distinguish rhetorical from nonrhetorical ads, and include additional interpretation heuristics to refine the conceptual and structural classes discussed thus far.

Step 1: Distinguishing Rhetorical from Nonrhetorical Ads

As we saw earlier, rhetorical figuration, either visual or verbal, can be defined as artful deviation from expectations by the viewer. Although the notion artful deviation is obviously at the core of visual rhetoric, it leaves much room for interpretation. First, the definition tacitly assumes that viewers expect advertisements to inform them by means of realistic pictures or descriptions, rather than nonliteral, figurative messages. True as this may be, it may just as well be the other way around. Browsing through a collection of recent ads by Wiedemann (2004), one gets the distinct impression that nonliteral deviation from reality may even be the default, rather than the exception. An ad that only tells us "This is our product, buy it and use it," seems to be a more marked deviation from expectation than rhetorical or otherwise deviant ads. Moreover, ads very often deviate from expectation without being rhetorical—think of a naked man recommending a certain perfume to us, to name but one recent Dutch example. And finally, the definition does not make clear when and why artful templates result in rhetorical effects.

Therefore, it is necessary to explicitly raise the question of whether an ad is rhetorical or not and what kind of deviations result in rhetorical figuration. We believe it would be wrong to just start classifying ads, and if we succeed, to conclude that the ad is rhetorical (as two of the three taxonomies in Table 11.1 seem to suggest). Take an advertisement that instantiates the well known before–after template, for example, the ads for Natan jewelry shown in Wiedemann (2004, 42). In all of the ads, the first plane shows an ugly male who offers a box of jewelry to an invisible female. The second plane shows the boxes just opened by beautiful female hands while the ugly male has turned into an attractive version. The ads are clearly based on a comparison template; they invite the viewer to compare the ugly man with his attractive counterpart and to infer that these altering states have been caused by the jewelry (i.e., in the eyes of a woman, this jewelry turns an ugly man into an attractive one). Structurally, the ads can be labeled a case of MP2 (Forceville 1996), juxtaposition (Phillips and McQuarrie 2004), or present–disjoint (Groupe Mu 1992). Yet, these characteristics do not render the ads rhetorical. Or, consider a recent ad for light milk that shows only the brand name and a human bone. We can label it a case of replacement (Phillips and McQuarrie 2004) or absence (Groupe Mu 1992) as the bottle of milk is absent and replaced by the human bone. But once again, in our view this is not a sufficient reason to label it rhetorical. Hence, it would seem that neither the meaning operation of comparison nor the formal templates are restricted to the realm of rhetoric.

What kinds of criteria can be used to decide on the rhetorical character of an ad? Although, at the moment, a watertight decision tree is not available, we see at least two necessary heuristics in deciding on the rhetorical nature of ads, one based on stylistic/perceptual characteristics and one based on conceptual characteristics.

Perceptual Heuristic

Consider Figure 11.3, an ad of the well-known endorsement or testimonial type. Structurally, it represents a case of juxtaposition (or MP2, or present–disjoint). The product is displayed on the lower right-hand side of the plane, and the large picture shows a cowboy scene. The scene aims at increasing the salience of a particular aspect of the cowboy in relation to the advertised product. Conceptually, the basic $X \sim Y$ message can be paraphrased as "This is the type of person (Y) who smokes our cigarettes (X)." The ad does not claim a similarity between X and Y (i.e., cigarettes are not like cowboys), rather, it suggests an association between the scene and the product. Now consider Figure 11.4, an ad showing an ice track and a smoked sausage. For Dutch viewers, this ad immediately triggers the idea of the winter season. As Figure 11.3, we can label it a case of juxtaposition. The conceptual load is highly similar as well: "This is the kind of season during which one eats smoked sausages." Hence, it invites a viewer to associate the product with this particular time of the year (usually, Dutch people indeed do consume this kind of food during the wintertime).

However comparable the messages may be, we claim that Figure 11.4 is rhetorical, while Figure 11.3 is not. Although the rhetorical function of what is shown is highly similar for the two ads, the crucial difference concerns the way the secondary objects are shown. Figure 11.4 invites the viewer to associate the ice track with the product by using deliberate formal signals: the shape and the spatial orientation of the ice track resonates the shape and orientation of the sausage. Hence, we witness here a stylistic or formal feature of an image that triggers or contributes

Figure 11.3   **Cigarette Ad (Marlboro)**   Figure 11.4   **Sausage Ad (Unox)**

to the conceptual import of the ad. Precisely these formal aspects render Figure 11.4 rhetorical. Figure 11.3 lacks such perceptual features. Here, the only thing that counts is what is shown to us, not how it is shown.

Advertisements such as the one presented in Figure 11.4 are far from exceptional. Designers of advertisements use visual perceptual factors such as perspective, distance, spatial orientation, and the like extensively to strengthen an associative relation conveyed by an ad. Just like phonology in language, these factors in general bear an arbitrary relation to the meaning of an image, but if employed in the highly marked way shown in Figure 11.4, they may provide additional support to the intended conceptual message of visual communication. Analogous to verbal rhetorical figures such as rhyme or other kinds of sound repetition, the visual rhetorical nature of Figure 11.4 operates at the level of visual perception strata, rather than conceptual strata. These perceptual templates are based on principles of Gestalt, such as proximity, good continuation, and similarity and provide an additional Prägnanz to the propositional message of the ad (for a comparable view on poetry, see Tsur 1992).

Based on these considerations, we hypothesize that an ad can be labeled rhetorical if it uses perceptual visual templates (in this case, similarity and visual repetition). Furthermore, we propose to label a visual figure a true case of perceptual rhetoric, if we can point out how perceptual factors are used to emphasize the propositional message rather than merely to embellish. In the case of Figure 11.4, perceptual devices are employed that aim to establish a semantic reflex linking the product to the ice track and thereby, metonymically, to the winter season.

Conceptual Heuristic

Now we turn to the ad in Figure 11.2 for Grolsch premium blond beer. This ad is built on the same structural template that underlies Figures 11.3 and 11.4. In addition, like the Marlboro ad, it does not seem to contain triggering elements that operate at the level of visual perception, which may lead us to decide that it is a nonrhetorical testimonial ad as well. But there is a conceptual question here that should be answered: Why does this ad show Marilyn Monroe together with the product? Note that while the cowboy in Figure 11.3 is probably meant to represent an ideal user of the product, we should certainly not consider Monroe as an idealized consumer of this brand of beer. Whereas the cowboy serves as a primary reference object for predication (*this is the person (Y) who smokes our brand of cigarettes*), the image of Monroe establishes a predicate to which the primary object (the product) can be compared, or even claimed to be similar (*our product (X) is similar to the other object (Y) in some highly salient respect*). This kind of conceptual link makes it possible to answer the three analytical questions proposed by Forceville to identify cases of visual rhetoric, which renders it a case of visual rhetoric on conceptual rather than perceptual grounds. The ad invites us to conceptualize the X object (the product) in terms of the Y object (Monroe), an operation that is not possible in the case of Figure 11.3. Types of visual rhetoric that involve the meaning of the objects depicted (*what* we see rather than *how* we see it) we label conceptual rhetoric. The reason that we consider the Grolsch ad rhetorical and the Marlboro ad not is that the Grolsch ad refers to only one entity (the product) rather than two. Reference to the other entity is made only to tell the viewer something about this one object: "Grolsch premium blond beer is as prominently blond as Marilyn Monroe." In cases of metaphors, these two types of referential domains are usually termed target and source, but since we believe that the distinction between the two kinds of referencing has a broader scope (visual hyperboles, for example, can be identified and analyzed accordingly), we prefer to use the more general terms referential domain and vehicle domain. In particular, a vehicle domain is not present in the Marlboro ad because this ad actually refers to both the cowboy (i.e., this is the kind of person) and the product (i.e., who smokes our cigarettes).

Summary

Without claiming to have solved the identification problem, we consider the next two heuristics crucial in determining the rhetorical nature of ads: (1) Does the ad contain perceptual cues that trigger a meaningful relation between X and Y? (2) Does

Figure 11.5   **Car Ad (Land Rover)**

it contain two objects or domains, one of which is to be conceptualized in terms of the other? If one or both of these questions can be answered affirmatively, we can identify the ad as a case of visual rhetoric. Figure 11.5, an ad for Land Rover jeeps, shows that ads can also *combine* the two types of rhetoric. Like the Grolsch ad, reference to the hippopotamus (Y) is made only in order to claim something about the primary object (X): the objects are similar in that they are both robust, strong, able to move on land and in the water, and so on. Apart from the conceptual level, the visual rhetoric also operates at the level of perception: the conceptual relation of similarity is given additional Prägnanz by the use of perceptual similarities (ears–rearview mirrors, eyes–headlights), perspective and spatial orientation (position in the water and the good continuation line connecting the three objects).

Table 11.2 sums up the analyzed features of the four ads. We consider a positive outcome of the perceptual or conceptual heuristic (or both) a necessary prerequisite for a further structural and conceptual classification of the visual rhetoric. In the next two sections we further refine the criteria for distinguishing structural and conceptual classes of visual rhetoric.

Step 2: Classifying the Conceptual Load of Visual Rhetoric

The taxonomies we discussed earlier distinguish a number of conceptual relations holding between X and Y, ranging from mere association to similarity to more complex relational types such as opposition. In this section, we argue that in analyzing the conceptual structure of an ad, two basic interpretation heuristics prove helpful, a schematic and a categorical heuristic, respectively. These heuristics are valuable in detecting and exploiting the interpretation process of visual rhetoric, in particular, the comparison between X and Y. The two heuristics are rooted in two

Table 11.2

Deciding on the Rhetorical Nature of Ads

	Figure 11.3 Marlboro	Figure 11.4 Unox	Figure 11.2 Grolsch	Figure 11.5 Land Rover
Perceptual heuristic?	No	Yes	No	Yes
Conceptual heuristic?	No	No	Yes	Yes
→ Visual rhetoric?	No	Yes	Yes	Yes

Table 11.3

Interpretation Heuristics and Types of Conceptual Relations

Schematic interpretation heuristic	Categorical interpretation heuristic
X fits in a particular relational scheme *Y*	*X* belongs to a particular category *Y*
As a result, a type of comparison between *Y* and *X* can be established	
Contiguity relations (similarity, causality, opposition, etc.) Mere association	Identity

different traditions in the interpretation of verbal metaphors and have been applied successfully to verbal metaphors by Shen (1999). It is typical of rhetorical ads that they evoke schemes or categories that are often ad hoc, idiosyncratic, and deviating from normal categories and schemas. The product is related to a deviating category of things or placed in a schema somehow deviating from our normal experiences, thus triggering the intended relation between the product and the qualification expressed in the basic proposition. Table 11.3 shows the two heuristics and the types of outcomes they deliver.

As Table 11.3 makes clear, we consider these heuristics as interpretative molds that facilitate the diagnosis of the type of comparison relationship involved in the ad. The two interpretation heuristics represent two basic ways of clustering and organizing knowledge, as they are at the heart of how we conceptualize and classify objects and attribute meaning to them. Put simply, any object can be seen either as a member of a category or as part of a whole. For example, we may consider a chair as a member of the set of objects we can use to sit on (or block the door with) or as part of a particular scene, for example, a living room or restaurant. The two heuristics also largely determine the way we structure cognitive constructs such as language. Meaning in language is a constant interaction between categorical and schematic classification. From a schematic point of view (clusters of) words can be seen as part of a whole (e.g., a sentence). From a categorical point of view,

Figure 11.6 **Motor Oil Ad (Mobil)**

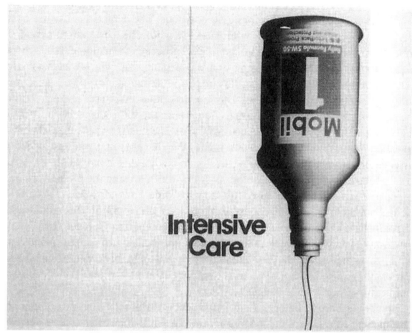

words or word clusters are members of a particular category (e.g., the category of verbs, noun phrases, or sentences).

Schematic Interpretation Heuristic: Domain as Schema

To introduce the schematic interpretation heuristic, based on Shen's notion of schematic source domain, consider the ad for Mobil motor oil in Figure 11.6 (taken from Forceville 1996). As Forceville points out, the image of the bottle together with the caption (intensive care) leads one to infer the analogy between motor oil and intravenous liquid. The central message is something like "Mobil oil is the lifeblood of a car." It tells the consumer that the product relates to a car the way an intravenous drip relates to the human body. Therefore, the additional inference can be made that by using this product, the purchaser relates to his/her car the way a doctor relates to his/her patients. Based on such inferences, the viewer may attribute notions such as professional care and expert treatment to the product.

The meaning of this ad can be considered "rich" in that it allows for many possible answers to the question, "How is this bottle of motor oil like a bottle of intravenous drip?" In terms of the Phillips and McQuarrie (2004) typology we are dealing with an example of similarity. The fused object of the intravenous bottle activates a medical schema, which consists of schematic elements such as doctors, medication, patients, hospitals, and so on. These components are related to each other via relations of contiguity (thematic, causal, spatial, temporal, and so on), which can be expressed as basic propositions. The depicted entity itself (the bottle) relates to the schema as a part relates to a whole, hence as part of a coherent network. Reconstructing the meaning of the ad proceeds by mapping these schema elements and relations to the target domain of motor oil, which yields schema-relevant inferences (e.g., by using this oil, I am taking care of my car as a good doctor cares for his patient), rather than schema-irrelevant inferences (e.g., bottles of motor oil and bottles of intravenous liquid have the same shape, are both made of plastic, etc.). The schematic heuristic both exhibits and explains the richness of the visual rhetoric in Figure 11.6 as it invites the viewer to map relevant attributes and relations from Y to X (doctor → consumer, medicine → motor oil, body → car, professional care Figure 11.6 Motor Oil Ad (Mobil) → using the product, etc.).

The relevance of schema-based inferences is widely acknowledged in cognitive science, psychology, and linguistics (e.g., Johnson-Laird 1983; Schank and Abelson 1977). With respect to metaphor processing, Clement and Gentner (1991) have demonstrated that in interpreting verbal metaphors or analogies such as "plant stems are like drinking straws," humans prefer the mapping of higher order, schema-based relations (e.g., used as a tool to nourish an organism) over low-level categorical qualifications (e.g., being thin and tubular).

In schema-based rhetorical advertisements, different types of comparison relationships can be exploited. Most common are relations of similarity between objects in different domains: motor oil is like an intravenous drip, washing powder is like fresh air or flowers, custard is like wine with a soft bouquet, and so on. Other schema-based ads trigger contrast relationships as in Figure 11.7, or causal relationships, as in Figure 11.1, an advertisement for light cheese. The tenet of Figure 11.1 is that Babybel light cheese is good for one's figure. This message is expressed by letting the consumer infer that mice (being prototypical consumers of cheese) get very slim by eating the product. The causal relationship evoked by this hyperbole figure requires a number of inferences and imaginings, based on an instantiated scheme of a mouse eating the light cheese and crawling into her hole without any trouble despite the hyperbolically small entry.

Another type of relationship, illustrated in Figures 11.4 and 11.8, is the mere association of the product with a schema evoked by the visual. Figure 11.8 evokes the schema of working with a toolbox and associates the Jupiler Blue Beer with this schema by replacing the tools in a toolbox with a can of beer in ice. Thus, the beer is associated with manual labor and presents itself as an evident and necessary tool for all working people. But schema-based associations can be very loosely related to the product as well. Examples can be found in magazines of airline companies all over the world. In many of these ads, products are associated with the airline company via a particular deviant schema or scenario (e.g., nightly airstrip lights that take the shape of a bottle of soft drink, an orange peeled like a globe, or a juice tetra brick with upper tips like wings). The association expressed in these ads does not

Figure 11.7   **Insurance Ad (Delta Lloyd)**

Figure 11.8   **Beer Ad (Jupiler Blue)**

seem to mean more than "This product is associated with the airline company."

In sum, schematic reasoning is a strong heuristic in interpreting the conceptual load of visual rhetoric. It provides viewers with an interpretation perspective that enables them to find the conceptual comparison between X and Y (ranging from mere association to different types of contiguity relations within the scheme, such as similarity, causality, or opposition).

Categorical Interpretation Heuristic: Domain as Category

The second interpretation heuristic is based on Shen's *domain-as-category* notion. The crucial characteristic of elements in categorical domains is that they are considered members of a set, rather than parts of a whole (Shen 1999). The metaphorical expression *John is a fox,* for example, is based on the taxonomic interpretation of a fox as an animal with specific attributes. According to Shen, the categorical interpretation is guided by the so-called diagnosticity principle, stating that the mapping of properties with a high diagnostic value is preferred over the mapping of properties with a low diagnostic value, an idea that is congruent with Ortony's salience imbalance theory of metaphor understanding (Ortony 1979). In the *John is a fox* metaphor, the diagnosticity principle predicts that the most relevant attributes are transferred from foxes to John, in particular, their slyness.

The categorical relation is especially productive in metaphorical political cartoons, in which personalities, situations, and objects are depicted as members of a specific class (e.g., Bush as a dangerous hawk, or Cuba as a naughty school boy). The categorical dimension has proved useful in explaining the (often) negative critical tenet of a political cartoon and in discovering the attributes that are responsible for its critical perspective (Schilperoord and Maes, forthcoming. Elements of the source domain are typically presented as bad or malicious specimens of the category.

Although such a critical tenet is almost absent in commercial ads, the categorical interpretation is crucial in frequently used types of commercials, typically in ads in which one attribute of a product is highlighted instead of a network of relations and attributes within a schema. Consider, again, Figures 11.2 and 11.5, the artful deviation of which is based on the activation of an ad hoc class of blond or robust things, respectively, with Marilyn Monroe and a hippo as prototypical members. Thus, typical class attributes of these prototypical members (e.g., attractive blondness or imperturbable robustness) are transferred rather than schematic properties (e.g., swimming in the water together, drinking beer with Marilyn).

There is another, very productive class of ads benefiting significantly from a categorical interpretation, the so-called real-thing ads. The message these ads communicate is essentially the same: the product *is like* the real thing: a carton of apple juice *is like* real apples, a can of salmon *is like* real salmon, a bottle of ketchup *is like* real tomatoes, and so on. In Figure 11.9, the orange is replaced by a carton of Tropicana, and the ad tells the viewer: "What you get if you drink

Figure 11.9   **Orange Juice Ad (Tropicana)**

Tropicana is the same as what you get when you squeeze oranges." Although the objects used in these ads intrinsically allow for relational and schematic extensions (e.g., eating oranges makes you stay healthy and fit), only one categorical property of this object is relevant here: the sheer fact that an orange is on all accounts the most prototypical member of the category of orange-like things. This means that the product is claimed to belong to the category of the thing it is made of. Note that these real-thing ads are problematic with respect to Phillips and McQuarrie's (2004) characterization of the difference between connection and similarity. On the one hand, Figure 11.9 is clearly a case of real similarity, even extreme similarity, rather than mere association. But unlike Phillips and McQuarrie's characterization of similarity, there is not a variety of answers to the question "How is X like Y?" but only one: freshness, and freshness only, is the relevant feature here. This unique feature would qualify them, incorrectly in our view, for the meaning operation of connection.

Summary

We contend that the conceptual interpretation and characterization of visual rhetoric should be guided by two heuristics, one based on schematic interpretation and one based on categorical interpretation. These heuristics pave the way to find the relevant type and degree of comparison between the relevant objects, ranging from loose association to similarity to near-identity. Based on the analyses presented in this section, we hypothesize that schema reasoning is related more naturally to different types of contiguity relations and to relational and multiple qualities, whereas category reasoning tends to trigger associations (as in Figure 11.4), simple attributive qualities (as in Figures 11.2 and 11.5) and the real-thing identity relationship (as in Figure 11.9).

The examples discussed in this section suggest that visual rhetoric is interpreted either schematically or categorically. Nothing, however, prevents schemas and categories from being at work together in the same rhetorical ad. Again, consider Figure 11.4. One can start from a schematic interpretation of the winter landscape (including the activity of skating) and associate the sausage with it as part of a whole. But we can also consider the ice track and the sausage as prototypical members of the set of wintry objects, hence relying on the potential of the categorical interpretation heuristic. In sum, we think that the combination of the two heuristics and the different types and degrees of comparison they give access to, adequately account for the conceptual richness of visual rhetoric.

Step 3: Classifying the Structural Dimension of Visual Rhetoric

The structural dimension of the taxonomies of visual rhetoric discussed earlier aims at classifying the various ways in which the two objects or domains are represented. Table 11.4 summarizes the three basic formal templates (which we refer to using Phillips and McQuarrie's terminology). As we suggested earlier, we consider juxtapositions the most subtle (and often disputable) rhetorical deviation. They constitute the borderline between rhetorical, nonrhetorical, and mere aesthetic or artistic ads. The deviation in replacements strongly depends on the visual context, which should enable the viewer to infer an absent object. Finally, fusion is the most obvious case of deviation, because it shows the physical integration of two objects coming from different conceptual or functional domains.

Table 11.4

Structural Classes of Visual Rhetoric

Groupe Mu	Forceville	Phillips and McQuarrie
present–disjoint	simile	juxtaposition
present–conjoined	MP2	fusion
absent–disjoint/conjoined	MP1	replacement

Despite the intuitive and analytical plausibility of the three structural templates, not all rhetorical ads can be classified unambiguously on a simple perceptual basis. Again, consider Figure 11.9. The categorical interpretation heuristic suggests a clear example of replacement. The prototypical member of the real-thing class (i.e., oranges) is replaced by a squeezed carton of Tropicana. But if we take a more schematic view, we see a breakfast ritual, in which two scenarios or domains are fused (i.e., drinking fresh Tropicana orange juice and squeezing fresh oranges). A similar ambiguity between replacement and fusion can be observed in many other ads, for example, Figure 11.6 or Figure 11.8. Things can be even more complicated, as is shown in Figure 11.7, an ad for an insurance company. This ad, a clear case of opposition, allows for various schematic interpretations, in turn resulting in different structural classes. First, we can define Y as the scheme of playing ice hockey, and hence "see" an absent ice hockey player, who is replaced by a figure skater. Or, we can consider the ad as a *fusion* of two conflicting schemes (i.e., playing ice hockey and figure skating). Finally, if we define X and Y as the figure skater and the group of ice hockey players, respectively, we see a lineup of these two objects, and thus a juxtaposition.

These examples suggest that rhetorical ads are often poly-interpretable, mainly for two reasons: their interpretation can differ based on the schematic versus categorical interpretation heuristic; and the definition and extension of the relevant comparison terms X and Y can differ considerably. These conceptual ambiguities result in structural ambiguities as well, which justifies the view of a structural taxonomy consisting of permeable rather than distinct categories.

This position can be supported by even more fine-grained cases of structural ambiguity that a taxonomy must be able to handle. First, consider the ad for Olay lipstick in Figure 11.10. We see here two pursed lips painted red, and a lead that reads *love your lips*. Due to both the fixed point of view of the ad and the color of the lips, the image also can be interpreted as a heart. So, conceptually the ad instantiates a $X \sim Y$ proposition by connecting the product to a heart (and thus to love). The ambiguous nature of the image makes it a complicated type between fusion and replacement. It is not a fusion proper, as one cannot visually identify the parts of the two merged objects or object domains. The image shows only one object that can be interpreted in two different ways. The fact that the viewer

Figure 11.10   **Lipstick Ad (Olay)**

is either aware of the lips or the heart leads to the judgment that the image is ambiguous. The lips cannot be considered a standard case of replacement either, since the image actually shows a heart rather than calling to mind the idea of a heart. In a standard case of replacement, one object is actually not shown, or is absent, as in Figure 11.9, whereas in this case both are somehow present. What one sees at a particular moment depends on which of the objects is currently accessible to awareness, a visual perception phenomenon that is often illustrated by the Necker cube.

The somewhat blurred boundary between fusions and replacements can further be illustrated if we look once again at Figures 11.8 and 11.9, typical specimens of replacement. They almost literally deviate from expectation: where we expect an orange or tools, we see cans of beer or a squeezed carton of orange juice. In all of these cases, the interpretation ultimately rests on a contextual interpretation of the perceptual field. The importance of this visual context is comparable to the role of context in cases of verbal replacement (i.e., metonymical or deferred reference; see Fauconnier 1985; or Ward 2004). In the sentence "Plato is on the top shelf," the interpretation of Plato as referring to the book instead of the person is exclusively based on the context of the sentence. Likewise, the squeezer and the toolbox are essential in successfully interpreting the replacement ads. The role of context is not always that clear-cut, however. Consider Figure 11.11, an ad for a brand of cooling fans, in which fans (X) are compared to ice cubes in a holder (Y). Conceptually, the ad is a case of similarity, but how are we to characterize the structural template, as fusion or replacement? Both seem possible, depending again on what we consider the extension of Y or where we draw the line between Y and the relevant context. Either we define Y as ice cubes, and the ice-cube holder as the visual background context—in this interpretation the ice cubes are replaced by fans—or we define Y as the ice-cube holder, in which case it can be seen as a fusion of an ice-cube holder and fans.

Figure 11.11   **Fan Ad (Voltas)**

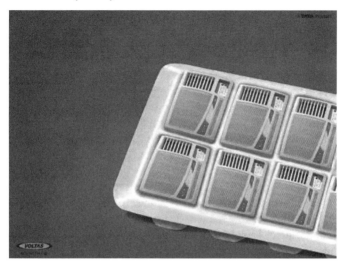

Summary

The examples given in this section illustrate complicated borderline cases between juxtaposition, fusion, and replacement, depending on the extension of X and Y and the interpretation of the visual context. Our own experience in applying the three structural classes tells us that many more such cases exist. This leads us even further away from a clear-cut division of structural classes and justifies the conclusion that the three classes are permeable rather than distinct. Ads often allow for different conceptualizations in terms of foreground and background and different extensions of X and Y. Of course, the basic heuristic value of the three templates remains valid. One can even find natural correspondences between these classes and conceptual types. For example, replacements depend on context, which often activates a schema, which in turn results in a schematic interpretation. But the many examples in which specific conceptualizations result in different structural classes render the templates a basis for the interpretation of visual rhetoric that should be taken with considerable caution. Additional heuristics will be needed to analyze these complicated cases. For example, we may classify an ad as a case of fusion (1) if both of the merged objects can be visually identified, and (2) if the objects constitute the two terms of the basic $X \sim Y$ proposition. These heuristics would solve the ambiguity displayed in the fan ad (Figure 11.11). Since the propositional template links the fan to ice cubes rather than to the ice-cube holder, fusion is ruled out, and hence the ad conforms to the replacement template. Obviously, one may disagree with this outcome, but in that case it is at least clear that this disagreement probably originates from the second "if" in the rule above. Further analytical work will have to clarify whether all borderline cases can be solved this way.

Relating Structural and Conceptual Classes to Readers' Responses

An important contribution of the taxonomy developed by Phillips and McQuarrie is that it relates the conceptual (meaning operation) and structural (visual structure) classes in the typology on the one hand, and readers' responses on the other (2004, 126–130). Connecting structural and conceptual characteristics of visual rhetoric to their pragmatic impact is crucial as it enables researchers to put the typology to the test, that is, by predicting the differential impact of advertisements on the basis of the type of visual structure and meaning operation they represent (see also McQuarrie in this volume). In this section, we refine two analytical notions that they use to predict pragmatic effects of classes of visual rhetoric (i.e., complexity and meaning richness).

Perceived complexity is a response factor associated with the structural templates of the taxonomy. Phillips and McQuarrie hypothesize that complexity will increase "as one moves along the visual structure dimension from juxtaposition to fusion to replacement" (2004, 118). This characterization, in our view, runs the risk of ambiguity as it seems to combine the objective analytical complexity of visual design with the subjective perceived complexity of viewers. Analytical complexity refers to formal and conceptual characteristics of the design of an image, which may range from more to less complex (i.e., the depiction of one or more objects, the number of pictorial details, visual richness, etc.). Perceived complexity, on the other hand, is a response variable as it refers to the cognitive demands placed on the viewer who processes the ad. To put this in somewhat simpler terms: a visual figuration can be hard to design, but easy to process, or the other way around. For example, the witty perceptual details of the Land Rover ad in Figure 11.5 may be hard to design, but they probably facilitate the conceptual connection between the objects for the user.

The distinction between analytical complexity and perceived complexity becomes vital in cases of replacement. Phillips and McQuarrie hypothesize that this template is more complex. As replacements crucially depend on visual context, they often display a rich visual context, as, for example, Figure 11.8 shows. In other words, replacements can be considered complex visual design. But this same visual design complexity may well make the interpretation easy, thus decreasing perceived complexity. The meaningful visual context may well facilitate processing just as a meaningful verbal context facilitates the processing of language. We actually tested this assumption experimentally by having people look at (fabricated) ads that were built either on the juxtaposition or the replacement template. For example, half of the subjects saw an ad for a brand of mineral water that showed two bottles of it juxtaposed to a battery holder containing two batteries with the lead *the water that energizes you*. The other half saw the same ad, but now with the two batteries replaced by the bottles. In the replacement case, the battery holder was the crucial context for the conceptual interpretation of the water. Prior to the experiment, the subjects were told that they were about to view a couple of ads on a computer screen and that they would be asked some questions about them. They were asked to look at the ads on a computer screen and to press a button once they felt able to answer questions about the ad. Perceived complexity was assessed by measuring the time interval between the moment the ads appeared on screen and the moment subjects pressed the button. We found significantly longer viewing times for the juxtaposed versions, which suggests a higher degree of perceived complexity for the juxtaposed versions of the ads. In constructing the stimuli, it was apparent that it was much more difficult to construct the replacement versions than the juxtapositions. It would thus seem that the distinction between analytical and perceived complexity results in more fine-grained assumptions about the processing demands of structural classes of visual rhetoric.

A similar refinement applies to the notion of meaning richness, which is assumed to relate to complexity as well. Again, one can distinguish between complexity as a rhetorical effect and complexity or richness as a characteristic of an ad. For example, the advertisement in Figure 11.6 is (analytically) rich or complex in meaning, in that one can distinguish analytically many different elements (attributes and relations) that can be transferred from the medical source domain to the domain of the product, as we have seen above. But it may well be that exactly this analytical richness makes the ad simple for the viewer because the evoked scheme contains many different triggers to understand the ad.

In sum, we consider the difference between analytical complexity (in terms of visual structure or meaning operation) and perceived complexity to be crucial in further refining the interaction between conceptual, structural, and response aspects of visual rhetoric.

Conclusion

In this chapter, we discussed a number of heuristics applicable to the three steps we consider crucial in defining the relevant conceptual and structural aspects of a rhetorical ad. These heuristics do not make up an analytical algorithm with a clear-cut and unambiguous result for each and every ad. Rather, they offer a systematic list of relevant analytical questions. In our view, the nature of heuristics naturally fits the often divergent and ambiguous interpretation of visual rhetoric. In Appendix 11.1, we summarize the heuristics discussed above in one scheme. In each step, more than one question can be answered positively, in which case more interpretation strategies apply.

Appendix 11.1. Flowchart for Rhetorical Categorization

1. Define X and Y
2. Step 1: Is this a rhetorical ad?
   - Does the ad contain perceptual cues that trigger a meaningful relation between X and Y?

      Yes → a case of perceptual rhetoric

      No → not a case of perceptual rhetoric

- Does the ad contain two objects or domains X and Y, one of which is to be conceptualized in terms of the other?

      Yes → a case of conceptual rhetoric

      No → not a case of conceptual rhetoric

3. Step 2: What is the conceptual interpretation of the ad?

- Does X fit in a particular relational schema Y?

      Yes → find the appropriate comparison relation between Y and X

      Association—contiguity relations—identity

- Does X belong to a particular class or category Y?

      Yes → find the appropriate comparison relation between Y and X

      Association—contiguity relations—identity

4. Step 3: What is the structural interpretation of the ad?

- Are X and Y both visually present (separately)?

      Yes → juxtaposition

- Are X and Y both visually present (merged)?

      Yes → fusion

- Is only X or Y present in a particular context?

      Yes → replacement

References

Clement, C.A., and Dedre Gentner. 1991. "Systematicity as a Selection Constraint in Analogical Mapping." *Cognitive Science: A Multidisciplinary Journal of Artificial Intelligence, Psychology, and Language* 15: 89–132.

Durand, Jacques. 1987. "Rhetorical Figures in the Advertising Image." In *Marketing and Semiotics: New Directions in the Study of Signs for Sale,* ed. J. Umiker-Sebeok, 295–318. Berlin: Mouton de Gruyter.

Fauconnier, Gilles. 1985. *Mental Spaces: Aspects of Meaning Construction in Natural Language.* Cambridge, MA: MIT Press.

Forceville, Charles. 1996. *Pictorial Metaphor in Advertising.* London: Routledge.

Groupe Mu. 1992. *Traité du Signe Visuel. Pour une Rhétorique de l'Image.* Paris: Seuil.

Johnson-Laird, P.N. 1983. *Mental Models.* Cambridge: Cambridge University Press.

Kennedy, John M. 1982. "Metaphor in Pictures." *Perception* 11: 589–605.

Kenney, Keith, and Linda M. Scott. 2003. "A Review of the Visual Rhetoric Literature." In *Persuasive Imagery: A Consumer Response Perspective,* ed. Scott and Rajeev Batra, 17–56. Mahwah, NJ: Erlbaum.

McQuarrie, Edward F., and David Glen Mick. 1996. "Figures of Rhetoric in Advertising Language." *Journal of Consumer Research* 22 (March): 424–438.

———, and ———. 1999. "Visual Rhetoric in Advertising: Text-Interpretive, Experimental, and Reader-Response Analyses." *Journal of Consumer Research* 26 (June): 37–54.

Ortony, Anthony. 1979. "Beyond Literal Similarity." *Psychological Review* 86: 161–180.

Phillips, Barbara J. 2003. "Understanding Visual Metaphor in Advertising." In *Persuasive Imagery: A Consumer Perspective,* ed. Linda M. Scott and Rajeev Batra, 297–310. Mahwah, NJ: Erlbaum.

————. and Edward F. McQuarrie. 2004. "Beyond Visual Metaphor: A New Typology of Visual Rhetoric in Advertising." *Marketing Theory* 4 (1/2): 113–136.

Schank, R.C., and R.P. Abelson. 1977. *Scripts, Plans, Goals and Understanding: An Inquiry into Human Knowledge Structures.* Hillsdale, NJ: Erlbaum.

Schilperoord, Joost, and Alfons Maes. Forthcoming. "Visual metaphoric conceptualization in political cartoons." In *Multimodal Metaphor,* ed. Charles Forceville and Eduardo Urios-Aparisi. Berlin: Mouton de Gruyter.

Scott, Linda M., and Rajeev Batra, eds. 2003. *Persuasive Imagery: A Consumer Response Perspective.* Mahwah, NJ: Erlbaum.

Shen, Yeshayahu. 1999. "Principles of Metaphor Interpretation and the Notion of 'Domain': A Proposal for a Hybrid Model." *Journal of Pragmatics* 31: 1631–1653.

Teng, Norman Y., and Sewen Sun. 2002. "Grouping, Simile, and Oxymoron in Pictures: A Design-Based Cognitive Approach." *Metaphor and Symbol: A Quarterly Journal* 17: 295–316.

Tsur, Reuven 1992. *Toward a Theory of Cognitive Poetics.* Amsterdam: Elsevier Science.

van Mulken, Margot 2003. "Analyzing Rhetorical Devices in Print Advertisements." *Document Design* 4: 114–128.

van Mulken, Margot; Renske van Enschot-van Dijk; and Hans Hoeken. 2005. "Puns, Relevance and Appreciation in Advertisements." *Journal of Pragmatics* 37: 707–721.

Ward, Gregory L. 2004. "Equatives and Deferred Reference." *Language: Journal of the Linguistic Society of America* 80: 262–289.

Wiedemann, Julius. 2004. *Advertising Now. Print.* Cologne: Taschen.

Part IV

The Toolbox
Unpacking the Inquiry Process

12

A Visit to the Rhetorician's Workbench

Developing a Toolkit for Differentiating Advertising Style

Edward F. McQuarrie

Chapter Summary

This chapter examines the activity of constructing a system for organizing catego-ries of rhetorical devices. I review existing categorization systems to abstract their essential characteristics. This produces a list of key properties that a good system of categories should possess (e.g., extensibility, inclusiveness, and generativity). I then demonstrate how a system of categories can be assembled from the ground up, using the example of pictorial layout in print advertisements. Along the way, I address a variety of issues that arise in connection with the activity of systemati-cally linking rhetorical categories. The chapter is conceived as a tutorial aimed at an audience of doctoral students or other beginning scholars, with the purpose of attracting scholars to the enterprise of systematically linking together rhetorical categories that differentiate advertising style.

As mentioned in Chapter 1, "Advertising Rhetoric: An Introduction," much of what rhetoricians do is differentiate the set of stylistic options available within a particular communication medium or advertising context. I have had the pleasure of constructing several such differentiations, focused variously on headlines in print advertising (McQuarrie and Mick 1996) and pictures in magazine advertising (McQuarrie 2007; Phillips and McQuarrie 2004). However, it seems to me that the differentiations thus far published, by myself and all my rhetorician colleagues put together, only scratch the surface of what is possible (and needed). It occurred to me that the best use of this chapter would not be to publish yet one more differentiation, or even to attempt a more comprehensive differentiation of, say, print advertisements, but rather, to write a short treatise on how to do it.

The best way to promote the scholarly activity of differentiating stylistic palettes is to recruit other scholars to the enterprise. And the best way to do that is to show in detail how it is done. Hence, this chapter is conceived as a visit to the workbench. My goal is to explain how to construct a conceptually integrated differentiation of the stylistic options available in a specified advertising domain. To do this, I first examine some of my past efforts, raising the hood as it were, so that the engine and transmission driving the system can be glimpsed. Next, I essay some new distinctions, to demonstrate the process of developing a system of differentiations from scratch. Although none of these novel distinctions will be developed in any depth here, the hope is that they can serve as a feedstock, helping to spark future efforts by the target audience, most especially doctoral students and scholars new to the enterprise of constructing rhetorical typologies.

Along the way the chapter will return continually to the idea that the best systems for stylistic differentiation are those that can be linked to consumer response by means of accepted psychological theories. Here again a workbench approach will be taken, designed to demonstrate the omnivorous nature of the rhetorical enterprise with respect to causal knowledge offered by other behavioral science disciplines.

Understanding Conceptual Structure in Systems of Stylistic Differentiation

Figures 12.1a and 12.1b (see pages 260–261) reproduce side by side the taxonomy of verbal rhetorical figures developed in McQuarrie and Mick (1996) and the typology of visual rhetorical figures developed in Phillips and McQuarrie (2004). The goal in juxtaposing these two systems (termed hereafter "MM system" and "PM system") is to identify common aspects of good systems of stylistic differentiation, and thus to facilitate abstraction to a more general level. Below are some of the shared structural elements that make each of these systems a model of the kind of differentiation I think rhetorical scholarship needs to pursue.

Multiplicity

Neither scheme contents itself with a simple dichotomy or a single dimension or axis. The MM system nests two distinctions below the main contrast of figurative and nonfigurative, distinguishing different degrees of deviation, and then different levels of complexity, to make a fourfold categorization. The PM system crosses two distinctions, between visual structure on the one hand, and meaning operation on the other, to make a ninefold categorization. As we shall see, multiplicity is one of the things that distinguishes rhetorical systems of differentiation from the comparatively more feeble efforts of psychologists to identify different kinds of ad stimuli.

Dimensionality

In each scheme the categories are arrayed along a dimension or continuum. In the MM system, not only are schemes distinguished from tropes, but also these are arrayed along a gradient of deviation. In the PM system, juxtaposition is not only distinguished from fusion and replacement as a distinct category of visual structure, but is also positioned as a simpler, less complex kind of structure. Later we will see the importance of dimensionality with respect to linking rhetorical systems of differentiation to consumer response.

Inheritance

Not directly visible in Figures 12.1a and 12.1b, but important to note, is that each scheme reuses elements drawn from distinctions offered by earlier scholars. The scheme–trope distinction in the MM system dates back to ancient times, and its application in the MM system hews closely to the ideas of Leech (1969). Likewise, the idea of a rhetorical operation (the bottom level of the MM system) was anticipated in Durand (1987). The visual structure dimension in the PM system picks up ideas from Forceville (1994), while the specific meaning operations owe much to Durand (1987), Groupe Mu, Plett, and other Continental authors (see Wenzel [1990] for a discussion). The point to note here is that it is highly unlikely, at this juncture, that a complex system of rhetorical differentiations is going to emerge de novo, without any mapping onto prior work. Good rhetoricians do not suffer from that sort of arrogance. Likewise, a good doctoral preparation for rhetorical scholarship entails exposure to the concepts and theories of a wide range of text-analytic disciplines, including poetics, aesthetics, semiotics, and linguistics. A student of advertising rhetoric rightly expects to mine these kindred disciplines for the raw material from which more comprehensive systems of stylistic differentiation, appropriate to the advertising context, can be constructed.

Comprehensive

A good system of stylistic differentiations is one that can credibly claim to contain all the stylistic options available within the target domain. Thus, the MM system claims that any verbal artful deviation that fits a template (their definition of a rhetorical figure) can be securely located within the taxonomy. The PM system similarly claims that all possible ways of constructing an artfully deviant two-dimensional arrangement of visual elements that conform to a template have a place in their system. These claims of comprehensiveness are of course falsifiable. And, as is well known, truly scientific ideas are distinguished by their falsifiability. By contrast, it is much harder to falsify a simple dichotomy. For instance, how would one go about showing that a particular kind of thinking did not correspond to either "left-brain" or "right-brain" thought (to mention but one

Figure 12.1a   **A Taxonomy of Rhetorical Figures in Advertising**

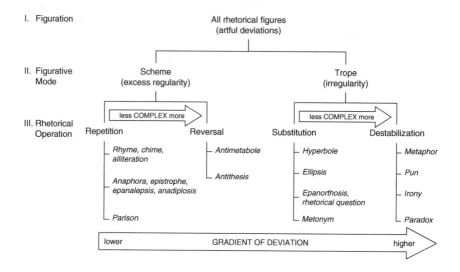

infamous example)? Simple, all-embracing dichotomies are difficult to falsify because, in order to incorporate everything, they have to be fuzzily defined, and such fuzziness makes it difficult to refute the application of the dichotomy to any specific case. To just that degree, all-embracing, stand-alone dichotomies fall short of one of the criteria by which we distinguish scientific thinking from mumbo jumbo.

Extensible

The flip side of being comprehensive, in a falsifiable way, is that good systems of differentiation are potentially extensible in future work. Conversely, a system that cannot be altered without destroying it is probably too Platonic in inspiration to be either suitable for empirical testing or effective in practice (and remember, rhetoricians are utterly pragmatic). For instance, Table 2 in McQuarrie and Mick (1996), which contains examples for each category in the taxonomy, actually gives some hints of how a fourth level of the taxonomy might be developed. Thus it distinguishes destabilization (i.e., liberation of multiple meanings) achieved by means of similarity on the one hand, and by opposition on the other. If it can be shown that consumer response (e.g., the particular kind of multiple meanings liberated or the manner in which these meanings are liberated) reliably differs when destabilization is evoked using similarity versus opposition, then the taxonomy ought to be extended to include this fourth level. Likewise, McQuarrie (2007) suggests that the PM system might be expanded to incorporate more than three

Figure 12.1b   **Typology of Visual Rhetoric Showing Classification of Ad Examples**

		RICHNESS →		
		Meaning Operation		
		Connection ("A is associated with B")	**Comparison**	
	Visual Structure		**Similarity** ("A is like B")	**Opposition** ("A is *not* like B")
COMPLEXITY ↓	**Juxtaposition** (Two side-by-side images)	Equal sweetener	Dexter shoes	Comfort fabric softener
	Fusion (Two combined images)	Discover card	Tide Reflex racquet	Kudos granola bar
	Replacement (Image present points to an absent image)	Silk Soy milk	Welch's juice	Canadian magazine industry Sunny Delight

distinct kinds of visual structure (see above). Such an extension leaves the overall system intact, but increases its claim to meaningfully and comprehensively identify "the available means of persuasion" within the circumscribed domain of visual rhetorical figures.

Constitutive

In a good system, locating a particular stylistic device within the system allows one to read off the key properties of that device. To see how valuable this can be, consider the situation of a scholar who must instead work outside of any such system of differentiations. In my view, many scholars whose stated interest is "metaphor" suffer from this fate. In defining "metaphor," they tend to oppose it to the "literal," but such a simple dichotomy reveals little. After all, puns are not literal, and neither are metonyms, nor are irony or hyperbole. Students of metaphor who labor in ignorance of the stylistic system of which metaphor is a part—the system of verbal rhetorical figures—inevitably run into difficulty when attempting to define the properties that specifically constitute a metaphor. A typical conflation is to attribute to metaphor properties possessed by all artful deviations—all figurative speech. This obscures understanding of both metaphor and figurative speech, to no one's benefit.

McQuarrie and Mick (1996, 429) are blunt on this score:

> [P]articular named rhetorical figures handed down by the classical tradition ought not to be considered as entities sui generis that have distinctive impacts on ad processing. In our framework individual rhetorical figures are not causal loci for explaining advertising effects but rather names that distinguish different applications of a rhetorical operation. Instead, it is artful deviation, irregularity, and complexity that explain the effects of a headline such as "Say hello to your child's new bodyguards," and not its assignment to the metaphor category.

This seems to me one of the most important assertions contained in that article. It states that the differences that matter, from a scientific standpoint, are only those differences embodied in the structure of the system of differentiations. Since pun and metaphor are both figures, are both tropes, and are both complex tropes relying on the rhetorical operation of destabilization, there should be no difference of note in their effect on consumer response. In other words, for descriptive purposes, a pun may be an entity that is very different from a metaphor. But for theoretical and scientific purposes, they may be conceptualized as one and the same causal agent: a complex trope of destabilization.

It is the constitutive property that allows rhetorical differentiation to be valorized as theory rather than impugned as mere description or cataloguing. The constitutive property is thus the key to rebutting Samuel Butler's gibe: "All the rhetorician's rules / Teach nothing but to name his tools." Absent the constitutive property, it would be more difficult to claim that rhetorical differentiation is a scientific activity. Put another way, our goal as rhetoricians should be classification systems that are akin to the periodic table in chemistry, which offers a predictive as well as a descriptive account of the properties of matter.

Generative

This is a more subtle property, and more an ideal than a prerequisite. A system is generative when at least some of its categories are rule-generated rather than simply listed, defined, or asserted. Returning to the analogy of the periodic table in chemistry, once elements were distinguished by their atomic weight, it became possible to identify missing entries (elements not yet distinguished as such), simply by finding substances with specific integer atomic weights that did not as yet have a name or a secure identity as a fundamental element.

More generally, any rule-generated set of categories has a couple of desirable properties. First, it has a clear stopping point, and thus a transparent claim to be exhaustive. Second, it is inherently systematic, so that one avoids the trap of cataloguing or mere description.

The visual structure dimension in the PM system serves as a good example of a generative scheme. Because of this fact, we can readily see how the three-part categorization of visual structure in Phillips and McQuarrie (2004) can be extended to a six-part categorization, as in McQuarrie (2007). To do this, we first translate the categories of visual structure into a notation or schematization (any true rule-generated set allows such a translation). Thus, the visual structure of juxtaposition can be redefined as "A besides B." As such, it is one of n possible arrangements of two elements. The rule becomes "generate all possible ways of arranging two visual elements on a page." Given this rule, the category of visual structures termed fusion can be understood as "A fused with B to create AB," and replacement can be understood as "A in place of B."

But why stop there? Logically, "A beside B" suggests "A inside of B"; similarly, "A fused with B to create AB" suggests "A combined with B to create C"; and "A in place of B" suggests "A and not B." Hence, a more complete set of visual structure categories, arrayed according to complexity as before, might look like Table 12.1.

Can more than six types of visual structure be identified? Time and human ingenuity will determine the answer. The test for further categories, and for the three new ones adduced above, is the same: on the one hand, do they occupy sufficiently distinct positions on the gradient of complexity to be reliably distinguished by knowledgeable judges, and on the other, do they produce measurable differences in consumer response? Thus, it seemed to Phillips and McQuarrie (2004) that juxtaposition was a distinct, measurably simpler, and easier-to-comprehend visual arrangement than fusion. If "inside" and "beside" can be distinguished by judgment, but do not evoke different consumer responses, then the typology may need to coin a term such as "proximally related," and use this single category in place of "juxtaposition" and "inclusion." Juxtaposition and inclusion then become analogous to pun and metaphor, or rhyme and anaphora in the MM system—two names of discriminable stylistic devices, that are not expected to differ in any causative way.

Causative

Implicit in the foregoing discussion of the dimensional, constitutive, and generative properties of good systems is the idea of causal power. Since I choose to consider myself a scientist as well as a rhetorician, I am most interested in systems of differentiation that yield testable hypotheses about consumer response to ads that can be located within the system. The MM system makes testable assertions about how scheme figures will differ from trope figures and about how simple figures will differ from complex figures. The PM system makes testable assertions based on the complexity of visual structure and the polysemy of the meaning operation. Both systems forge a link to causation by mapping key structural elements of the system onto preexisting psychological constructs. The artful deviation that defines a rhetorical figure in the MM system links to Berlyne's (1971) ideas about incongruity. Polysemy in the PM system links to the idea of elaboration that is central to cognitive response theories. And, complexity has its own tradition dating to before Berlyne (see Huhmann [page 85] and Lowrey [page 159] in this volume).

Table 12.1

Visual Structure Categories

Category	Notation
Juxtaposition	• A beside B
Inclusion	• A inside B
Combination	• A combined with B to form C
Fusion	• A fused with B to form AB
Replacement	• A in place of B
Removal	• A and not B

Note: Italicized categories do not appear in the original Phillips and McQuarrie (2004) typology.

The way this part of system building works then, is to secure, as part of one's education, a reasonable background in psychological or other cognitive science disciplines concerned with how human beings respond to stimuli—especially complex and meaningful artifactual stimuli (like ads). One then iterates between the text-analytic mind-set, which seeks out differences in text artifacts (like ad headlines), the theorist's mind-set, which seeks ways to systematize and conceptualize the discovered differences, and the psychologist's mind-set, which seeks to relate elements of the constructed system to known causal agents that shape human response to stimuli.

An example of this iteration would be the genesis of the MM system for verbal rhetoric. David Mick and I were well versed in text-analytic disciplines, so the scheme–trope distinction was ready to hand. We had a theoretical mind-set, so we were attracted to a systematization of the scheme–trope distinction that made each of these a specific kind of deviation from regularity (excess for schemes like rhyme, deficient for tropes like the pun). Last, our education had included exposure to a range of psychological theorists, like Berlyne, so that we readily made the link between deviation and incongruity, which in turn allowed us to generate testable hypotheses about schemes and tropes in ads.

Grounded

Finally, and this is only implicit in the published accounts of the MM and PM systems, I think one must be immersed in the advertising phenomenon under study if one is to make a contribution to its rhetorical systematization. That is, I believe it is essential to spend large amounts of relatively unstructured and unhurried time looking at actual advertisements. Literary critics are always reading literature, art critics gaze long at paintings, and students of advertising rhetoric need to be immersed in real advertisements. Reflective engagement is the heart of the process of system development: What is going on in this concrete specific advertisement? Why this picture? Why these words, just so?

Development of a Rhetorical System: How to Begin

So you like the idea of developing your own system of rhetorical differentiations—now where do you start? I think the crucial first step is to decide on the particular kind of advertisement that is going to be your area of specialization. That is, I do not think it is possible to develop a rhetorical differentiation of "advertising"—the category of "advertising" is too big, too amorphous, comprised of too many distinct subphenomena, to provide a useful focus. Here, again, we see the crucial difference in emphasis between rhetoricians, who seek contextualized knowledge, and psychologists, who have been taught to seek universals. Attempting to meaningfully differentiate "advertising" is the same trap as attempting to theorize about "persuasion" or "communication"—which is simply to say that useful (broad) boundaries for academic disciplines and journals need not be useful boundaries for focusing the kind of specific differentiation attempts pursued by rhetoricians. At a minimum, one has to tighten the focus to something like "magazine advertising," or "banner ads on the Web."

My sense is that any distinction among advertising situations or media types that gets a regular mention in advertising textbooks provides one place to start. Thus, magazines are generally distinguished as a particular type of print advertising, different from newspapers, both of which can be distinguished from broadcast media such as television or radio. The reason that "magazine advertising" exists as a category within the textbook literature is simply that large numbers of practitioners are prone to think of magazine ads as matching a particular kind of marketing strategy, having their own design rules, aimed at a particular kind of consumer, and processed in a characteristic way. This is the minimum that you need: a distinct category of advertising text, with a bounded set of expected consumer responses.

It may sometimes be useful to narrow the focus even further. For instance, business-to-business magazines are quite distinct from consumer magazines. Magazine advertisements for consumer-packaged goods may likewise be distinct from magazine ads for consumer durables. Magazine ads for technologically innovative products might even constitute a distinct subcategory within the consumer-durables set. All right, then—where does this progressive narrowing stop? If the goal is causal scientific knowledge, then I think we draw the line at the product–*category* X media level, and preferably at the product-*class* X media level. We should not try to drill down to the ads of a particular brand—this can produce meritorious history, or biography, or cultural criticism (Holt 2004), but not good rhetorical science. Conversely, we probably can meaningfully study "television ads for beer" (in part because there are dozens of brands, and literally thousands of executions available). However, to my taste, we would be somewhat better off if the domain were instead specified at the product class level, as "television ads for alcoholic beverages." At this level, we can assume a common underlying consumer motivation, but possibly make use of the different shades of motivation that characterize the consumption of beer versus wine versus spirits, to assist us in building our system of differentiations.

In short, the first point to make is that specialization is one of those endeavors where the optimum does not equal the maximum; it is a Goldilocks problem. The second point to make is that you must have a natural affinity for the category of advertising on which you will focus. In my case, I was a heavy consumer of magazines as a young adult. I generally had four or five subscriptions going at any one time, spent hours every week reading magazines, and I was a bona fide member of the target audience for many of the ads appearing in those magazines. Conversely, it is unlikely that I will ever make a scholarly contribution to the rhetorical differentiation of television advertising. I more or less stopped watching TV in my teens, and did not own a television for many years. I do not have a feel for this medium, nor do I have the necessary history of exposure to ads in this medium.

The reason you must specialize in a particular ad medium, or on ads for a particular product class, is that you are going to have to spend a great deal of time immersed in examples of ads within your area of focus. This is going to be relatively unstructured time with no immediate tangible output of any note. You will not be motivated to spend that time unless you have a basic tropism toward the specific advertising phenomenon under study. I *like* to look through magazines (even magazines for which I am not the target audience). That is one reason my rhetorical scholarship has been focused on magazine advertisements.

In terms of what you will be doing as you immerse yourself in your chosen category of ads, any of the treatises on grounded theory development may be helpful (Strauss and Corbin 1990). More broadly, if you are still a doctoral student, you would do well to take courses on ethnography. Ethnographers, and anthropologists generally, have always emphasized the idea that great gobs of observation must precede the development of conceptual and theoretical structure. It behooves you to get some exposure to expert practitioners of the craft of grounded theory development, and these will often be ethnographers.

An education in ethnography may be particularly important if much of your doctoral education has been focused on psychological theory as developed through laboratory experiments (as was mine). It strikes me that much social psychological theory, although it is supposed to generalize to everything, is not about anything in particular (only applied psychologists study particular social phenomena, and they do not set the tone for the discipline). Doing social psychological theory means designing experiments that test patterns of results obtained in previous experiments, which tested patterns of results from earlier experiments, and so forth (McQuarrie 2004). One can get lots of ideas for good experiments by reading other experiments; but no literature of this kind is going to help you develop a new scheme of rhetorical differentiation. For that, you have to return to the advertising phenomenon itself and try to look at it afresh. If you will only take the time to look at the phenomenon, then an education in experimental psychology may be very helpful in structuring what you see—as will an education in poetics or art criticism. But first and foremost, you have to be immersed in the phenomenon to do rhetoric.

The Procedure of Differentiation

So what exactly are you supposed to be doing as you immerse yourself in actual examples of ads from a particular domain? Here I will take magazine ads as an example, and unpack the process by which I have developed several differentiations concerning magazine ads. Fundamentally, I look for differences and multiple instances (i.e., multiple tokens instantiating some type). This is really no more than unleashing the human mind's natural propensity to find patterns (the brain is a pattern-finding organ, it has been said). The inspiration for this approach is the often-heard dictum in stylistics, that "style is difference." As I immerse myself, I am seeking differences in style, and differences that occur often enough that I can define a rule for classifying the ad in front of me as belonging to some type: "oh, that's another one of *those*." Put another way, I am simply identifying the available means of persuasion in magazine advertising, by looking at each individual ad I encounter and asking, "To what *type* might this ad (or ad component) belong?"

Here a couple of caveats are in order. Logically, one cannot execute the approach just described on the first ad that one sees. In fact, it is difficult to execute the procedure on the first ten ads, or even the first hundred ads that you observe; and it may not even be possible to do this at all during your first immersion session. But if you will look at a hundred or more ads, striving to observe each with an open mind, and if you sleep on it, and then return for another immersion session with another hundred ads, then it will be almost impossible *not* to begin the process of generating typologies of ads—if you have any proclivity for this line of work at all.

The second caveat is that it is a matter of divisive philosophical debate whether anything close to pure observation is even possible. It is probably better to assume that you bring a considerable amount of theoretical and conceptual baggage to your initial immersion session. Some of this is probably useful and represents the fruits of past observers' efforts. Some of it is probably misguided, or just plain wrong. A little reading in phenomenological philosophy will not hurt; it helps to know the idea of *epoche,* the attempt to identify and then bracket (hold only tentatively) one's presuppositions.

Here is an example. Observe the two ads in Figures 12.2a and 12.2b. If we had to parse these ads into their components, most of us would distinguish "picture" from "text" elements. We might further distinguish the brand block as a third kind of element that combines picture and text elements (most notably in the Sears ad). Most would also distinguish the small piece of text that appears in a much larger typeface as a "headline," to be treated separately from the remaining text ("body copy"). Some might note that the Wishbone ads have a second piece of large font text placed at the bottom of the ad, and treat it separately as well ("tagline").

Figure 12.2a **Comparing and Parsing Ads: Sears Financial Network
and Wish-Bone Italian Dressing**

Thus far, we are simply reproducing categorizations that we may have tacitly or uncritically absorbed after skimming an introductory textbook or browsing the reminiscences of a practitioner. It is almost impossible for a contemporary observer not to distinguish "picture," "headline," and "brand" when looking at the ads in Figures 12.2a and 12.2b. Some would go even so far as to define a magazine ad as an assemblage whose fundamental elements consist exactly of picture, text, and brand elements that occupy varying proportions of the page. The value of immersion is that as we encounter more and more ads, the probability increases of an "aha!" experience, in which our assumptions about "picture," "text," and "brand" are suddenly reconfigured.

Figure 12.2b **Comparing and Parsing Ads: Sears Financial Network and Wish-Bone Italian Dressing**

Observe now the three ads in Figures 12.3a–c (see pages 271–273). Here are things I notice when I move back and forth between these two sets:

- The Tostitos® and Wrigley's ads have no headline as conventionally understood.
- Neither the Tostitos®, nor the Pampers®, nor the Wrigley's ad has a brand block analogous to that in the Sears ad. A package shot within the picture has replaced the stand-alone brand block.
- In all of the Figures 12.3a–c ads, the picture has taken over the ad, rather than being confined to its own patch of real estate. Each of these ads *is* a picture.
- Each of the Figures 12.3a–b ads contains over a hundred words of body copy; the Figures 12.3a–c ads contain one or two dozen words (Tostitos®, Pampers®), or less than a dozen (Wrigleys). The few words that do appear are embossed onto the picture—they also no longer occupy a distinct patch of real estate.

We can say with some certainty that the *style* of the ads in Figures 12.3a–c differs considerably from the style seen in the Figures 12.3a–b ads. In fact, the head-to-head comparison renders visible a style dimension that had been *in*visible when we remained within the confines of the orthodox description of a magazine ad as a deployment of picture, text, and brand block on the page. The invisible dimension is sometimes referred to as layout. The separate deployment of picture, text, and brand, each to its own patch of real estate, turns out not to be constitutive of magazine advertising at all; rather it is simply one among several possible styles of layout. Thus, the ads in Figures 12.2a–b conform to what has been termed the "picture-window layout." Only ads in this one particular style are optimally parsed into geographically separate headline, picture, body copy, and brand components. The separate deployment of these elements turns out to be an accidental rather than fundamental property of magazine advertising style.

I hope the contrast between the ads in Figures 12.2a–b and Figures 12.3a–c provides a useful example of the sort of fruits that may be expected to result from the effort of immersing oneself in large quantities of actual ads. Of course, as any ethnographer will tell you, simply noting and describing differences among observed phenomena is only the first step in making a scholarly contribution or advancing theoretical understanding. The next step is to ask, What difference might these stylistic differences make? Put another way, *why* would an advertiser choose to craft ads in the style of Figures 12.3a–b, versus ads in the style of Figures 12.3a–c?

I have attempted to answer this question elsewhere in more detail (McQuarrie 2007; McQuarrie and Phillips forthcoming; Phillips and McQuarrie 2002), and do not want to linger on the issue here; briefly, the style of ads in Figures 12.3a–c should be more effective for consumers who are disinclined to read or otherwise intensively engage ads, and who are only willing to glance briefly at a picture. We may sum up the distinction between the two sets of ads in Figures 12.2a–b and 12.3a–c in terms of documentary versus pictorial style. The first set of ads can be thought of as documents to be read; the second set of ads is pictures to be viewed. The consumer targeted by the first set is a reader who examines; the consumer targeted by the second set is a viewer who glances. Documents directed at viewers will fall flat; that is the causal importance of this stylistic distinction.

I have been at some pains to disabuse you of the practice of resting content with simple dichotomies, so I do not want to stop with this distinction between documentary and pictorial ads. Let me sketch out the next step in the development of what is turning out to be a typology of layouts linked to a typology of pictures. Look back at Figures 12.3a–c and see if you can articulate a distinction between the Wrigleys ad on the one hand, and the Pampers® and Tostitos® ads on the other. Both ads use a pictorial rather than documentary layout. But to my eye, there are two different kinds of pictures here.

The Pampers® and Tostitos® ads contain "look-through" pictures, while the Wrigley's ad is a "look-at" picture. By this I mean that in the Pampers® and Tostitos® ads, the depicted object is the point of the picture. We are supposed to

Figure 12.3a **Comparing and Parsing Ads: Tostitos® Tortilla Chips, Pampers®, and Wrigley's Gum**

look through the picture itself, as if it were a clear glass window, and focus our interpretations on the objects. We are to recognize the Tostitos® package if we should see it on the shelf, and perhaps, we are to salivate at the sight of the salsa. We are definitely supposed to draw inferences about fresh taste from the ingredients

Figure 12.3b   **Comparing and Parsing Ads: Tostitos® Tortilla Chips, Pampers®, and Wrigley's Gum**

shown. In the Pampers® ad, we are to feel the baby's anguish and feel the mothers concern. We are to infer raw red bottom from the red scrunched up face.

By contrast, the Wrigley's ad is not a picture of a busy urban street. It is a tableau filled with glyphs: the stressed-out cell-phone user, the impatient drivers, and so

Figure 12.3c **Comparing and Parsing Ads: Tostitos® Tortilla Chips, Pampers®, and Wrigley's Gum**

forth. In the Wrigley's ad, the picture is an end in itself. The picture is not a picture of a consumption object, or of users consuming; the picture is a consumption object itself, meant to hold the gaze a little longer than a depiction of objects would. Time on ad, enhanced brand salience, and reinforced brand positioning (Wrigleys = refreshing alternative) are the goals.

You can see the rest of this emerging typology developed at greater length in McQuarrie (2007). What I wanted to demonstrate here was the process of embedding one stylistic distinction within another to create a multilevel typology. Thus far, we have a simple tree diagram, with documentary versus pictorial layout at the top level, and then a differentiation of pictorial layout as involving either look-through or look-at pictures. A tree diagram is one major approach to developing a system of differentiations (MM is basically a tree diagram), and a matrix or cube, consisting of completely crossed dimensions (like the PM system), is the other. Whether tree diagram or matrix, either approach takes you far beyond simple dichotomies and all-inclusive contrasts.

The Importance of Sampling

The final point I want to make with the aid of the ads in Figures 12.2a–b and Figures 12.3a–c will emerge when I share with you this fact: the ads in Figures 12.2a–b are about twenty years older than the ads in Figures 12.3a–c, having appeared in the middle 1980s, whereas the ads in Figures 12.3a–c appeared after 2000. Does that suggest some possible explanations for the stylistic differences between the two sets of ads? Of course it does! Once we place the ads within a temporal frame, all kinds of inferences pop up, not the least of which is that the relationship between consumers and magazine advertisers, or the mode in which consumers process magazine ads, may have changed in important ways over the past twenty years. Such inferences are developed further in the papers cited above.

From a workbench perspective, here is the point: sampling plans, and diligent attention to issues of sampling, are just as important to a rhetorician seeking to differentiate ad style as to a more conventional social scientist studying audience response. Immersion in actual ads is not going to be that effective if you execute it by simply picking up the six magazine issues that happened to be lying by your easy chair this afternoon. Whatever insights may emerge from a comparison of Figures 12.2a–b and Figures 12.3a–c ads will flow in part from the underlying decision to systematically sample magazine ads from different time periods (McQuarrie and Phillips forthcoming; Phillips and McQuarrie 2002).

The same argument explains why one is better off sampling ads at the product-class level rather than the product-category level. If we examine alcoholic beverage ads, rather than simply beer ads, then we have built-in intrasample differences on which we can test tentative explanations. Thus, if we are inclined to think that mass/class differences drive some stylistic choices in liquor advertising, then we can compare wine ads and beer ads. If we think the presence or absence of a social drinking mind-set is perspicuous, then we can compare wine and beer ads as against liquor ads (where more pressing intrapsychic purchase motives may override sociability concerns). If we think imported beer ads use a different style because of their foreign origin, we can investigate whether this foreign-domestic contrast is replicated in the case of imported wine and imported liquor.

Claiming that sampling is important is part and parcel of presenting rhetorical analysis as a scientific, causal endeavor. It also reflects my belief that a structured approach to sampling is no less important for qualitative text-analytic disciplines as for quantitative empirical disciplines. The focus of sampling is different—rhetoricians, in developing differentiations, are primarily concerned to sample properly from the population of texts, rather than from the population of consumers. But the logic (and the power) of a disciplined approach to sampling is the same, regardless of whether one is sampling people or texts.

If you are receptive to these reflections on the importance of sampling, here is one final tip from the workbench. After almost two decades of systematically sampling magazines in order to observe ads, it now seems to me that for any given rhetorical inquiry, some media vehicles will provide richer troves of particular sorts of interesting stylistic devices than other, superficially similar vehicles. For instance, I continue to be interested in the sort of visual rhetorical figures described in Phillips and McQuarrie (2004). I have learned that *Good Housekeeping* magazine is a better source of such visual figures than, say, *Cosmopolitan*; and that *Better Homes and Gardens* is an even more prolific source. In the second stage of inquiry, when the rhetorician seeks to explain the stylistic differences discovered in the first phase, it is crucial to note which vehicles have been particularly fruitful sources. This almost certainly reflects some difference in either the uses and gratifications sought by those who consume this particular media vehicle, or the product mix that appears in ads in that vehicle, or the lifestyle or psychographics of the audience drawn to the editorial matter appearing in that vehicle. For the crucial first phase, however, when discovery is the goal, it behooves you to first sample broadly and shallowly, and then later to focus on the vehicles that seem to provide the richest trove of the sort of stylistic difference that interests you.

Summary

The gist of this article is that many opportunities remain to develop new systems for differentiating stylistic options within one or another category of advertising. The field is open to newcomers, and much remains to be done. After reviewing the characteristics of good systems of differentiations, I suggested a step-by-step process to follow if you want to take up the challenge and develop from scratch your own typology of stylistic differentiations.

1. Get cross-disciplinary exposure to both text-analytic disciplines such as semiotics or literary criticism and to cognitive-science disciplines such as experimental social psychology.
2. Cultivate the mental habit of systematically conceptualizing linked, multilevel distinctions. Do not get hung up on simple dichotomies or all-embracing contrasts.

3. Immerse yourself in a circumscribed category of advertisements. Select a category of ads where you have some native sympathy or long history of exposure. Spend at least as much time looking at actual ads as reviewing past literature.

4. After your initial period of immersion, construct structured samples of ads and reimmerse. Start the process of linking differences in style to external differentiating factors.

5. Drive toward a tree diagram or matrix. Link each branch or dimension to an appropriate psychological construct. Specify how consumers will respond differently to stylistic options located at different points in the system.

I look forward to seeing the results of your efforts.

References

Berlyne, Daniel. 1971. *Aesthetics and Psychobiology.* New York: Appleton.

Durand, Jacques. 1987. "Rhetorical Figures in the Advertising Image." In *Marketing and Semiotics: New Directions in the Study of Signs for Sale,* ed. Jean Umiker-Sebeok, 295–318. New York: Mouton.

Forceville, Charles. 1994. *Pictorial Metaphor in Advertising.* Wageningen, the Netherlands: Ponsen & Looijen.

Holt, Douglas B. 2004. *How Brands Become Icons: The Principles of Cultural Branding.* Cambridge, MA: Harvard Business School.

Leech, Geoffrey N. 1969. *A Linguistic Guide to English Poetry.* London: Longman.

McQuarrie, Edward F. 2004. "Integration of Construct and External Validity by Means of Proximal Similarity: Implications for Laboratory Experiments in Marketing." *Journal of Business Research* 57: 142–153.

———. 2007. "Differentiating the Pictorial Element of Advertising: A Rhetorical Perspective." In *Visual Marketing,* eds. Michel Wedel and Rik Pieters, 91–112. Mahwah, NJ: Erlbaum.

———, and David Glen Mick. 1996. "Figures of Rhetoric in Advertising Language." *Journal of Consumer Research* 22 (March): 424–438.

———, and Barbara J. Phillips. Forthcoming. "Not Your Father's Magazine Ad: Magnitude and Direction of Recent Changes in Ad Style." *Journal of Advertising.*

Phillips, Barbara J., and Edward F. McQuarrie. 2002. "The Development, Change, and Transformation of Rhetorical Style in Magazine Advertisements." *Journal of Advertising* 31 (4): 1–13.

———, and ———. 2004. "Beyond Visual Metaphor: A New Typology of Visual Rhetoric in Advertising." *Marketing Theory* 4 (1/2): 113–136.

Strauss, Anselm L., and Juliet Corbin. 1990. *Basics of Qualitative Research: Techniques and Procedures for Developing Grounded Theory.* Thousand Oaks, CA: Sage.

Wenzel, Peter. 1990. "Rhetoric and Semiotics." In *Semiotics in the Individual Sciences,* vol. 2, ed. Walter A. Koch, 551–558. Bochum, Germany: Brockmeyer.

13

Visual Analysis of Images in Brand Culture

Jonathan E. Schroeder

Chapter Summary

Cultural codes, ideological discourse, and rhetorical processes have been acknowledged as influences on consumers' relationships with advertising, brands, and mass media. If brands exist as cultural, ideological, and rhetorical objects, then researchers require tools developed to understand culture, ideology, and rhetoric, in conjunction with more typical branding concepts, such as equity, identity, and value. This chapter argues for an art historical imagination within advertising, branding, and consumer research, one that reveals how representational conventions—or common patterns of portraying objects, people, or identities—work alongside rhetorical processes in ways that often elude advertising research. Several new theoretical concepts, including snapshot aesthetics—the growing use of snapshot-like imagery in marketing communication—and the transformational mirror of consumption—which reflects basic assumptions about how advertising works—provide productive directions for research.

The persuasive power of marketing images depends largely upon the rhetorical representational conventions of photographic reproduction; that is, advertising, corporate reports, packaging, product catalogs, promotional materials, and Web graphics rely heavily upon photographic information technology to help produce meaning and create value. Advertising images, brand images, corporate images, and Web sites all depend upon compelling visual rhetoric. Variously referred to as the attention economy, the aesthetic economy, and the experience economy, this visual turn in marketing may call for new perspectives and research approaches. How do images communicate? In what ways do images create value? How does the

277

handling of images in the allied fields of visual studies, art history, and photography shed light on the relationships between visual processes and consumption?

This chapter discusses methodological and theoretical issues of visual images as they pertain to brands via interdisciplinary research examples and exemplars. Representation plays a key role in the analysis, emphasizing the cultural aspects of images, which provides a useful complement to the visual rhetoric tradition, as it draws upon theory and method from disciplines such as art history, cultural studies, and semiotics. In focusing on *representational conventions,* I place visual issues within a broader theoretical perspective of *brand culture*—the cultural dimensions or codes of brands—history, images, myths, art, theater—that influence brand meaning in the marketplace. This *critical visual analysis* cuts across methodological and topical boundary lines—the possibilities and problems of visual approaches encompass experimental and interpretive realms, and include such varied topics as information processing, image interpretation, and research techniques.

The Image

Many battles of the brands take place within the visual domain. The World Wide Web mandates visualizing almost every aspect of corporate strategy, operations, and communication—Web design has brought visual issues into the mainstream of strategic thinking, and spurred research and thinking about perception and preference of visual information. Visual images exist within a distinctive sociolegal environment—unlike textual or verbal statements, such as product claims or political promises, pictures cannot generally be held to be true or false—images often sidestep issues of deception, false claims, or puffery in advertising.

From the consumer perspective, visual experiences dominate the Web, as consumers navigate through a computer-mediated environment almost entirely dependent upon their sense of sight. Photography—including digital, film, and video—remains a key component of many information technologies—digital incorporation of scanned photographic images helped transform the Internet into the visually rich environment of the World Wide Web. Photography, in turn, was heavily influenced by the older traditions of painting in its commercial and artistic production, reception, and recognition, and profoundly shapes how consumers think about identity (e.g., Cotton 2004; Schroeder 2002; Sobieszek 1999). Today, we live in a photographic-image-saturated world, from television, video, computer games, the World Wide Web, one that often includes images of ourselves, via surveillance, security, identity photos, and Web site photos, what sociologist John Thompson calls "the new visibility" (2005, 31).

Even when consumers realize that an image or image-based scenario is not "real"—for example, when it appears as part of a strategic marketing campaign—these images influence how they perceive and respond to their world. Images give us a sense that we know places, times, and peoples that we have never experienced (e.g., Schroeder 1998). Thus, images in marketing communication—in addition to other visual forms—play cultural as well as persuasive roles. Given such wide-ranging influence, recent work in marketing scholarship urges us to consider marketing images as cultural texts, and not merely as accurate or true strategic pictures that transparently record faces, families, or familiar products, services, and sights (see Mick et al. [2004], for a review; Phillips and McQuarrie 2005; Schroeder 2002).

Images in marketing communication frequently stand in for experience, especially when other information sources have less prominence, and serve as a foundation for future attempts to comprehend and construct the world around us (Borgerson and Schroeder 2005). As a result, images in brand culture understandably have attracted attention from marketing strategists, advertising practitioners, and consumer researchers, and have increasingly evoked criticism from consumer advocacy groups, cultural theorists, and policymakers. Marketing images contribute to the "reality" into which contemporary consumers are socialized and often evade notions of creative interpretation and critical resistance.

Visual images constitute much corporate communication about brands, corporate identity, and economic performance, and also inform efforts to create positive attitudes for citizens, consumers, and organizations. Viewers make sense of these visual images in a number of ways, many of which are automatic or without awareness (e.g., Bargh 2002). Many perceptual processes fluctuate between conscious and unconscious control. For example, cognitive as well as physiological processes govern eye movement, attention, and awareness. Perceptual codes influence visual information processing—Westerners generally read from left to right, and from top to bottom. Further, perceptual cues, such as relative size, shape, color, and symmetry contribute to consumer cognition at a level that most are perhaps only dimly aware (e.g., Arnheim 1974; Larson, Luna, and Peracchio 2004). Objects or people that appear larger in the visual frame are generally ascribed more perceptual and symbolic importance than those that appear small. Representational conventions—or common patterns of portraying objects, people, or identities—work in conjunction with these perceptual and cultural processes in ways that often elude marketing communication research (Borgerson and Schroeder 2005).

Many contemporary ads consist of photographic images with little or no ad copy, few verbal or text-based brand claims, and minimal product information of the traditional sort—technical specifications, performance claims, or text-based arguments. Photographs are used so often and so fluidly for civil, commercial, judicial, and scientific purposes that it can be difficult to keep in mind that photographs are culturally produced images that exist within shifting planes of meaning and significance. As a cultural historian reminds us:

> The range of contexts within which photographs have been used to sell products or services is so enormous that we are almost unaware of the medium of photography and the language which has been created to convey commercial messages. Photographs for commerce appear on everything from the glossy, high-quality billboard and magazine advertisement to small, cheap flyers on estate agents' blurbs. Between these two areas there is a breadth of usage, including the mundane

images in mail-order information and catalogues, the seemingly matter-of-fact but high-quality documentary-style images of company annual reports, the varied quality of commodity packaging, and of course the photography on marketing materials such as calendars, produced by companies to enhance their status.
(Ramamurthy 2004, 204)

Photographs often appear as if they just *are,* mere visual records of what has happened, how people look, or where events took place. Upon reflection, however, "all photographs are representations, in that they tell us as much about the photographer, the technology used to produce the image, and their intended uses as they tell us about the events or things they depicted" (McCauley 1997, 63). Furthermore, as graphic designers Gavin Ambrose and Paul Harris point out, "in our age of vast digital technologies, nearly all images presented for public consumption are altered, enhanced or 'improved' in some way before they are printed or published" (2005, 110). Researchers must acknowledge the malleability of photographic representation within the visual landscape that everyday consumers encounter, pausing to remember that someone takes a range of photographs and then selects one or two that juxtapose product and text in the frame that we see as an ordinary advertisement, Web-page graphic, or brochure illustration. This apparent realism undergirds photography's persuasive power.

In the next section, I present three examples of critical visual analysis of advertising, Web sites, and corporate communication that reveal cultural foundations of visual rhetoric. I focus on the *ad system,* that is, the visual elements within the ad, more than the *human system* (McQuarrie and Mick 2003), drawing upon concepts of *style, types,* and *tropes,* in an attempt to reveal the cultural foundations of contemporary branding. First, I introduce what I call *snapshot aesthetics* to characterize the growing use of snapshot-like imagery in marketing communication. Next, I focus on the mirror as a consumer metaphor and visual trope, borrowed from fairy tale, myth, and painting, within what I term the *transformational mirror of consumption.* Finally, I look at the *visual language of architecture* and its role in the development, growth, and worldwide success of the financial industry. These three aspects of strategic image management serve to illustrate an interpretive, interdisciplinary approach to visual rhetoric—one that offers researchers many avenues for further study.

Snapshot Aesthetics

Digital photography signals a qualitative shift in image production, one that helped shape the World Wide Web, emerged as a cell-phone "killer application," and spurred the growth of online photographic sites, so-called *photoblogs.* Small, easy-to-use, digital cameras, such as the Contax T2, Webcams, and cell-phone cameras have profoundly transformed the way photographs are taken, by both amateurs and professionals (Lenman 2005; Schroeder and McDonagh 2006). For example, Figure 13.1 captures travelers on a tour boat, with the two main subjects semi-posed. In

Figure 13.1   **Example of a Digital Photograph: Travelers on a Boat**

characteristic digital snapshot style, a woman's head emerges behind the figure on the left, the other's eyes scrunch up in a squint, and a cell phone appears awkwardly at his neck, perhaps lending some visual appeal to an ordinary photograph.

The snapshot, a straightforward, generally unposed photograph of everyday life, has emerged as an important style in contemporary marketing communication. Many recent ads portray models in classic snapshot poses—out of focus, eyes closed, poorly framed—in contrast to more traditional and historical patterns of formal studio shots or highly posed tableaux. Companies such as Volkswagen, IKEA, Ford Motor Company, Apple, and Coca-Cola present snapshot-like images in their print, television, and Internet communications. These snapshots often appear less formal, more everyday or "real"—more "authentic" (Nickel 1998).

As internationally celebrated fashion photographer Terry Richardson explains: "Ninety percent of the images I've ever taken have been done with a small camera. You don't have to focus it or do a light reading. You can't fuck up. And because you don't have full control over it, they allow for accident. . . . Those cameras aren't invasive. It's less formal" (quoted in Braddock 2002, 161). *Vogue* magazine editor Robin Derrick agrees: "Snap cameras, rather than elaborate technical cameras, put the emphasis back on the photographer as auteur, rather than as technician. . . . With point-and-shoot cameras, what becomes interesting is what you point it at" (quoted in Braddock 2002, 161). The snapshot, along with its close relatives paparazzi photography, reality TV, and photoblogs, offers strategic branding possibilities.

I contend that snapshot aesthetics—an increasingly prominent style of advertising imagery—accelerates photography's apparent realism. In this way, in advertising that employs snapshots, or images that appear as snapshots, several strategic goals might be met. First, these photographs appear *authentic,* as if they are beyond the artificially constructed world of typical advertising photography. This visual quality can be harnessed to promote brands as authentic, to invoke the "average consumer" as a credible product endorser, and to demonstrate how the brand might fit in with the regular consumer's lifestyle. Furthermore, authenticity has been argued as a key component of consumer interaction with brands (e.g., Arnould and Price 2000; Elliott and Davies 2006; Holt 2002). Thus, an authentic-looking image may support authentic brands, or at least an authentic use of brand values, by appearing honest, sincere, and unstaged.

Second, snapshot aesthetics supports a *casual* image of brands, particularly consumer lifestyle brands. Many brands appeal to less formal consumption—from family dinners to online financial management. Popular fashion brands, in particular, court casual images for their brands and subbrands. Moreover, as the casual clothing market has grown in recent years, fueled by "dress-down Fridays," expanded demand for men's clothing in between suits and blue jeans, and haute couture designers' turn toward basic, everyday clothing in their secondary lines—casual wear such as jeans and T-shirts—the aesthetic regime of the snapshot has developed into a potent marketing tool. Well-known examples include Burberry, Diesel, and Sisley—each deploy snapshot-like photographs in high profile branding campaigns for their everyday clothing lines. Benetton has elevated the snapshot, along with journalistic imagery, to style icon in its long running, often criticized, and widely imitated United Colors of Benetton campaign (e.g., Borgerson, Magnusson, and Magnusson 2006). Thus, clothing companies offering casual product lines often rely on snapshot-like imagery in the ads, catalogs, and on Web sites, both to show their products intended use and to signal their casual style.

In this way, photographic style helps articulate market segmentation strategy. For example, Italian designer Giorgio Armani's Collezioni clothing—his most expensive ready-to-wear collection—generally appears in classically composed black-and-white promotional images, whereas the Armani Jeans line—a more recent, entry-level brand—usually features snapshot-like images of sexualized bodies. Moreover, Burberry's successful rebranding from conservative classic to contemporary cool seemed to have benefited greatly from snapshot-like photographs, featuring the likes of supermodels Kate Moss and Stella Tennant (Schroeder 2006). Of course, Burberry's rebranding encompassed many other strategic initiatives, but I contend that for consumers, their iconic early 2000s black-and-white photographic ad campaign remains the most visible and persuasive rhetorical device.

Snapshot aesthetics provide a *visual frame* for marketing images—a "here and now," contemporary look, by (appearing to) capture a moment, offering a fresh, posed look to the image. Snapshots often appear rushed, carelessly composed, taken almost by chance, thus revealing subjects unposed, "natural" (e.g., Nickel 1998). As advertising photographer John Spinks explains: "The style is basically a recontextualisation of documentary practice. The equipment is rudimentary, but the lie is far more sophisticated, it appears to be verité but it's not. It can be set up and contrived and as much of a fantasy as more technical shoots. A lot of the work is in the edit" (quoted in Braddock 2002, 162). Snapshots within strategic brand communication invoke a *realist* effect that supports a range of brand associations. I argue that this realist aspect of snapshot aesthetics underlines the fashion element of many products—up-to-date, hip, and cool—distinguishing them from classic, boring, or yesterday's goods. In this way, the snapshot look may help to accelerate fashion cycles and trends.

Finally, snapshot aesthetics further blurs the line between strategic marketing communication and popular photography. Advertising excels in appropriating or borrowing cultural codes and styles—snapshot aesthetics draws on the codes and conventions of popular, home photography, but transforms the humble snapshot into a powerful strategic tool. Furthermore, many snapshot ads appear as if produced by average consumers. With the rise of Web sites that allow users to post their own photographs and videos, such as Facebook, Flickr, MySpace, and YouTube, the snapshot enjoys higher circulation than ever (see Cohen 2005; Currie and Long 2006; Smith 2001; Web sites such as Collected Visions, and fotolog.com; as well as Google image and Yahoo! image search engines).

Furthermore, many consumers happily create their own ads, which are often in the snapshot or documentary style. Web sites such as Current TV and YouTube offer consumers a forum to try their hand at brand communication—and occasionally successful specimens are snapped up by brand managers for more conventional broadcast. Other companies sponsor consumer-generated ads, including Converse, MasterCard, and Sony (Petrecca 2006). As Colin Decker, creative director at Current TV, explains, the coveted eighteen- to thirty-four-year-old demographic "does not respond positively to something overly produced and (that is) a hard sell" (quoted in Mills 2006). Snapshot aesthetics may work against an overly produced, hard sell appearance.

The snapshot aesthetic concept offers researchers a host of questions to pursue. What associations do snapshot aesthetics help consumers build? What products and brands are appropriate for this style of promotion? Many luxury goods draw on snapshot aesthetics, will this erode their brand image? Should companies utilize consumer-generated imagery that draws upon snapshot aesthetics? And will this transform the advertising industry? What are the cultural connections of the snapshot, and how might these work within visual communication? What is the visual genealogy of snapshot aesthetics? Is it a fad that may soon fade away?

The Transformative Mirror of Consumption

In a recent paper focused on masculine identity and consumption, Schroeder and Zwick (2004) argued that advertising imagery helps consumers resolve cultural contradictions. They assessed several contemporary advertising exemplars that articulate a set of contradictions, providing illustrative examples for reflecting on masculinity, identity, and desire. This method does not claim that this set of examples is representative, but rather that they are meaningful, compelling images worthy of close analysis. In this way, this approach follows interpretive work that focuses on a limited range of materials in order to make broader points about representation and identity in visual materials (e.g., Gombrich 1999).

One of Schroeder and Zwick's (2004) illustrative ads reads: "She was impressed that he ordered their Mudslides with Coloma. Which did wonders for his self-confidence." This late 1990s print ad for Coloma "100% Colombian Licor de Cafe" features a black-and-white photograph of a white man and woman at a bar or restaurant table with a superimposed color photograph of a Coloma bottle next to a lowball glass that presumably contains a Mudslide drink.

The action takes place in an oval, gilt-framed mirror hanging to the left of the couple. The bespectacled man gazes at his reflection, which has curiously transformed him into a much more classically attractive figure. In the mirror's reflection, the man appears to be in his mid- to late twenties, tall, dark, with a rakish curl of hair falling seductively down his forehead. He has lost "his" eyeglasses, pointed nose, unstyled hair, and oversize chin—he might be said to resemble Pierce Brosnan as James Bond. The woman—not reflected in the image that we see—seems to peer across her companion to admire his rugged reflection. She models a clingy cocktail dress, which reveals a slim figure, a conservative, shoulder-length haircut, and makeup that exaggerates her facial expression—one of bemusement. She appears to be enjoying herself—her right arm reaches over and intimately grasps the man's right arm. His right hand curls around his Coloma Mudslide, maintaining its fetish-like powers of transformation.

We suggest that the ad represents a portrait of a male-female couple with the addition of another male peering in on them from behind the mirror. This mirror image may be read in several ways, as the sage from whom the man learned the codes of alcohol consumption, or the self transformed by demonstrating taste. To know the right product (even the choice of the restaurant) expresses the man's cultural capital in the field of middle-class consumer culture. Thus, the ornamental femininity of his date further enhances his capital accumulation, and her apparent pleasure at his beverage brand reaffirms his masculinity, attractiveness, and taste in one go. Perhaps more attractive mirror-man admires less attractive man's drinking partner, thus conferring male status on his ability to attract a desirable date? The alchemical mirror embodies contradictions of the consuming male; one must be vain and attractive, as well as rational and sophisticated.

Furthermore, the tropes of alcohol involve taste, the pleasures of imbibing, the ability to "control one's liquor," and, at a more fundamental level, a ritual of adulthood, especially the male variety. In sociologist Pierre Bourdieu's theory of symbolic capital, the conversion of one form of capital into another is precisely what makes it so valuable to vie for various forms of capital in different social fields. Here, we see the conversion of cultural capital into social capital by virtue of acquiring more desirable "body-for-others" (Bourdieu 1984, 207). Either way, we have a provocative message of physicality and product use.

The "homely" man seems caught, Narcissus-like, gazing at his more handsome reflection, looking away from his date. Mirrors are a traditional trope of vanity, narcissism, lust, and pride in Western art. Usually, mirrors are linked to women, revealing, reflecting, and reinforcing feminine attributes of beauty and vanity. In this ad, the mirror plays a double role—casting a reflection of the newly self-confident man, and echoing the female role of mirroring male identity. Thus, the feminine mirrors the masculine, reflecting back self-confidence, consumer expertise, and embodied transformation. Furthermore, the woman stands in as a mirror. He looks to her to gain a flattering conception of himself—*she was impressed, which did wonders for his self-confidence.*

This ad stands out for its representation of the male gaze, and suggests a reordering of limits within the male discourse. The image appears to invert, or perhaps expand, the object of gaze; the man seems quite concerned with himself as an object of beauty, as he vainly pays more attention to his image than to his date. His self-doubts fade—thanks to the woman's positive impression—his masculinity reaffirmed. However, one might read this ad in other ways, as men to men, perhaps the striking man in the mirror attracts the gaze of the homely man, doubly disrupting the gaze, and transforming the ad into a potentially gay image (e.g., Stern and Schroeder 1994). This queer perspective finds homoerotic overtones in the gaze between the two men—one reflecting, one reflected—who wink at themselves while wooing others.

A similar visual theme occupies an early 2000s print ad for Gateway computers, *The Way Things Should Be.* In this example, another apparently unattractive man gazes into a mirrored wall to see a more conventionally good-looking "reflection," transformed, in this case, by his "smart, sexy, and always on the go" Gateway notebook computer. His "improved" reflection has more hair, a more conventionally masculine face, complete with a "strong" jaw, and his clothes seem to fit him better. As in the Coloma ad, he grasps the talismanic product with his right hand, as he straightens his necktie with his left, perhaps signaling grooming rituals that underlie contemporary notions of masculine regimes of appearance. Here, however, the modernist office environment provides the setting, subtly suggesting that looks count on the job as well as on the make.

Motorola adopts the transformative mirror of consumption in its 2006 campaign for Moto KRZR, a slim cell phone with integrated camera, music player, and a reflective, mirrored case. A series of ads revolves around reflected figures—one right side up, and another seemingly reflected, upside down—that generally reveal subtle changes in appearance. For example, one young female model, staring quite seriously into the camera in the "right side up" image, smiles and looks away in her "reflected" image. Another young man holds a pair of drumsticks in his "reflection." In a third version of the basic ad, a woman's "reflection" reveals windblown hair, a slightly tighter necklace, and an elaborate tattoo, hidden in the "right side

Figure 13.2 **Transformative Mirror Example: Motorola**

up" image (Figure 13.2). In each of these "spot the differences" ads, the phone appears at the reflection's edge—thus not reflected itself—acting as a hinge of the reflected image. Seemingly, the power of the phone, or at least its technological capabilities for sound and image production and reproduction, enables consumers expression in new, or at least formally hidden, ways, revealing the transformative mirror of consumption.

The mirror of transformation, as identified across several ads from various product categories, reveals some of the visual building blocks of brand meaning. The classic visual analysis technique of *comparing* and *contrasting* helps uncover themes common across product categories and brand campaigns, helping shift our focus to cultural concerns that are broader than those of market-focused studies, and opening up consumer research to interdisciplinary inquiry. In particular, it helps illuminate the visual building blocks of brand meaning and value. Questions worth pursuing include: How do art historical and mythical figures and tropes work in marketing communication? Do consumers understand the uses of items like the mirror as a metaphorical device? How do ads draw upon ancient representational conventions for their rhetorical power? Is there a useful "set" of conventions, culled from history, or does advertising create its own conventions?

The Visual Language of Architecture

In a *visual genealogy* of contemporary marketing communication and branding efforts, this study analyzed banking Web sites, corporate reports, and marketing communication to reveal the staying power of classicism for transmitting certain key values about banks and building brand images for global financial institutions (Schroeder 2003). This type of research project requires interdisciplinary sources, and often a good introductory book from a relevant discipline offers a useful start—such as, in this case, Hazel Conway and Rowan Roenisch's wonderfully concise *Understanding Architecture* (2005). I studied bank Web sites, financial institutions' brand campaigns, credit card advertising, and corporate reports, and found the classical language of architecture remains, despite massive changes in banking and the financial sector. Although space and time are transfigured within the information-based electronic world of contemporary commerce, classical architecture remains a viable method for communicating consumer values, revealing how visual rhetoric adapts to new communication technologies and evolving marketing strategies.

Architecture has played a key role in persuading consumers about the merits of banks:

> Created by private capital to serve a pragmatic function for its owners, bank architecture at the same time turns a public face to its community in a vigorous attempt to communicate, persuade, assure, impress, and convince. . . . Contemporary attitudes regarding money, respectability, security, and corporate aesthetics are reflected . . . bank architecture thus communicates the importance of banks as institutions, assuring us of their stability, prosperity, and permanence and inviting us inside to do business. (Nisbet 1990, 8)

Architecture provided a strategic method for banks to communicate key attributes of stability, strength, and security. The classical form visually generates "a sense of longevity, stability, rectitude, even stable power" (O'Gorman 1998, 94). Customers entrust banks with their savings—this distinguishes banking from many other business concerns. Although most consumers are aware that banks do not delegate space to store their particular deposits—money is represented by computer databases now—the physical attributes of the bank have played an important role in projecting a proper image, including stability over time, financial and material strength, and financial and physical security. Classicism helped legitimize banking, a role it played for the nascent United States commercial system:

> Classicism, like language, is precise but flexible. It can suggest commercial probity, as we see in the classical architecture of bank buildings and above all, in the New York Stock Exchange. It can radiate culture, as in the neoclassical art museum in Philadelphia and many another city. In the early nineteenth century, the Greek temple form pledged allegiance to the democratic principles that Americans traced back to ancient Athens. (O'Gorman 1998, 95)

Each of these strategic banking values—*stability, strength,* and *security*—has a psychological dimension as well as a material solution. Stability, expressed in visual form by a sturdy structure, provides a metaphor for long-term endurance—"this is why the posts, pillars, and columns which have assured people in many cultures of the buildings' structural stability have been just as critical in resolving other uncertainties and anxieties" (Onians 1988, 3). Colossal columns, heavy materials, and symmetrical form contribute to a building's appearance of strength. Of course, bank customers also desire financial strength, and an ability to withstand economic cycles. Security, for so long largely dependent on architectural fortresses, walled cities, and massive structures, also relates to psychological anxiety about financial matters. The closed form of most banks was meant to signal protection—a secure institution to entrust one's future. Furthermore, the use of the temple form created a visual of a special building protecting its valuables, allowing only certain people access to the interior space, and promoting a ritual element of bank visit. Banks are not just depositories of money; they are repositories of hopes, dreams, and anxieties—a modern temple (Figure 13.3).

Information technology drove many changes in the banking industry—money and financial matters are not confined to pieces of paper that must be sorted and stored in ways that leave a ledger and an audit trail. Instead, they are electronic entries, generated via computers, and disconnected from particular spaces or buildings. This transformation was instrumental in overhauling the banking system from a loose network of numerous small local banks interacting with the Federal Reserve System to the current deregulated arrangement of mega banks, online banking, and international markets. The small-town bank of the past, where customers knew the tellers, and met personally with the loan officer to discuss their mortgage, is mostly gone, replaced by automated teller machines (ATMs), computerized forms, and secondary markets for mortgages (Cross 1993): more efficient, certainly, but possibly less human. Perhaps this points to the continuing significance of classical architecture—it alone remains to symbolize banking's connection with the past by tapping into classicism as a powerful referent system. Although the premises of

Figure 13.3   **Classical Form Example: Old Stone Bank**

banking have changed, the promises of the banking industry have not.

A fourth banking attribute emerged along with the electronic revolution: *speed.* Now banks need to communicate the four S's: Stability, Strength, Security, and Speed, as customers expect quick and efficient transactions supported by computerized operations (e.g., Zwick and Dholakia 2006). However, the other values remain, and basic relationships between the consumer and the bank continue to require symbolic association. The giant Wells Fargo Bank's 1999 annual report announced that "the basic financial needs of our customers, however, do not change that much. They want to borrow, invest, transact, and be insured. They want convenience, security, trust and dependability" (Wells Fargo 2000, 4). What role does the classical form play today? Certainly, banks are no longer primarily physical places—they are name brands that occupy space in the consumer's mind. I am not concerned here with recently built banks, or general architectural trends. Rather, I am interested in how the classical form resides in contemporary marketing communication—advertising, corporate reports, Web sites, and the ephemera of electronic banking—for these are the crux of brand building and meaning making within strategic communication.

In this way, architecture functions as a heuristic for consumers in a cluttered marketplace of images. It is not necessary for viewers to identify columns as "Ionic" or "Doric"—or know much about the history of classicism—for ads to work as a reference to tradition, dialogue and debate, and the classical past. By juxtaposing old and new styles, brand communication sets up an implicit contrast as well as an allusion to time by abstracting the physical aspects of architecture into two-dimensional and electronic space.

Traditionally, consumers have valued three qualities in a bank: stability, strength, and security (Schroeder 2003). Banks adopted classical architectural form to persuade the public. In the electronic age, architecture no longer confines banking, nor do most consumer banking transactions take place within a bank's headquarters. Therefore, a change might be expected in communicative tools, and classical motifs might seem outmoded or old-fashioned for the information society. However, banks have shifted the symbolic domain from the building to the marketing message, adopting architectural symbols for use in digitized images that carry on the communicative tradition of classical forms. Advertising, Internet sites, and ATM banking still incorporate abstracted architectural symbols, and buildings continue to provide many metaphors for the banking industry.

VeriSign, an online financial security firm, echoes these architectural themes in their brand communications, which feature images of classical buildings—but not their buildings. Furthermore, a recent VeriSign (2002) ad's copy refers to the brand promise of stability, strength, and security. The ad shows an immense classical atrium with a beautiful, ornate dome. The copy states:

> You trust that the ravages of 400 years have not weakened the bases.
> You trust the granite bases to support the 24-foot high Corinthian columns.
> You trust nothing more than eight columns to sustain a 15,000-ton dome above your head.
> Yet you're wary of using a credit card online?

Here, we might consider that trusting "the ravages of 400 years have not weakened the bases" obliquely refers to stability; trusting "the granite bases to support the 24-foot high Corinthian columns" to strength; and "nothing more than eight columns to sustain a 15,000-ton dome above your head" to security. In this way, I suggest that VeriSign offers a playful invocation of the classical values of bank architecture, promoting their brand as a contemporary, safe solution to long-standing financial concerns. Thus, the high-tech, electronic VeriSign brand invokes the legacy of the classical form in a neat comparative statement that marries the old and the new, placing an Internet business within the long legacy of architectural signification.

Banks today are in the business of building brands as much as physical structures.

Consumer researcher Benoît Heilbrunn argues that brands are transformative devices that allow contradictory principles to coincide, such as nature and culture, the real and the imaginary, the past and the present, and the very distant and the here and now (Heilbrunn 2006). Classicism reinforces this notion, linking an ancient past to the present via rhetorical devices perfected during the classical era. Of course, these persuasive visual rhetorical tools are augmented via marketing information technology, selling the past to the future (Berger 1972).

Classicism remains a central cultural referent structure. Architecture provides spatial, historical, and psychological images easily appropriated by visual media. Furthermore, architecture provides basic metaphorical structures for perception and cognition—indeed, it "presents embodiments of thought when it invents and builds shapes" (Arnheim 1977, 274). These shapes, translated into two dimensions, abstracted and isolated, are the building blocks of meaning making.

By tracing visual genealogies such as classicism—and how these metamorphose over time—we gain an appreciation of the complex composition of contemporary brand culture. Further research might investigate how rhetorical systems such as classicism function within other product categories, and how architecture itself interacts with communication and promotion—a relatively overlooked area of inquiry within advertising research. Other questions remain about the continuing significance of classicism, and the role that trends, fads, fashions, nostalgia, and retro-marketing plays within marketing communication. How do long-established cultural systems such as architecture intersect with advertising?

Discussion and Insights

To more fully understand brands, researchers must investigate the cultural, historical, and representational conventions that shape brand communication. If brands exist as cultural, ideological, and rhetorical objects, then brand researchers require tools developed to understand culture, rhetoric, and ideology, in conjunction with more typical branding concepts, such as equity, strategy, and value. Within the brand culture perspective, *brand identity* forms the strategic heart of the brand—what the brand manager imagines brand to be, and *brand image* reflects psychological aspects of brands—how the brand image rests within the minds of the consumer, gauged by consumer response (Figure 13.4). *Brand culture* refers to the cultural dimensions or codes of brands—history, images, myths, art, theater—that influence brand meaning in the marketplace (Schroeder 2005).

Many insights emerge from critical visual analysis that would be difficult to generate with traditional social science approaches. Links to the tradition of fine art serve to remind us that advertisements have a visual and historical genealogy. Genre analysis produces generalizable insights into contemporary marketing images. Quoting or mimicking an art historical tradition helps ground images for viewers, by drawing associations to familiar visual traditions. By noting and investigating the links between new images with rhetorical traditions, we generate

Figure 13.4   **Brand Dimensions**

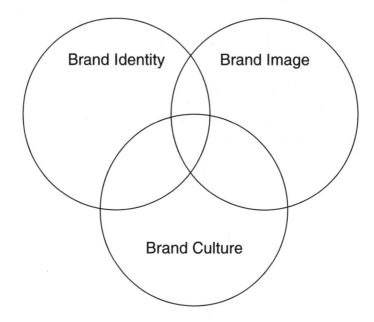

clues into how advertising helps strengthen brands through visual representations that transcend the here and now.

Critical visual analysis reveals limitations in an information-processing model of consumption, one in which culture, history, and style are attenuated (see also Allen, Fournier, and Miller 2007). For example, the "white space" of the many advertising images—the blank background, neutral surround, or studio backdrop—does not neatly fit into cognitive models; from a strictly "decision-making" or "persuasion" perspective, this white space carries no "information," it is "lost" amid persuasive or rhetorical devices (Pracejus, Olsen, and O'Guinn 2006). In contrast, critical visual analysis helps point out how white space imbues images with meaning. In other words, white space is not "nothing," it helps to situate subjects within images, and its use links images to a broader cultural world of aesthetics, luxury, and value.

Critical visual analysis points to the cultural and visual context of ads within the flow of mass culture, underscoring the powerful role marketing plays in both the political economy and in the constitution of consuming subjects. A key element of critical visual analysis often entails constructing a visual genealogy of contemporary images, to contextualize and historicize them, and point to the cultural domain of contemporary visual consumption. An important issue to consider is how the representational conventions discussed affect viewers' perceptions. Most consumers are not necessarily visually literate, and art historical references and conventions may not consciously inform their viewing of an ad. Likewise, most language speakers have a limited awareness of the linguistic horizon that shapes their use of vocabulary, grammar, and syntax; nor do they have a well-developed sense of how language developed over time. However, historical conventions shape communication. This does not imply that all consumers read images in the same way, of course (e.g., Phillips 2003); rather that each image carries with it a historical and cultural genealogy that helps us to understand how it produces, reflects, and initiates meaning. I urge visual rhetoric researchers to engage their *art historical imagination* when considering how visual images work, why they draw consumers' attention, and how they help create brand value.

Conclusion

Greater awareness of the associations between the traditions and conventions of visual culture and the production and consumption of brand images helps to position and understand advertising as a global representational system. Future research on images in brand culture must acknowledge images' representational and rhetorical power both as cultural artifacts and as engaging and deceptive bearers of meaning, reflecting broad societal, cultural, and ideological codes. Questions remain about how verbal and visual issues intersect (Stern and Schroeder 1994). Studies that extend previous work on visual representation into past, cultural, and art historical realms, may provide an essential bridge between visual meaning residing within producer intention or wholly subsumed by individual response, and between aesthetics and ethics. In other words, along with brand identity and brand image, the realm of brand culture serves as a necessary complement to understanding brand meaning and brand creation (Schroeder and Salzer-Mörling 2006).

Brand research focused on the rhetorical, social, and economic implications of images, fueled by an understanding of the historical conditions influencing their production and consumption may require cross-disciplinary training and collaboration. Key questions remain about the relationships between vision and value—why certain images are celebrated, criticized, or condemned. Understanding the role that visual consumption plays in consumer preference, cultural production, and representation signals a step toward understanding how images inform and influence basic consumer issues of attention, branding, identity, and meaning making.

Acknowledgments

Thanks to Janet Borgerson, Detlev Zwick, Jennifer Davis, David Vaver, Jane Ginsburg, Lionel Bentley, John Balmer, T.C. Melewar, Stefano Puntoni, Marcus Gianneshi, Eric Guthey, Linda Scott, and my students in the Masters in Fashion Experience and Design program at Bocconi University, Milan, for comments and interest in this project. Thank you to Jane Blackwell and Bruce Schroeder for help with images, and also to Victoria-Tamara Lee at Motorola for kind permission to reproduce the Moto KRZR ad. A preliminary version of this chapter was presented

to the Interdisciplinary Trade Marks Workshop at Cambridge University's Centre
for Intellectual Property and Information Law, July 2006.

References

Allen, Chris T.; Susan Fournier; and Felicia Miller. 2007. "Brands and Their Meaning Makers." In *Handbook of Consumer Psychology,* ed. Curtis P. Haugtvedt, Paul M. Herr, and Frank R. Kardes. Mahwah, NJ: Erlbaum.

Ambrose, Gavin, and Paul Harris. 2005. *Image.* Lausanne: Ava.

Arnheim, Rudolf. 1974. *Art and Visual Perception.* Berkeley: University of California Press.

———. 1977. *The Dynamics of Architectural Form.* Berkeley: University of California Press.

Arnould, Eric, and Linda Price. 2000. "Authenticating Acts and Authoritative Performances: Questing for Self and Community." In *The Why of Consumption: Contemporary Perspectives on Consumer Motives, Goals and Desires,* ed. Cynthia Huffman, S. Ratneshwar, and David Glen Mick, 140–163. London: Routledge.

Bargh, John A. 2002. "Losing Consciousness: Automatic Influences on Consumer Judgment, Behavior, and Motivation." *Journal of Consumer Research* 29 (September): 280–285.

Berger, John. 1972. *Ways of Seeing.* London: Penguin/BBC.

Borgerson, Janet, and Jonathan E. Schroeder. 2005. "Identity in Marketing Communications: An Ethics of Visual Representation." In *Marketing Communication: Emerging Trends and Developments,* ed. Allan J. Kimmel, 256–277. Oxford: Oxford University Press.

———; Martin Escudero Magnusson; and Frank Magnusson. 2006. "Branding Ethics: Negotiating Benetton's Identity and Image." In *Brand Culture,* ed. Jonathan E. Schroeder and Miriam Salzer-Mörling, 171–185. London: Routledge.

Bourdieu, Pierre. 1984. *Distinction—A Social Critique of the Judgment of Taste.* Cambridge, MA: Harvard University Press.

Braddock, Kevin. 2002. "Vision Express." *The Face* (October): 157–161.

Cohen, Kris R. 2005. "What Does the Photoblog Want?" *Media, Culture & Society* 27 (6): 883–901.

Collected Visions. 2006. http://cvisions.nyu.edu (accessed April 4, 2006).

Conway, Hazel, and Roenisch, Rowan. 2005. *Understanding Architecture: An Introduction to Architecture and Architectural History,* 2d ed. London: Routledge.

Cotton, Charlotte. 2004. *The Photograph as Contemporary Art.* London: Thames & Hudson.

Cross, Gary. 1993. *Time and Money: The Making of Consumer Culture.* New York: Routledge.

Currie, Nick, and Andrew Long. 2006. *fotolog.book: A Global Snapshot for the Digital Age.* London: Thames & Hudson.

Elliott, Richard, and Andrea Davies. 2006. "Symbolic Brands and Authenticity of Identity Performance." In *Brand Culture,* ed. Jonathan E. Schroeder and Miriam Salzer-Mörling, 155–170. London: Routledge.

Fotolog. 2006. www.fotolog.com (accessed April 11, 2006).

Gombrich, Ernst H. 1999. *The Use of Images: Studies in the Social Function of Art and Visual Communication.* London: Phaidon.

Heilbrunn, Benoît. 2006. "Cultural Branding between Utopia and A-topia." In *Brand Culture,* ed. Jonathan E. Schroeder and Miriam Salzer-Mörling, 103–117. London: Routledge.

Holt, Douglas B. 2002. "Why Do Brands Cause Trouble? A Dialectical Theory of Consumer Culture and Branding." *Journal of Consumer Research* 29 (June): 70–90.

Larson, Val; David Luna; and Laura A. Peracchio. 2004. "Points of View and Pieces of

Time: A Taxonomy of Image Attributes." *Journal of Consumer Research* 31 (March): 102–111.

Lenman, Robin, ed. 2005. *The Oxford Companion to the Photograph.* New York: Oxford University Press.

McCauley, Elizabeth A. 1997. "Photography." In *A Short Guide to Writing about Art,* 5th ed, ed. Sylvan Barnet, 61–71. New York: Longman.

McQuarrie, Edward F., and David Glen Mick. 2003. "The Contribution of Semiotic and Rhetorical Perspectives to the Explanation of Visual Persuasion in Advertising." In *Persuasive Imagery: A Consumer Response Perspective,* ed. Linda M. Scott and Rajeev Batra, 191–221. Mahwah, NJ: Erlbaum.

Mick, David Glen; James F. Burroughs; Patrick Hetzel; and Mary Yoko Brannen. 2004. "Pursuing the Meaning of Meaning in the Commercial World: An International Review of Marketing and Consumer Research Founded on Semiotics." *Semiotica* 152 (1/4): 1–74.

Mills, Elinor. 2006. "Perhaps the Best Sony 'Ad' Last Year Was Created by a Consumer." *CNET News,* April 4. www.news.com (accessed September 20, 2006).

Nickel, Douglas R. 1998. *Snapshots: The Photography of Everyday Life 1888 to the Present.* San Francisco: San Francisco Museum of Modern Art.

Nisbet, Robert. 1990. "Men and Money: Reflections by a Sociologist." In *Money Matters: A Critical Look at Bank Architecture,* ed. Joel Stein and Caroline Levine, 7–14. New York: McGraw-Hill.

O'Gorman, James F. 1998. *A B C of Architecture.* Philadelphia: University of Pennsylvania Press.

Onians, John. 1988. *Bearers of Meaning: The Classical Orders in Antiquity, the Middle Ages, and the Renaissance.* Princeton: Princeton University Press.

Petrecca, Laura. 2006. "Amateur Advertisers Get a Chance." *USA Today* online, March 3. www.usatoday.com (accessed September 20, 2006).

Phillips, Barbara J. 2003. "Understanding Visual Metaphor in Advertising." In *Persuasive Imagery: A Consumer Response Perspective,* ed. Linda M. Scott and Rajeev Batra, 297–310. Mahwah, NJ: Erlbaum.

———, and Edward F. McQuarrie. 2004. "Beyond Visual Metaphor: A New Typology of Visual Rhetoric in Advertising." *Marketing Theory* 4 (1/2): 113–136.

Pracejus, John W.; Douglas G. Olsen; and Thomas C. O'Guinn. 2006. "How Nothing Became Something: White Space, History, Meaning and Rhetoric." *Journal of Consumer Research* 23 (June): 82–90.

Ramamurthy, Annadi. 2004. "Spectacles and Illusions: Photography and Commodity Culture." In *Photography: A Critical Introduction,* ed. Liz Wells, 193–245. London: Routledge.

Schroeder, Jonathan E. 1998. "Consuming Representation: A Visual Approach to Consumer Research." In *Representing Consumers: Voices, Views, and Visions,* ed. Barbara B. Stern, 193–230. New York: Routledge.

———. 2002. *Visual Consumption.* London: Routledge.

———. 2003. "Building Brands: Architectural Expression in the Electronic Age." In *Persuasive Imagery: A Consumer Response Perspective,* ed. Linda M. Scott and Rajeev Batra, 349–382. Mahwah, NJ: Erlbaum.

———. 2005. "The Artist and the Brand." *European Journal of Marketing* 39 (11/12): 1291–1305.

———. 2006. "Critical Visual Analysis." In *Handbook of Qualitative Research Methods in Marketing,* ed. Russell W. Belk, 303–321. Aldershot, UK: Edward Elgar.

———, and Pierre McDonagh. 2006. "The Logic of Pornography in Digital Camera Promotion." In *Sex in Consumer Culture: The Erotic Content of Media and Marketing,* ed. Tom Reichert and Jacqueline Lambiase, 219–242. Mahwah, NJ: Erlbaum.

———, and Miriam Salzer-Mörling. 2006. *Brand Culture.* London: Routledge.

———, and Detlev Zwick. 2004. "Mirrors of Masculinity: Representation and Identity in Advertising Images." *Consumption, Markets, and Culture* 7 (1): 21–51.

Scott, Linda M., and Rajeev Batra, eds. 2003. *Persuasive Imagery: A Consumer Response Perspective*. Mahwah, NJ: Erlbaum.

Sobieszek, Robert A. 1999. *Ghost in the Shell: Photography and the Human Soul, 1850–2000*. Cambridge, MA: Los Angeles Museum of Contemporary Art and MIT Press.

Smith, Joel. 2001. "Roll Over—Analysis of Snapshot Photography, Photos of Everyday Life Not Initially Produced as Art." *Afterimage* (September): 1–10.

Stern, Barbara B., and Jonathan E. Schroeder. 1994. "Interpretive Methodology from Art and Literary Criticism: A Humanistic Approach to Advertising Imagery." *European Journal of Marketing* 28: 114–132.

Thompson, John. 2005. "The New Visibility." *Theory, Culture & Society* 22 (6): 31–51.

Wells Fargo Bank. 2000. *Annual Report, 1999*. San Francisco, California.

Zwick, Detlev, and Nikhilesh Dholakia. 2006. "Bringing the Market to Life: Screen Aesthetics and the Epistemic Consumption Object." *Marketing Theory* 6 (1): 41–62.

14

Expanding Rhetoric

Linda M. Scott

> *There is always just beneath the surface of the antirhetorical stance a powerful and corrosive elitism.*
>
> —Stanley Fish

"Rhetoric" is people using symbols to get their way. This is my contemporized restatement of definitions offered by rhetoricians ranging from Aristotle to Kenneth Burke. The definition can encompass a wide variety of forms, any individual or group of humans, and all situations in which some jockeying for advantage is in the offing. Given this range, it is easy to see why rhetoric, the oldest language theory in history, has traveled so well (Davis and Schleifer 1989; Jost and Olmsted 2006; Rivkin and Ryan 2004).

Just a few steps more and we also can see the basis for rhetoric's current fashionability across a range of disciplines. Thinkers like Derrida and Barthes have made us comfortable with applying the term "symbol" to a variety of forms, so it would be typical of our times to see studies of rhetoric that focused not just on language or voice or gesture, but also images, music, and narrative—or scents, dress, and décor. Marx and Foucault have taught us to understand the struggle for power as a ubiquitous dynamic of human interaction, so it is nothing strange to take a rhetorical view of advertisers, as well as statesmen, clergy, scientists, and, yes, academics. With our recently acquired appreciation for the ways that reality is constructed by the tools we have devised to express it (courtesy of scholars from Geertz to Einstein), we are able to see that rhetoric can claim legitimate province over not only television commercials but also scientific treatises, revolutionary manifestos, and tenure decisions. I hope, then, that readers can begin to see why many contemporary thinkers are allied with a "globalized" concept of rhetoric: "Rhetoric's 'globalization' can best be understood as a project or intellectual movement, at the center of which is a proposed disciplinary reframing: from the study of rhetoric as a delimited object of study—as circumscribed by the classical tradition—to rhetoric as a perspective or set of perspectives on virtually all human acts and artifacts" (Simons 2006, 154; see also Best and Kellner 1997; Fish 1990).

In the advertising and marketing literature, however, studies under the banner of "rhetoric" have had a fairly traditional application. When constrained most narrowly, rhetoric is a study of the formal devices employed to achieve persuasion. Thus, research that measures consumer response to particular formal strategies in advertising, from the employment of tropes to the use of drama, fits into this more limited notion of the purview of rhetoric. That stream of research has been remarkably fruitful, producing what is in my opinion the only consistent record of results in the entire literature on advertising response. Nevertheless, it barely scratches the surface of what is possible to include in a rhetorical approach. In this chapter, I identify several other studies—of consumer response, of practitioners' intent, of industrial struggle—that, while the authors may not use the word "rhetoric," do fit under that rubric. I also point to some ways in which our future avenues of inquiry may be expanded through a full use of the scope of rhetoric.

My proposed definition, however, is also aimed to advance purposefully toward more recent evolutions in rhetoric's application: the study of how people *get their way* by the use of symbols, especially when they are allegedly doing something disinterested. So I will end this chapter by addressing the ways that our own field constructs the rhetoric of inquiry, wrapping itself in a cloak of impartial science, thus allowing particular scholarly adherents to get their way, and, in the process, serving a particular locus of power.

Placing Rhetoric

To date, the only literary theory most marketing academics recognize by name is semiotics. Since that theory preemptively calls itself "the science of signs," I often find that scholars in our own field have trouble understanding where to place rhetoric. Thus, I suspect it would be helpful to begin with a thumbnail sketch of rhetoric's province and history. If there is to be space for the rest of my argument, I can only summarize, so I advise readers to follow up with the citations for more detail (especially Davis and Schliefer 1989; Eagleton 1983; Jost and Olmsted 2006; Rivkin and Ryan 2006).

Like semiotics, rhetoric is only one in a stable of theories used for the study of literature. Anthologies of criticism consistently categorize these and other approaches (formalism, Marxism, and feminism are others) as distinctly separate slots in a shared taxonomy from which critics variously draw. Sometimes, individual critics are strongly associated with particular theories (as Cleanth Brooks was with the New Criticism and Stanley Fish is with reader-response theory), but it is equally common for critics to move among theories, employing what seems appropriate to analyze a certain work or make a particular point. As a result, the distinctions among the theories can seem blurry in practice. Nevertheless, rhetoric is usually distinguished from other approaches.

Rhetoric is conventionally characterized as a form of criticism focusing on the ways that texts are created to elicit particular responses from readers. Thus, in the practice of criticism, rhetoric often takes a historical tack, looking at the context in which a novel was written, for instance. A rhetorical analysis may also involve analyzing the responses of actual readers (as in the work of I.A. Richards), but more likely would be a critical outline of the way the formal devices of a text suggest the existence of a particular reader or guide readers through a certain reading experience (as in the works of Stanley Fish) (see Tompkins 1980). (Please note that reader-response is essentially a subgenre of rhetoric and is therefore often put in the same section in anthologies.) If the critic tries to reconstruct the circumstances under which a book became a best seller or a play became "a hit," it would be rhetorical criticism but would be more likely specifically labeled "reception theory" (another subgenre of rhetoric that usually appears in the same sections of anthologies).

Within individual examples of criticism, a little blurring around the edges of the received taxonomy always exists. In practice, for instance, rhetorical analysis often involves close formal exegesis, just as New Criticism and Russian Formalism do. Structuralism is generally seen as the conceptual opposite of rhetoric because of its formalism, scientism, implied order, and explicit orientation toward some philosophical center or "Truth." Even so, the practitioners of "semiotics" often step over into areas, such as reader response, that are typically considered the province of rhetoric. Historicism and more overtly political theories, such as Marxism and feminism, are often hard to distinguish from rhetorical analysis because the first is focused on context and the latter on the use of language (or symbols generally) in the maintenance of power, both of which are also typical of rhetoric. Poststructuralism is very similar to rhetoric in both its concept of how language works and its rejection of timeless truths (my own opinion is that poststructuralism is simply the latest incarnation of rhetoric, a sort of *rhétorique du jour*). Stanley Fish remarks that, "Indeed deconstructive or poststructuralist thought is in its operation a rhetorical machine: it systematically asserts and demonstrates the mediated, constructed, partial, socially constituted nature of all realities, whether they be phenomenal, linguistic, or psychological" (1990, 214). Nevertheless, rhetoric is often seen to be less nihilistic than poststructuralism because of its insistence on the possibility of communication, more grounded because of its ties to pragmatism, more robust because of its focus on the function of language as symbolic action, and more hopeful because of its comparatively comedic attitude (Blakesley 1998; Simons 2006).

I think the unique feature of rhetoric is its focus on the interaction between intentions and outcomes. The New Critics eschewed both intention and effect. Structuralism, in its formalistic approaches and its desire to rise to a level above individual speech acts, does not attend to either intentions or outcomes. Political literary theories tend to assert broadscale effects without consideration of either evidence or circumstances—and such theories usually reject the legitimacy of intention as a dimension of analysis. So the marriage of intention to effect is, to a very large degree, rhetoric's exclusive domain. From this focus, all the rest eventually comes, beginning with the close attention to the details of particular speech acts, moving to the context in which they are performed, advancing to the motives the rhetors seek to satisfy, and finally turning to address audience response, material outcomes, theoretical implications, and, increasingly, social and moral responsibilities

Rhetorical analysis is very much concerned with particularities—of texts, of writers, of readers, of cultures, of historical moments. As a theory, it has few general principles and little inclination toward grand scientific explanations of the working of language. The basis for communication, in the rhetorical view, is the loose and ever-changing accumulation of social contracts—called "conventions"—by which you and I simply agree that, for the moment anyway, "cat" will refer to a certain furry, four-legged animal, and so on. In more modernist approaches to language (e.g., structuralism), communication is based on an elaborate, preexisting, and more or less permanent architecture of grammars and denotations. In rhetoric, language is more like the film that floats and flows on the surface of water, the outlines clear and the colors consistent, but always moving and changing and never tethered to anything concrete.

It is important to understand, however, that communication is not thought to be completely random in rhetoric. Instead, because every text is so grounded in the social constructions of its time, the response to it is, in some ways, predictable and, at the very least, intelligible, even from a distance. People will react to a text in a consistent manner, except that their responses will vary according to (1) their own particular characteristics as readers (memberships in certain cultural subgroups, for instance), or (2) the author's skill or ability to assess the situation, or (3) the time in which the audience confronts the text (it is not presumed, in rhetoric, that the value ascribed a text would be "timeless"). Thus, even rejection of the text will be explainable in light of the circumstances of its delivery and the characteristics of its audience. This ability to predict within certain constraints is the reason the rhetorical framework for advertising research has been able to produce such robust results—but it is also the reason it has been able to demonstrate systematic variation according to the characteristics of readers.

As an outgrowth of the study of symbols as persuasive devices, rhetoric came to examine the ways in which the very signs with which we communicate are constitutive of thought and foundational to knowledge. Rhetoric has been concerned with "the way language contains embedded within it schemas for understanding the world in a particular way," in which "language shapes people's perceptions of the world" and "also actively constructs social reality" (Rivkin and Ryan 2004, 128). The symbolic scope of influence has expanded with technological advances, causing a restructuring of both thought and discourse (Ong 1982; Scott 1993; Scott and Vargas 2007). Therefore, the potential power in the ability to control the rhetoric of a particular discourse has itself become a major focus of inquiry for rhetoric scholars. Terry Eagleton writes in his widely read book, *Literary Theory*, "Discourses, sign-systems and signifying practices of all kinds, from film and television to fiction and the languages of natural science, produce effects, shape forms of consciousness and unconsciousness, which are closely related to the maintenance or transformation of our existing systems of power" (1983, 210).

In the last years of the twentieth century, during which rhetoric had enjoyed a major renaissance, rhetorical analysis was used to debunk discourses thought to be somehow above reproach—most notably scientific, literary, philosophical, and economic dialogues—and revealed them to be, at base, concerned with protecting interests, maintaining influence, shoring up comfort levels, and the like. Works such as Thomas Kuhn's *The Structure of Scientific Revolutions* (1970) and Donald McCloskey's *The Rhetoric of Economics* (1985) shook the faith that many had in knowledge production as an impartial, orderly enterprise. The leading thinker of twentieth-century rhetoric was the mercurial, multitalented Kenneth Burke. Increasingly associated with philosophical pragmatists like Richard Rorty and renegade theorists like Stanley Fish, however, rhetoric began, first, to signify a rapacious challenge to the-truth-as-we-know-it and, then, to take on a clear philosophical viewpoint. This viewpoint, though it vociferously rejects normal earmarks of philosophy such as "basic principles" or "essential truths" has nevertheless become identifiable as "rhetoricality" (Bender and Wellbery 1990).

Because rhetoric not only acknowledges but also seeks out multiple readings and provisional circumstances, rhetoricality is radically relativist in orientation. Further, since this approach acknowledges the instability of symbols themselves, it does not approach a text with the same sense of authority that inheres in other language theories. In fact, rhetoric, like history (a close philosophical cousin), is at base an antitheory. Because it rejects ideas like "truth," "objectivity," and "structure"—and does not orient in any way toward a philosophical "center" (like "parole" or "aesthetic value" or even "God")—rhetoric is said to be "antifoundationalist" as a theory or as a philosophy. Thus, it is profoundly postmodern in outlook, in spite of its ancient pedigree.

Rhetoric in Research

Rhetorical Devices

To begin identifying the places where rhetoric could be most easily and immediately expanded within advertising research, it makes sense to start with formal devices and practices. McQuarrie, Mick, and Phillips have already demonstrated that studying consumer response to tropes and schemes is a profitable area (McQuarrie and Mick 1992, 1996, 1999; Phillips 1997; Phillips and McQuarrie 2002). Similarly, some beginning efforts have been made with particular genres (lectures and dramas) (Deighton, Romer, and McQueen 1989) as well as character (Mulvey and Medina 2002). These areas could all be studied further, but efforts could also extend to include other elements, such as motif or rhyme, and other forms such as music or dance (Scott 1990). To date, no studies have looked at the ways formal features are used to constitute an implied author (or "brand personality") nor the tactics that invite a certain mock reader (Scott 1994). Working toward a genre theory specific to advertising (where the genres are "testimonial," "torture test," "slice-of-life," and the like, rather than borrowed constructs such as "lyric" or "epic") would also be an important tool for future research.

Responses of Readers

Researchers have also studied readers' holistic responses to advertisements. Mick and Buhl (1992) offered an early empirical study of a small sample of readers interpreting advertisements. This study made it clear that consumers responded to ads in a very situated and skeptical manner—and, importantly, that ads affected consumers primarily in the context of their own life themes and projects. Other works made close investigations of the match between life projects or themes and the appeals of ads (e.g., Grier and Brumbaugh 1999; Motley, Henderson, and Baker 2003; Parker 1998; Stevens, Maclaren, and Brown 2003). Taken in sum, this body of research shows starkly that individual life projects—rather than manufacturer's intentions or formal tricks—is most central to consumers' responses to ads. Furthermore, membership in certain subcultural communities, does, as initially articulated in the theoretical work (Scott 1994) have an effect on how ads are read and evaluated. Grier and Brumbaugh (1999) showed, for instance, that the subcultural status of readers (by race and sexual preference) formed the reading strategy and ultimately had a strong impact on response to ads. Thus, when Douglas Holt (2004) published *How Brands Become Icons,* in which he says brands become "cultural icons" only by speaking to the identity projects of large groups of consumers, his position was solidly underpinned by this body of research about the responses of readers.

Some research also suggests that ordinary consumers approach ads with a politically informed, critical consciousness. Ahuvia (1998) tested the assertions of an established critic, who had already interpreted an ad for Airwalk shoes as carrying a message supporting a "culture of rape" as well as racial stereotyping. Ahuvia's respondents shared some of the critic's interpretation, but not all of it. Even so, the verbatims suggested respondents saw themselves as situated in oppressive social structures and were able to see the function of ads to support that configuration of relations. British women viewing spots for *Red* magazine showed a similar ability when they expressed discomfort over the use of striptease, even if with a surprising "twist" at the end: "it's just, again, there we are—taking off our clothes to sell a magazine" (Stevens, Maclaran, and Brown 2003, 39). Further, Motley, Henderson, and Baker (2003) found that African-American respondents often interpreted offensive commercial racial memorabilia in a way that helped them confront, understand, and work through their historical past—while not denying its oppressive and dehumanizing nature.

Ritson and Elliott's (1999) study of British adolescents focused on the ways that consumers quoted, reinterpreted, and reused ads as part of an ongoing local social discourse. Though the authors do not cite Kenneth Burke or situate their study in rhetoric, the research itself is directly in the line of what Burke called for in one of his most famous essays, "Literature as Equipment for Living" (1973). In this study, the appearance of ads in conversation as phatic communication, shared jokes, ways of poking fun at teachers and friends was a sharp reminder that humans consume to live, not live to consume—and that ads fall into a larger, complex "text" of other media materials and actual face-to-face dialogue rather than being isolated, privileged missives of information.

Consumers are shown by this literature to be enmeshed in a symbolic environment that is rife with persuasive attempts—as any rhetorical theorist would avow. Freistad and Wright (1994) have argued that this very environment has led to the emergence of a folk theory of persuasion that helps consumers resist advertisers' attempts to get into their pocketbooks. Yet, despite the critical readings, social uses, and resistance tactics that have been documented, there still remains no systematic study of active consumer rejection of advertisements in the literature (Scott 1994b).

Intentions and Institutions

The practices of advertisers, including especially copywriters and art directors, is an area that has also seen a bit of work. Some have documented creatives' intentionalities (Kover 1995). Others have studied the interactions between creatives, clients, and other parties to this multiauthored form (Cronin 2004a, 2004b; Hackley 2003a, 2003b, 2003c; Kover and Goldberg 1995). This research focuses on a previously understudied aspect of advertising practice, intentionality, and so adds necessary balance to the analysis of ads-as-texts or consumers-as-readers: "Whilst practitioners certainly cannot be said to determine viewers' reception of their texts, completely excluding practitioners from the analysis skews understanding of the significance of advertising practice and its textual products" (Cronin 2004a, 352–353).

Many of the "great men" of advertising history—from Albert Lasker to Claude Hopkins to David Ogilvy to John O'Toole—left treatises and memoirs that recorded their personal theories of advertising as well as their own experiences of the struggle that characterizes its production (for just a few examples, see Calkins 1922; Hopkins 1960; Lasker 1963; Ogilvy 1963; O'Toole 1977; Sullivan 2003). At this point, quite a number of works have documented the tension between advertisers and clients, between research departments and creatives, as well as the variation of philosophies within these groups and the high level of uncertainty that typifies the enterprise (Fox 1985; Holt 2004; Schudson 1985).

The Rhetoric of Markets

Indeed, virtually all of the published research characterizes advertising practice as agonistic, fragmented, uncertain, fluid, and stressful, suggesting further that the task of producing advertising itself is subject to multiple strategies, homilies, agendas, and interpretations (Cronin 2004a, 2004b; Hackley 2003a, 2003b, 2003c; Kover 1995; Kover and Goldberg 1995). Such adversarial struggles emerge from very different philosophies and agendas among those who produce advertising—and from the anxious belief that most ads fail (Schudson 1985). Economic anthropology's most basic text, Marcel Mauss's *The Gift* (1990), characterizes exchange in even the most archaic and remote societies as a continuous clash of rivalries, embedded in a never-ending web of reciprocity. Thus, it would seem that the backdrop of ubiquitous symbolic combat in which rhetoric places every text is particularly fitting to the study of advertising.

Mauss further argues that it is pointless to try to separate the acts of exchange from interactions with other institutions—art, church, and kinship. New histories, in fact, are emerging to document the ways that the practice of advertising has been put in the service of agendas that seem at first to be far removed from its business. For instance, Jason Chambers (2007) painstakingly documents the efforts that many in the African-American community put into building their own advertising industry so as to legitimize themselves in the eyes of the world's biggest consumer democracy, as well as to counter and replace racial stereotyping in the mainstream industry's work. Similarly, Jean Grow and Joyce Wolberg (2006) documented the conscious attempts of the women at Weiden+Kennedy to express a feminist perspective in the Nike advertising of the 1990s. Evidence of such political activism among practicing advertising people is not hard to find (Berman, Fedewa, and Caggiano 2006; Fischer 2004; Kreshel 2004). Indeed, one of the highest profile campaigns today is Product Red, the campaign led by U2 singer Bono to harness the power of the globe's leading brands in conquering AIDs in Africa.

Reconceptualizing the work of advertising this way, however, also complicates the imagined audience. Not only do agencies seek consumers-as-citizens to help combat world problems, they also often expect advertising to persuade and motivate internal audiences (Gilly and Wolfinbarger 1998)—and to tout their services to potential clients and rival agencies. This is not to mention the "green" and Fair Trade campaigns designed to pacify governments and nongovernmental organizations. Researching the multiple intentionalities and conflicting agendas that actually characterize advertising would be an important avenue for correcting the mischaracterization of the industry as a monolith in the traditional research of the field.

Rhetoric of Objects

To the degree that brands are employed for the purposes of humanitarian aid and that athletic shoes become a feminist statement, we can certainly see that the objects featured in advertising can become signs in a form of material rhetoric. The idea that goods are meaningful as signs, over and above their utilitarian functions, introduced to our field by Grant McCracken (1987), has been axiomatic in economic anthropology for decades. In fact, Mary Douglas and Baron Isherwood argue not only that goods are more important for communication than for sustenance, but that objects, like words or pictures, are tools for thought: "Forget the idea of consumer irrationality. Forget that commodities are good for eating, clothing, and shelter; forget their usefulness and try instead the idea that commodities are good for thinking; treat them as a nonverbal medium for the human creative faculty" (1990, 40–41). Advertising functions as a form of ritual that consecrates goods with a distinctive social meaning (Otnes and Scott 1996; Scott 2005). Chris Hackley, who has extensively studied (2003a, 2003b, 2003c) the efforts of advertising account planners to understand and articulate the views and voice of consumers, argues that advertising professionals, like anthropologists have come to view consumer behavior "as an imaginative activity realized through symbolic consumption as opposed to a merely instrumental activity driven by rational product evaluation" and thus an "activity 'inspired' by the beauty of persuasive and alluring images and ideas" (2003c, 2). In practice, we can see that global campaigns like MasterCard make clear use of the knowledge that the main reason to consume is to connect with other people ("MasterCard Roundtable" 2006; Schudson 1985).

Yet it is in the nature of rhetoric—and therefore goods-as-rhetoric—to exclude as well as to include. The use of trade sanctions to break an enemy is as old as recorded history, as current as today's MSN headlines. Withholding access to goods is a time-marked way for elites to reduce despised subcultures (Scott 2005). Particularly given the widening gap among the haves and have-nots, it would seem that more research should be directed toward the messages that exclude as well as include audiences. As Douglas and Isherwood remark: "Goods are neutral, their uses are social; they can be used as fences or bridges" (1990, xv).

The instability of conventions, the polysemy of texts, the activity of readers, the politics of goods, and the agonistic aims of authors, together, create a scene for which rhetoric seems uniquely suited. And yet, even in the presence of empirical substantiation, the rhetorical approach remains marginalized in the field of marketing.

The Rhetoric of Inquiry

Stanley Fish argues that the whole history of Western thought could be written as a quarrel between a rhetorical worldview and an idealist one. "In one version written many times, the mists of religion, magic, and verbal incantation . . . are displaced by the Enlightenment rediscovery of reason and science," he writes, while "in another version . . . a carnivalesque world of exuberance and possibility is drastically impoverished by the ascendancy of a soulless reason, a brutally narrow perspective that claims to be objective and proceeds in a repressive manner to enforce its claims" (1990, 209). In the recent past, the idealist view is most famously exemplified in the scientific model, one in which "independent facts are first collected by objective methods and then built up into a picture of nature, a picture that nature herself either confirms or rejects in the context of controlled experiments" (210).

Fish's intentional caricature of "the ascendancy of a soulless reason" and the "world of exuberance and possibility" is reminiscent of the rhetoric that accompanied the legendary paradigm conflict in marketing research during the 1980s and 1990s. Based on the accumulation-of-observations model, however, we would now expect the scientific community that still dominates this area of academe to be showing changes in the ways they conduct their studies of advertising response. Instead, their work seems to stubbornly hew to a business-as-usual ethic and to ignore the evidence mounting around them (see, for instance, Scott and Vargas 2007). Originally heralded as a "paradigm shift" similar to the one that affected the other social sciences in the late twentieth century (the shift to rhetoricality of which I have been writing here), the emergence of textual, historical, and ethnographic perspectives in marketing research appears instead to have produced separate silos in which scientists and interpretivists pursue their own agendas. I now turn to a closer look at the rhetoric of inquiry that enforces this isolation.

Let us begin by going back to the original source of the term "paradigm shift." Thomas Kuhn coined both "paradigm" and "paradigm shift" in his landmark work, *The Structure of Scientific Revolutions* (1970), a rhetorical analysis of the conduct of research in the natural sciences over several hundred years. His story, which ranges from astronomy to biology to physics and beyond, is consistently one in which groups of scientists who subscribe to a shared view of a phenomenon and who also share a prescribed set of tools, standards, theories, prejudices, and blinkers for studying it, work to maintain their control of training, publication, and advancement by constraining the topics and methods of inquiry. The group and its arena of control is called "normal science" and the tradition from which the members work is called a "paradigm."

Kuhn argues that the most famous breakthroughs in science are not, according to the actual historical record, the result of a gradual accumulation of evidence, but come about in a volatile, sudden, "revolutionary" way. He documents, across multiple cases, how a field of research will stall out, having reached the limits of what the existing paradigm can explain. As anomalies in the data pile up, the institutions of normal science are used to defend the paradigm from potential intruders. The intruders are often new to the field, either young recruits or mature scholars coming in from another discipline. Their outsider perspective allows them to see the impending death of the old paradigm, gives them the tools to challenge the falseness of its assumptions, and provides a framework for a fresh perspective. Usually, a long and bitter struggle ensues but, eventually, the corpus of data implodes from the weight of its own anomalies and, in a moment of "scientific revolution," a new paradigm comes into being.

From the moment of this paradigm shift, the old guard of normal science is disgraced and disenfranchised, just as they had feared all along. Hence, the story of paradigm shifts is usually one of long and vicious struggle, rather than the dispassionate gathering and review of data. That is because, in some sense, it is not about data at all. It is about power, and the protection of interests. Or, in the "ordinary language" aesthetic of rhetoric, it is about some scholars getting their way at the expense of others—and using symbols (textbooks, measurements, journal articles) to do it.

Interestingly, Kuhn remarks that advances in fields where an external social need—he specifically enumerates medicine and law—is the "principal *raison d'être*" for the discipline, the institutions of normal science do not operate this way. I remark on this because, in the first place, one might expect that business schools could claim engagement in pressing social issues (economics, material provisioning, etc.), and second, the justification for the dominant paradigm in marketing so often is the existence of outside auditors (e.g., marketers).

Indeed, the interests of an imagined beneficiary community—advertisers—is often the guiding principle in research on advertising response, and it certainly infuses the exemplary article to which I now to turn. Demetrios Vakratas and Tim Ambler published an ambitious review, "How Advertising Works: What Do We Really Know?" in the *Journal of Marketing* (1999). In this article, the authors set out their mission in terms typical of normal science: they aim not only to document, analyze, and categorize past achievements (a key to power maintenance to which Kuhn specifically points), but also "to identify what *should* be known." My italics in that last quotation are intended to emphasize the prescriptive function of review articles to set (and constrain) future agendas for research—again one of Kuhn's list of normal science's typical features—but I also want to make salient the implicit value judgment about what we *should* want to know, what is *worthwhile* pursuing as knowledge, what is a *legitimate* topic of research, and, as we shall see, who is a *worthy* beneficiary of our findings.

We begin to see very quickly what is to be delegitimized and who is to be kept outside when the authors begin to enumerate their strategy for including or excluding studies from their analysis. From the abstract through to the conclusions, the beneficiaries of the research are identified as "advertisers." However, there seems to be little awareness of the multiple players, various intentions, and competing theories that make up "advertisers" in reality. Instead the beneficiary is treated as a monolith. But then, the actual beneficiaries themselves, "advertising practitioners," are excluded from the list of publications to be surveyed on the basis that "they don't publish" (Vakratas and Ambler 1999, 26). As I mentioned before, the vanity of advertising men has produced a substantial literature of theories and memoirs from which Vakratas and Ambler could have drawn. But herein lies the true point—practitioners may publish, but they do not publish in "the right journals" (that is, the narrow and seldom-read journals of this tiny corner of normal science). We can see that policing the paradigm is the actual task at hand. "Advertisers" is just a straw man, a beneficiary imagined for the purpose of rhetoric, like a character in a fiction (Booth 1961).

The locus of power to be served, however, is abundantly clear. The authors specifically exclude any study that looks at broad social or economic effects, though it is certainly arguable that their stated goal "to establish what is and should be known about how advertising affects the consumer" (Vakratas and Ambler 1999,

26) could logically include environmental damage, rampant materialism, racial stereotyping, and price inflation. They also exclude any study not published in English, yet disingenuously claim, "Our study also has an international flavor, because it examines research by academics and practitioners in the United States, United Kingdom, Australia, and the Netherlands" (27). If there were any doubt, the authors specifically state that the ultimate purpose of this field's research agenda is to help advertisers "formulate more effective advertising strategies" (26). What is allegedly to be served by this rhetoric, therefore, are the interests of Western corporations.

A false concession to their own exclusivity ("we make no claim that this selection is complete") turns quickly into a claim that their selections "include every significant and current theory of how advertising works" (27). They list and painstakingly analyze five categories drawn from this highly circumscribed literature. The diagram used for their exegesis has "inputs": "message content, media scheduling, and repetition," not interested human attempts to persuade. The dimensions of consumer response are limited to cognition, affect, and experience. Only in "experience" can we see potential for the realm of the social to intrude on this model—but "experience" is specifically defined as memories of product use (not news stories about abusive labor practices or impressions of sexist imagery), which can easily be produced in the laboratory. Indeed, the laboratory language of psychology is pervasive throughout: consumers do not listen to, argue with, or reject ads, for instance, they have responses that are "triggered" (26). Amazingly, though the avowed justification for this review is that "much advertising expenditure is wasted," there is no potential acknowledged anywhere in the article for the subjects to reject the proposition (though they may be too unskilled or too passive to process it). So it would seem that advertising is wasted, not because consumers reject ads, but because they are too stupid and lazy to look at them.

In one particularly telling passage, the authors claim that, "According to one historian (Nevett 1982), advertising, from its earliest days, has been regarded as providing strictly factual information" (27). This statement is risible to anyone who has read even a small subset of the many books on advertising history published in the past twenty years. Commercial speech has been known for outlandish hyperbole for at least three centuries. Indeed, the oldest book-length treatment of advertising history, *The History and Development of Advertising* by Frank Presbrey (1929) contains drawings of outrageous signs used in preliterate England to advertise a range of establishments from cobblers to taverns. Probably the oldest joke about advertising comes from Samuel Johnson, writing in 1759: "Promise, large promise is the soul of an advertisement." Johnson's text provides more evidence of the pervasiveness of advertising gimmickry, many years ago: "Whatever is common is despised. Advertisements are now so numerous that they are very negligently perused, and it is therefore become necessary to gain attention by magnificence of promises, and by eloquence sometimes sublime and sometimes pathetick" (Samuel Johnson, *Idler* #40, January 20, 1759).

Dr. Johnson shows us that the carnivalesque ground of advertising has been in place for quite some time, yet the rhetoric of science changes history to make its object fit the tools (and the objectives). A field that calls itself "information processing" needs very badly to define advertising in a way that matches its language and methods. Even here, though, it is long overdue to recognize that this idea of human cognition is based on an analogy to computers. It is an interesting tool for thinking, but there is no particular reason to believe that our brains work like the machines we created. Indeed, at this point, our field's emphasis on words and numbers as the form in which "information" must come is itself lagging behind the technology it believes we mimic (Scott and Vargas 2007). At base, "information processing" is just a very powerful *trope*. Just as McCloskey (1985) showed economics to be engaged in the measurement of metaphors rather than of objective realities, we, too, are in thrall to a simile employed to persuade.

By the time Vakratsas and Ambler's article appeared, several of the empirical rhetorical studies I have reported in this chapter were already published in the scholarly literature (for instance, Ahuvia 1998; Deighton, Romer, and McQueen 1989; Gilly and Wolfinbarger 1998; Kover 1995; Kover and Goldberg 1995; McQuarrie and Mick 1992, 1996; Mick and Buhl 1992; Parker 1998; Phillips 1997). But those studies do not appear in Vakratsas and Ambler's taxonomy or even in their reference list. Instead, the authors cite only a few theoretical pieces (none of which draw on rhetoric) that they promptly cast into an "all others" category, and then dismiss as "philosophic." This catchall category turns out, not surprisingly, to be the smallest category in the taxonomy, thus allowing Vakratsas and Ambler to execute yet another rhetorical finesse: "This proved to be the smallest category, which in itself provides some support for the classification methodology" (1999, 34). The authors do acknowledge that the "postpositivist" pieces are more "person-centered" than the studies that bulge from their own taxonomy, but they reduce this advantage to "an extension of a basic reinforcement model." Finally, they dismiss the "all others" studies, in the spirit of McCloskey's economists, because they allegedly had not measured their effects (in fact, several of the studies mentioned at the top of this paragraph employed traditional measurements).

Most damning, though, is the authors' judgment that "the postpositivists have, thus far, broadened the width of our understanding, but not the depth. For example, we have not found research to advise the practitioner as to which measures predict advertising effectiveness" (35). It is astonishing to see that what counts as "depth" in this research paradigm is the ability to tell advertisers, indiscriminantly, how to sell more stuff.

Please consider this objective closely. If advertising researchers could identify an advertising appeal or form that would reliably sell anything (since "advertisers" is an undelimited beneficiary) to anyone ("consumers," similarly, refers to all humanity), what would the social and economic outcome be? Without any way to screen, ignore, resist, or reject an advertising proposition, consumers everywhere would be buying without the constraints of budget, tastes, sanctions, or needs.

Sixth-graders would be buying adult diapers and hockey players would purchase tampons. Poor families would be unable to save; rich families to invest. Diabetics would gobble candy bars and alcoholics everywhere would fall off the wagon. Retailers could not predict their inventories and factories could not forecast labor needs. Complete social and economic chaos would ensue, bulldozing the lives of marketing scholars as certainly as it demolished everything else. Why would anybody embrace this research objective?

Well, of course, no one would. I do not believe that any of the participants in this discourse actually believe they are ever going to reach this goal—otherwise, they would be running as fast as they could in the opposite direction. Instead, this scenario is merely part of the rhetoric of normal science in advertising research. Yet it does speak poorly of our discipline that so many have publicly claimed their life goal to be to find a way to predict (in order to control) the behavior of their fellow humans. This is a cruelly arrogant proposition and, since one can only assume that the proponents feel they would be immune to whatever devices were shown to manipulate others, it is also outrageously elitist.

It is true that, when this field began, the founders imagined that the best strategy for winning credibility (and funding and consultancies) for their fledgling enterprise was to embrace science and imagine themselves at the service of industry. But it was just that—an act of imagination. Since most marketing programs are in state universities, the early scholars could just as easily have imagined themselves in the service of the tax-paying public or even the government (also sources of grant money and other goodies). The founders chose corporate America instead and have acted ever since to exclude the broader concerns of citizens. Yet all that is required to reverse this constraint is a second act of imagination. An axiom of rhetoric—"the writer's audience is always a fiction"—can free us to address other agendas, if we are only willing (Ong 1989).

The time for that would seem to be at hand. The business schools, at least in America, are under fire. As it turns out, the scientific research agenda, instead of generating useful managerial insights and tools for control, has produced a body of work that is seen by business as irrelevant and has led to charges that narrow technocrats instead of managers are being trained. Because this realization comes at a time when corporate greed and corruption is splashed across the press, industry is blaming business schools for failing to inculcate a sense of moral and social responsibility in students (Bennis and O'Toole 2005; Quelch 2005). It seems that the cynical ethos of control attributed by Vakratsas and Ambler (as well as a whole generation of scholars) to "advertisers" is not what industry had ordered up after all.

Indeed, as someone who has spent all of her adult life engaged, directly and often, with members of the advertising community, it has always puzzled me that academics thought the industry expected these things. In my experience, most advertising people are intelligent, educated people, most of whom have a pretty well-developed sense of social responsibility. Certainly they would not endorse the vision of socioeconomic chaos outlined above—indeed, what would be the advantage to any one advertiser to have a set of magic bullets good for all targets? I have found, instead, that most industry professionals respect the independence of universities as institutions and even envy scholars their freedom to study and report outside the controls of proprietary market research. Most would think it inappropriate for schools to prostitute themselves to this imagined industry directive to help sell more stuff. And, besides, none of them find the promise—a set of advertising features good for selling all things at all times—even remotely plausible. So, the whole enterprise has always struck me as a pipedream puffed by people who do not get out much.

If we were instead to expand inquiry to encompass the entire rhetorical enterprise of exchange, all institutions and players, as well as all the potential ways that advertising might affect them could be considered legitimate subjects of study. There would be no need to limit the methods of research to quantification, or for that matter to exclude quantification from the toolbox. Numbers, as any sophisticated statistician will tell you, are just as easy to put in the service of rhetoric as words. Indeed, the scientists of our own field have been using numbers to advance their rhetoric—that is, to get their way—for a very long time.

"Theories, in short, are themselves rhetorics whose usefulness is a function of contingent circumstances," writes Professor Fish. "It is ends—specific goals in local contexts—that rule the invocation of theories, not theories that determine goals and the means by which they can be reached" (1990, 221). If we were to reimagine the purposes and beneficiaries of research on advertising, we might make enough room in the field for it to become a discipline that has impact, rather than pretending, as we do now, that anyone cares. We might be able to provide the basis for social and moral accountability in exchange, instead of feeding a vision of corporate greed unchecked by any other institution. For certain, we could take as our goals more worthy ends, something we could each feel good about dedicating a life to, rather than feigning interest in an outcome that would, if reached, destroy the very social fabric that connects us, holds us, and even shapes our thoughts.

References

Ahuvia, Aaron C. 1998. "Social Criticism of Advertising." *Journal of Advertising* 27 (1): 143–163.

Bender, John, and David Wellbery, eds. 1990. *The Ends of Rhetoric: History, Theory, Practice.* Stanford: Stanford University Press.

Bennis, Warren G., and James O'Toole. 2005. "How Business Schools Lost Their Way." *Harvard Business Review* (May): 1–9.

Berman, Cheryl; Denise Fedewa; and Jeanie Caggiano. 2006. "Still Miss Understood: She's Not Buying Your Ads." *Advertising & Society Review* 7(2).

Best, Steven, and Douglas Kellner. 1997. *The Postmodern Turn.* London: Guilford Press.

Blakesley, David. 1998. "Kenneth Burke's Pragmatism—Old and New." In *Kenneth Burke and the 21st Century,* ed. Bernard L. Brock, 71–95. Albany: State University of New York.

Booth, Wayne. 1961. *The Rhetoric of Fiction.* Chicago: University of Chicago Press.

Burke, Kenneth. 1973. "Literature as Equipment for Living." In Burke, *The Philosophy of Literary Form*, 293–304. Berkeley: University of California Press.

Calkins, Earnest Elmo. 1922. *The Advertising Man*. New York: Scribner's.

Chambers, Jason P. 2007. *Madison Avenue and the Color Line: African Americans in the Advertising Industry*. Philadelphia: University of Pennsylvania Press.

Cronin, Anne M. 2004a. "Regimes of Mediation: Advertising Practitioners as Cultural Intermediaries?" *Consumption, Culture, and Markets* 7 (4): 349–369.

———. 2004b. "Currencies of Commercial Exchange." *Journal of Consumer Culture* 4 (3): 339–360.

Davis, Robert Con, and Ronald Schleifer, eds. 1989. *Contemporary Literary Criticism*, 2d ed. New York: Longman.

Deighton, John; Daniel Romer; and Josh McQueen. 1989. "Using Drama to Persuade." *Journal of Consumer Research* 16 (December): 335–343.

Douglas, Mary, and Baron Isherwood. 1996. *The World of Goods*. London: Routledge.

Eagleton, Terry. 1983. *Literary Theory*. Minneapolis: University of Minnesota Press.

Fischer, Eileen. 2004. "Working for Women Within the Organization: Eileen Fischer (York University Interviews Denise Fedewa of LeoShe)." *Advertising & Society Review* 4 (4).

Fish, Stanley. 1990. "Rhetoric." In *Critical Terms for Literary Study*, ed. Frank Lentricchia and Thomas McLaughlin, 203–224. Chicago: University of Chicago Press.

Fox, Stephen R. 1985. *The Mirror-Makers: A History of American Advertising and Its Creators*. New York: Vintage.

Freistad, Marian, and Peter Wright. 1994. "The Persuasion Knowledge Model: How People Cope with Persuasion Attempts." *Journal of Consumer Research* 21 (June): 1–31.

Geertz, Clifford. 1973. *The Interpretation of Cultures*. New York: Basic Books.

Gilly, Mary C., and Mary Wolfinbarger. 1998. "Advertising's Internal Audience." *Journal of Marketing* 62 (1): 69–89.

Grier, Sonya A., and Anne M. Brumbaugh. 1999. "Noticing Cultural Differences: Ad Meanings Created by Target and Non-Target Markets." *Journal of Advertising* 28 (1).

Grow, Jean, and Joyce Wolburg. 2006. "Selling Truth: How Nike's Advertising to Women Claimed a Contested Reality." *Advertising & Society Review* 7 (2).

Hackley, Christopher E. 2003a. "Divergent Representation Practices in Advertising and Consumer Research." *Qualitative Market Research* 6 (3): 175–184.

———. 2003b. "Accounting Planning: A Review of Current Practitioner Perspectives from Leading London and New York Agencies." *Journal of Advertising Research* (June): 1–11.

———. 2003c. "The Implicit Epistemological Models Underlying Intra-Account Team Conflict in International Advertising Agencies." *International Journal of Advertising* 23: 1–19.

Holt, Douglas B. 2004. *How Brands Become Icons*. Boston: Harvard Business School Press.

Hopkins, Claude. 1960. *Scientific Advertising*. New York: Bell.

Jost, Walter, and Wendy Olmsted, eds. 2006. *A Companion to Rhetoric and Rhetorical Criticism*. Oxford: Blackwell.

Kover, Arthur J. 1995. "Copywriters' Implicit Theories of Communication: An Exploration." *Journal of Consumer Research* 31 (March): 596–611.

———, and Stephen M. Goldberg. 1995. "The Games Copywriters Play: Conflict, Quasi-Control, A New Proposal." *Journal of Advertising Research* (July/August): 52–62.

Kreshel, Peggy. 2004. "The Industry's Feminist Conscience: Peggy Kreshel (University of Georgia) Interviews Liz Schroeder and Margie Goldsmith of the Advertising Women of New York (AWNY)." *Advertising & Society Review* 4 (4).

Kuhn, Thomas. 1970. *The Structure of Scientific Revolutions*, 2d. ed. Chicago: University of Chicago Press.

Lasker, Albert. 1963. *The Lasker Story.* Chicago: Advertising Publications.

"MasterCard Roundtable." 2006. *Advertising & Society Review* 7 (1).

Mauss, Marcel. 1990. *The Gift: The Form and Reason for Exchange in Archaic Societies,* trans. W.D. Halls. New York: Norton.

McCloskey, Donald. 1985. *The Rhetoric of Economics.* Madison: University of Wisconsin Press.

McCracken, Grant. 1987. "Advertising: Meaning or Information." *Advances in Consumer Research* 14: 121–124.

McQuarrie, Edward F., and David Glen Mick. 1992. "On Resonance." *Journal of Consumer Research* 19 (March): 180–197.

———, and ———. 1996. "Figures of Rhetoric in Advertising Language." *Journal of Consumer Research* 22 (December): 424–438.

———, and ———. 1999. "Visual Rhetoric in Advertising: Text-Interpretive, Experimental, and Reader-Response Analyses." *Journal of Consumer Research* 26 (June): 37–54.

Mick, David Glen, and Claus Buhl. 1992. "A Meaning-Based Model of Advertising Experiences." *Journal of Consumer Research* 19 (September): 317–338.

Motley, Carol M.; Geraldine R. Henderson; and Stacey Menzel Baker. 2003. "Exploring Collective Memories Associated with African-American Advertising Memorabilia." *Journal of Advertising* 32 (Spring): 47–57.

Mulvey, Michael S., and Carmen Medina. 2002. "Invoking the Rhetorical Power of Character to Create Identifications." In *Persuasive Imagery: A Consumer Response Perspective,* ed. Linda M. Scott and Rajeev Batra, 223–246. Mahwah, NJ: Erlbaum.

Nevett, T.R. 1982. *Advertising in Britain.* London: Heinemann.

Ogilvy, David. 1963. *Confessions of an Advertising Man.* New York: Atheneum.

Ong, Walter J. 1989. "The Writer's Audience Is Always a Fiction." In *Contemporary Literary Criticism,* ed. Robert Con Davis and Ronald Schleifer, 82–99. New York: Longman.

———. 1982. *Orality and Literacy.* London: Methuen.

O'Toole, John. 1977. *From One Person to Another.* New York: Foote, Cone & Belding.

Otnes, Cornelia, and Linda M. Scott. 1996. "Something Old, Something New: Exploring the Interaction between Ritual and Advertising." *Journal of Advertising* 25 (Spring): 33–50.

Parker, Betty J. 1998. "Exploring Life Themes and Myths in Alcohol Advertisements Through a Meaning-Based Model of Advertising Experiences." *Journal of Advertising* 27 (Spring): 97–112.

Phillips Barbara J. 1997. "Thinking Into It: Consumer Interpretation of Complex Advertising Images." *Journal of Advertising* 26 (2): 77–87.

———, and Edward F. McQuarrie. 2002. "The Development, Change, and Transformation of Rhetorical Style in Magazine Advertisements, 1954–1999." *Journal of Advertising* 31 (4): 1–13.

Presbrey, Frank. 1929. *The History and Development of Advertising.* Garden City, NY: Doubleday.

Quelch, John. 2005. "A New Agenda for Business Schools." *Chronicle of Higher Education,* December 2, B19.

Ritson, Mark, and Richard Elliott. 1999. "The Social Uses of Advertising: An Ethnographic Study of Adolescent Advertising Audiences." *Journal of Consumer Research* 26 (3): 260–277.

Rivkin, Julie, and Michael Ryan, eds. 2004. *Literary Theory.* Oxford: Blackwell.

Schudson, Michael. 1985. *Advertising, the Uneasy Persuasion.* New York: Basic Books.

Scott, Linda M. 1990. "Understanding Jingles and Needledrop: A Rhetorical Approach to Music in Advertising." *Journal of Consumer Research* 17 (September): 223–236.

———. 1993. "Spectacular Vernacular: Literacy and Commercial Culture in the Postmodern Age." *International Journal of Research in Marketing* 10 (June): 251–275.

————. 1994. "The Bridge from Text to Mind: Adapting Reader-Response Theory for Consumer Research." *Journal of Consumer Research* 19 (December): 461–490.

————. 2005. *Fresh Lipstick: Redressing Fashion and Feminism.* New York: Palgrave Macmillan.

————, and Patrick Vargas. 2007. "Writing with Pictures: Toward a Unifying Theory of Consumer Response to Visuals." *Journal of Consumer Research,* in press.

Simons, Herbert W. 2006. "The Rhetorical Legacy of Kenneth Burke." *Rhetoric and Rhetorical Criticism,* ed. Walter Jost and Wendy Olmsted, 152–168. Oxford: Blackwell.

Stevens, Lorna; Pauline Maclaran; and Stephen Brown. 2003. "*Red* Time Is Me Time: Advertising, Ambivalence, and Women's Magazines." *Journal of Advertising* 32 (1): 35–45.

Sullivan, Luke. 2003. *Hey, Whipple, Squeeze This: A Guide to Creating Great Ads,* 2d ed. Hoboken, NJ: Wiley.

Tompkins, Jane, ed. 1980. *Reader-Response Criticism: From Formalism to Post-Structuralism.* Baltimore, MD: Johns Hopkins University Press.

Vakratsas, Demetrios, and Tim Ambler. 1999. "How Advertising Works: What Do We Really Know?" *Journal of Marketing* 63 (January): 26–43.

About the Editors and Contributors

Johannes W.J. Beentjes is a professor of communication science at the Radboud University Nijmegen, Department of Communication Science, the Netherlands. He received his PhD from Leiden University. His research interests include the production, nature, and effects of persuasive communication. He is a scientific adviser for *Sesamstraat,* the Dutch version of Sesame Street, and the *Kijkwijzer,* the Dutch classification system for television programs and movies.

Mark A. Callister is an associate professor of communications at Brigham Young University in Provo, Utah, where he teaches courses in advertising, consumer behavior, and research methods. He received his MBA at Brigham Young University and PhD in communication at the University of Arizona. His research interests focus on visual rhetoric in advertising. In addition, he conducts research into media effects and the family.

Eric D. DeRosia is an assistant professor of business management at the Marriott School of Management, Brigham Young University, where he teaches consumer behavior and marketing management. He earned an undergraduate degree in business management from Brigham Young University and a PhD in business administration from the University of Michigan.

Charles Forceville is employed in the University of Amsterdam's Media Studies Department, where he coordinates the Research Masters Program. After publishing *Pictorial Metaphor in Advertising*, his current research encompasses multimodal metaphor in moving and multipanel (as opposed to static, stand-alone) images in various genres, and is embedded in a Relevance Theory framework. His papers have appeared in journals including *Metaphor and Symbol, Journal of Pragmatics, Poetics, Poetics Today, Language and Literature,* and the *New Review of Film and Televi-*

sion Studies. He teaches courses on documentary film, animation, and multimodal metaphor. Narrativity never lost its scholarly appeal for him after he studied English language and literature at the Vrije Universiteit Amsterdam. Forceville is at present co-editing, with Eduardo Urios-Aparisi, *Multimodal Metaphor.* Generally formulated, his interests pertain to the structure and rhetoric of multimodal discourse and to how research in this field can contribute to an understanding of human cognition.

Bruce A. Huhmann (PhD, University of Alabama) is an associate professor of marketing at New Mexico State University, where he teaches undergraduate courses in consumer decision processes, retail management, and the design and delivery of goods and services, as well as doctoral courses in marketing models and advertising methods and research. His primary stream of research focuses on verbal and visual appeals in advertising. He has conducted extensive research on the effects of rhetorical language on advertising information processing. Some results of this research have recently appeared in the *Journal of Consumer Research* and *IEEE Transactions on Professional Communications.* His other research interests include emotional appeals in advertising, information search behavior, and international advertising. In 2004, he won an award for Outstanding Scholarly Research–Junior Faculty from the College of Business at New Mexico State University. He received his PhD from the University of Alabama.

Paul Ketelaar is an assistant professor in the Department of Communication Science at the Radboud University of Nijmegen (the Netherlands), where he has been teaching communication science and marketing communications since 1992. He received an MA in psychology and in communication science, and a PhD in social sciences from the Radboud University. He is director of Marketing Symbolics, a foundation that aims to increase cooperation between business and science and to make communication research results more widely known. Before this, he was co-owner of a communication agency in health communication. His research program focuses on the effects of marketing-communication strategies on consumer behavior. More specifically, he focuses on the occurrence and effects of open advertisements and advertising-avoidance behavior across media.

Val Larsen is an associate professor of marketing at James Madison University, where he teaches consumer behavior and database marketing. He earned undergraduate degrees in philosophy and English from Brigham Young University, an MA and PhD in English from the University of Virginia, and a PhD in marketing from Virginia Tech. His research interests include the semiotics of visual persuasion and the economics of privacy.

Tina M. Lowrey is a professor of marketing at the University of Texas at San Antonio. She received her PhD from the University of Illinois. Her main research interests include psycholinguistic analyses of advertising, and gift-giving and ritualistic consumption. Her work has appeared in numerous journals, including the *Journal of Consumer Research, Journal of Consumer Psychology,* and *Journal of Advertising.* She has chapters in *Contemporary Consumption Rituals: A Research Anthology* (which she co-edited with Cele C. Otnes); *Marketing Communication: New Approaches, Technologies, and Styles; Gender Issues and Consumer Behavior; Gift Giving: A Research Anthology;* and *New Developments and Approaches in Consumer Behavior Research.* She serves on the editorial boards of *Journal of Advertising, Media Psychology,* and *Psychology & Marketing.*

Alfons Maes is a professor in the Humanities Faculty at Tilburg University and head of the research program Multimodality and Cognition. His research focuses on the role of multimodal aspects of human communication. Topics include multimodal metaphoric conceptualization, computer-mediated multimodal reference, spatial processes in using hyperlinked documents, and multimodal information presentation.

Edward F. McQuarrie is a professor of marketing at the Leavey School of Business, Santa Clara University. He received his PhD from the University of Cincinnati. His research interests include qualitative research techniques and market research appropriate to technology products, on the one hand, and advertising research, rhetoric, and semiotics, on the other. He has written two books, *Customer Visits: Building a Better Market Focus,* and *The Market Research Toolbox: A Concise Guide for Beginners,* and published articles in the *Journal of Consumer Research, Journal of Consumer Psychology, Journal of the Market Research Society, Journal of Advertising Research, Journal of Advertising, Marketing Theory,* and elsewhere. With Barbara J. Phillips, he has twice received the Best Paper Award from *Journal of Advertising* (2002, 2005). He serves on the editorial board of the *Journal of Consumer Research.*

Laura A. Peracchio is professor of marketing at the University of Wisconsin–Milwaukee. She received her PhD from Northwestern University. Her areas of research interest are visual persuasion, language and culture, and food and nutrition issues. Her work has appeared in the *Journal of Consumer Research, Journal of Consumer Psychology,* and *Journal of Advertising.* She is an associate editor of the *Journal of Consumer Research* and president of the Society for Consumer Psychology, an international organization composed of marketing and psychology scholars and a division of the American Psychological Association.

Barbara J. Phillips is the Rawlco Scholar in Advertising and a professor of marketing at the University of Saskatchewan, where she has been teaching integrated marketing communications, consumer behavior, and other marketing courses since 1996. She received her MA and PhD in advertising from the University of Texas at Austin. Her research program focuses on visual images in advertising and their influence on consumer response. She has published articles in peer-reviewed journals, books, and conference proceedings, such as the *Journal of Advertising* and *Marketing Theory*. With Edward F. McQuarrie, she has twice received the Best Article Award from the *Journal of Advertising* (2002, 2005) and the Dunn Award from the University of Illinois (2004) for excellence in advertising research.

Joost Schilperoord is an associate professor in the Humanities Faculty at Tilburg University and member of the research program Discourse Studies. His research interests include the role of prefabs in human communication and the study of verbal and visual metaphor and rhetoric.

Jonathan E. Schroeder is a professor of marketing in the School of Business and Economics, University of Exeter. He is also visiting professor in marketing semiotics at Bocconi University in Milan, visiting professor in design management at the Indian School of Business, Hyderabad, and associate faculty, University of the Arts, London. He received his BA in psychology from the University of Michigan, and his MA and PhD in social psychology from the University of California, Berkeley. His research focuses on the production and consumption of images. He is the author of *Visual Consumption* and co-editor of *Brand Culture*. He is an editor of *Consumption Markets & Culture,* and serves on the editorial boards of *Advertising and Society Review, European Journal of Marketing,* and *Marketing Theory*.

Linda M. Scott is a reader in marketing at the Saïd School of Business, Oxford University, in the United Kingdom. She has published several articles that argue for a rhetorical approach to research in advertising. She has also published two books, *Persuasive Imagery: A Consumer Response Perspective* (with Rajeev Batra), and *Fresh Lipstick: Redressing Fashion and Feminism.* Her training is primarily in arts theory, with an emphasis on literary theory, and she has held appointments in art, women's studies, and communications, in addition to advertising and marketing.

Barbara B. Stern is a professor of marketing and vice-chair of the department at Rutgers Business School. Her research focuses on the meaning of texts in consumer behavior, and she uses textual analysis adapted from literary theory to examine stimuli such as ads and marketing communications associated with consumer responses such as attitudes to ads, product placement in television programs, and verbal protocols. Her research has appeared in the *Journal of Consumer Research, Journal of Marketing, Journal of Advertising, International Journal of Electronic Commerce, Journal of the Academy of Marketing Science (JAMS),* and other publications. She is the founding co-editor of the journal *Marketing Theory,* which she continues to co-edit, and serves or has served on over a dozen editorial boards including the *Journal of Consumer Research, Journal of Marketing, Journal of the Academy of Marketing Science, and Journal of Advertising.* She received the American Advertising Association Award for Outstanding Contribution to Research in 1997, and in her premarketing life, the Leavey Award for Excellence in Private Enterprise Education, and the Women's Institute for Freedom of the Press Award.

Lesa A. Stern is currently an associate professor of communication studies at Westmont College in Santa Barbara, California. She was previously at Southern Illinois University Edwardsville for thirteen years. Her areas of teaching and research involve interpersonal conflict management and communication assessment. Lesa also functions as Mark Callister's partner in conducting research in rhetorical figures in advertising. She received her BA from UCLA and her MA and PhD from the University of Arizona.

Marnix S. van Gisbergen works as a manager of research development at De Vos & Jansen Marketing Group, a full-service research company in the Netherlands. He received his MA and PhD in communication science from the Radboud University of Nijmegen (the Netherlands). He also worked as an assistant professor in communication science at the same university. His research interests include leisure management and the effects of communication strategies, such as openness in advertising, on consumer behavior. He has published in several national and international magazines, journals, and books, and has spoken at various international conferences.

Kai-Yu Wang is a PhD candidate in marketing at the University of Wisconsin–Milwaukee. He received his MBA degree from National Dong Hwa University and undergraduate degree in psychology from Chung-Yuan Christian University in Taiwan. His research interests include advertising effects, information processing, and consumer persuasion processes.

Index

Paradox, 90*t*, 230
Parallelism, 87*t*
Parison, 87*t*
Parody, 89*t*
Paronomasis pun, 89*t*
Pepsi, 147
Pepto-Bismol, 90*t*
Periphrasis, 88*t*
Personification, 89*t*
Persuasion
  cognitive processing model, 92*f*, 95–96, 102, 104
  soap operas, 57–60
Persuasion knowledge
  cognitive processing model, 105, 106
  open advertisement, 117
Peter Island Hotel, 90*t*
Peugeot, 189–90, 196, 200
Phaedrus (Plato), 24, 25*t*
Philips Senseo coffee machine, 192, 200
Phillips, B., 234–35, 235*f*, 247*t*
Photography
  brand culture images, 278, 279–83, 281*f*
  icon-symbol distinction, 70–71
Photoshop, 13, 199
Pictorial metaphor. *See* Metaphor
Plato, 24, 25*t*
PlayStation, 89*t*, 103
PLJ, 88*t*
PMS Escape, 89*t*
Poetics, 8, 52–53
Poetics (Aristotle), 25*t*, 52–53
Polyptoton, 87*t*
Pond's, 89*t*
Porsche, 122
PowerBar, 88*t*
Pragmatism, 7–9
Presbrey, Frank, 308
Prior knowledge, 105–6
Proctor & Gamble, 57
Product category expertise, 105, 106
Product Red, 304
Product schema incongruity, 146–47
Program, 87*t*
Pyrex Ware, 89*t*

Quaker Oats, 89*t*
Quintilian, 25*t*, 26, 30, 31, 32, 33, 34, 35, 36, 38, 39, 40–41, 42, 43, 44, 46

Reader's Digest, 150
Reality-deviating schema, 149–50
Recall, 125, 127, 128, 129, 131–32
  See also Memory
Red, 302
Reflex, 261*f*
Relevancy, 139–41
Relpax, 86
Repetition
  rhetorical figures, 86, 87*t*, 90, 93–94, 97, 101
  visual stylistic properties, 216–17

Resonance, 90*t*, 180–81
Resource demand, 92*f*, 93, 97, 99, 100–2, 103, 104–10
Resource-matching theory
  cognitive processing model, 85–86, 91, 93, 99, 103, 107–10
  complexity continuum, 174
  visual stylistic properties, 208, 220–21
Reversal scheme, 86, 87*t*, 93–94, 101
Rhetorica ad Herennium, 24, 25*t*, 26, 30, 40, 41, 42, 44
Rhetorical analysis
  classical scholarship
    advertising rhetoric, 4, 5–7, 13
    audience response, 5–6, 24–25, 26, 30, 31, 32, 33, 34, 35, 36, 38, 39, 40–41, 42, 43, 44, 45–47
    dramatic context, 52–53
  criticism, 8, 298–99
  defined, 298
  disciplinary application, 297–301
  inquiry rhetoric, 305–11
  semiotics, 298–301
Rhetorical figures
  aesthetic information, 102–3
  alliteration-chime, 87*t*
  allusion, 89*t*
  anadiplosis-epizeuxis, 87*t*
  anaphora, 5, 86, 87*t*, 97
  antanaclasis pun, 89*t*
  anthimeria, 88*t*
  antithesis, 5, 87*t*, 93–94
  assonance, 87*t*, 103
  audience response
    affective response, 28–29*t*, 39–42, 45–46
    attention, 26, 27*t*, 30–31
    classical scholarship, 5–6, 24–25, 26, 30, 31, 32, 33, 34, 35, 36, 38, 39, 40–41, 42, 43, 44, 45–47
    cognitive processing, 28*t*, 35–39
    comprehension, 27–28*t*, 31–35
    contemporary scholarship, 23–24, 26, 27–29*t*, 30–32, 33–35, 36–38, 39–40, 41–44, 45, 46, 47
    counterarguing, 36–38
    diminishing effects, 44–46
    extrafigurative effects, 29*t*, 44–46
    mental imagery, 38–39
    motivation factors, 37–38
    source evaluation, 29*t*, 42–44
  defined, 23–24
  elements, 86, 93–97, 99, 102, 103
  ellipsis-aposiopesis, 88*t*
  epanalepsis-chiasmus, 87*t*, 102
  epanorthosis, 88*t*
  epiphora, 87*t*, 99
  euphemism, 88*t*
  homonym pun, 89*t*, 94
  hyperbaton-anastrophe, 87*t*
  hyperbole, 88*t*, 90, 149, 181
  idiom, 89*t*, 98, 105